THE INVESTMENT
READER

THE INVESTMENTS READER

Edited by
Jay Wilbanks

Dow Jones-Irwin Homewood, Illinois 60430

The editor does not intend that this book or any of the readings be taken as a recommendation to invest in any product, security, or property. The readings presented in this book give the opinions and insights of the authors, not of the editor.

Many of the readings in this book are from the American Association of Individual Investors' *AAII Journal*, a nonprofit organization dedicated to the presentation of investment issues in a clear and concise manner. Students and professionals should consider the *AAII Journal* as one source of information to remain informed about products and methods of investing throughout their career.

Sponsoring editor: Tony Frankos
Project editor: Jean Roberts
Production manager: Ann Cassady
Cover designer: Mike Finkelman
Compositor: Precision Typographers, Inc.
Typeface: 11/13 Times Roman
Printer: R. R. Donnelley & Sons Company

Library of Congress Cataloging-in-Publication Data

The Investments reader.

    1. Investments.   I. Wilbanks, Jay.
HG4515.I58 1989   332.6   89–7729
ISBN 1–55623–237–3
ISBN 1–55623–273–X (pbk.)

Printed in the United States of America
1 2 3 4 5 6 7 8 9 0 DO 6 5 4 3 2 1 0 9

The editor wishes to thank Mark Pederson, Dave Lockwood, and Tony Frankos for their encouragement and help with this project.

PREFACE

The field of investments is continually growing as new innovations and products come to light almost daily. Without some marked effort, professionals and students may end up knowing a little about everything, but not enough about anything. This book can be used, at the option of the reader, to either add to this confusion or contribute to the development of a broad base of knowledge in investments.

This book is designed to accompany a basic textbook in investments. It also stands alone as a sampling of new products and ideas presented in a highly readable format for the investments professional. The readings here present a collection of ideas and viewpoints about investments, portfolios, and markets. Readings have been chosen to provide information that is normally not covered in textbooks, or topics that investments textbooks do present, but in a highly academic fashion. In particular, readings in the last section give ideas about portfolio management that are realistic and practical, but that are in stark contrast to the classical portfolio construction theories presented in most textbooks. It is the editor's hope that this book will be used to add to a practical knowledge of the broad field of investments.

Jay Wilbanks

CONTENTS

THE INVESTMENTS READER

PART 1

INTRODUCTION TO INVESTING

READING 1

INVESTMENT BASICS: A GUIDE FOR THE NEWCOMER

Maria Crawford Scott

This article is aimed at those individuals with little investment knowledge who are thrown into deep financial waters and are told to sink or swim. It won't tell you what to do; instead, it is an overview that should provide you with a base on which to make your own investment decisions.

WHERE TO START: THE BASICS

Where does one start when they know absolutely nothing about investing? I'll assume that the preliminary work has been done, such as budgeting and gathering information on current wealth. These are not insignificant tasks. However, here we're concerned with an investment problem.

The first step is to learn some basic investment concepts. You should understand these concepts whether you go on to do your own investing, or whether you decide to turn to an adviser for help.

The most basic concept is very straightforward: Never invest in anything that you do not understand. If this means that you are restricted to certificates of deposit (in banks that are insured), then so be it.

Other important concepts are somewhat more complex: risk, the risk-return relationship, and the importance of diversification.

Source: *AAII Journal*, August 1988. Used with permission.

BASIC CONCEPTS: RISK

Many investors, when viewing investment alternatives, focus on potential returns. Equally important, however, is risk. All investments carry some risk.

What is risk? It can best be defined as uncertainty—of not knowing what is going to happen to your investment. There are different ways of viewing this uncertainty risk; you should be aware of all of them when comparing investments. These include:

- The risk of not getting the return you expected. In the worst instances, this would include losing some or all of your original investment.
- The risk of not being able to get out of the investment at any time with the original investment amount intact. This is also known as liquidity risk, and it can occur either because the market is not active (for instance, it takes some time to sell a house) or because the market is very volatile (and you may have to sell at a significant loss).
- The risk of bankruptcy or default of the business in which you are investing. This affects not just the holders of stocks, but also bondholders and those who purchase certificates of deposit from banks that are not federally insured.
- The risk of not keeping up with inflation. This risk is often ignored. However, if your assets are earning less than the inflation rate, you are losing ground—your investment will not be able to buy as much in the future as it can today.
- The risk of being forced to increase your commitment in order to maintain the investment. Some investments, such as futures, options, those that use margin, and some limited partnerships, hold you liable for more than what you put up initially. These are extremely risky and should be avoided, particularly by those new to investing.

THE RISK-RETURN TRADEOFF

An important element of risk is its relationship to return. This relationship exists *on average,* and not in every single instance. On average, the returns from an investment should compensate for the level of risk undertaken:

Investment Basics

- Never invest in anything you don't understand.
- Risk is uncertainty. Always be aware of the risks in terms of:
  - Not getting what you expected.
  - Lack of liquidity.
  - Bankruptcy or default.
  - Loss of purchasing power.
  - Additional liabilities.
- Always relate risk to return, and don't take on risks that you will not be compensated for through higher returns. Lower-risk investments produce lower returns; higher-risk investments should produce higher returns. High returns are *not* produced by low-risk investments—be wary of claims to the contrary.
- Return expectations should be reasonable, based on past experience. However, history may not repeat itself—that's part of the risk. Always take transaction costs and taxes into consideration—they will lower your return. The less frequently you make changes, the less costs you will incur.
- Diversification is an important way to lower risk without lowering returns. Always diversify among securities (by holding 10 or more) and among investment categories (stocks, bonds, cash, and real estate).
- Diversification is also important across different market environments—the longer the holding period, the better. Don't invest in stocks or other volatile investments if you will remain invested for less than five years.

Riskier investments can be expected to have higher returns, and low-risk investments can be expected to have lower returns. In order to earn a higher return, you must take on more risk; and in order to have low risks, you must accept lower returns. That's why low-risk investments—money market funds and money market deposit accounts—have lower long-term returns on average than higher-risk investments, such as longer-term bonds (with moderate risk and somewhat higher expected returns) and stocks (moderate to high risk and higher expected returns).

Sometimes, riskier investments will not produce higher returns—these are "inefficient" investments (they are also lousy investments). The converse rarely occurs—low-risk investments do not produce high returns; any claims that an investment will produce high returns at low risk is hype and should be viewed skeptically. The important point is that you should always look at both returns *and* risk when comparing investments: If you are considering two investments, for instance, and one has a slightly higher expected return but is much riskier, it is not as desirable.

In order to judge the risk-return tradeoff, you must have some idea of what kinds of returns to expect. Ideally, you are seeking the highest return for the level of risk you have decided that you can stomach. But your expectations should mesh with reality.

Most expectations are based on what happened in the past and, unfortunately, history doesn't always repeat itself. On the other hand, there is little else to go on, and reasonable conclusions about future returns can be reached by looking at the past, with the understanding that these returns are not guaranteed.

Over the last 30 years, stocks have produced returns that average between 10 percent to 14 percent annually; long-term bonds have produced average annual returns of between 6 percent to 10 percent and money market funds have averaged 6 percent to 9 percent annually. These returns reflect the risk-return tradeoff: higher-risk stocks tend to do better than medium-risk bonds, which tend to do better than low-risk money market funds.

You should not expect returns much higher than these for the various investment categories. In fact, your actual returns will probably be somewhat lower, because you will incur transaction costs (such as sales commissions and other fees), and you will have to pay taxes on income and gains. Cost considerations should not override investment decisions, but you should keep a keen eye on them. The bulk of these costs are incurred only when you make a transaction; the fewer changes you make, the lower your costs.

BASIC CONCEPTS: DIVERSIFICATION

Another extremely important investment concept is diversification. In fact, it is related to the risk-return concept. Numerous studies have shown that the best returns at a given risk level are achieved through diversification—being invested in more than one investment category (for instance, stocks, bonds and cash). It is also important to be diversified *within* most investment categories—in the stock category, for instance, this consists of investing in 10 unrelated stocks rather than just one.

The reason why diversification is so important is more complicated than the notion of simply not putting all of one's eggs in one basket, and it is well worth understanding the reason.

Diversification is an important part of the risk-return relationship. Returns compensate for risk, but they do not compensate for all risk. Diversification eliminates those risks that are not compensated for through greater returns. For example, if you invest in only one bond, you face a significant default risk: If your one bond defaults, you will suffer a substantial loss. However, if you invest in a large number of bonds, a single default will have considerably less impact, and your return for the group will be similar to that of a single bond that did not default. Another example would be if you put all of your assets in a savings account. This is generally considered to be a very low risk, and it is. But it does have one kind of risk—the risk that those assets will not keep up with inflation. That inflation risk can be reduced by diversifying into other asset categories—for instance, by putting a small amount in common stock mutual funds—and over the long term your average return will not be lowered.

The importance of diversification can be seen by restating it in the negative: If you don't diversify, you are taking on a considerable risk for which you will *not* be compensated.

There is another type of diversification that is also extremely important, yet it is frequently ignored. It is known as time diversification—remaining invested over different market cycles. "Time heals all wounds"—including investment wounds. Remaining invested over longer time periods substantially reduces the risk that, at the end of your investment period, you will not have earned the return that could be expected based on the risk that you took.

The stock market provides the best example of the benefits of time diversification. In the stock market, investors face the substantial risk that their investments will suffer an actual loss in value. However, as the length of time invested in the stock market is increased, the risk of suffering a loss is substantially reduced. Since World War II, investors who remained in the market for only one year could have suffered a loss of as much as 26.5 percent of the value of their assets; their chances of seeing a loss were also greater, since there were 10 one-year time periods in which the stock market suffered a loss. In contrast, investors who remained in the market for 10 years on average faced no risk of an actual loss to their portfolio.

Time diversification has much more of an impact on investments that have a high degree of volatility, such as stocks, where prices can fluctuate wildly over the short term; longer time periods smooth those fluctuations. Time diversification is less important for relatively stable investments, such as certificates of deposit, money market funds and short-term bonds. That's why these investments are usually recommended for investors who plan on remaining invested only for short time periods (less than five years); you should not be invested in the stock market or other risky investments if you plan on remaining invested for less than five years. This is a sound approach for short-term investors even if it is undertaken at the expense of diversification across investment categories—if, for instance, you must exclude stocks.

One other aspect of time diversification comes into play when investing or withdrawing large sums of money. In general, it is better to do so gradually over time, rather than doing so all at once. This process is known as dollar cost averaging.

CONCENTRATING YOUR EFFORTS

It is traditional, after laying the groundwork, to survey the investment media, such as stocks, bonds, insurance investments, etc. Many investment books do this quite well, and it is certainly important to have a general understanding of these categories, particularly in terms of the risks and returns you can expect. However, individuals who are new to investing should be careful about spending too much time (and money) trying to master investments that are too complex to start with. Which investments are these?

- Individual stocks and bonds.
- Insurance investment products (whole and universal life, for instance; this does *not* include straight insurance, such as term, which is not an investment).
- Futures, options and margined investments.
- Limited partnerships.

Limited partnerships and insurance investment products are extremely difficult to analyze. In general, the terms of the contracts are complex and vary considerably; comparisons among products are difficult.

Futures, options, and margined investments are very risky—most likely beyond the risk that most individuals can tolerate, particularly new-comers.

Picking individual stocks and bonds can also be tough. First, the group of stocks or bonds chosen must be diversified. Second, you could spend years trying to learn all of the various techniques that are espoused for se-lecting the "right" stock or bond.

Instead, newer investors should be concentrating their efforts on no-load mutual funds. These funds are a low-cost way of tapping into profes-sional investment advice, and provide investors with a full array of invest-ment categories, including stock funds, bond funds, and money market funds. The "Individual Investor's Guide to No-Load Mutual Funds," sent to all AAII members in June, is the single best source of information for investing in these funds.

THE NEXT STEP: ASSET ALLOCATION

Once an investor understands the concepts, the next step is applying them to individual circumstances. That means determining what portions of your wealth are invested in the various investment categories. This is known as asset allocation, and it is the single most important investment decision you will make. It has far more of an impact on long-term future returns than such decisions as individual stock picks, assuming you are properly diversified.

Unfortunately, it is difficult to come up with generalizations that can be applied to asset allocation. The decision has to be made by the individ-ual, because it is based on personal circumstances, such as income needs, time horizon, and the amount of risk the individual is willing to take on. However, you should be diversified among the various investment catego-ries: stocks, bonds, cash, and real estate (including your own home). One simple approach (which excludes your home for the calculation) would be to put a minimum of 25 percent in each of three categories: stock mutual funds, bond mutual funds, and money market funds, and to apportion the remainder according to your risk and return preferences; if you are con-servative, you would apportion the remainder to money market funds and bond funds.

The specific kinds of mutual funds chosen depends not only on your own risk-return tradeoff, but also on your income needs and tax stance. If you need income, you may want to consider for your stock portion those funds that invest in conservative, high dividend-paying stocks; if you are in a high tax bracket, you may want to consider municipal bond funds for your bond portion. Beware, however, when choosing among bond funds, whether municipal or taxable: The longer the maturity of a bond, the greater the risk. Long-term bonds with maturities of 20 years or more have risk levels approaching the risk of stocks. When choosing bond funds, stick to the shorter maturity funds—those with less than five years' maturity.

Asset allocation is complex—it could be the subject of numerous articles; two approaches have been the subject of articles in the *AAII Journal*. Any asset allocation decision, however, should be based on the investment concepts discussed here.

FINDING SHALLOWER WATERS

The investment concepts outlined here . . . should provide you with a base—a life preserver, so to speak. With time, as you gain more knowledge and become more accustomed to the waters, perhaps they won't seem quite so deep.

READING 2

THE SEC: ORGANIZATION AND FUNCTIONS

U.S. Securities and Exchange Commission

INTRODUCTION

The U.S. Securities and Exchange Commission's mission is to administer federal securities laws that seek to provide protection for investors. The purpose of these laws is to ensure that the securities markets are fair and honest and to provide the means to enforce the securities laws through sanctions where necessary. Laws administered by the commission are the:

- Securities Act of 1933.
- Securities Exchange Act of 1934.
- Public Utility Holding Company Act of 1935.
- Trust Indenture Act of 1939.
- Investment Company Act of 1940.
- Investment Advisers Act of 1940.

The commission also serves as adviser to federal courts in corporate reorganization proceedings under Chapter 11 of the Bankruptcy Reform Act of 1978 and, in cases begun prior to October 1, 1979, Chapter X of the National Bankruptcy Act. The commission reports annually to Congress on administration of the securities laws.

From Sumner N. Levine, ed., *The Financial Analyst's Handbook*, 2nd ed. (Homewood, Ill.: Dow Jones-Irwin, 1988). Used with permission.

Source: U.S. Securities and Exchange Commission, *The Work of the SEC*, 1986.

Under the Securities Exchange Act of 1934, Congress created the Securities and Exchange Commission (SEC). The SEC is an independent, nonpartisan, quasi-judicial regulatory agency.

The commission is composed of five members: a chairman and four commissioners. Commission members are appointed by the president, with the advice and consent of the Senate, for five-year terms. The chairman is designated by the president. Terms are staggered; one expires on June 5th of every year. Not more than three members may be of the same political party.

Under the direction of the chairman and commissioners, the staff ensures that publicly held entities, broker-dealers in securities, investment companies and advisers, and other participants in the securities markets comply with federal securities laws. These laws were designed to facilitate informed investment analyses and decisions by the investing public, primarily by ensuring adequate disclosure of material (significant) information. Conformance with federal securities laws and regulations does not imply merit. If information essential to informed investment analysis is properly disclosed, the commission cannot bar the sale of securities which analysis may show to be of questionable value. It is the investor, not the commission, who must make the ultimate judgment of the worth of securities offered for sale.

The commission's staff is composed of lawyers, accountants, financial analysts and examiners, engineers, and other professionals. The staff is divided into divisions and offices (including 14 regional and branch offices), each directed by officials appointed by the chairman.

This chapter describes the work of the SEC by discussing the laws it administers, the organization of the commission, the ways in which it carries out its statutory mandates, and the sanctions it can bring to bear to enforce federal securities laws.

SECURITIES ACT OF 1933

This "truth in securities" law has two basic objectives:

- To require that investors be provided with material information concerning securities offered for public sale.
- To prevent misrepresentation, deceit, and other fraud in the sale of securities.

A primary means of accomplishing these objectives is disclosure of financial information by registering securities. Securities subject to registration are most corporate debt and equity securities. Government (state and federal) and mortgage-related debt are not. Certain securities qualify for exemptions from registration provisions; these exemptions are discussed below.

Purpose of Registration

Registration is intended to provide adequate and accurate disclosure of material facts concerning the company and the securities it proposes to sell. Thus, investors may make a realistic appraisal of the merits of the securities and then exercise informed judgment in determining whether to purchase them.

Registration requires, but does not guarantee, the accuracy of the facts represented in the registration statement and prospectus. However, the law does prohibit false and misleading statements under penalty of fine, imprisonment, or both. And investors who purchase securities and suffer losses have important recovery rights under the law if they can prove that there was incomplete or inaccurate disclosure of material facts in the registration statement or prospectus. If such misstatements are proven, the following could be liable for investor losses sustained in the securities purchase: the issuing company, its responsible directors and officers, the underwriters, controlling interests, the sellers of the securities, and others. These rights must be asserted in an appropriate federal or state court (not before the commission, which has no power to award damages).

Registration of securities does not preclude the sale of stock in risky, poorly managed, or unprofitable companies. Nor does the commission approve or disapprove securities on their merits; it is unlawful to represent otherwise in the sale of securities. The only standard which must be met when registering securities is adequate and accurate disclosure of required material facts concerning the company and the securities it proposes to sell. The fairness of the terms, the issuing company's prospects for successful operation, and other factors affecting the merits of investing in the securities (whether price, promoters' or underwriters' profits, or otherwise) have no bearing on the question of whether securities may be registered.

The Registration Process

To facilitate registration by different types of companies, the commission has special forms. These vary in their disclosure requirements but generally provide essential facts while minimizing the burden and expense of complying with the law. In general, registration forms call for disclosure of information such as:

- Description of the registrant's properties and business.
- Description of the significant provisions of the security to be offered for sale and its relationship to the registrant's other capital securities.
- Information about the management of the registrant.
- Financial statements certified by independent public accountants.

Registration statements and prospectuses on securities become public immediately upon filing with the commission. After the registration statement is filed, securities may be offered orally or by certain summaries of the information in the registration statement as permitted by commission rules. However, it is unlawful to sell the securities until the effective date. The act provides that most registration statements shall become effective on the 20th day after filing (or on the 20th day after filing the last amendment). At its discretion, the commission may advance the effective date if deemed appropriate considering the interests of investors and the public, the adequacy of publicly available information, and the ease with which the facts about the new offering can be disseminated and understood.

Registration statements are examined for compliance with disclosure requirements. If a statement appears to be materially incomplete or inaccurate, the registrant usually is informed by letter and given an opportunity to file correcting or clarifying amendments. The commission, however, has authority to refuse or suspend the effectiveness of any registration statement if it finds that material representations are misleading, inaccurate, or incomplete.

The commission may conclude that material deficiencies in some registration statements appear to stem from a deliberate attempt to conceal or mislead, or that the deficiencies do not lend themselves to correction through the informal letter process. In these cases, the commission may decide that it is in the public interest to conduct a hearing to develop the facts by evidence. This determines if a "stop order" should be issued to refuse or suspend effectiveness of the statement. The commission may issue stop orders after the sale of securities has been commenced or completed. A stop order is not a permanent bar to the effectiveness of the registration statement or to the sale of the securities. If amendments are filed correcting the statement in accordance with the stop order decision, the order must be lifted and the statement declared effective.

Although losses which may have been suffered in the purchase of securities are not restored to investors by the stop order, the commission's order precludes future public sales. Also, the decision and the evidence on which it is based may serve to notify investors of their rights and aid them in their own recovery suits.

Exemptions from Registration

In general, registration requirements apply to securities of both domestic and foreign issuers and to securities of foreign governments (or their instrumentalities) sold in domestic securities markets. There are, however, certain exemptions. Among these are:

- Private offerings to a limited number of persons or institutions who have access to the kind of information that registration would disclose and who do not propose to redistribute the securities.
- Offerings restricted to residents of the state in which the issuing company is organized and doing business.
- Securities of municipal, state, federal, and other governmental instrumentalities as well as charitable institutions, banks, and carriers subject to the Interstate Commerce Act.
- Offerings not exceeding certain specified amounts made in compliance with regulations of the commission.
- Offerings of "small business investment companies" made in accordance with rules and regulations of the commission.

Whether or not the securities are exempt from registration, antifraud provisions apply to all sales of securities involving interstate commerce or the mails.

Among the special exemptions from the registration requirement, the "small issue exemption" was adopted by Congress primarily as an aid to small business. The law provides that offerings of securities under $5 million may be exempted from registration, subject to conditions the commission prescribes to protect investors. The commission's Regulation A permits certain domestic and Canadian companies to make exempt offerings. A similar regulation is available for offerings under $500,000 by small business investment companies licensed by the Small Business Administration. The commission's Regulation D permits certain companies to make exempt offerings under $500,000 with only minimal federal restrictions; more extensive disclosure requirements and other conditions apply for offerings exceeding that amount but less than $5 million.

Exemptions are available when certain specified conditions are met. These conditions include the prior filing of a notification with the appropriate SEC regional office and the use of an offering circular containing certain basic information in the sale of the securities. For a more complete discussion of these and other special provisions adopted by the commission to facilitate capital formation by small business, please request a copy of "Q & A: Small Business and the SEC," available from the Public Reference Branch of the commission.

SECURITIES EXCHANGE ACT OF 1934

By this act, Congress extended the "disclosure" doctrine of investor protection to securities listed and registered for public trading on our national securities exchanges. Thirty years later, the Securities Act Amendments of 1964 extended disclosure and reporting provisions to equity securities in the over-the-counter market. This included hundreds of companies with assets exceeding $1 million and shareholders numbering 500 or more. (Today, securities of thousands of companies are traded over the counter.) The act seeks to ensure fair and orderly securities markets by prohibiting certain types of activities and by setting forth rules regarding the operation of the markets and participants.

Corporate Reporting

Companies seeking to have their securities registered and listed for public trading on an exchange must file a registration application with the exchange and the SEC. If they meet the size test described above, companies whose equity securities are traded over the counter must file a similar registration form. Commission rules prescribe the nature and content of these registration statements and require certified financial statements. These are generally compared to, but less extensive than, the disclosures required in Securities Act registration statements. Following the registration of their securities, companies must file annual and other periodic reports to update information contained in the original filing. In addition, issuers must send certain reports to requesting shareholders.

Reports may be read at the commission's public reference rooms, copied there at nominal cost, or obtained from a copying service under contract to the commission.

Proxy Solicitations

Another provision of this law governs soliciting proxies (votes) from holders of registered securities, both listed and over-the-counter, for the election of directors and/or for approval of other corporate action. Solicitations, whether by management or minority groups, must disclose all material facts concerning matters on which holders are asked to vote. Holders also must be given an opportunity to vote "yes" or "no" on each matter. Where a contest for control of corporate management is involved, the rules require disclosure of the names and interests of all "participants" in the proxy contest. Thus, holders are enabled to vote intelligently on corporate actions requiring their approval. The commission's rules require that proposed proxy material be filed in advance for examination by the commission for compliance with the disclosure requirements. In addition, the rules permit shareholders to submit proposals for a vote at the annual meetings.

Tender Offer Solicitations

In 1968 Congress amended the Exchange Act to extend its reporting and disclosure provisions to situations where control of a company is sought through a tender offer or other planned stock acquisition of over 10 percent of a company's equity securities. Commonly called the Williams Act, this amendment was further amended in 1970 to reduce the stock acquisition threshold to 5 percent. These amendments, and commission rules under the act, require disclosure of pertinent information by anyone seeking to acquire over 5 percent of a company's securities by direct purchase or by tender offer. This disclosure is also required by anyone soliciting shareholders to accept or reject a tender offer. Thus, as with the proxy rules, public investors holding stock in these corporations may now make more informed decisions on takeover bids.

Disclosure provisions are supplemented by certain other provisions to help ensure investor protection in tender offers.

Insider Trading

Insider trading prohibitions are designed to curb misuse of material confidential information not available to the general public. Examples of such misuse are buying or selling securities to make profits or avoid losses based on material nonpublic information—or by telling others of the information so that they may buy or sell securities—before such information is generally available to all shareholders. The commission has brought numerous civil actions in federal court against persons whose use of material nonpublic information constituted fraud under the securities laws. Additionally, the commission supported legislation to increase the penalties that can be imposed by the courts on those found guilty of insider trading. The Insider Trading Sanctions Act, signed into law on August 10, 1984, allows imposing fines up to three times the profit gained or loss avoided by use of material nonpublic information.

Another provision requires that all officers and directors of a company (and beneficial owners of more than 10 percent of its registered equity securities) must file an initial report with the commission and with the exchange on which the stock may be listed showing their holdings of each of the company's equity securities. Thereafter, they must file reports for any month during which there was any change in those holdings. In addition, the law provides that profits obtained by them from purchases and sales (or sales and purchases) of such equity securities within any six-month period may be recovered by the company or any security holder on its behalf. This recovery right must be asserted in the appropriate U.S. district court. Such "insiders" are also prohibited from making short sales of their company's equity securities.

Margin Trading

Margin trading in securities also falls under certain provisions of the act. The board of governors of the Federal Reserve System is authorized to set limitations on the amount of credit which may be extended for the purpose of purchasing or carrying securities. (The Federal Reserve periodically reviews these limitations.) The objective is to restrict excessive use of the nation's credit in the securities markets. While the credit restrictions are set by the board, investigation and enforcement is the responsibility of the SEC.

Trading and Sales Practices

Securities trading and sales practices on the exchanges and in the over-the-counter markets are subject to provisions that are designed to protect the interests of investors and the public. These provisions seek to curb misrepresentations and deceit, market manipulation, and other fraudulent acts and practices. They also strive to establish and maintain just and equitable principles of trade conducive to maintaining open, fair, and orderly markets.

These provisions of the law establish the general regulatory pattern. The commission is responsible for promulgating rules and regulations for its implementation. Thus, the commission has adopted regulations which, among other things:

- Define acts or practices which constitute a "manipulative or deceptive device or contrivance" prohibited by the statute.
- Regulate short selling, stabilizing transactions, and similar matters.
- Regulate hypothecation (use of customers' securities as collateral for loans).
- Provide safeguards with respect to the financial responsibility of brokers and dealers.

Registration of Exchanges and Others

As amended, the 1934 act requires registration with the commission of:

- "National securities exchanges" (those having a substantial securities trading volume).
- Brokers and dealers who conduct securities business in interstate commerce.
- Transfer agents.
- Clearing agencies.
- Municipal brokers and dealers.
- Securities information processors.

To obtain registration, exchanges must show that they are organized to comply with the provisions of the statute as well as the rules and regulations of the commission. The registering exchanges must also show that their rules contain just and adequate provisions to ensure fair dealing and to protect investors.

Each exchange is a self-regulatory organization. Its rules must provide for the expulsion, suspension, or other disciplining of member broker-dealers for conduct inconsistent with just and equitable principles of trade. The law intends that exchanges shall have full opportunity to establish self-regulatory measures ensuring fair dealing and investor protection. However, it empowers the SEC (by order, rule, or regulation) to approve proposed rule changes of exchanges concerning various activities and trading practices if necessary to effect the statutory objective. Exchange rules and revisions, proposed by exchanges or by the commission, generally reach their final form after discussions between representatives of both bodies without resort to formal proceedings.

By a 1938 amendment to the 1934 act, Congress also provided for creation of a national securities association. The only such association, the National Association of Securities Dealers, Inc., is registered with the commission under this provision of the law. This association is responsible for preventing fraudulent and manipulative acts and practices and for promoting just and equitable trade principles among over-the-counter brokers and dealers. The establishment, maintenance, and enforcement of a voluntary code of business ethics is one of the principal features of this provision of the law.

Broker-Dealer Registration

The registration of brokers and dealers engaged in soliciting and executing securities transactions is an important part of the regulatory plan of the act. Broker-dealers must apply for registration with the commission and amend registrations to show significant changes in financial conditions or other important facts. Applications and amendments are examined by the commission. Brokers and dealers must conform their business practices to the standards prescribed by the law and the commission's regulations for protecting investors and to rules on fair trade practices of their association. Additionally, brokers and dealers violating these regulations risk suspension or loss of registration with the commission (and thus the right to continue conducting an interstate securities business) or of suspension or expulsion from a self-regulatory organization.

PUBLIC UTILITY HOLDING COMPANY ACT OF 1935

Interstate holding companies engaged, through subsidiaries, in the electric utility business or in the retail distribution of natural or manufactured gas are subject to regulation under this act. Today, 13 systems are registered;

12 are active. These systems must register with the commission and file initial and periodic reports. Detailed information concerning the organization, financial structure, and operations of the holding company and its subsidiaries is contained in these reports. (However, if a holding company or its subsidiary meets certain specifications, the commission may exempt it from part or all of the duties and obligations otherwise imposed by statute.) Holding companies are subject to SEC regulations on matters such as structure of the system, acquisitions, combinations, and issue and sales of securities.

Integration and Simplification

The most important provisions of the act were the requirements for physical integration and corporate simplification of holding company systems. Integration standards restrict a holding company's operations to an "integrated utility system." Such a system is defined as one:

- Capable of economical operation as a single coordinated system.
- Confined to a single area or region in one or more states.
- Not so large that it negates the advantage of localized management, efficient operation, and effective regulation.

The capital structure and continued existence of any company in a holding company system must not unnecessarily complicate the corporate structure of the system or distribute voting power inequitably among security holders of the system.

The commission may determine what action, if any, must be taken by registered holding companies and their subsidiaries to comply with act requirements. The SEC may apply to federal courts for orders compelling compliance with commission directives.

Voluntary reorganization plans for many divestments of nonretainable subsidiaries and properties, recapitalizations, dissolutions of companies, and other adjustments may be used to satisfy act requirements. The SEC may approve voluntary plans it finds to be fair and equitable to all affected persons and to be necessary to further the objectives of the act. If the company requests, the commission will apply to a federal district court for an order approving the plan and directing its enforcement. All interested persons, including state commissions and other governmental agencies, have full opportunity to be heard in proceedings before the commission and before the federal courts.

Acquisitions

To be authorized by the SEC, the acquisition of securities and utility assets by holding companies and their subsidiaries must meet the following standards:

- The acquisition must not tend toward interlocking relations or concentrating control to an extent detrimental to investors or the public.
- Any consideration paid for the acquisition (including fees, commissions, and other remuneration) must not be unreasonable.
- The acquisition must not complicate the capital structure of the holding company system or have a detrimental effect on system functions.
- The acquisition must tend toward economical, efficient development of an integrated public utility system.

Issuance and Sale of Securities

Proposed security issues by any holding company must be analyzed and evaluated by the staff and approved by the commission to ensure that the issues meet the following tests under prescribed standards of the law:

- The security must be reasonably adapted to the security structure of the issuer and of other companies in the same holding company system.
- The security must be reasonably adapted to the earning power of the company.
- The proposed issue must be necessary and appropriate to the economical and efficient operation of the company's business.
- The fees, commissions, and other remuneration paid in connection with the issue must not be unreasonable.
- The terms and conditions of the issue or sale of the security must not be detrimental to the public or investor interest.

Other Regulatory Provisions

Other phases of the act provide for regulating dividend payments (in circumstances where payments might result in corporate abuses); intercompany loans; solicitation of proxies, consents, and other authorizations; and insider trading. "Upstream" loans from subsidiaries to their parents and "upstream" or "cross-stream" loans from public utility companies to any holding company in the same holding company system require commission approval. The act also requires that all services performed for any company in a holding company system by a service company in that system be rendered at a fair and equitably allocated cost.

TRUST INDENTURE ACT OF 1939

This act applies to bonds, debentures, notes, and similar debt securities offered for public sale and issued under trust indentures with more than $1 million of securities outstanding at any one time. Even though such securities may be registered under the Securities Act, they may not be offered for sale to the public unless the trust indenture conforms to statutory standards of this act. Designed to safeguard the rights and interests of the purchasers, the act also:

- Prohibits the indenture trustee from conflicting interests which might interfere with exercising its duties on behalf of the securities purchasers.
- Requires the trustee to be a corporation with minimum combined capital and surplus.
- Imposes high standards of conduct and responsibility on the trustee.
- Precludes, in the event of default, preferential collection of certain claims owing to the trustee by the issuer.
- Provides that the issuer supply to the trustee evidence of compliance with indenture terms and conditions (such as those relating to the release or substitution of mortgaged property, issue of new securities, or satisfaction of the indenture).
- Requires the trustee to provide reports and notices to security holders.

Other provisions of the act prohibit impairing the security holder's right to sue individually for principal and interest, except under certain circumstances. It also requires maintaining a list of security holders for their use in communicating with each other regarding their rights as security holders.

Applications for qualification of trust indentures are examined by the SEC's Division of Corporation Finance for compliance with the law and the commission's rules.

INVESTMENT COMPANY ACT OF 1940

The Public Utility Holding Company Act of 1935 required Congress to direct the SEC to study the activities of investment companies and investment advisers. The study results were sent to Congress in a series of reports filed in 1938, 1939, and 1940, causing the creation of the Investment Advisers Act of 1940 and the Investment Company Act of 1940. The legislation was supported by both the commission and the industry.

Activities of companies engaged primarily in investing, reinvesting, and trading in securities, and whose own securities are offered to the investing public, are subject to certain statutory prohibitions and to commission regulation under this act. Also, public offerings of investment company securities must be registered under the Securities Act of 1933.

Investors must understand, however, that the commission does not supervise the investment activities of these companies and that regulation by the commission does not imply safety of investment.

In addition to the registration requirement for such companies, the law requires they disclose their financial condition and investment policies to provide investors complete information about their activities. This act also:

- Prohibits such companies from substantially changing the nature of their business or investment policies without stockholder approval.
- Bars persons guilty of security frauds from serving as officers and directors.
- Prevents underwriters, investment bankers, or brokers from constituting more than a minority of the directors of such companies.
- Requires that management contracts (and any material changes) be submitted to security holders for their approval.
- Prohibits transactions between such companies and their directors,

officers, or affiliated companies or persons, except when approved by the SEC.
- Forbids such companies to issue senior securities except under specified conditions and upon specified terms.
- Prohibits pyramiding of such companies and cross-ownership of their securities.

Other provisions of this act involve advisory fees not conforming to an adviser's fiduciary duty, sales and repurchases of securities issued by investment companies, exchange offers, and other activities of investment companies, including special provisions for periodic payment plan and face-amount certificate companies.

Regarding reorganization plans of investment companies, the commission is authorized to institute court proceedings to prohibit plans that do not appear to be fair and equitable to security holders. The commission may also institute court action to remove management officials who have engaged in personal misconduct constituting a breach of fiduciary duty.

Investment company securities must also be registered under the Securities Act. Investment companies must file periodic reports and are subject to the commission's proxy and "insider" trading rules.

INVESTMENT ADVISERS ACT OF 1940

This law establishes a pattern of regulating investment advisers. In some respects, it has provisions similar to Securities Exchange Act provisions governing the conduct of brokers and dealers. With certain exceptions, this act requires that persons or firms compensated for advising others about securities investment must register with the commission and conform to statutory standards designed to protect investors.

The commission may deny, suspend, or revoke investment adviser registrations if, after notice and hearing, it finds that a statutory disqualification exists and that the action is in the public interest. Disqualifications include conviction for certain financial crimes or securities violations, injunctions based on such activities, conviction for violating the Mail Fraud Statute, willfully filing false reports with the commission, and willfully violating the Advisers Act, the Securities Act, the Securities Exchange Act, the Investment Company Act, or the rules of the Municipal Securities Rulemaking Board. In addition to the administrative sanction of denial, suspension, or revocation, the commission may obtain injunctions prohibiting further violations of this law. The SEC may also recommend prosecution by the Department of Justice for fraudulent misconduct or willful violation of the law or commission rules.

The law contains antifraud provisions and empowers the commission to adopt rules defining fraudulent, deceptive, or manipulative acts and practices. It also requires that investment advisers:

- Disclose the nature of their interest in transactions executed for their clients.
- Maintain books and records according to commission rules.
- Make books and records available to the commission for inspections.

CORPORATE REORGANIZATION

Reorganization proceedings in the U.S. courts under Chapter 11 of the Bankruptcy Code are begun by a debtor, voluntarily, or by its creditors. Federal bankruptcy law allows a debtor in reorganization to continue operating under the court's protection while it attempts to rehabilitate its business and work out a plan to pay its debts. If a debtor corporation has publicly issued securities outstanding, the reorganization process may raise many issues that materially affect the rights of public investors.

Chapter 11 of the Bankruptcy Code authorizes the SEC to appear in any reorganization case and to present its views on any issue. Although Chapter 11 applies to all types of business reorganizations, the commission generally limits its participation to proceedings involving significant public investor interest—protecting public investors holding the debtor's securities and participating in legal and policy issues of concern to public investors. The SEC also continues to address matters of traditional commission expertise and interest relating to securities. Where appropriate, it comments on the adequacy of reorganization plan disclosure statements and participates where there is a commission law enforcement interest.

Under Chapter 11, the debtor, official committees, and institutional creditors negotiate the terms of a reorganization plan. The court can confirm a reorganization plan if it is accepted by creditors for:

- At least two thirds of the amounts of allowed claims.

- More than one half the number of allowed claims.
- At least two thirds in amount of the allowed shareholder interest.

The principal safeguard for public investors is the requirement that a disclosure statement containing adequate information be transmitted by a debtor or plan proponent in connection with soliciting votes on the plan. In addition, reorganization plans involving publicly held debtors usually provide for issuing new securities to creditors and shareholders which may be exempt from registration under Section 5 of the Securities Act of 1933.

ORGANIZATION OF THE COMMISSION

The commission carries out its work, in both Washington headquarters and the regional offices around the country, through divisions and offices charged with specific responsibilities under the securities laws. Additionally, there are offices responsible for the smooth and effective administration of the commission itself. Overall responsibility for carrying out the SEC mission rests with the commissioners.

The Commissioners

The Securities Exchange Act of 1934 formally created the Securities and Exchange Commission on June 1, 1934. (The Securities Act of 1933 was administered by the Federal Trade Commission until creation of the SEC.) Among other provisions, this act set forth the composition of the commission, which remains unchanged today. Five commissioners are appointed by the president, with the advice and consent of the Senate, for five-year terms. Terms are staggered; one expires in June of every year. The chairman is generally of the same political party as the president, but no more than three of the five commissioners may belong to the same political party. The result is that the commission is an independent, nonpartisan agency.

A deliberative collegial body, the commission meets numerous times monthly to debate and decide upon regulatory issues. Like other regulatory agencies, the commission has two types of meetings. Under the Government in the Sunshine Act, meetings may be open to the public and to members of the press. However, if necessary to protect the commission's ability to conduct investigations and/or protect the rights of individuals and entities which may be the subject of commission inquiries, meetings may be closed.

Commission meetings are generally held to deliberate on the resolve issues that staff brings before the commissioners. Issues may be interpretations of federal securities laws, amendments to existing rules under the laws, new rules (often to reflect changed conditions in the marketplace), actions to enforce the laws or to discipline those subject to direct regulation, legislation to be proposed by the commission, and matters concerning administration of the commission itself. Matters not requiring joint deliberation may be resolved by procedures set forth in the Code of Federal Regulation.

Resolution of the issues brought before the commission may take the form of new rules or amendments to existing ones, enforcement actions, or disciplinary actions. The most common activity is rulemaking. Rulemaking is generally the result of staff recommendations made to the commissioners.

The Commission Staff

The staff is organized into divisions (with subordinate offices) and major offices with specific areas of responsibility for various segments of the federal securities laws.

For the past several years, the divisions have been Enforcement, Corporation Finance, Market Regulation, and Investment Management. The Office of the General Counsel serves as the chief legal officer for the commission. As such, it is responsible for appellate and other litigation as well as certain other legal matters.

At present, the offices are those of Chief Accountant, Opinions and Review, Chief Economist, Administrative Law Judges, Secretary, and the Directorate of Economic and Policy Analysis.

Other offices provide administration and carry out certain necessary functions for the commission. These include the Office of Executive Director, Comptroller, Consumer Affairs and Information Services, Personnel, Administrative Service, Applications and Reports Services, Information Systems Management, and Public Affairs.

The Divisions

The Division of Corporation Finance
Corporation Finance has the overall responsibility of ensuring that disclosure requirements are met by publicly held companies registered with the commission. Its work includes reviewing registration statements for new securities, proxy material and annual reports the commission requires

from publicly held companies, documents concerning tender offers, and mergers and acquisitions in general.

This division renders administrative interpretations of the Securities Act of 1933 and its regulations to the public, prospective registrants, and others. It is also responsible for certain statutes and regulations pertaining to small businesses and for the Trust Indenture Act of 1939. Applications for qualification of trust indentures are examined for compliance with the applicable requirements of the law and the commission's rules. The Division of Corporation Finance works closely with the Office of the Chief Accountant in drafting rules and regulations which prescribe requirements for financial statements.

The Division of Market Regulation
Market Regulation is responsible for oversight of activity in the secondary markets—registration and regulation of broker-dealers, oversight of the self-regulatory organizations (such as the nation's stock exchanges), and oversight of other participants in the secondary markets (such as transfer agents and clearing organizations).

Financial responsibility of these entities, trading and sales practices, policies affecting operation of the securities markets, and surveillance fall under the purview of this division. In addition, it carries out activities aimed at achieving the goal of a national market system set forth in the Securities Act Amendments of 1975. Market Regulation develops and presents market structure issues to the commissioners for their consideration. The division also oversees the Securities Investor Protection Corporation and the Municipal Securities Rulemaking Board.

The Division of Investment Management
Investment Management has basic responsibility for the Investment Company Act of 1940 and the Investment Advisers Act of 1940. In 1985 it assumed responsibility for administering the Public Utility Holding Company Act of 1935.

The division staff ensures compliance with regulations regarding the registration, financial responsibility, sales practices, and advertising of mutual funds and of investment advisers. New products offered by these entities also are reviewed by staff in this division. They also process investment company registration statements, proxy statements, and periodic reports under the Securities Act.

The division's Office of Public Utility Regulation oversees the activities of the 12 active registered holding company systems, ensuring that their corporate structures and financings are permissible according to certain tests set up in the Holding Company Act. The staff analyzes legal, financial, accounting, engineering, and other issues arising under the act. The office participates in hearings to develop the factual records where necessary, files briefs and participates in oral arguments before the commission, and makes recommendations regarding the commission's findings and decisions in cases which arise in administration of the law. All hearings are conducted in accordance with the commission's Rules of Practice.

The Division of Enforcement

This division is charged with enforcing federal securities laws. Enforcement responsibilities include investigating possible violations of federal securities laws and recommending appropriate remedies for consideration by the commission. Possible violations may come to light through the Enforcement Division's own inquiries, through referrals from other divisions of the commission, from outside sources such as the self-regulatory organizations, or by other means.

When possible violations of federal securities laws warrant further investigation by the staff, the commission is consulted before proceeding. The commission's decisions may result in issuing subpoenas, formal orders of investigation, or other means of proceeding with actions. At the conclusion of investigations, the commission may authorize the staff to proceed with injunctions preventing further violative conduct, with administrative proceedings in the case of entities directly regulated by the commission, or with other remedies as appropriate.

Activities of Divisions

Each of the divisions, often in cooperation with an office or offices, engages in a variety of activities.

Interpretation and Guidance

On the basis of responsibilities and powers assigned under federal securities laws, each division provides guidance and counseling to registrants, prospective registrants, the public, and others. This information is provided to help determine the application of the law and its regulations and to aid in complying with the law. For example, this advice might include an informal expression of opinion about whether the offering of a particular security is subject to the registration requirements of the law and, if so, advice on compliance with disclosure requirements of the applicable registration form. These interpretations of the rules and laws help ensure conformity on the part of the registrants. Also, most divisions occasionally issue "no action" letters which indicate they will take no action on matters regarding registrants in certain circumstances.

Rulemaking

One of the most common activities engaged in by the divisions is rulemaking.

The commission's objective of requiring regulated entities to provide effective disclosure, with a minimum of burden and expense, calls for constant review of practical operations of the rules and registration forms adopted. If experience shows that a particular requirement fails to achieve its objective, or if a rule appears unduly burdensome in relation to the resulting benefits, the staff presents the problem to the commission. The commission then considers modifying the rule or other requirement. Based on their particular area of expertise, the divisions and offices are often asked to contribute specific analyses.

Many suggestions for rule modification follow extensive consultation with industry representatives and others affected. The commission normally gives advance public notice of proposals to adopt new or amended rules or registration forms and affords the opportunity for interested members of the public to comment on them.

The commission decides, generally in open meetings, whether the new rules or amendments to existing rules are warranted. Proposals approved by the commission become mandatory, usually within a specific time period, after publication in the Federal Register.

The commission's work is remedial, not punitive. Its primary activities are to ensure investor protection through full disclosure of material information and to ensure that the securities markets are fair and honest in compliance with federal securities laws and rules under those laws. Interpretations, counseling, rulemaking, and similar activities are all aimed at ensuring compliance with the law.

The commission, however, does have civil authority to enforce federal securities laws and does so when it has reason to believe that the laws have been, or in some cases are about to be, violated. The commission also works closely with criminal authorities in matters of mutual interest.

Investigations

Under the laws it administers, the commission has a duty to investigate complaints and other indications of possible law violations in securities transactions. Most arise under the Securities Act of 1933 and the Securities Exchange Act of 1934. (Fraud prohibitions of the Securities Act are similar to those contained in the securities Exchange Act of 1934.) Investigation and any subsequent enforcement work is conducted primarily by the commission's regional offices and the Division of Enforcement.

Most of the commission's investigations are conducted privately. Facts are developed to the fullest extent possible through informal inquiry, interviewing witnesses, examining brokerage records and other documents, reviewing and trading data, and similar means. The commission is empowered to issue subpoenas requiring sworn testimony and the production of books, records, and other documents pertinent to the subject matter under investigation. In the event of refusal to respond to a subpoena, the commission may apply to a federal court for an order compelling obedience.

Inquiring and complaints by investors and the general public are primary sources of leads for detecting law violations in securities transactions. Another source is surprise inspections by regional offices and the Division of Market Regulation of the books and records of regulated persons and organizations to determine whether their business practices conform to the prescribed rules. Still another means is conducting inquiries into market fluctuations in particular stocks which don't appear to result from general market trends or from known developments affecting the issuing company.

Investigations frequently concern the sale without registration of securities subject to the registration requirement of the Securities Act. Misrepresentation or omission of material facts concerning securities offered for sale, whether or not registration is required, is another common subject of investigation. The antifraud provisions of the law also apply to the purchase of securities, whether involving outright misrepresentations or the withholding or omission of pertinent facts to which the seller was entitled. For example, it is unlawful in certain situations to purchase securities from another person while withholding material information which would indicate that the securities have a value substantially greater than that at which they are being acquired. These provisions apply not only to transactions between brokers and dealers and their customers but also to the reacquisition of securities by an issuing company or its "insiders."

Other types of inquiries relate to manipulating market prices of securities; misappropriating or illegally hypothecating customers' funds or securities; conducting a securities business while insolvent; broker-dealers buying or selling securities from or to customers at prices not reasonably related to current market prices; and broker-dealers violating their responsibilities to treat customers fairly.

A common type of violation involves the broker-dealer who gains the customer's trust and then takes undisclosed profits in securities transactions with or for the customer over and above the agreed commission. For example, the broker-dealer may have purchased securities from customers at prices far below, or sold securities to customers at prices far above, their current market prices. In most of these cases, the broker-dealer risks no loss; the purchases from customers are made only if simultaneous sales can be made at prices substantially higher than those paid to the customers. Conversely, sales to customers are made only if simultaneous purchases can be made at prices substantially lower than those charged the customer. Another type of violation involves firms engaging in large-scale in-and-out transactions for the customer's account (called *churning*) to generate increased commissions, usually without regard to any resulting benefit to the customer.

There is a fundamental distinction between a broker and a dealer. The broker serves as the customer's agent in buying or selling securities for the customer. The broker owes the customer the highest fiduciary responsibility and may charge only such agency commission as has been agreed to by the customer. On the other hand, a dealer acts as a principal and buys securities from or sells securities to customers. The dealer's profit is the difference between the prices for which the securities are bought and sold. The dealer normally will not disclose the fee or commission charged for services rendered. The law requires that the customer receive a written "confirmation" of each securities transaction. This confirmation discloses whether the securities firm is acting as a dealer (a principal for its own account) or as a broker (an agent for the customer). If the latter, the confirmation must also disclose the broker's compensation from all sources as well as other information about the transaction.

Statutory Sanctions

Commission investigations, usually conducted in private, are essentially fact-finding inquiries. The facts developed by the staff are considered by the commission to determine whether there is valid evidence of a law violation; whether action should begin to determine if a violation actually occurred; and, if so, whether some sanction should be imposed.

When facts show possible fraud or other law violation, the laws provide several courses of action which the commission may pursue:

- Civil injunction where the commission may apply to an appropriate U.S. district court for an order prohibiting the acts or practices alleged to violate the law or commission rules.
- Administrative remedy, where the commission may take specific action after hearings. It may issue orders to suspend or expel members from exchanges or over-the-counter dealers association; deny, suspend, or revoke broker-dealer registrations; or censure for misconduct or bar individuals (temporarily or permanently) from employment with a registered firm.

Broker-Dealer Revocations

In the case of exchange or association members, registered brokers or dealers, or individuals who may associate with any such firm, the administrative remedy is generally invoked. In these administrative proceedings, the commission issues an order specifying illegal acts or practices allegedly committed and directs that a hearing be held for the purpose of taking evidence. At the hearing, counsel for the Division of Enforcement (often a regional office attorney) undertakes to establish those facts supporting the charge. Respondents have full opportunity to cross-examine witnesses and to present evidence in defense. If the commission ultimately finds that the respondents violated the law, it may take remedial action in the form of statutory sanctions as indicated above. The respondent has the right to seek judicial review of the decision by the appropriate U.S. Court of Appeals. Remedial action may effectively bar a firm from conducting a securities business in interstate commerce or on exchanges, or an individual from association with a registered firm.

The many instances in which these legal sanctions have been invoked present a formidable record. Of great significance to the investing public is the deterrent effect of the very existence of the fraud prohibitions of the law and the commission's powers of investigation and enforcement. These provisions of the law, coupled with the disclosure requirements applicable to new security offerings and to other registered securities, tend to inhibit fraudulent stock promotions and operations. They also increase public confidence in securities as an investment medium. This facilitates financing through the public sale of securities, which contributes to the economic growth of the nation.

Administrative Proceedings

All formal administrative proceedings of the commission follow its Rules of Practice which conform to the Administrative Procedure Act. These rules establish procedural "due process" safeguards to protect the rights and interests of parties to these proceedings. Included are requirements for timely notice of the proceeding and for a sufficient specification of the issues or charges involved to enable parties to prepare their cases adequately. All parties, including counsel for the interested SEC division or office, may appear at the hearing and present evidence and cross-examine witnesses. In addition, other interested persons may intervene or be given limited rights to participate. In some cases, the relevant facts may be stipulated instead of conducting an evidentiary hearing.

Hearings are conducted before a hearing officer, normally an administrative law judge appointed by the commission. The hearing officer, who is independent of the interested division or office, rules on the admissibility of evidence and on other issues arising during the course of the hearing. At the conclusion of the hearing, participants may urge in writing that the hearing officer adopt specific findings of fact and conclusions of law. The hearing officer then prepares and files an initial decision (unless waived), stating conclusions to the facts established by the evidence and including an order disposing of the issues. Copies of the initial decision are served on the parties and participants, who may seek commission review. If review is not sought and the commission does not order review on its own motion, the initial decision becomes final and the hearing officer's order becomes effective.

If the commission reviews the initial decision, the parties and participants may file briefs and be heard in oral argument before the commission. On the basis of an independent review of the record, the SEC prepares and issues its own decision. The Office of Opinions and Review aids the commission in this process. The laws provide that any person or firm aggrieved by a decision order of the commission may seek review by the appropriate U.S. Court of Appeals. The initial decisions of hearing officers as well as the commission decisions are made public. Ultimately, the commission decisions (as well as initial decisions which have become final and are of precedential significance) are printed and published.

The commission has only civil authority. However, if fraud or other willful law violation is indicated, the commission may refer the facts to the

Department of Justice with a recommendation for criminal prosecution of the offending persons. That department, through its local U.S. attorneys (who frequently are assisted by commission attorneys), may present the evidence to a federal grand jury and seek an indictment.

In its investigation and enforcement actions, the SEC cooperates closely with other federal, state, and local law enforcement officials.

The Offices

The Office of the General Counsel
The Office of the General Counsel serves as the focal point for handling all appellate and other litigation brought by the commission, either in connection with the securities laws or against the commission or its staff. The general counsel is the chief legal officer of the commission.

Duties of this office include representing the commission in judicial proceedings, handling multidivisional legal matters, and providing advice and assistance to the commission, its operating divisions, and regional offices. Advice concerns statutory interpretation, rulemaking, legislative matters and other legal problems, public or private investigations, and congressional hearings and investigations. The general counsel directs and supervises all contested civil litigation and SEC responsibilities under the Bankruptcy Code and all related litigation. It also represents the commission in all cases in the appellate courts, filing briefs and presenting oral arguments on behalf of the commission. In private litigation involving the statutes the commission administers, this office represents the SEC as a friend of the court on legal issues of general importance.

The commission's work is primarily legal in nature. Occasional questions of legality regarding the commission's own decisions or legal decisions affecting the federal securities laws are handled by the general counsel.

The commission also recommends revisions in the statutes which it administers. In addition, the SEC prepares comments on proposed legislation which might affect its work or when asked for its views by congressional committees. The Office of the General Counsel, together with the division affected by such legislation, prepares this legislative material.

The Office of the Chief Accountant
The chief accountant consults with representatives of the accounting profession and the standard-setting bodies designated by the profession regarding the promulgation of new or revised accounting and auditing stan-

dards. This implements a major SEC objective to improve accounting and auditing standards and to maintain high standards of professional conduct by the independent accountants.

This office also drafts rules and regulations prescribing requirements for financial statements. Many of the accounting rules are embodied in Regulation S-X, adopted by the commission. Regulation S-X, together with the generally accepted accounting principles promulgated by the profession's standard-setting bodies and a number of opinions issued as "Accounting Series Releases" or "Financial Reporting Releases," governs the form and content of most of the financial statements filed with the SEC.

This office administers the commission's statutes and rules which require that accountants examining financial statements filed with the SEC be independent of their clients. This office also makes recommendations on cases arising under the commission's Rules of Practice which specify reasons an accountant may be denied the privilege of practicing before the commission. These reasons include lack of character or integrity, lack of qualifications to represent others, unethical or unprofessional conduct, or the willful violation of (or the willful aiding and abetting of violation of) any of the federal securities laws, rules, or regulations. The chief accountant supervises the procedures followed in accounting investigations conducted by the commission staff.

The Directorate of Economic and Policy Analysis
This group deals with the economic and empirical issues which are inextricably associated with the commission's regulatory activities. The directorate usually works closely with the divisions responsible for rule proposals. Whether working with one of the operating divisions or serving the commission independently, the directorate analyzes impacts and benefits of proposed regulations and conducts studies on specific rules.

More specifically, the directorate analyzes rule changes and engages in long-term research and policy planning. To accomplish this, it builds and maintains diverse computer databases, designs programs to access data, and develops and tests alternative methodologies. The directorate assesses the impact of securities market regulations on issuers (in particular, small or high technology issuers), broker-dealers, investors, and the economy in general. One area it monitors is the emerging national market structure and regulation changes affecting the ability of small businesses to raise capital. The directorate also collects, processes, and publishes (in its SEC Monthly Statistical Review) data on the financial condition of the securities industry, registered securities issues, and trading volume and value of exchange-listed equity securities.

The Office of the Chief Economist

The Office of the Chief Economist analyzes potentially significant developments in the marketplace. Its work includes gathering and analyzing data on a wide range of market activities that may require attention by the commission. Examples are new types of securities, actions by publicly held entities and their impact on investors, and new or emerging trends in the securities markets.

Results of this work are used internally as part of the process to determine whether commission action is necessary and to keep abreast of trends in the marketplace. Occasionally, subject to approval of the commission, the research of this office is published.

The Office of Administrative Law Judges

The administrative law judges are responsible for scheduling and conducting hearings on administrative proceedings instituted by the commission and appeals of proceedings instituted by others. Opinions and orders resulting from these hearings are prepared by the Office of Opinions and Review.

The Office of the Executive Director

The executive director develops and executes the overall management policies of the commission for all its operating divisions and offices. The executive director administers programs to implement certain statutes, regulations, and executive orders. Program functions include appointing program officials; reviewing and approving program policies, procedures, and regulations; authorizing and transmitting reports; and assuring appropriate resource requirements to implement the program.

The Office of Consumer Affairs and Information Services

This office of the commission provides direct assistance to the investing public. It reviews public complaints against entities regulated by the commission and disseminates public information about these entities as well as commission activities.

The office's Investor Services Branch reviews all complaints from the investing public and typically obtains written responses from firms mentioned in the complaint. Information suggesting a possible violation of federal securities laws is referred to appropriate commission staff. When complaints entail private disputes between parties, commission staff attempt informally to assist the parties in resolving the problem. The commission is not authorized to arbitrate private disputes or intercede on behalf of a private party to recover losses from the purchase or sale of securities or otherwise act as a collection agency for an individual. Investors must seek a financial judgment through civil litigation or binding arbitration. Laws which provide investors with important recovery rights if they have been defrauded can be used in private lawsuits.

Through the office's Public Reference and Freedom of Information Branches, the public may obtain a wide range of information including all public reports filed by registered entities and internal commission information on completed investigations and official actions.

Quarterly (10-Q) and annual (10-K) reports, registration statements, proxy material, and other reports filed by corporations, mutual funds, or broker-dealers are available for inspection in the Public Reference Room of the commission's headquarters office in Washington, D.C., and in the New York and Chicago regional offices. Registration statements (and subsequent reports) filed by companies traded over-the-counter and by those registered under the 1964 Amendments to the Exchange Act are also available in regional offices.

READING 3

DEFINING YIELD: A WORD OF MANY MEANINGS

John Markese

The term *yield* is thrown about often by the financial press and others. The trouble is that yield has many different meanings and implications for investors. This workshop will try and sort out some of the major differences. It will not, however, attempt to present mathematically all the possible yield calculations created by institutions and financial instruments.

The basic dilemma is that yield may or may not be synonymous with total return—the bottom line for investors. Newspaper listings for both stocks and bonds tend to add to the confusion.

STOCK YIELDS

The stock pages in newspapers list yield, among other statistics. Generally, the yield figure is close to the current annual dividend figure, but many investors may not know how the two are related. For example, Figure 1 shows a typical listing for several stocks; look in particular at the figures for IBM.

A considerable amount of information is presented along with the yield figure. Yield in this case is dividend yield, and it is calculated by dividing the annual cash dividend by the closing price of the stock. For IBM, with an an-

Source: *AAII Journal*, September 1987. Used with permission.

FIGURE 1
A Typical Newspaper Listing for Stocks and Bonds

Stock Listing

52 Weeks		Stock	Div.	Yield %	P/E Ratio	Sales 100s	Week's			Net Chg.
High	Low						High	Low	Close	
169⅞	115¾	IBM	4.40	2.6%	23	22634	169⅞	166½	168	+½
60¼	43	Lockhd	1.40	2.4	9	31128	58¾	55⅝	57½	+1⅝
38¾	14½	USX	1.20	3.1	—	84124	38¾	35⅜	38¾	+3⅛

Bond Listing

52 Weeks		Bond and Coupon	Cur. Yld.	Vol.	Week's			Net Chg.
High	Low				High	Low	Close	
91¾	77⅝	ATT 7s01	8.5%	111	81⅞	81⅝	81⅞	−⅛
57⅞	41⅛	Bkam zr93s	—	171	53¼	52⅝	52⅝	—
128¾	110½	IBM 7⅞ 04	cv	737	128¾	127⅝	128	−¼

nual cash dividend of $4.40 and a closing price of $168, the yield is: $4.40/$168 = 0.0262 = 2.6 percent—the yield quoted in the paper.

If you had purchased IBM at $140 per share, held the stock for a year, and received quarterly total dividends of $4.40 without reinvesting the dividends, your total return before taxes would have been 23.1 percent. This total return would have been composed of a 20 percent capital gain and a 3.1 percent dividend yield (based on the purchase price). It was calculated as follows:

$$\frac{\$168 - \$140 + \$4.40}{\$140} = 23.1\%$$

What does the yield in the paper mean? Simply that the historic annual dividend relative to the current market price is 2.6 percent—a number that may prove to be irrelevant to your return experience.

BOND YIELDS

Turning to the corporate bond page, the yield reported is termed current yield. Examples of bond quotations appear in the bottom half of Figure 1.

Current yield, which is 8.5 percent for the ATT 7 percent coupon bond maturing in 2001, is calculated by dividing the annual interest payment ($70 or 7 percent coupon times $1,000 of maturity value) by the current market price of $818.75 (81 7/8 or 81.875 percent of a $1,000 maturity value).

The current yield, much like the dividend yield, only captures one aspect of total return—the income generated by the investment. It ignores any changes in capital value.

The Bank America bond is a zero-coupon bond, sold at a discount to mature in 1993 and paying no annual interest, so no current yield can be calculated. The IBM bond is a convertible bond, convertible into common stock and selling more as a stock than a bond. The ATT and the IBM bonds have similar coupon rates and maturities, yet the IBM bond is selling for 128 percent of its maturity value and the ATT is selling at a substantial discount. The premium on the IBM indicates that its common stock conversion value is greater than its straight bond value. In the case of convertible bonds, the current yield is not given and may be irrelevant if it were.

The discount on the ATT bond highlights a distinction between the current yield reported in the newspaper and the total return focus that investors should have. The coupon rate on the ATT bond is low relative to the level of current interest rates, so the market adjusts the bond price down. If interest rates rise in the market, the prices of existing bonds fall; the bonds with the longest time to maturity and the lowest coupons fall the most in price. A long-term zero-coupon bond would be the most price-volatile with respect to interest rate changes.

Total return incorporates capital gains and losses, and yield. Using the ATT bond example and assuming a bond price decline due to rising interest rates, the one-year total return on the bond would be calculated as follows:

$$\frac{B_c - B_b + I}{B_b} = \text{Total return}$$

Where: B_b = Bond price at beginning of year
B_c = Bond price at end of year
I = Annual interest payments

For the ATT bond, assuming a price at the beginning of the year of $918.75 and an end-year price of $818.75, the one-year total return would be:

$$\frac{\$818.75 - \$918.75 + \$70}{\$918.75} = -3.27\%$$

This negative return is in contrast to the 8.5 percent current yield. The calculation does not assume any reinvestment of interest and is a before-tax return. Looking just at current yield masks the impact of capital gains and losses on return.

One other bond yield that is reported in the financial press is the yield to maturity. This concept of yield assumes that the bond is held to maturity and all interest payments are reinvested and compounded at the yield to maturity. In most newspapers, the yield to maturity is only given for U.S. government and agency bonds and sometimes for selected municipal bonds, although municipal bonds are not reported generally.

The precise math for yield to maturity is fairly complex and either requires financial tables, a computer, or a sophisticated hand-held calculator. A simple approximation is useful:

$$\frac{I + \dfrac{B_m - B_t}{Yrs.}}{0.40(B_m) + 0.60(B_t)} = YTM$$

Where: B_m = Bond value at maturity
B_t = Bond price today
Yrs. = Years to maturity

Again, using the ATT bond, the yield to maturity would be:

$$\frac{\$70 + \dfrac{\$1,000 - \$818.75}{14}}{0.40(\$1,000) + 0.60(\$818.75)} = 9.3\%$$

The calculation adds the annual interest payment to the average annual capital gain to maturity and then relates this total average annual amount to a weighted average of the current price and the maturity value. The unequal weights (40 percent and 60 percent) have been found to improve the accuracy of the approximation over an equal weighting system.

This is very close to the precise yield to maturity and, for most investors, it is sufficient for making investment decisions. Because the yield to maturity assumes that interest payments are reinvested at the same yield to maturity rate each period, if interest rates rise, the realized yield to maturity will be higher and, conversely, if interest rates fall, the realized yield to maturity will fall. Of course, if the bond is sold before maturity, any yield, including a negative one, is possible.

For corporate bonds, Moody's Bond Record and Standard & Poor's Bond Guide provide yield to maturity figures.

Yield to maturity is useful for individual investment decisions but makes some rather rigid assumptions. On the other hand, the total return

TABLE 1
Yield Definitions

Dividend yield: The annual cash dividend relative to the current market price of the common or preferred stock.

Current yield: The annual interest payment of a bond relative to the current market price of the bond.

Yield to maturity: The compound annual return on the bond if held to maturity and if all interest payments are reinvested at the yield to maturity.

Total return: For any period, the cash dividends or interest plus the change in value of the stock or bond relative to the beginning value or purchase price.

---

for any period can be calculated by the individual investor and is specific to the individual investor's particular experience (i.e., purchase price, holding period, end of period value).

CONCLUSIONS

The bottom line to an individual investor is total return. Current yield and dividend yield only reflect one part of total return. They ignore capital gains and losses, which can be a significant portion of the total return component. While yield figures are useful in analyzing an investment, investors should understand what yield figures do and do not measure. Table 1 presents some short definitions of the yields discussed in this article.

PART 2

BOND MARKET INVESTING

READING 4

INTRODUCTION TO BONDS AND BOND PRICING

Frank J. Fabozzi
T. Dessa Fabozzi

A bond is an instrument in which the issue (debtor/borrower) promises to repay to the lender/investor the amount borrowed plus interest over some specified period of time. Prior to the 1970s, a typical ("plain vanilla") bond issued in the United States would specify (1) a fixed date at which the amount borrowed (principal) is due and (2) the contractual amount of interest that would be paid every six months. The date on which the principal is required to be repaid is called the *maturity date*. The interest rate that the issuer agrees to pay annually on the principal is called the *coupon rate*. Assuming that the issuer does not default or redeem the issue before the maturity date, an investor who holds this bond until the maturity date would be assured of a known cash flow pattern.

The high and volatile interest rates that prevailed in the United States in the late 1970s and the early 1980s brought a wide variety of new types of "bonds" issued by corporations and municipalities designed to make them more attractive to investors. These included: (1) *zero-coupon bonds,* in which there are no periodic coupon payments, but instead the entire principal and interest are paid at the maturity date; (2) *adjustable-rate* or *floating-rate* bonds, in which the coupon payments are indexed to some

Source: From Fabozzi/Fabozzi, BOND MARKETS, ANALYSIS AND STRATEGIES, © 1989, pp. 1–30. Adapted by permission of Prentice-Hall, Inc., Englewood Cliffs, NJ.

EXHIBIT 1

Composition of the U.S. Bond Market as of December 31, 1987 (Dollars in Billions; Based on Par Value)

U.S. government securities					$1,713	(26%)
U.S. government agencies (excluding agency pass-through securities)					275	(4%)
Corporate bonds					1,023	(15%)
State and local (municipal) securities					776	(12%)
Mortgages					2,849	(43%)
Residential mortgages			2,113	(32%)		
Nonsecuritized	1,432	(22%)				
Securitized (mortgage pass-throughs)	681	(10%)				
Commercial mortgages			649	(10%)		
Farm mortgages			87	(1%)		
Total of all bond markets					$6,636	

Source: This exhibit was prepared from data supplied by Salomon Brothers, Inc.

financial or commodity benchmark; (3) *bonds with embedded options,* such as the option to sell ("put") the bond back to the issuer at predetermined time periods or the option to buy an additional bond; and (4) *bonds issued in the United States* in which the contractual interest payments and/or principal payments are *in a foreign currency* rather than U.S. dollars.

In the residential mortgage market new types of mortgages, such as adjustable-rate mortgages and graduated-payment mortgages, became commonplace. The pooling of individual mortgages to form mortgage pass-through securities increased dramatically. Using the basic instruments in the mortgage market (mortgages and mortgage pass-through securities), derivative instruments, such as collateralized mortgage obligations and stripped mortgage-backed securities, were created to meet the specific investment needs of a broadening range of institutional investors.

Exhibit 1 shows the composition of the U.S. bond market as of December 31, 1987. Of the $6.636 trillion total bond market, the largest component is by far the mortgage market. Within the mortgage market, the largest sector is the residential mortgage sector. Approximately 32 percent of residential mortgages have been securitized. That is, they have been pooled to create mortgage pass-through securities. The second-largest section of the bond market is the market for U.S. government securities, while the smallest sector is the U.S. government agency market (excluding mortgage pass-through securities guaranteed by any agency).

RISKS ASSOCIATED WITH INVESTING IN BONDS

The investor in bonds may be exposed to one or more of the following risks: (1) interest rate risk; (2) reinvestment risk; (3) default risk; (4) call risk (prepayment risk in the case of mortgage-backed securities); (5) inflation risk; (6) foreign-exchange rate risk; and (7) marketability/liquidity risk. Here we provide a brief description of each.

Interest Rate Risk

A bond's price moves in the opposite direction of the change in interest rates. As interest rates rise (fall), the price of a bond will fall (rise). For an investor who plans to hold a bond to maturity, the change in the bond's price prior to maturity is not of concern; however, for an investor who may have to sell the bond before the maturity date, an increase in interest rates after the bond was purchased will mean the realization of a capital loss. The risk is referred to as *interest rate risk.*[1] Not all bonds have the same degree of interest rate risk.

Reinvestment Risk

The dollar return from investing in a bond comes from three sources: (1) coupon interest payments; (2) any capital gain (or capital loss) when the bond is redeemed, sold, or matures; and (3) interest earned from reinvesting the interim cash flows (coupon payments or principal repayments).[2] In order for an investor to realize a yield equal to the stated yield at the time the bond is purchased, these interim cash flows must be reinvested at an

---

[1] Interest rate risk is also referred to as *price risk* or *market risk*.

[2] The importance of interest earned from reinvesting the interim cash flows was first highlighted in a now-classic book by Sidney Homer and Martin L. Leibowitz, *Inside the Yield Book* (Englewood Cliffs, N.J.: Prentice-Hall; and New York: New York Institute of Finance, 1972).

interest rate equal to the stated yield when the bond is purchased. The risk that interim cash flows will have to be reinvested at such a lower rate that the investor will earn a lower yield than the stated yield at the time the bond is purchased is called *reinvestment risk.*

Default Risk

Default risk, also known as *credit risk,* is the risk that the issuer will default on its contractual payments of interest and/or principal. The obligations of the U.S. government are perceived to be free of default risk. For other issuers, the risk of default is gauged by quality ratings assigned by commercial rating companies such as Moody's Investor Service, Standard & Poor's Corporation, Duff & Phelps, and Fitch Investors Service, as well as credit research staffs of dealer firms and institutional investor concerns.

Call Risk

One of the provisions in the contract between the issuer and the bondholder might be that the issuer has the right to retire or "call" all or part of the issue before the maturity date. The issuer wants this right so that if at some time in the future market interest rates decline below the coupon rate on the issue, the issuer can retire the issue and replace it with new bonds issued at a lower interest rate. Early redemption is simply the exercising of an option by the issuer to refinance debt on more favorable terms.

From the investor's perspective, there are three disadvantages of the call provision. First, the cash flow pattern of a callable bond is not known with certainty. Second, because the issuer will call the bonds when interest rates have dropped, the investor is exposed to reinvestment rate risk. That is, the investor will have to reinvest the proceeds received when the bond is called at a lower interest rate than the yield when the bond was purchased. Finally, the capital appreciation potential of a bond will be reduced. For example, when interest rates fall, the price of a bond will rise. However, because the bond may be called, the price of a callable bond may not rise much above the price the issuer will pay if the bond is called. Every callable bond indenture and prospectus specifies a call price schedule. In many instances, the price at which the issuer may call the bond is higher than the bond's face value.

Holding aside default risk, the key characteristic that distinguishes U.S. Treasury obligations, corporate bonds, municipal bonds, and mortgage-backed securities is the degree of certainty of the cash flow pattern. In the case of Treasury securities, with the exception of some outstanding Treasury bonds that are callable, the cash flow is known with certainty. Since almost all long-term corporate and municipal bonds are callable by the issuer prior to maturity, the cash flow pattern of these securities is not known with certainty. Typically, however, the issue has a provision prohibiting the issuer from calling or refunding the issue until a specified number of years after issuance. Moreover, investors generally can expect that the issuer will not call or refund an issue when the current market interest rate is greater than the issue's coupon interest rate.

Mortgage-backed securities also expose the investor to uncertainty about the timing of the cash flow because the investor has effectively granted *each* borrower/homeowner in the pool of mortgages underlying the mortgage-backed security the option to prepay part or all of the mortgage at any time. In fact, the uncertainty of the timing of the cash flow is even greater for mortgage-backed securities than for corporate and municipal bonds because exercising the option to prepay a mortgage does not depend solely on the current market interest rate. It depends also on the unique circumstances facing each homeowner (such as relocations or defaults). These circumstances may cause principal prepayments when the current market interest rate is greater than the mortgage interest rate. Thus a homeowner's decision to prepay a mortgage may be less a purely economic decision than a chief financial officer's decision to refund corporate debt obligations.

Inflation Risk

Inflation risk or *purchasing power risk* is the risk that the return realized from investing in a bond will not be sufficient to offset the loss in purchasing power due to inflation. For example, if an investor purchases a five-year bond in which he can realize a yield of 7 percent, but the rate of inflation is 8 percent, then the purchasing power value of the investment has declined. For all but adjustable- or floating-rate bonds, an investor is exposed to inflation risk because the interest rate that the issuer promises to make is fixed.

Foreign-Exchange Rate Risk

A U.S. investor who purchases a bond in which the issuer promises to make payments in a foreign currency does not know what the resulting cash flow of the bond will be in U.S. dollars. The cash flow will depend on the foreign-exchange rate at the time the cash flow is received. Thus the investor is exposed to *foreign-exchange rate* or *currency risk.*

Marketability Risk

Marketability risk (or *liquidity risk*) involves the ease with which an issue can be sold at or near the prevailing market price. The primary measure of marketability/liquidity is the size of the spread between the bid price (the price at which the issue can be sold) and the ask price (the price at which an issue can be purchased) quoted by a dealer. The greater the dealer spread, the greater the marketability/liquidity risk. The number of active market makers will influence the size of the bid-ask spread; the larger the number of active market makers, the smaller the bid-ask spread. For an investor who plans to hold the bond until the maturity date, marketability/liquidity risk is not important.

OVERVIEW OF FRAMEWORK FOR
EVALUATING BONDS

A wide variety of bonds are available in the marketplace. The price that an investor will pay for a bond will depend on market interest rates, the risks associated with the particular issue, and unique features of the particular issue.

In general, the price that an investor will pay for a bond can be expressed as follows (assuming identical maturity and coupon):

> Price of a "comparable" Treasury bond
>> minus
> Value of the risk premium for accepting the credit risk associated with the issue
>> minus
> Value of any options the bondholder grants to the issuer
>> plus
> Value of any options the issuer grants to the bondholder
>> minus
> Value of the risk premium required for accepting foreign-exchange rate risk for a nondollar-denominated bond
>> plus
> Value of any tax advantage associated with the issue
>> minus
> Value of the premium required for accepting marketability risk

The key to evaluating bonds is determining the value of each of these components. The starting point is the valuation of a "comparable" Treasury security.

While we have set forth the basic valuation framework in terms of price, the framework can be recast in terms of yield as follows (assuming the same maturity and coupon):

> Yield on a "comparable" Treasury bond
> > plus
> Yield premium required for accepting the credit risk associated with the issue
> > plus
> Yield premium required for any options the bondholder grants to the issuer
> > minus
> Yield give-up for any options the issuer grants the bondholder
> > plus
> Yield premium required for accepting foreign exchange rate risk for a nondollar-denominated bond
> > minus
> Yield give-up for any tax advantage associated with the issue
> > plus
> Yield premium required for accepting marketability risk

Notice that there is an inverse relationship between price and yield. A feature of a particular bond issue that increases risk and/or makes the bond less attractive decreases the price of the bond and thus increases its yield.

PORTFOLIO OBJECTIVES AND MANAGEMENT POLICIES FOR BOND INVESTORS

Why do individuals and institutions invest in bonds? The reason is that bonds have cash flow characteristics that make them attractive to investors who have certain portfolio objectives to satisfy.[3]

---

[3]For a more detailed discussion, see Richard W. McEnally, "Portfolio Objectives and Management Policies for Fixed Income Investors," in Frank J. Fabozzi and T. Dessa Garlicki, eds., *Advances in Bond Analysis and Portfolio Strategies* (Chicago: Probus Publishing, 1987).

The traditional reason for investing in bonds is that they provide the investor with a steady income stream (unless callable), where income is equated with coupon payments. Thus by monitoring credit and call risk and adequately diversifying a portfolio by type of issuer, an investor can expect the promised cash flow with a high degree of certainty.

For institutional investors such as pension funds, life insurance companies, trusts, banks, and thrifts, funds must be invested to satisfy contractual obligations. These liabilities may be a single sum at a future date (called a *bullet liability*) or a stream of liabilities. If properly constructed, the cash flow from a portfolio of bonds can be used to satisfy either a bullet liability or a stream of liabilities.

There are investment advisors whose portfolio objective is to maximize the total return over some holding period for a given level of risk. The total return over some holding period is simply the ending value of the portfolio plus any cash received during the holding period minus the beginning value of the portfolio, all divided by the beginning value of the portfolio. An institution that seeks to maximize the holding-period return can follow one or both of the following strategies: (1) timely shifting of funds between bonds and stocks; and (2) changing the composition of a bond portfolio to capitalize on expected changes in market interest rates and/or changes in spreads between different sectors of the bond market.

Unfortunately, there are some investment advisors who attempt to maximize some accounting "yield" measure rather than total return.

PRICING A BOND

The price of any financial instrument is equal to the present value of the *expected* cash flows from the financial instrument. Therefore, to determine the price requires the following information:

1. Estimate of the expected cash flows.
2. Estimate of the appropriate required yield.

The expected cash flows for some financial instruments are simple to compute; for others, the task is more difficult. The required yield reflects the yield for financial instruments with *comparable* risk, or so-called alternative (or substitute) investments.

The first step in determining the price of a bond is to determine its cash flows. The cash flows in which the issuer cannot retire the bond issue prior to its stated maturity date (i.e., a noncallable bond) consist of:

1. Periodic coupon interest payments to the maturity date.
2. The par (or maturity) value at maturity.

In our illustrations of bond pricing we make the following three assumptions to simplify the analysis:

1. The coupon payments are made every six months. (For most domestic bond issues coupon interest is in fact paid semiannually.)
2. The next coupon payment for the bond is received exactly six months from now.
3. The coupon interest is fixed for the term of the bond.

Consequently, the cash flow for a noncallable bond consists of an annuity of a fixed coupon interest payment paid semiannually and the par or maturity value. For example, a 20-year bond with a 10 percent coupon rate and a par or maturity value of $1,000 has the following cash flows from coupon interest:

$$\text{Annual coupon interest} = \$1,000 \times .10$$
$$= \$100$$
$$\text{Semiannual coupon interest} = \$100/2$$
$$= \$50$$

Therefore, there are 40 semiannual cash flows of $50, and a $1,000 cash flow 40 six-month periods from now.

Notice the treatment of the par value. It is *not* treated as if it is received 20 years from now. Instead, it is treated on a basis consistent with the coupon payments, which are semiannual.

The required yield is determined by investigating the yields offered on comparable bonds in the market. By comparable, we mean noncallable bonds of the same credit quality and the same maturity. The required yield is typically expressed as an annual interest rate. When the cash flows occur semiannually, the market convention is to use one half the annual interest rate as the periodic interest rate with which to discount the cash flows.

Given the cash flows of a bond and the required yield, we have all the analytical tools to price a bond. Since the price of a bond is the present value of the cash flows, it is determined by adding these two present values:

1. The present value of the semiannual coupon payments.

2. The present value of the par or maturity value at the maturity date.

In general, the price of a bond can be computed from the following formula:

$$P = \frac{C}{(1 + r)^1} + \frac{C}{(1 + r)^2} + \frac{C}{(1 + r)^3} + \ldots + \frac{C}{(1 + r)^n} + \frac{M}{(1 + r)^n}$$

or

$$P = \sum_{t=1}^{n} \frac{C}{(1 + r)^t} + \frac{M}{(1 + r)^n} \tag{1}$$

where: P = Price (in $)
C = Semiannual coupon payment (in $)
M = Maturity value
n = Number of periods (number of years times 2)
r = Periodic interest rate (required annual yield divided by 2)

Since the semiannual coupon payments are equivalent to an ordinary annuity, the following equation gives the present value of the coupon payments:

$$C \left[\frac{1 - \dfrac{1}{(1 + r)^n}}{r} \right] \tag{2}$$

To illustrate how to compute the price of a bond, consider a 20-year 10 percent coupon bond with a par value of $1,000. Let's suppose that the required yield on this bond is 11 percent. The cash flows for this bond are as follows:

1. 40 semiannual coupon payments of $50.
2. $1,000 to be received 40 six-month periods from now.

The semiannual or periodic required yield is 5.5 percent (11 percent divided by 2).

The present value of the 40 semiannual coupon payments of $50 discounted at 5.5 percent is $802.31, as shown:

$$C = \$50$$
$$n = 40$$
$$r = .055$$

$$= \$50 \left[\frac{1 - \frac{1}{(1.055)^{40}}}{.055} \right]$$

$$= \$50 \left[\frac{1 - \frac{1}{8.51332}}{.055} \right]$$

$$= \$50 \left[\frac{1 - .117463}{.055} \right]$$

$$= \$50 \, (16.04613)$$

$$= \$802.31$$

The present value of the par or maturity value of $1,000 received *40 six-month periods from now*, discounted at 5.5 percent, is $117.46, as shown:

$$\frac{\$1,000}{(1.055)^{40}}$$

$$= \frac{\$1,000}{8.51332}$$

$$= \$117.46$$

The price of the bond is then equal to the sum of the two present values:[4]

	Present value of coupon payments	=	$802.31
+	Present value of par (maturity) value	=	117.46
	Price	=	$919.77

Suppose that instead of an 11 percent required yield, the required yield is 6.8 percent. The price of the bond would then be $1,347.04, as the following calculations demonstrate:

The present value of the coupon payments using a periodic interest rate of 3.4 percent (6.8 percent/2) is:

---

[4]*Note:* To compute the price of this bond using a financial calculator: $n = 40$, $i = 5.5$, $PMT = 50$, $FV = 1,000$, and the bond price is the computed present value, $PV = \$919.77$.

$$\$50 \left[\frac{1 - \frac{1}{(1.034)^{40}}}{.034} \right]$$

$$= \$50 \quad (21.69029)$$

$$= \$1,084.51$$

The present value of the par or maturity value of $1,000 received *40 six-month periods from now* discounted at 3.4 percent is:

$$\frac{\$1,000}{(1.034)^{40}} = \$262.53$$

The price of the bond is then:

Present value of coupon payments	=	$1,084.51
+ Present value of par (maturity) value	=	262.53
Price	=	$1,347.04

If the required yield is equal to the coupon rate of 10 percent, the price of the bond would be its par value, $1,000, as the following calculations demonstrate.

Using a periodic interest rate of 5.0 percent (10 percent/2), the present value of the coupon payments is:

$$\$50 \left[\frac{1 - \frac{1}{(1.050)^{40}}}{.050} \right]$$

$$= \$50 \quad (17.15909)$$

$$= \$857.95$$

The present value of the par or maturity value of $1,000 received *40 six-month periods from now* discounted at 5 percent is:

$$\frac{\$1,000}{(1.050)^{40}} = \$142.05$$

The price of the bond is then:

Present value of coupon payments	=	$ 857.95
+ Present value of par (maturity) value	=	142.05
Price	=	$1,000.00

Pricing Zero-Coupon Bonds

Some bonds do not make any periodic coupon payments. Instead, the investor realizes interest as the difference between the maturity value and the purchase price. These bonds are called *zero-coupon bonds*. The price of a zero-coupon bond is calculated by substituting zero for C in equation (1):

$$P = \frac{M}{(1 + r)^n} \qquad (3)$$

Equation (3) states that the price of a zero-coupon bond is simply the present value of the maturity value. Notice that in the present value computation the number of periods used for discounting is not the number of years to maturity of the bond, but rather *double* the number of years. Remember that the discount rate is one half the required annual yield.

For example, the price of a zero-coupon bond that matures 15 years from now, if the maturity value is $1,000 and the required yield at 9.4 percent is $252.12, as shown:

$$M = \$1,000$$

$$r = .047 \, (.094/2)$$

$$n = 30 \, (2 \times 15)$$

$$P = \frac{\$1,000}{(1.047)^{30}}$$

$$= \frac{\$1,000}{3.96644}$$

$$= \$252.12$$

EXHIBIT 2
Price/Yield Relationship for a 20-Year 20 Percent Coupon Bond

Yield	Price
0.045%	$1,720.32
0.050	1,627.57
0.055	1,541.76
0.060	1,462.30
0.065	1,388.65
0.070	1,320.33
0.075	1,256.89
0.080	1,197.93
0.085	1,143.08
0.090	1,092.01
0.095	1,044.41
0.100	1,000.00
0.105	958.53
0.110	919.77
0.115	883.50
0.120	849.54
0.125	817.70
0.130	787.82
0.135	759.75
0.140	733.37
0.145	708.53
0.150	685.14
0.155	663.08
0.160	642.26
0.165	622.59

Price/Yield Relationship

A fundamental property of a bond is that its price changes in the opposite
direction of the change in the required yield. The reason is that the price of
the bond is the present value of the cash flows. As the required yield increases, the present value of the cash flows decreases; hence, the price decreases. The opposite is true when the required yield decreases: the present
value of the cash flows increases and, therefore, the price of the bond increases. This can be seen by examining the price for the 20-year 20 percent
bond when the required yield is 11 percent, 10 percent, and 6.8 percent.
Exhibit 2 shows the price of the 20-year 20 percent coupon bond for various required yields.

If we graph the price/yield relationship for any noncallable bond, we

EXHIBIT 3
Shape of Price/Yield Relationship

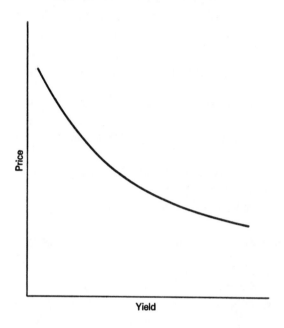

will find that it has the "bowed" shape shown in Exhibit 3. This shape is referred to as *convex*. The convexity of the price/yield relationship has important implications for the investment properties of a bond.

The Relationship between Coupon Rate, Required Yield, and Price

As yields in the marketplace change, the only variable that can change to compensate an investor for the new required yield in the market is the price of the bond. When the coupon rate is equal to the required yield, the price of the bond will be equal to its par value, as we demonstrated for the 20-year 20 percent coupon bond.

When yields in the marketplace rise above the coupon rate at *a given point in time,* the price of the bond adjusts so that the investor can realize some additional interest. If it did not, investors would sell the bond for an alternative, higher-yielding issue, and the resulting lack of demand would cause the price to fall and thus the yield on the bond to increase. This is how a bond's price falls below its par value. The capital appreciation realized by holding the bond to maturity represents a form of interest to the investor to compensate for a coupon rate that is lower than the required yield. When a bond sells below its par value, it is said to be selling at a *discount*. In our earlier calculation of bond price we saw that, when the required yield is greater than the coupon rate, the price of the bond is always less than the par value ($1,000).

When the required yield in the market is below the coupon rate, the price of the bond must sell above its par value. This is because investors who would have the opportunity to purchase the bond at par would be getting a coupon rate in excess of what the market requires. As a result, investors would bid up the price of the bond because its yield is so attractive. The price would eventually be bid up to a level where the bond offered the required yield in the market. A bond whose price is above its par value is said to be selling at a *premium*.

The relationship between coupon rate, required yield, and price can be summarized as follows:

Coupon rate < required yield ⟷ price < par (discount bond)
Coupon rate = required yield ⟷ price = par
Coupon rate > required yield ⟷ price > par (premium bond)

Relationship between Bond Price and Time if Interest Rates Are Unchanged

If the required yield does not change between the time the bond is purchased and the maturity date, what will happen to the price of the bond? For a bond selling at par value, the coupon rate is equal to the required yield. As the bond moves closer to maturity, the bond will continue to sell at par value. Its price will remain constant as the bond moves toward the maturity date.

The price of the bond will *not* remain constant for a bond selling at a premium or a discount. Exhibit 4 shows the time path of a 20-year 10 percent coupon bond selling at a discount and the same bond selling at a premium as it approaches maturity. Notice that the discount bond increases in price as it approaches maturity, assuming the required yield does not change. For a premium bond, the opposite occurs. For both bonds, the price will equal par value at the maturity date.

EXHIBIT 4

Time Path for the Price of a 20-Year 10 Percent Bond Selling at a Discount and Premium as It Approaches Maturity

Year	Discount Bond Selling to Yield 12 Percent	Premium Bond Selling to Yield 7.8 Percent
	Price	Price
20.0	$ 849.54	$1,221.00
19.5	850.51	1,218.62
19.0	851.54	1,216.14
18.5	852.63	1,213.57
18.0	853.79	1,210.90
17.5	855.02	1,208.13
17.0	856.32	1,205.24
16.5	857.70	1,202.25
16.0	859.16	1,199.14
15.5	860.71	1,195.90
15.0	862.35	1,192.54
14.5	864.09	1,189.05
14.0	865.94	1,185.43
13.5	867.89	1,181.66
13.0	869.97	1,177.74
12.5	872.17	1,173.67
12.0	874.50	1,169.45
11.5	876.97	1,165.06
11.0	879.58	1,160.49
10.5	882.36	1,155.75
10.0	885.30	1,150.83
9.5	888.42	1,145.71
9.0	891.72	1,140.39
8.5	895.23	1,134.87
8.0	898.94	1,129.13
7.5	902.88	1,123.16
7.0	907.05	1,116.97
6.5	911.47	1,110.53
6.0	916.16	1,103.84
5.5	921.13	1,096.89
5.0	926.40	1,089.67
4.5	931.98	1,082.16
4.0	937.90	1,074.37
3.5	944.18	1,066.27
3.0	950.83	1,057.85
2.5	957.88	1,049.11
2.0	965.35	1,040.02
1.5	973.27	1,030.58
1.0	981.67	1,020.78
0.5	990.57	1,010.59
0.0	1,000.00	1,000.00

Reasons for the Change in the Price of a Bond

The price of a bond will change for one or more of the following three reasons:

1. There is a change in the required yield owing to changes in the credit quality of the issuer.
2. There is a change in the price of the bond selling at a premium or a discount, without any change in the required yield, simply because the bond is moving toward maturity.
3. There is a change in the required yield owing to a change in the yield on comparable bonds (that is, a change in the yield required by the market).

Reasons 2 and 3 for a change in price were discussed here. Predicting a change in an issue's credit quality (reason 1) before that change is recognized by the market is one of the challenges of investment management.

COMPLICATIONS

The framework for pricing a bond discussed here assumed that:

1. The next coupon payment was exactly six months away.
2. The cash flows are known.
3. The appropriate required yield can be determined.

Let's look at the implications of each assumption for the pricing of a bond.

Next Coupon Payment Due in Less Than Six Months

When an investor purchases a bond whose next coupon payment is due in less than six months, the method adopted by the Street for computing the price of the bond is as follows:

$$P = \sum_{t=1}^{n} \frac{C}{(1 + r)^v (1 + r)^{t-1}} + \frac{M}{(1 + r)^v (1 + r)^{n-1}} \tag{4}$$

where

$$v = \frac{\text{Days between settlement and next coupon}}{\text{Days in six-month period}}$$

Note that when v is 1 (that is, when the next coupon payment is 6 months away), equation (4) reduces to equation (1).

The Cash Flows May Not Be Known

For noncallable bonds, assuming that the issuer does not default, the cash flows are known. For most bonds, however, the cash flows are not known with certainty. This is because an issuer may call a bond before the stated maturity date. With callable bonds, the cash flow will, in fact, depend on the level of current interest rates relative to the coupon rate. For example, the issuer will typically call a bond when interest rates drop far enough below the coupon rate so that it is economic to retire the bond issue prior to maturity and issue new bonds at a lower coupon rate. Consequently, the cash flows of bonds that may be called prior to maturity are dependent on current interest rates in the marketplace.

PRICE QUOTES, ACCRUED INTEREST, AND INVOICE PRICE

Price Quotes

Throughout this reading we have assumed that the maturity or par value of a bond is $1,000. A bond may have a maturity or par value greater or less than $1,000. Consequently, when quoting bond prices, traders quote the price as a percentage of par value.

A bond selling at par is quoted as 100, meaning 100 percent of its par value. A bond selling at a discount will be selling for less than 100; a bond selling at a premium will be selling for more than 100. The following examples illustrate how a price quote is converted into a dollar price.

Price Quote (1)	Converted to a Decimal (2) [= (1)/100]	Par Value (3)	Dollar Price (4) = [(2) × (3)]
97	0.9700000	$ 10,000	$ 9,700.00
85$1/2$	0.8550000	100,000	85,500.00
90$1/4$	0.9025000	5,000	4,512.50
80$1/8$	0.8012500	10,000	8,012.50
76$5/32$	0.7615625	1,000,000	761,562.50
86$11/64$	0.8617188	100,000	86,171.88
100	1.0000000	50,000	50,000.00
109	1.0900000	1,000	1,090.00
103$3/4$	1.0375000	100,000	103,750.00
105$3/8$	1.0537500	25,000	26,343.75
103$19/32$	1.0359375	1,000,000	1,035,937.50

Accrued Interest

When an investor purchases a bond between coupon payments, the investor must compensate the seller of the bond for the coupon interest earned from the time of the last coupon payment to the settlement date of the bond.[5] This amount is called *accrued interest*. The computation of accrued interest depends on the type of bond. With a Treasury coupon security, accrued interest is based on the actual number of days the bond is held by the seller. For corporate and municipal bonds, accrued interest is based on a 360-day year, with each month having 30 days.

Invoice Price

The invoice price is the total proceeds that the buyer of the bond pays the seller. The invoice price is equal to the price agreed upon by the buyer and the seller plus accrued interest. This is often referred to as the *full price* of a bond.

SUMMARY

This reading showed how to determine the price of a noncallable bond. The price is simply the present value of the bond's expected cash flows, the discount rate being equal to the yield offered on comparable bonds. For a noncallable bond, the cash flows are the coupon payments and the par value or maturity value. For a zero-coupon bond, there are no coupon payments. The price is equal to the present value of the maturity value, where the number of periods used to compute the present value is double the number of years and the discount rate is a semiannual yield.

The higher (lower) the required yield, the lower (higher) the price of a bond. Therefore a bond's price changes in the opposite direction to the change in the required yield. When the coupon rate is equal to the required yield, the bond will sell at its par value. When the coupon rate is less (greater) than the required yield, the bond will sell for less (more) than its par value and is said to be selling at a discount (premium).

---

[5]The exceptions are bonds that are in default. Such bonds are said to be quoted *flat*—that is, without accrued interest.

Over time, the price of a premium or discount bond will change even if the required yield does not change. Assuming the credit quality of the issuer is unchanged, the price change on any bond can be decomposed into a portion attributed to a change in the required yield and a portion attributed to the time path of the bond.

READING 5

BOND RATINGS

Sumner N. Levine

STANDARD & POOR'S*

Rating Definitions

Debt

A Standard & Poor's corporate or municipal debt rating is a current assessment of the creditworthiness of an obligor with respect to a specific obligation. This assessment may take into consideration obligors such as guarantors, insurers, or lessees.

The debt rating is not a recommendation to purchase, sell, or hold a security, inasmuch as it does not comment as to market price or suitability for a particular investor.

The ratings are based on current information furnished by the issuer or obtained by Standard & Poor's from other sources it considers reliable. Standard & Poor's does not perform any audit in connection with any rating and may, on occasion, rely on unaudited financial information. The ratings may be changed, suspended, or withdrawn as a result of changes in, or unavailability of, such information, or for other circumstances.

From Sumner N. Levine, ed., *The Financial Analyst's Handbook,* 2nd ed. (Homewood, Ill.: Dow Jones-Irwin, 1988).

*Source: Standard & Poor's Corporation, 25 Broadway, New York, New York 10004.

The ratings are based, in varying degrees, on the following considerations:

1. Likelihood of default-capacity and willingness of the obligor as to the timely payment of interest and repayment of principal in accordance with the terms of the obligation.
2. Nature of and provisions of the obligation.
3. Protection afforded by, and relative position of, the obligation in the event of bankruptcy, reorganization, or other arrangement under the laws of bankruptcy and other laws affecting creditors' rights.

AAA. Debt rated AAA has the highest rating assigned by Standard & Poor's. Capacity to pay interest and repay principal is extremely strong.

AA. Debt rated AA has a very strong capacity to pay interest and repay principal and differs from the higher rated issues only in small degree.

A. Debt rated A has a strong capacity to pay interest and repay principal although it is somewhat more susceptible to the adverse effects of changes in circumstances and economic conditions than debt in higher rated categories.

BBB. Debt rated BBB is regarded as having an adequate capacity to pay interest and repay principal. Whereas it normally exhibits adequate protection parameters, adverse economic conditions or changing circumstances are more likely to lead to a weakened capacity to pay interest and repay principal for debt in this category than in higher rated categories.

BB, B, CCC, CC, C. Debt rated BB, B, CCC, CC and C is regarded, on balance, as predominantly speculative with respect to capacity to pay interest and repay principal in accordance with the terms of the obligation. BB indicates the lowest degree of speculation and C the highest degree of speculation. While such debt will likely have some quality and protective characteristics, these are outweighed by large uncertainties or major risk exposures to adverse conditions.

BB. Debt rated BB has less near term vulnerability to default than other speculative issues. However, it faces major ongoing uncertainties or exposure to adverse business, financial or economic conditions which could lead to inadequate capacity to meet timely interest and principal payments.

B. Debt rated B has a greater vulnerability to default but presently has adequate capacity to meet interest payments and principal repayments.

Adverse business, financial or economic conditions will likely impair capacity or willingness to pay interest and repay principal.

CCC. Debt rated CCC has a currently identifiable vulnerability to default, and is dependent upon favorable business, financial, and economic conditions to meet timely payment of interest and repayment of principal. In the event of adverse business, financial or economic conditions, it is not likely to have the capacity to pay interest and repay principal.

CC. The rating CC is typically applied to debt subordinated to senior debt which is assigned an actual or implied CCC rating.

C. The rating C is typically applied to debt subordinated to senior debt which is assigned an actual or implied CCC-debt rating.

CI. The rating CI is reserved for income bonds on which no interest is being paid.

D. Debt rated D is in default, and payment of interest and/or repayment of principal is in arrears.

Plus (+) or minus (−). The ratings from "AA" to "CCC" may be modified by the addition of a plus or minus sign to show relative standing within the major rating categories.

Provisional ratings. The letter "p" indicates that the rating is provisional. A provisional rating assumes the successful completion of the project being financed by the debt being rated and indicates that payment of debt service requirements is largely or entirely dependent upon the successful and timely completion of the project. This rating, however, while addressing credit quality subsequent to completion of the project, makes no comment on the likelihood of, or the risk of default upon failure of such completion. The investor should exercise his own judgment with respect to such likelihood and risk.

L. The letter "L" indicates that the rating pertains to the principal amount of those bonds where the underlying deposit collateral is fully insured by the Federal Savings & Loan Insurance Corp. or the Federal Deposit Insurance Corp.

Continuance of the rating is contingent upon S&P's receipt of an executed copy of the escrow agreement or closing documentation confirming investments and cash flows.

NR. This indicates that no rating has been requested, that there is insufficient information on which to base a rating, or that S&P does not rate a particular type of obligation as a matter of policy.

Debt obligations of issuers outside the United States and its terri-

tories. These are rated on the same basis as domestic corporate and municipal issues. The ratings measure the creditworthiness of the obligor but do not take into account currency exchange and related uncertainties.

Bond investment quality standards. Under present commercial bank regulation issued by the Comptroller of the Currency, bonds rated in the top four categories (AAA, AA, A, BBB, commonly known as "Investment Grade" ratings) are generally regarded as eligible for bank investment. In addition, the Legal Investment Laws of various states may impose certain rating or other standards for obligations eligible for investment by savings banks, trust companies, insurance companies and fiduciaries generally.

CreditWatch. CreditWatch highlights potential changes in ratings of bonds and other fixed income securities. It focuses on events and trends that place companies and government units under special surveillance by S&P's analytical staff. These may include mergers, voter referendums, actions by regulatory authorities, or developments gleaned from analytical reviews. Unless otherwise noted, a rating decision will be made within 90 days. Issues appear on CreditWatch where an event, situation, or deviation from trend has occurred and needs to be evaluated as to its impact on credit ratings. A listing, however, does not mean a rating change is inevitable. Since S&P continuously monitors all of its ratings, CreditWatch is not intended to include all issues under review. Thus, rating changes will occur without issues appearing on CreditWatch.

Rating "outlook." To highlight rating direction, credit analyses include an "outlook" covering a three-year period. There are four designations: *positive* indicates the rating may be raised; *negative,* it may be lowered; *stable,* it is not likely to change; and *developing* means the rating may be raised or lowered. The outlook focuses on alternatives that could result in a change. Rating actions may differ from the outlook based on unexpected events.

Commercial Paper

A Standard & Poor's commercial paper rating is a current assessment of the likelihood of timely payment of debt having an original maturity of no more than 365 days. Ratings are graded into four categories, ranging from "A" for the highest quality obligations to "D" for the lowest. The four categories are as follows:

A. Issues assigned this highest rating are regarded as having the greatest capacity for timely payment. Issues in this category are delineated with the numbers 1, 2, and 3 to indicate the relative degree of safety.

A-1. This designation indicates that the degree of safety regarding timely payment is either overwhelming or very strong. Those issues determined to possess overwhelming safety characteristics are denoted with a plus (+) sign designation.

A-2. Capacity for timely payment on issues with this designation is strong. However, the relative degree of safety is not as high as for issues designated "A-1".

A-3. Issues carrying this designation have a satisfactory capacity for timely payment. They are, however, somewhat more vulnerable to the adverse effects of changes in circumstances than obligations carrying the higher designations.

B. Issues rated "B" are regarded as having only an adequate capacity for timely payment. However, such capacity may be damaged by changing conditions or short-term adversities.

C. This rating is assigned to short-term debt obligations with a doubtful capacity for payment.

D. This rating indicates that the issue is either in default or is expected to be in default upon maturity.

The commercial paper rating is not a recommendation to purchase or sell a security. The ratings are based on current information furnished to Standard & Poor's by the issuer or obtained from other sources it considers reliable. The ratings may be changed, suspended, or withdrawn as a result of changes in or unavailability of such information.

Municipal Notes
A Standard & Poor's note rating reflects the liquidity concerns and market access risks unique to notes. Notes due in three years or less will likely receive a note rating. Notes maturing beyond three years will most likely receive a long-term debt rating. The following criteria will be used in making that assessment.

- Amortization schedule (the larger the final maturity relative to other maturities the more likely it will be treated as a note).
- Source of Payment (the more dependent the issue is on the market for its refinancing, the more likely it will be treated as a note).

Note-rating symbols are as follows:

SP-1   Very strong or strong capacity to pay principal and interest.
Those issues determined to possess overwhelming safety characteristics will be given a plus (+) designation.

SP-2   Satisfactory capacity to pay principal and interest.

SP-3   Speculative capacity to pay principal and interest.

Tax-Exempt Demand Bonds

Standard & Poor's assigns "dual" ratings to all long-term debt issues that
have as part of their provisions a demand or double feature.

The first rating addresses the likelihood of repayment of principal and
interest as due, and the second rating addresses only the demand feature.
The long-term debt rating symbols are used for bonds to denote the long-
term maturity and the commercial paper rating symbols are used to denote
the put option (for example, "AAA/A-1+"). For the newer "demand
notes," S&P's note rating symbols, combined with the commercial paper
symbols, are used (for example, "SP-1+/A-1+").

MOODY'S*

Rating Definitions

Short-Term Debt Ratings

Moody's short-term debt ratings are opinions of the ability of issuers to
repay punctually senior debt obligations which have an original maturity
not exceeding one year.

Among the obligations covered are commercial paper, Eurocommer-
cial paper, bank deposits, bankers' acceptances, and obligations to deliver
foreign exchange. Obligations relying upon support mechanisms, such as
letters-of-credit and bonds of indemnity, are excluded unless explicitly
rated.

Moody's employs the following three designations, all judged to be
investment grade, to indicate the relative repayment ability of rated issuers:

---

*Source: Moody's Investors Service Publishing and Executive Offices, 99 Church Street, New
York, New York 10007.

- Issuers rated **Prime-1** (or supporting institutions) have a superior ability for repayment of senior short-term debt obligations. Prime-1 repayment ability will often be evidenced by many of the following characteristics:

  Leading market positions in well-established industries.

  High rates of return on funds employed.

  Conservative capitalization structure with moderate reliance on debt and ample asset protection.

  Broad margins in earnings coverage of fixed financial charges and high internal cash generation.

  Well-established access to a range of financial markets and assured sources of alternate liquidity.

- Issuers rated **Prime-2** (or supporting institutions) have a strong ability for repayment of senior short-term debt obligations. This will normally be evidenced by many of the characteristics cited above but to a lesser degree. Earnings trends and coverage ratios, while sound, may be more subject to variation. Capitalization characteristics, while still appropriate, may be more affected by external conditions. Ample alternate liquidity is maintained.

- Issuers rated **Prime-3** (or supporting institutions) have an acceptable ability for repayment of senior short-term obligations. The effect of industry characteristics and market compositions may be more pronounced. Variability in earnings and profitability may result in changes in the level of debt protection measurements and may require relatively high financial leverage. Adequate alternate liquidity is maintained.

- Issuers rated **Not Prime** do not fall within any of the Prime rating categories.

Obligations of a branch of a bank are considered to be domiciled in the country in which the branch is located. Unless noted as an exception, Moody's rating on a bank's ability to repay senior obligations extends only to branches located in countries which carry a Moody's sovereign rating. Such branch obligations are rated at the lower of the bank's rating or Moody's sovereign rating for bank deposits for the country in which the bank is located.

When the currency in which an obligation is denominated is not the same as the currency of the country in which the obligation is domiciled, Moody's ratings do not incorporate an opinion as to whether payment of the obligation will be affected by actions of the government controlling the currency of denomination. In addition, risks associated with bilateral conflicts between an investor's home country and either the issuer's home country or the country where an issuer's branch is located are not incorporated into Moody's short-term debt ratings.

Moody's makes no representation that the rated obligations are exempt from the registration under the U.S. Securities Act of 1933 or issued in conformity with any other applicable law or regulation. Nor does Moody's represent that any specific obligation is legally enforceable or a valid senior obligation of a rated issuer.

If an issuer represents to Moody's that its short-term debt obligations are supported by the credit of another entity or entities, then the name or names of such supporting entity or entities are listed within the parenthesis beneath the name of the issuer, or there is a footnote referring the reader to another page for the name or names of the supporting entity or entities. In assigning ratings to such issuers, Moody's evaluates the financial strength of the affiliated corporations, commercial banks, insurance companies, foreign governments or other entities, but only as one factor in the total rating assessment. Moody's makes no representation and gives no opinion on legal validity or enforceability of any support arrangement.

Moody's ratings are opinions, not recommendations to buy or sell, and their accuracy is not guaranteed. A rating should be weighed solely as one factor in an investment decision and you should make your own study and evaluation of any issuer whose securities or debt obligations you consider buying or selling.

Note: Moody's ratings are subject to change. Because of the possible time lapse between Moody's assignment or change of a rating and your use of this publication, we suggest you verify the current rating of any security or issuer in which you are interested.

Long-Term Debt Ratings[1]

Aaa.   Bonds which are rated Aaa are judged to be of the best quality. They carry the smallest degree of investment risk and are generally referred to as "gilt edged." Interest payments are protected by a large or by an exceptionally stable margin and principal is secure. While the various

---

[1]Preferred stock ratings are the same as long-term debt but lowercase with quotation marks.

protective elements are likely to change, such changes as can be visualized are most unlikely to impair the fundamentally strong position of such issues.

Aa. Bonds which are rated Aa are judged to be of high quality by all standards. Together with the Aaa group they comprise what are generally known as high-grade bonds. They are rated lower than the best bonds because margins of protection may not be as large as in Aaa securities or fluctuation of protective elements may be of greater amplitude or there may be other elements present which make the long-term risk appear somewhat larger than the Aaa securities.

A. Bonds which are rated A possess many favorable investment attributes and are to be considered as upper-medium-grade obligations. Factors giving security to principal and interest are considered adequate, but elements may be present which suggest a susceptibility to impairment some time in the future.

Baa. Bonds which are rated Baa are considered as medium-grade obligations (i.e., they are neither highly protected nor poorly secured). Interest payments and principal security appear adequate for the present but certain protective elements may be lacking or may be characteristically unreliable over any great length of time. Such bonds lack outstanding investment characteristics and in fact have speculative characteristics as well.

Ba. Bonds which are rated Ba are judged to have speculative elements; their future cannot be considered as well-assured. Often the protection of interest and principal payments may be very moderate, and thereby not well safeguarded during both good and bad times over the future. Uncertainty of position characterizes bonds in this class.

B. Bonds which are rated B generally lack characteristics of the desirable investment. Assurance of interest and principal payments or of maintenance of other terms of the contract over any long period of time may be small.

Caa. Bonds which are rated Caa are of poor standing. Such issues may be in default or they may present elements of danger with respect to principal or interest.

Ca. Bonds which are rated Ca represent obligations which are speculative in a high degree. Such issues are often in default or have other marked shortcomings.

C. Bonds which are rated C are the lowest rated class of bonds, and issues so rated can be regarded as having extremely poor prospects of ever attaining any real investment standing.

Note: Moody's applies numerical modifiers, 1, 2, and 3 in each generic rating classification from Aa through B in its corporate bond rating system. The modifier 1 indicates that the security ranks in the higher end of its generic rating category; the modifier 2 indicates a mid-range ranking; and the modifier 3 indicates that the issue ranks in the lower end of its generic rating category.

Moody's bond ratings, where specified, are applied to senior bank obligations with an original maturity in excess of one year. Among the bank obligations covered are bank deposits and obligations to deliver foreign exchange. Obligations relying upon support mechanisms such as letters-of-credit are excluded unless explicitly rated.

Obligations of a branch of a bank are considered to be domiciled in the country in which the branch is located. Unless noted as an exception, Moody's rating on a bank's ability to repay senior obligations extends only to branches located in countries which carry a Moody's sovereign rating. Such branch obligations are rated at the lower of the bank's rating or Moody's sovereign rating for the bank deposits for the country in which the branch is located. When the currency in which the obligation is denominated is not the same as the currency of the country in which the obligation is domiciled, Moody's ratings do not incorporate an opinion as to whether payment of the obligation will be affected by the actions of the government controlling the currency of denomination. In addition, risk associated with bilateral conflicts between an investor's home country and either the issuer's home country or the country where an issuer branch is located are not incorporated into Moody's ratings.

Moody's makes no representation that rated bank obligations are exempt from registration under the U.S. Securities Act of 1933 or issued in conformity with any other applicable law or regulation. Nor does Moody's represent any specific bank obligation as legally enforceable or a valid senior obligation of a rated issuer.

Long-Term Municipal Ratings
Moody's ratings represent the opinion of Moody's Investors Service as to the relative investment classification of bonds. As such, they should be used in conjunction with the description and statistics appearing in Moody's Municipal & Government Manual and Municipal Credit Reports. Reference should be made to those for information regarding the issuer.

Aaa. Bonds which are rated Aaa are judged to be of the best quality. They carry the smallest degree of investment risk and are generally referred to as "gilt edge." Interest payments are protected by a large or by an exceptionally stable margin and principal is secure. While the various protective elements are likely to change, such changes as can be visualized are most unlikely to impair the fundamentally strong position of such issues.

Aa. Bonds which are rated Aa are judged to be of high quality by all standards. Together with the Aaa group they comprise what are generally known as high grade bonds. They are rated lower than the best bonds because margins of protection may not be as large as in Aaa securities or fluctuation of protective elements may be of greater amplitude or there may be other elements present which make the long-term risks appear somewhat larger than in Aaa securities.

A. Bonds which are rated A possess many favorable investment attributes and are to be considered as upper medium grade obligations. Factors giving security to principal and interest are considered adequate, but elements may be present which suggest a susceptibility to impairment sometime in the future.

Baa. Bonds which are rated Baa are considered as medium grade obligations; i.e., they are neither highly protected nor poorly secured. Interest payments and principal security appear adequate for the present, but certain protective elements may be lacking or may be characteristically unreliable over any great length of time. Such bonds lack outstanding investment characteristics and in fact have speculative characteristics as well.

Ba. Bonds which are rated Ba are judged to have speculative elements; their future cannot be considered as well assured. Often the protection of interest and principal payments may be very moderate, and thereby not well safeguarded during both good and bad times over the future. Uncertainty of position characterizes bonds in this class.

B. Bonds which are rated B generally lack characteristics of the desirable investment. Assurance of interest and principal payments or of maintenance of other terms of the contract over any long period of time may be small.

Caa. Bonds which are rated Caa are of poor standing. Such issues may be in default or there may be present elements of danger with respect to principal or interest.

Ca. Bonds which are rated Ca represent obligations which are speculative in a high degree. Such issues are often in default or have other marked shortcomings.

C. Bonds which are rated C are the lowest rated class of bonds, and issues so rated can be regarded as having extremely poor prospects of ever attaining any real investment standing.

Con. (. . .). Bonds for which the security depends upon the completion of some act or the fulfillment of some condition are rated conditionally. These are bonds secured by (a) earnings of projects under construction, (b) earnings of projects unseasoned in operation experience, (c) rentals which begin when facilities are completed, or (d) payments to which some other limiting condition attaches. Parenthetical rating denotes probable credit stature upon completion of construction or elimination of basis of condition.

Note: These bonds in the Aa, A, Baa, Ba, and B groups which Moody's believes possess the strongest investment attributes are designated by the symbols Aa 1, A 1 Baa 1, and B 1.

Short-Term Municipal Loan Ratings

Ratings. Moody's ratings for state and municipal short-term obligations will be designated Moody's Investment Grade or **(MIG).** Such ratings recognize the differences between short-term credit risk and long-term risk. Factors affecting the liquidity of the borrower and short-term cyclical elements are critical in short-term ratings, while other factors of major importance in bond risk, long-term secular trends for example, may be less important over the short run.

A short-term rating may also be assigned on an issue having a demand feature-variable rate demand obligation (VRDO). Such ratings will be designated as **VMIG** or, if the demand feature is not rated, as **NR.** Short-term ratings on issues with demand features are differentiated by the use of the **VMIG** symbol to reflect such characteristics as payment upon periodic demand rather than fixed maturity dates and payment relying on external liquidity. Additionally, investors should be alert to the fact that the source of payment may be limited to the external liquidity with no or limited legal recourse to the issuer in the event the demand is not met.

A VMIG rating may also be assigned to commercial paper programs. Such programs are characterized as having variable short-term maturities but having neither a variable rate nor demand feature.

Definitions: Moody's short-term ratings are designated Moody's Investment Grade as **MIG 1** or **VMIG 1** through **MIG 4** or **VMIG 4.** As the name implies, when Moody's assigns a **MIG** or **VMIG** rating, all categories define an investment grade situation.

The purpose of the **MIG** or **VMIG** ratings is to provide investors with a simple system by which the relative investment qualities of short-term obligations may be evaluated.

Gradations of investment quality are indicated by rating symbols, with each symbol representing a group in which the quality characteristics are broadly the same.

Changes in Rating. A change in rating may occur at any time in the case of an individual issue. Such a rating occurs because Moody's observed some alteration in the investment risks of the short-term obligation or because the previous rating does not fully reflect the quality as now seen. Such rating changes may include the suspension or withdrawal of a rating.

Limitations to Uses of Ratings. Short-term obligations carrying the same rating are not claimed to be of absolutely equal quality. In a broad sense they are alike in position, but since there are only four rating levels used in grading thousands of short-term obligations, the symbols cannot reflect fine shadings of risks. Therefore, it should be evident to the user of ratings that two short-term obligations identically rated are unlikely to be precisely the same in investment quality.

As ratings are designed exclusively for the purpose of grading short-term obligations according to their investment qualities, they should not be used alone as a basis for investment decisions. For example, they have limited value in forecasting the direction of future trends of market price. Market price movements are influenced not only by the quality of individual issues but also by length of maturity. During its life even the best quality short-term obligation may have wide price movements, while its investment status remains unchanged.

The matter of market price has no bearing whatsoever on the determination of ratings, which are not to be construed as recommendations with respect to attractiveness. The attractiveness of a given short-term obligation will depend on its yield, its maturity date and other factors as well as on its investment quality, the only characteristic to which the rating refers.

Since ratings involve judgments about the future, an effort is made when assigning ratings to look at worst potentialities in the visible future, rather than solely at the past record and current status. Therefore, investors should be aware that a rating includes the recognition of many nonstatistical factors.

Moody's ratings represent the opinion of Moody's Investors Service as to the relative investment classification of short-term obligations. As such, they should be used in conjunction with the information on the issuer appearing in Moody's Municipal & Government Manual and Municipal Credit Reports. Reference should be made to these for information regarding the issuer.

Absence of Rating.   Should no rating be assigned, among other reasons, it may be for one of the following:

1. An application for rating was not received or accepted.
2. The issue or issuer belongs to a group of securities that are not rated as a matter of policy.
3. There is a lack of essential data pertaining to the issue or issuer.
4. The issue was privately placed, in which case the rating is not published in Moody's publications.
5. The issue was judged not to be of investment grade.

Where no rating has been assigned or where a rating has been suspended or withdrawn, it may be for reasons unrelated to the quality of the issue. When no rating is applied to either the long- or short-term aspect of the VRDO, it will be designated **NR.**

Because of the generally short-term nature of these obligations, the user of these ratings should monitor them closely in case any change in investment status may occur.

Short-Term Municipal Loan Ratings

MIG 1/VMIG 1.   This designation denotes best quality. There is present strong protection by established cash flows, superior liquidity support or demonstrated broad-based access to the market for refinancing.

MIG 2/VMIG 2.   This designation denotes high quality. Margins of protection are ample although not so large as in the preceding group.

MIG 3/VMIG 3.   This designation denotes favorable quality. All security elements are accounted for but there is lacking the undeniable strength of the preceding grades. Liquidity and cash flow protection may be narrow and market access for refinancing is likely to be less well established.

MIG 4/VMIG 4.   This designation denotes adequate quality. Protection commonly regarded as required of an investment security is present and although not distinctly or predominantly speculative, there is specific risk.

Issues or the features associated with **MIG** or **VMIG** ratings are identified by date of issue, date of maturity or maturities or rating expiration date and description to distinguish each rating from other ratings. Each rating designation is unique with no implication as to any other similar issue of the same obligor. **MIG** ratings terminate at the retirement of the obligation while **VMIG** rating expiration will be a function of each issue's specific structural or credit features.

Note: Moody's ratings are subject to change. Because of the possible time lapse between Moody's assignment or change of a rating and your use of this publication, we suggest you verify the current rating of any security or issuer in which you are interested.

READING 6

INTEREST RATE CHANGES AND THEIR EFFECT ON BOND PRICES

John Markese

Bonds, bond mutual funds, and unit investment trusts have recently been hit hard by movements in interest rates. Whether the interest rate movements are caused by inflation fears, weakness in the dollar, or Federal Reserve actions, the impact on the bond investor is the same: Rising interest rates reduce bond values and falling rates increase bond values.

How will your bond investments be affected by changes in interest rates? Since bonds differ by maturity and coupon rate as well as by type of issuer (municipal, U.S. government, corporation) and other factors, figuring out how your bond portfolio will be affected by interest rate changes can be complex. This workshop will endeavor to give you some basic guidelines for judging the price volatility of your bonds.

WHAT AFFECTS VOLATILITY?

The longer the maturity of your bond investments, the greater their price volatility. Why? Without going into the mathematics of bond valuations, the reason that long-term bonds are more affected by interest rate changes

---

Source: *AAII Journal,* November 1987. Used with permission.

than short-term bonds is that the maturity value of the long-term bond as well as many of the interest payments are cash flows to the investor at very distant points in the future. What a bond sells for in the market today is the sum of all future cash flows discounted in value because they are not available today. A dollar tomorrow is worth less to us than a dollar today. The discount rate used is the rate of interest prevailing in the market for bonds of the same risk and maturity. If interest rates rise, those very distant cash flows of the long-term bond are discounted in value significantly and the price of the long-term bond falls in the market abruptly.

Coupon rates—the interest paid by the issuer of the bond—also affect bond price volatility. A higher coupon means that more cash in the form of interest payments flows to the investor before maturity than is the case with a lower coupon bond. What this means is that when interest rates rise and future cash flows are discounted at a higher rate, the lower coupon bond has relatively more cash flow in the distant future and its value today will fall relatively more.

Combining these characteristics produces the riskiest bonds in terms of price volatility: The longer maturity, lower coupon bonds are the most price volatile. A long-term zero-coupon bond defines the outer boundary for riskiness. Investors who are risk averse should look for bonds and bond mutual funds that have shorter average maturities—those with less than five years—and should avoid zero-coupon bonds, particularly long-term zero-coupon bonds.

HOW MUCH WILL PRICES CHANGE?

The accompanying tables indicate just how much bond prices can change when interest rates change. The tables show the percentage change in bond price for a given interest rate change for bonds of different maturities and coupon rates. These tables are based upon the assumptions of semiannual interest payments and bonds selling at their maturity (face) value.

As an example of how to read the table, assume that you have a bond with a 30-year maturity and a 10 percent coupon rate. If you anticipate that interest rates will rise 4 percentage points, say from 10 percent to 14 percent, your bond will drop in price by 28.1 percent. A bond selling at a face value of $1,000 before the interest rate rise would drop to $719 for a capital loss of $281. On the bright side, however, if interest rates instead fell to 6 percent, your bond would increase in value by 55.4 percent to $1,554 for a capital gain of $554. Both these interest rate changes are extreme but not impossible, and the gains and losses are large because the bond maturity is so long. A higher coupon rate for the same maturity would result in smaller but still very significant price changes. The only way to effectively reduce bond price volatility is to shorten maturities. As a note, the gains are always larger than the losses for the same interest rate change because of the mathematics of the relative change.

With some minor adjustments, you can use these tables as an estimate of potential bond price change even if a bond in your portfolio is currently selling at a discount or premium to face value. For example, if you have an 8 percent coupon bond but interest rates are currently 10 percent, the bond will sell at a discount—for a $1,000 bond with 20 years to maturity, the price would be approximately $828 (see Table 2). If interest rates rose another 2 percentage points to 12 percent, the bond would have a value of $699, for a total loss of 30.1 percent from the original value of $1,000. However, your loss from $828 to $699 is only 15.6 percent of $828. Thus, if you want to determine how much your bond price will change, you can calculate its current value, find the actual expected price change from its face value, and then calculate the resulting percentage change from the current value. Table 4 presents an example of the calculation, using the above example and the information contained in Tables 1, 2 and 3.

If you are concerned about the price volatility of a portfolio of bonds, such as a bond mutual fund, you can use the portfolio's average maturity and the average coupon rate for a rough idea of the price volatility of the overall portfolio. For mutual funds, this information can be found using simple arithmetic and the information on the fund's portfolio composition contained in the fund's annual, semi-annual and quarterly reports. The volatility indicated will be only a rough idea of what to expect, because the mutual fund portfolio manager may lengthen or shorten the average maturities over time in anticipation of interest rate changes. However, the mutual fund's investment objective statement found in the prospectus generally restricts major changes in maturity.

OTHER FACTORS AFFECTING VOLATILITY

There are also some important qualitative factors that affect bond price changes. The tables detail price changes for bonds generically. The realities of the market place are that when interest rates rise, lower-rated

TABLE 1
Bond Price Changes When Interest Rates Rise or Fall: 1 Percentage Point

Years to Maturity	8% Coupon		9% Coupon		10% Coupon		11% Coupon		12% Coupon	
	If Rates:		If Rates:		If Rates:		If Rates:		If Rates:	
	Rise	Fall	Rise	Fall	Rise	Fall	Rise	Fall	Rise	Fall
	The Value of the Bond Will Change by:									
1	− 0.9%	+ 1.0%	− 0.9%	+ 0.9%	− 0.9%	+ 0.9%	− 0.9%	+ 0.9%	− 0.9%	+ 0.9%
2	− 1.8	+ 1.8	− 1.8	+ 1.8	− 1.8	+ 1.8	− 1.7	+ 1.8	− 1.7	+ 1.8
3	− 2.6	+ 2.7	− 2.5	+ 2.6	− 2.5	+ 2.6	− 2.5	+ 2.5	− 2.4	+ 2.5
4	− 3.3	+ 3.4	− 3.2	+ 3.4	− 3.2	+ 3.3	− 3.1	+ 3.2	− 3.0	+ 3.2
5	− 4.0	+ 4.2	− 3.9	+ 4.1	− 3.8	+ 4.0	− 3.7	+ 3.9	− 3.6	+ 3.8
10	− 6.5	+ 7.1	− 6.2	+ 6.8	− 6.0	+ 6.5	− 5.7	+ 6.2	− 5.5	+ 6.0
20	− 9.2	+ 10.7	− 8.6	+ 9.9	− 8.0	+ 9.2	− 7.5	+ 8.6	− 7.1	+ 8.0
30	−10.3	+ 12.5	− 9.5	+ 11.3	− 8.7	+ 10.3	− 8.1	+ 9.5	− 7.5	+ 8.7

TABLE 2
Bond Price Changes When Interest Rates Rise or Fall: 2 Percentage Points

Years to Maturity	8% Coupon		9% Coupon		10% Coupon		11% Coupon		12% Coupon	
	If Rates: Rise	Fall	If Rates: Rise	Fall	If Rates: Rise	Fall	If Rates: Rise	Fall	If Rates: Rise	Fall
	The Value of the Bond Will Change by:									
1	− 1.9%	+ 1.9%	− 1.9%	+ 1.9%	− 1.8%	+ 1.9%	− 1.8%	+ 1.9%	− 1.8%	+ 1.9%
2	− 3.6	+ 3.7	− 3.5	+ 3.7	− 3.5	+ 3.6	− 3.4	+ 3.6	− 3.4	+ 3.6
3	− 5.1	+ 5.4	− 5.0	+ 5.3	− 4.9	+ 5.2	− 4.8	+ 5.2	− 4.8	+ 5.1
4	− 6.5	+ 7.0	− 6.3	+ 6.9	− 6.2	+ 6.7	− 6.1	+ 6.6	− 6.0	+ 6.5
5	− 7.7	+ 8.5	− 7.5	+ 8.3	− 7.4	+ 8.1	− 7.2	+ 7.9	− 7.0	+ 7.7
10	− 12.5	+ 14.9	− 12.0	+ 14.2	− 11.5	+ 13.6	− 11.0	+ 13.0	− 10.6	+ 12.5
20	− 17.2	+ 23.1	− 16.1	+ 21.4	− 15.1	+ 19.8	− 14.2	+ 18.4	− 13.3	+ 17.2
30	− 18.9	+ 27.7	− 17.5	+ 24.9	− 16.2	+ 22.6	− 15.0	+ 20.6	− 14.0	+ 18.9

TABLE 3

Bond Price Changes When Interest Rates Rise or Fall: 4 Percentage Points

The Value of the Bond Will Change by:

Years to Maturity	8% Coupon If Rates:		9% Coupon If Rates:		10% Coupon If Rates:		11% Coupon If Rates:		12% Coupon If Rates:	
	Rise	Fall	Rise	Fall	Rise	Fall	Rise	Fall	Rise	Fall
1	− 3.7%	+ 3.9%	− 3.6%	+ 3.9%	− 3.6%	+ 3.8%	− 3.6%	+ 3.8%	− 3.6%	+ 3.8%
2	− 6.9	+ 7.6	− 6.9	+ 7.5	− 6.8	+ 7.4	− 6.7	+ 7.4	− 6.6	+ 7.3
3	− 9.8	+ 11.2	− 9.7	+ 11.0	− 9.5	+ 10.8	− 9.4	+ 10.7	− 9.3	+ 10.5
4	− 12.4	+ 14.7	− 12.2	+ 14.3	− 11.9	+ 14.0	− 11.7	+ 13.8	− 11.5	+ 13.5
5	− 14.7	+ 18.0	− 14.4	+ 17.5	− 14.1	+ 17.1	− 13.7	+ 16.6	− 13.4	+ 16.2
10	− 22.9	+ 32.7	− 22.0	+ 31.2	− 21.2	+ 29.8	− 20.4	+ 28.4	− 19.6	+ 27.2
20	− 30.1	+ 54.7	− 28.3	+ 50.2	− 26.7	+ 46.2	− 25.2	+ 42.7	− 23.9	+ 39.6
30	− 32.3	+ 69.5	− 30.1	+ 61.8	− 28.1	+ 55.4	− 26.3	+ 49.9	− 24.8	+ 45.3

TABLE 4
Determining Volatility for Bonds Not Selling at Face Value

Step 1: Determine bond's current price.

For example: An investor wants to purchase an 8% coupon bond with a 20-year maturity after interest rates have risen by 2 percentage points to 10 percent. Thus, he will buy the bond at a discount, and its current price would be 17.2 percent less than face value, based on information contained in Table 2. Thus, the bond's current price (the investor's purchase price) would be:

$$\$1,000 - (\$1,000 \times 0.172) = \$828$$

Step 2: Determine the bond's value if interest rates were to rise further.

For example: If interest rates were anticipated to rise another 2 percentage points to 12 percent, the total percentage point change from the time that the bond sold at face value is 4 percentage points; the price would decline by 30.1 percent from its original face value, based on information contained in Table 3:

$$\$1,000 - (\$1,000 \times 0.301) = \$699$$

Step 3: Subtract the anticipated price (if rates were to change) from the current price and divide the result by the current price to determine the percentage change in price for a bond not selling at face value:

$$(\$699 - \$828)/\$828 = -15.6\%$$

Thus, an 8 percent coupon bond selling at a discount and with a 20-year maturity would suffer a price decline of 15.6 percent if interest rates were to rise from 10 percent to 12 percent.

---

bonds—those with the higher default risks—tend to fall faster in price. This distinction holds for corporate and municipal bonds alike, but is obviously not relevant for U.S. government bonds. A rise in interest rates in a deteriorating economic environment would drop the price of a low-rated bond—a junk bond—much faster than the price of a triple-A rated corporate bond of the same coupon and maturity.

The tables should give investors a feel for bond price volatility without going through the actual mathematics of calculating bond price changes. Even though a bond you hold may not have the exact coupon or maturity combination found in the table, you can "eyeball" the tables for a useful estimate of bond price change in the event of interest rate changes.

Remember that long-term zero-coupon bonds are extremely volatile. As a general rule, the losses on a zero-coupon bond, given an interest rate rise, would be twice the losses of the 8 percent coupon bond and the gains would be three times the gains of an 8 percent coupon bond of the same maturity. If interest rates rose from 8 percent to 12 percent, a 30-year zero-coupon bond would fall in price by about 66 percent and if interest rates fell from 8 percent to 4 percent, the zero would rise in price by about 210 percent.

A look at the tables should leave you with the thought that conservative investors who are risk averse should stay with short-term bonds and bond funds. If you feel that you can forecast the direction of interest rates—at best a pastime with many disappointments—then an expectation of interest rate declines should trigger a move into longer-term, low coupon investments, and an expectation of rising rates should trigger a move into short-term high coupon issues. Transaction costs and tax considerations alone make bond interest rate anticipation switches costly. The rewards along with the risks are great.

READING 7

U.S. GOVERNMENT SECURITIES: BUYING DIRECT FROM THE FACTORY

John Markese

For many investors, money market mutual funds, bond mutual funds, and bank certificates of deposit come to mind long before direct purchase of government securities. Ease of purchase, transaction costs, liquidity, safety, insured accounts, and diversification are all important investment concepts. Direct purchase of U.S. government securities does not suffer by comparison with other investments, but investors may not be aware of their choices simply because the federal government is not as adept at advertising.

Treasury securities come in three designations: bills, notes, and bonds. Bills are short term and are sold at a discount, maturing at face value. Investors in bills do not receive separate interest payments as they do with Treasury notes and bonds. The only significant distinction between notes and bonds is the time to maturity from when the securities are originally issued—bonds have longer maturities. The minimum investment also varies by type of security. Table 1 lists the maturities, minimum investments, and a generalized schedule of the frequency of new issues; the schedule, however, is subject to change without notice.

The Treasury sells these securities through the Federal Reserve at auc-

---

Source: *AAII Journal*, August 1988. Used with permission.

TABLE 1
Maturity, Minimum Investment, and Issue Schedule

	Treasury Bills	
13-Week	$10,000 initial min. followed by $5,000 increments	Every Monday
26-Week	(same)	Every Monday
52-Week	(same)	Every 4th Thursday
	Treasury Notes	
2-Year	$5,000 initial min. followed by $5,000 increments	Every 3rd Wednesday
3-Year	(same)	2nd week of Feb., May, August, and Nov.
4-Year	(same)	End of March, June, Sept. and Dec.
5-Year	$1,000 initial min. followed by $1,000 increments	End of Feb., May, August, and Nov.
7-Year	(same)	Beginning of Jan., April, July, and Oct.
10-Year	(same)	2nd week of Feb., May, August, and Nov.
	Treasury Bonds	
30-Year	$1,000 initial min. followed by $1,000 increments	2nd week of Feb., May, August, and Nov.

tion on both a competitive and a noncompetitive basis. A competitive basis requires an investor to bid a specific price on yield for an issue; depending upon other bids made at the time of the auction, the investor may or may not receive the desired securities. Competitive bids require a very specific and detailed knowledge of the current bond markets and are usually made by institutions and professional traders.

Noncompetitive bids allow individual investors to participate, since these bids simply require the investor to request securities without specifying a price on yield. All non-competitive requests are accepted and filled at the average of all the accepted competitive bids.

Noncompetitive bids can be accomplished by mail, and the required forms along with comprehensive brochures are available from the Federal Re-

TABLE 2
Walk-In Addresses and Phone Numbers of Federal Reserve Banks
(Alphabetical by City)

104 Marietta Street, NW
Atlanta, GA
(404) 521-8657

502 South Sharp Street
Baltimore, MD
(301) 576-3300

1801 Fifth Avenue, North
Birmingham, AL
(205) 252-3141, Ext. 215 or
264

600 Atlantic Avenue
Boston, MA
(617) 973-3805 or 3810

160 Delaware Avenue
Buffalo, NY
(716) 849-5046

401 South Tryon Street
Charlotte, NC
(704) 336-7100

230 South LaSalle Street
Chicago, IL
(312) 322-5369

150 East Fourth Street
Cincinnati, OH
(513) 721-4787, Ext. 334

1455 East Sixth Street
Cleveland, OH
(216) 579-2490

400 South Akard Street
Dallas, TX
(214) 651-6362

1020 16th Street
Denver, CO
(303) 572-2473 or 2470

160 West Fort Street
Detroit, MI
(313) 963-0080
(313) 964-6157

301 East Main Street
El Paso, TX
(915) 544-4730

1701 San Jacinto Street
Houston, TX
(713) 659-4433

515 Julia Street
Jacksonville, FL
(904) 632-4245

925 Grand Avenue
Kansas City, MO
(816) 881-2783 or 2109

325 West Capitol Avenue
Little Rock, AR
(501) 372-5451, Ext. 288

409 West Olympic Boulevard
Los Angeles, CA
(213) 683-8546

410 South Fifth Street
Louisville, KY
(502) 568-9236 or 9238

200 North Main Street
Memphis, TN
(901) 523-7171, Ext. 225 or
641

9100 N.W. 36th Street
Miami, FL
(305) 593-9923

250 Marquette Avenue
Minneapolis, MN
(612) 340-2075

301 Eighth Avenue, North
Nashville, TN
(615) 259-4006

525 St. Charles Avenue
New Orleans, LA
(504) 586-1505, Ext. 293

33 Liberty Street
New York, NY
(212) 791-6619
(212) 791-5823 (24 hr.
recording)

226 Dean A. McGee Avenue
Oklahoma City, OK
(405) 235-1721, Ext. 182

2201 Farnam Street
Omaha, NE
(402) 221-5633

10 Independence Mall
Philadelphia, PA
(215) 574-6680

717 Grant Street
Pittsburgh, PA
(412) 261-7988

915 S.W. Stark Street
Portland, OR
(503) 221-5921 or 5931

701 East Byrd Street
Richmond, VA
(804) 643-1250

120 South State Street
Salt Lake City, UT
(801) 322-7911 or
(801) 355-3131

126 East Nueva Street
San Antonio, TX
(512) 224-2141, Ext. 303 or
305

101 Market Street
San Francisco, CA
(415) 392-6640 or 6650

1015 Second Avenue
Seattle, WA
(206) 442-1650

411 Locust Street
St. Louis, MO
(314) 444-8602

serve offices listed in Table 2. You can either walk in to any of these offices
with your bid by 1:00 P.M. Eastern time on the day of auction, or you can mail
in the bid, postmarked no later than the day before the auction.

The forms, called tenders, are simple and you can pay with cash, cash-
ier's check, certified personal check, or maturing Treasury securities. The
government has gone to considerable effort to make the process easy.
Since all government securities are book entry, they don't send the certificates. This system allows the investor to automatically reinvest the proceeds from maturing Treasury bills for two years before a reinvestment
renewal request is required. Interest earned can also be directly deposited
into your account at a financial institution.

Any hitches? The system described above is called *Treasury Direct*
and is designed for individual investors who intend to hold their securities
until maturity. What if you want to sell before maturity? You must transfer
to the commercial book-entry system—a simple process, but another step
nonetheless.

Buying through a broker or through a financial institution puts you in
the commercial book-entry system from the beginning. Selling before maturity is easier and you avoid the necessity of filing the tender form, although this requires minimal effort. What are the advantages of purchasing
directly rather than through a broker or financial institution? You avoid
any charges, fees, or brokerage commissions. A survey of charges for
buying and selling Treasury securities found that they ranged from $25 to
$39 for minimum purchases and sales, with only small increases in costs
for large denominations. On a $10,000 purchase, $39 represents only 0.39
percent but on a $1,000 purchase, the charge represents a substantial 3.9
percent.

SHOULD THEY BE IN YOUR PORTFOLIO?

Procedures aside, do Treasury securities have a place in your portfolio?
They are reasonably liquid—more so than certificates of deposit, but less
so than money market mutual funds or bond mutual funds.

Risk? Default risk is, of course, nonexistent for Treasuries, but the
risk of an insured certificate of deposit, money market fund, or bond fund
that holds nothing but Treasuries is essentially the same.

The ability to control interest rate risk, however, does differ. Interest
rate risk is the risk of changing market value of the security as interest rates

TABLE 3
Treasury Bonds, Notes, and Bills (as Reported in *The Wall Street Journal:* 6–27–88)

Treasury Bonds and Notes

Rate	Mat.	Date	Bid	Asked	Bid Chg.	Yld.
6⅝	1988	Jul p	99–28	99–31	......	6.79
6⅛	1989	Jan n	99–06	99–10	......	7.32
14⅝	1989	Jan n	104	104–04	......	6.79
8	1989	Feb p	100–07	100–11	− 01	7.41
6¼	1989	Feb p	99–03	99–07	− 01	7.44
11⅜	1989	Feb n	102 07	102–11	− 01	7.48
9⅞	1990	Aug p	103 07	103–11	− 04	8.13
10¾	1990	Aug n	104–30	105–02	− 05	8.11
6¾	1990	Sep p	97–03	97–07	− 04	8.12
11½	1990	Oct n	106–23	106–27	− 04	8.16
8	1990	Nov p	99–17	99–21	− 06	8.15
9⅝	1990	Nov k	102–31	103–03	− 05	8.16
13	1990	Nov n	110–04	110–08	− 06	8.16
6⅝	1990	Dec p	96–15	96–19	− 05	8.16
11¼	1995	Feb p	112–04	112–08	− 18	8.77
8⅜	1995	Apr p	97–27	97–31	− 16	8.77
10⅜	1995	May	108–04	108–08	− 15	8.75
11¼	1995	May p	112–13	112–17	− 15	8.78
12⅝	1995	May	119–26	119–30	− 15	8.71
10½	1995	Aug p	108–23	108–27	− 13	8.80
9½	1995	Nov p	103–17	103–21	− 14	8.81
11½	1995	Nov	114–15	114–19	− 16	8.77
8⅞	1996	Feb p	100	100–04	− 19	8.85
7⅜	1996	May p	91–13	91–17	− 17	8.89
7¼	1996	Nov p	90–06	90–10	− 17	8.91
8⅝	1997	Aug k	97–27	97–31	− 24	8.95
8½	1997	May k	97–08	97–12	− 20	8.93
8⅛	1998	Feb p	94–16	94–20	− 21	8.97
9	1998	May p	100–11	100–15	− 22	8.92
10⅝	2015	Aug k	114–26	115	− 1–07	9.12
9⅞	2015	Nov	107–07	107–13	− 1–02	9.13
9¼	2016	Feb k	101–05	101–11	− 1–01	9.11
7¼	2016	May k	81–03	81–09	− 1–00	9.11
7½	2016	Nov k	83–19	83–25	− 30	9.10
8¾	2017	May k	96–09	96–15	− 1–04	9.10
8⅞	2017	Aug k	97–22	97–28	− 1–02	9.08
9⅛	2018	May k	101–20	101–26	− 1–00	8.95

TABLE 3—Continued

| Treasury Bills | | | | | | | |
Mat. Date	Bid Discount	Asked Discount	Yield	Mat. Date	Bid Discount	Asked Discount	Yield
−1988−				10–20	6.65	6.58	6.81
6–30	4.26	3.74	3.79	10–27	6.66	6.60	6.84
7– 7	6.31	6.24	6.34	11– 3	6.67	6.61	6.86
7–14	5.66	5.59	5.68	11–10	6.72	6.66	6.93
7–21	6.00	5.93	6.04	11–17	6.73	6.67	6.95
7–28	6.08	6.01	6.12	11–25	6.77	6.71	7.00
8– 4	6.45	6.38	6.51	12– 1	6.75	6.69	6.99
8–11	6.40	6.33	6.47	12– 8	6.78	6.72	7.03
8–18	6.35	6.28	6.42	12–15	6.82	6.76	7.08
8–25	6.37	6.30	6.45	12–22	6.83	6.79	7.12
9– 1	6.53	6.49	6.66	−1989−			
9– 8	6.45	6.41	6.58	1–19	6.89	6.83	7.18
9–15	6.47	6.43	6.61	2–16	6.95	6.89	7.25
9–22	6.57	6.53	6.73	3–16	6.98	6.92	7.31
9–29	6.55	6.48	6.68	4–13	7.01	6.95	7.36
10– 6	6.57	6.50	6.71	5–11	7.05	6.99	7.43
10–13	6.56	6.49	6.71	6– 8	7.05	7.01	7.49

change. When interest rates rise, the prices of existing securities fall; the fall in market value is greater for bonds with longer maturities and lower coupon rates. (The coupon rate is the stated interest rate of the bond.) Certificates of deposit, unless they are the large denomination negotiable type, have no market interest rate risk because they have no market price. They do, however, have a substantial penalty if cashed in early, a risk similar in many respects to interest rate risk. Money market mutual funds are short-term and designed to maintain a fixed value per share so that they effectively have no interest rate risk. Bond mutual funds have significant interest rate risk, particularly the funds that hold long-term bonds.

Treasury securities run the gamut in terms of interest rate risk. Short-term Treasury bills, because of their maturities, have little interest rate risk, but Treasury notes and especially 30-year Treasury bonds have significant risk of market value fluctuations when market interest rates change.

Holding Treasury securities directly, rather than through a mutual fund, has some important implications. Even though some securities in a money market fund or a bond fund will be held to maturity, the mutual fund itself cannot be held to maturity—there is no maturity date for a mutual fund. On the other hand, individual bills, notes, or bonds can be held to maturity and a minimum return is guaranteed—with higher than a minimum return possible if the periodic interest payments on notes and bonds can be reinvested at any positive rate. While market prices can fluctuate with changes in market interest rates, capital losses can be avoided by holding the securities directly and to maturity. On the other hand, the price volatility caused by interest rate movements and the extremely long-term maturity of the 30-year bond sold at auction argues strongly that individuals should leave purchase of these to life insurance companies and other institutions.

OBTAINING INFORMATION

For an idea of the yields available on Treasury securities, *The Wall Street Journal* carries a listing of representative prices and yields for bills, notes, and bonds. These quotes are for large denominations, but they can give you a general idea of yields in each of the available maturities. All of these securities have already been issued, but you can draw some conclusions.

Part of the listing is represented in Table 3. For bonds and notes, the rate in the first column is the coupon rate, or stated rate—6-5/8, for example, means that the security pays 6-5/8 percent of its face value in interest annually. The year and month of maturity are followed by the bid price (what dealers are willing to pay for the bond) and asked price (what dealers are willing to sell the bond for). These prices are stated in bond points, where one point equals 1 percent of the face value of the bond. A price of 99-28 translates to 99 28/32 or 99.875, just slightly below face value. The yield to maturity, which is the rate of return if the bond is held to maturity and all interest payments are reinvested at that same rate, is given in the last column.

The Treasury bills are quoted differently, since they do not have a coupon rate but instead are sold at a discount to mature at face value. The bid and asked figures are quoted in terms of the discount, but this statistic is generally not important for individual investors; the yield figures are the most important.

How might you use Table 3? As an example, from Table 1 you know that seven-year notes are auctioned at the beginning of January, April, July, and October. A call to your nearest Federal Reserve Bank office can confirm the specific date. The date that the example listing was taken from *The Wall Street Journal* (Table 3) is late June. Looking at notes (designated by n or p) that mature in 1995, about a seven-year maturity, you can see that yields may fall in the high 8 percent range if rates do not change dramatically over the next few weeks. Looking at the overall yield structure for the various maturities, it is also clear that investing in a 30-year bond with a 2018 maturity would only marginally increase your yield. You can also compare the bill yields to certificate of deposit rates. Because you cannot hold money market mutual funds or bond mutual funds to maturity, and thereby lock in a minimum return, the yields on mutual funds are not comparable.

Given the risk characteristics of investing directly in shorter-term Treasury securities, and the low cost and simplicity of maintaining a Treasury direct account, these securities and the direct purchase option are worth considering in your portfolio plans.

READING 8

MUNICIPAL BONDS

Sylvan G. Feldstein
Frank J. Fabozzi

Municipal bonds are securities issued by state and local governments and their creations such as "authorities" and special districts. Most recent available information indicates that approximately 37,000 different states, counties, school districts, special districts, towns, and other public issuing bodies have issued municipal bonds. Although some investors buy municipal bonds as a way of supporting public improvements such as schools, playgrounds, and parks, the vast majority buy them because interest income from such bonds generally is exempt from federal income taxes. Consequently, municipal bonds are purchased by those who are in high marginal tax brackets, because on an aftertax basis they offer a yield that is greater than comparable bonds that are fully taxable.

Municipal bonds come in a variety of types, with different redemption features, credit risks, and marketability. Consequently, the holder of municipal bonds is exposed to the same risks as the holder of corporate and Treasury bonds: interest rate risk, reinvestment risk, and call risk. Moreover, the holder of a municipal bond, like the holder of a corporate bond, faces credit risk.

In this reading we describe the basic characteristics of municipal bonds as well as the municipal bond industry.

Source: From Sumner N. Levine, ed. *The Financial Analyst's Handbook*, 2nd ed. (Homewood, Ill.: Dow Jones-Irwin, 1988).

TYPES OF MUNICIPAL OBLIGATIONS

Bonds

In terms of municipal bond security structures, there are basically two different types. The first type is the general obligation bond, and the second is the revenue bond.

General obligation bonds are debt instruments issued by states, counties, special districts, cities, towns, and school districts. They are secured by the issuer's general taxing powers. Usually, a general obligation bond is secured by the issuer's unlimited taxing power. For smaller governmental jurisdictions such as school districts and towns, the only available unlimited taxing power is on property. For larger general obligation bond issuers, such as states and big cities, the tax revenues are more diverse and may include corporate and individual income taxes, sales taxes, and property taxes. The security pledges for these larger issuers such as states are sometimes referred to as being *full faith and credit obligations*.

Additionally, certain general obligation bonds are secured not only by the issuer's general taxing powers to create monies accumulated in the general fund but also from certain identified fees, grants, and special charges, which provide additional revenues from outside the general fund. Such bonds are known as being *double-barreled* in security because of the dual nature of the revenue sources.

Also, not all general obligation bonds are secured by unlimited taxing powers. Some have pledged taxes that are limited as to revenue sources and maximum property tax millage amounts. Such bonds are known as *limited-tax general obligation bonds*.

The second basic type of security structure is found in a revenue bond. Such bonds are issued for either project or enterprise financings in which the bond issuers pledge to the bondholders the revenues generated by the operating projects financed. Below are examples of the specific types of revenue bonds that have been issued over the years.

Airport Revenue Bonds. The revenues securing airport revenue bonds usually come from either traffic-generated sources—such as landing fees, concession fees, and airline apron-use and fueling fees—or lease revenues from one or more airlines for the use of a specific facility such as a terminal or hangar.

College and University Revenue Bonds.   The revenues securing college and university revenue bonds usually include dormitory room rental fees, tuition payments, and sometimes the general assets of the college or university as well.

Hospital Revenue Bonds.   The security for hospital revenue bonds is usually dependent on federal and state reimbursement programs (such as Medicaid and Medicare), third-party commercial payers (such as Blue Cross and private insurance), and individual patient payments.

Single-Family Mortgage Revenue Bonds.   Single-family mortgage revenue bonds are usually secured by the mortgages and mortgage loan repayments on single-family homes. Security features vary but can include Federal Housing Administration (FHA), Veterans Administration (VA), or private mortgage insurance.

Multifamily Revenue Bonds.   These revenue bonds are usually issued for multifamily housing projects for senior citizens and low-income families. Some housing revenue bonds are usually secured by mortgages that are federally insured; others receive federal government operating subsidies, such as under section 8, or interest-cost subsidies, such as under section 236; and still others receive only local property tax reductions as subsidies.

Industrial Development and Pollution Control Revenue Bonds. Bonds have been issued for a variety of industrial and commercial activities that range from manufacturing plants to shopping centers. They are usually secured by payments to be made by the corporations or businesses that use the facilities.

Public Power Revenue Bonds.   Public power revenue bonds are secured by revenues to be produced from electrical operating plants. Some bonds are for a single issuer, who constructs and operates power plants and then sells the electricity. Other public power revenue bonds are issued by groups of public and private investor-owned utilities for the joint financing of the construction of one or more power plants. This last arrangement is known as a *joint power* financing structure.

Resource Recovery Revenue Bonds.   A resource recovery facility converts refuse (solid waste) into commercially salable energy, recoverable products, and a residue to be landfilled. The major revenues for a resource recovery revenue bond usually are (1) the "tipping fees" per ton paid by those who deliver the garbage to the facility for disposal, (2) revenues from steam, electricity, or refuse-derived fuel sold to either an electric power company or another energy user; and (3) revenues from the sale of recoverable materials such as aluminum and steel scrap.

Seaport Revenue Bonds.   The security for seaport revenue bonds can include specific lease agreements with the benefiting companies or pledged marine terminal and cargo tonnage fees.

Sewer Revenue Bonds.   Revenues for sewer revenue bonds come from hookup fees and user charges. For many older sewer bond issuers, substantial portions of their construction budgets have been financed with federal grants.

Sports Complex and Convention Center Revenue Bonds.   Sports complex and convention center revenue bonds usually receive revenues from sporting or convention events held at the facilities and, in some instances, from earmarked outside revenues such as local motel and hotel room taxes.

Student Loan Revenue Bonds.   Student loan repayments under student loan revenue bond programs are sometimes 100 percent guaranteed either directly by the federal government—under the Federal Insured Student Loan program (FISL) for 100 percent of bond principal and interest— or by a state guaranty agency under a more recent federal insurance program, the Federal Guaranteed Student Loan program (GSL). In addition to these two federally backed programs, student loan bonds are also sometimes secured by the general revenues of the specific colleges involved.

Toll Road and Gas Tax Revenue Bonds.   There are generally two types of highway revenue bonds. The bond proceeds of the first type are used to build such specific revenue-producing facilities as toll roads, bridges, and tunnels. For these pure enterprise-type revenue bonds, the pledged revenues usually are the monies collected through the tolls. The second type of highway bond is one in which the bondholders are paid by earmarked revenues outside of toll collections, such as gasoline taxes, automobile registration payments, and driver's license fees.

Water Revenue Bonds. Water revenue bonds are issued to finance the construction of water treatment plants, pumping stations, collection facilities, and distribution systems. Revenues usually come from connection fees and charges paid by the users of the water systems.

Hybrid and Special Bond Securities

Though having certain characteristics of general obligation and revenue bonds, there are some municipal bonds that have more unique security structures as well. They include the following:

Federal Savings and Loan Insurance Corporation-Backed Bonds. In this security structure, the proceeds of a bond sale were deposited in a savings and loan association that, in turn, issued a certificate of deposit (CD). The CD was insured by the Federal Savings and Loan Insurance Corporation (FSLIC) up to a limit of $100,000 of combined principal and interest for each bondholder. The savings and loan association used the money to finance low- and moderate-income rental housing developments. While these bonds are no longer issued, there are billions of dollars of these bonds in the secondary market.

Insured Bonds. These are bonds that, in addition to being secured by the issuer's revenues, also are backed by insurance policies written by commercial insurance companies. The insurance, usually structured as a surety type insurance policy, is supposed to provide prompt payment to the bondholders if a default should occur.

Lease-Backed Bonds. Lease-backed bonds are usually structured as revenue-type bonds with annual rent payments. In some instances the rental payments may only come from earmarked tax revenues, student tuition payments, or patient fees. In other instances the underlying lessee governmental unit is required to make annual appropriations from its general fund.

Letter of Credit–Backed Bonds.   Some municipal bonds, in addition to being secured by the issuer's cash flow revenues, also are backed by commercial bank letters of credit. In some instances the letters of credit are irrevocable and, if necessary, can be used to pay the bondholders. In other instances the issuers are required to maintain investment quality worthiness before the letters of credit can be drawn upon.

Life Care Residence Revenue Bonds.   Life care residence bonds are issued to construct long-term residential facilities for older citizens. Revenues are usually derived from initial lump-sum payments made by the residents.

Moral Obligation Bonds.   A moral obligation bond is a security structure for state-issued bonds that indicates that if revenues are needed for paying bondholders, the state legislature involved is legally authorized, though not required, to make an appropriation out of general state tax revenues.

Municipal Utility District Revenue Bonds.   These are bonds that are usually issued to finance the construction of water and sewer systems as well as roadways in underdeveloped areas. The security is usually dependent on the commercial success of the specific development project involved, which can range from the sale of new homes to the renting of space in shopping centers and office buildings.

New Housing Authority Bonds.   These bonds are secured by a contractual pledge of annual contributions from HUD. Monies from Washington are paid directly to the paying agent for the bonds, and the bondholders are given specific legal rights to enforce the pledge. These bonds can no longer be issued.

Tax Allocation Bonds.   These bonds are usually issued to finance the construction of office buildings and other new buildings in formerly blighted areas. They are secured by property taxes collected on the improved real estate.

"Territorial" Bonds.   These are bonds issued by U.S. territorial possessions such as Puerto Rico, the Virgin Islands, and Guam. The bonds are tax exempt throughout most of the country. Also, the economies of these issuers are influenced by positive special features of the U.S. corporate tax codes that are not available to the states.

"Troubled City" Bailout Bonds.   There are certain bonds that are structured to appear as pure revenue bonds but in essence are not. Revenues come from general-purpose taxes and revenues that otherwise would have gone to a state's or city's general fund. Their bond structures were created to bail out underlying general obligation bond issuers from severe budget deficits. Examples are the New York State *Municipal Assistance Corporation for the City of New York Bonds (MAC)* and the State of Illinois *Chicago School Finance Authority Bonds.*

Refunded Bonds.   These are bonds that originally may have been issued as general obligation or revenue bonds but are now secured by an "escrow fund" consisting entirely of direct U.S. government obligations that are sufficient for paying the bondholders. *They are among the safest of all municipal bonds if the escrow is properly structured.*

Notes

Tax-exempt debt issued for periods ranging not beyond three years is usually considered to be short term in nature. Below are descriptions of some of these debt instruments.

Tax, Revenue, Grant, and Bond Anticipation Notes: TANs, RANs, GANs, and BANs.   These are temporary borrowings by states, local governments, and special jurisdictions. Usually, notes are issued for a period of 12 months, though it is not uncommon for notes to be issued for periods of as short as three months and for as long as three years. TANs and RANs (also known as TRANs) are issued in anticipation of the collection of taxes or other expected revenues. These are borrowings to even out the cash flows caused by the irregular flows of income into the treasuries of the states and local units of government. BANs are issued in anticipation of the sale of long-term bonds.

Construction Loan Notes: CLNs.   CLNs are usually issued for periods up to three years to provide short-term construction financing for multifamily housing projects. The CLNs generally are repaid by the proceeds of long-term bonds, which are provided after the housing projects are completed.

Tax-Exempt Commercial Paper.   This short-term borrowing instrument is issued for periods ranging from 30 to 270 days. Generally the tax-exempt commercial paper has backstop commercial bank agreements, which can include an irrevocable letter of credit, a revolving credit agreement, or a line of credit.

In this chapter we shall refer to both municipal bonds and municipal notes as simply municipal bonds.

Newer Market-Sensitive Debt Instruments

Municipal bonds are usually issued with one of two debt retirement structures or a combination of both. Either a bond has a "serial" maturity structure (wherein a portion of the loan is retired each year), or a bond has a "term" maturity (wherein the loan is repaid on a final date). Usually term bonds have maturities ranging from 20 to 40 years and retirement schedules (which are known as sinking funds) that begin 5 to 10 years before the final term maturity.

Because of the sharply upward-sloping yield curve that existed in the municipal bond market between 1979 and 1986, many investment bankers introduced innovative financing instruments priced at short or intermediate yield levels. These debt instruments are intended to raise money for long-term capital projects at reduced interest rates. Below are descriptions of some of these more innovative debt structures.

Put or Option Tender Bonds.   A "put" or "option tender" bond is one in which the bondholder has the right to return the bond at a price of par to the bond trustee prior to its stated long-term maturity. The put period can be as short as one day or as long as 10 years. Usually, put bonds are backed by either commercial bank letters of credit in addition to the issuer's cash flow revenues or entirely by the cash flow revenues of the issuer.

Super Sinkers.   A "super sinker" is a specifically identified maturity for a single-family housing revenue bond issue to which all funds from early mortgage prepayments are used to retire bonds. A super sinker has a long stated maturity but a shorter, albeit unknown, actual life. Because of this unique characteristic, investors have the opportunity to realize an attractive return when the municipal yield curve is upward sloping on a bond that is priced as if it had a maturity considerably longer that its anticipated life.

Variable-Rate Notes.   Variable-rate notes have coupon rates that change. When a variable-rate note has a put feature it is called a *variable-rate demand obligation* which may be puttable after one day, seven days, quarterly, semiannually, annually, or longer The coupon rate is tied to one of various indexes. Specific examples include percents of the prime rate, the J.J. Kenney Municipal Index, the Merrill Lynch Index, or a percent of the 90-day Treasury bill rate. A bank letter of credit is usually required as liquidity backup for variable-rate demand obligations.

A variation of variable-rate obligations is one in which the investor in advance selects the interest rate and interest payment date from 1 up to 90 to 180 days. The security may have a nominal 30-year maturity. Such a bond has a put feature of a variable-rate demand obligation and the maturity flexibility of tax-exempt commercial paper. One version of this new investment vehicle is called UPDATES (Unit Priced Demand Adjustable Tax-Exempt Securities).

Zero-Coupon Bonds.   A zero-coupon bond is one in which no coupon interest payments are paid to the bondholder. Instead, the bond is purchased at a very deep discount and matures at par. The difference between the original-issue discount price and par represents a specified compounded annual yield. In the municipal bond market there is also a variant of the zero-coupon bond called a "municipal multiplier" or "compound interest bond." It is a bond that is issued at par and *does* actually have interest payments. However, the interest payments are not distributed to the holder of the bond until maturity. Rather, the issuer agrees to reinvest the undistributed interest payments at the bond's yield to maturity when it was issued. For example, suppose that a 10 percent, 10-year bond with a par value of $5,000 is sold at par to yield 10 percent. Every six months, the maturity value of the bond is increased by 5 percent of the maturity value of the previous six months. So at the end of 10 years, the maturity value of the bond will be equal to $13,267 [$= \$5,000 \times (1.05)^{20}$]. In the case of a 10-year zero-coupon bond priced to yield 10 percent, the bond would have a maturity value of $5,000 but sell for $1,884 when it is issued.[1]

---

[1]Variations on the zero-coupon bond were introduced to allow municipal issuers to circumvent restrictions on the amount of par value that they were legally permitted to issue.

THE LEGAL OPINION

Municipal bonds have legal opinions. The relationship of the legal opinion to the safety of municipal bonds for both general obligation and revenue bonds is threefold. First, bond counsel should check to determine if the issuer is indeed legally able to issue the bonds. Second, bond counsel is to see that the issuer has properly prepared for the bond sale by having enacted the various required ordinances, resolutions, and trust indentures and without violating any other laws and regulations. This preparation is particularly important in the highly technical areas of determining whether the bond issue is qualified for tax exemption under federal law and whether the issue has not been structured in such a way as to violate federal arbitrage regulations. Third, bond counsel is to certify that the security safeguards and remedies provided for the bondholders and pledged either by the bond issuer or by third parties, such as banks with letter-of-credit agreements, are actually supported by federal, state, and local government laws and regulations.

The popular notion is that much of the legal work done in a bond issue is boilerplate in nature, but from the bondholder's point of view the legal opinions and document reviews should be the ultimate security provisions. This is because if all else fails, the bondholder may have to go to court to enforce his or her security rights. Therefore, the integrity and competency of the lawyers who review the documents and write the legal opinions that usually are summarized and stated in the official statements are very important.[2]

THE COMMERCIAL CREDIT RATING OF
MUNICIPAL BONDS

Of the municipal bonds that were rated by a commercial rating company in 1929 and plunged into default in 1932, 78 percent had been rated double-A or better, and 48 percent had been rated triple-A. Since then, the ability of rating agencies to assess the creditworthiness of municipal obligations has

---

[2]For specific studies on recent problems with legal opinions, see Chapter 11 on contemporary defaults and related problems in Sylvan G. Feldstein and Frank J. Fabozzi, *Dow Jones-Irwin Guide to Municipal Bonds* (Homewood, Ill.: Dow Jones-Irwin, 1987).

evolved to a level of general industry acceptance and respectability. In most instances, they adequately describe the financial conditions of the issuers and identify the credit-risk factors. However, a small but significant number of recent instances have caused market participants to reexamine their reliance on the opinions of the rating agencies.

As an example, the troubled bonds of the Washington Public Power Supply System (WPPSS) should be mentioned. Two major commercial rating companies—Moody's and Standard & Poor's—gave their highest ratings to these bonds in the early 1980s. Moody's gave the WPPSS Projects 1, 2, and 3 bonds its very highest credit rating of Aaa and the Projects 4 and 5 bonds its rating of A1. This latter investment-grade rating is defined as having the strongest investment attributes within the upper medium grade of creditworthiness. Standard & Poor's also had given the WPPSS Projects 1, 2, and 3 bonds its highest rating of AAA and Projects 4 and 5 its rating of A+. While these high-quality ratings were in effect, WPPSS sold over $8 billion in long-term bonds. By 1986, over $2 billion of these bonds were in default.

In fact, since 1975 all of the major municipal defaults in the industry initially had been given investment-grade ratings by these two commercial rating companies. Of course, it should be noted that in the majority of instances, ratings of the commercial rating companies adequately reflect the condition of the credit. However, unlike 25 years ago when the commerical rating companies would not rate many kinds of revenue bond issues, today they seem to view themselves as assisting in the capital formation process.[3] The commercial rating companies now receive fairly substantial fees from issuers for their ratings, and they are part of large, growth-oriented conglomerates. Moody's is an operating unit of the Dun & Bradstreet Corporation and Standard & Poor's is part of the McGraw-Hill Corporation.

Today, many institutional investors, underwriters, and traders rely on their own in-house municipal credit analysts for determining the creditworthiness of municipal bonds. However, other investors do not perform their own credit-risk analysis, but, instead, rely upon credit-risk ratings by Moody's and Standard & Poor's. In this section we discuss the rating categories of these two commercial rating companies.

---

[3]See Victor F. Zonana and Daniel Hertzberg, "Moody's Dominance in Municipals Market Is Slowly Being Eroded," *The Wall Street Journal,* November 1, 1981, pp. 1 and 23; and Peter Brimelow, "Shock Waves from Whoops Roll East," *Fortune,* July 25, 1983, pp. 46–48.

Moody's Investors Service

The municipal bond rating system used by Moody's grades the investment quality of municipal bonds in a nine-symbol system that ranges from the highest investment quality, which is Aaa, to the lowest credit rating, which is C. The respective nine alphabetical ratings and their definitions are the following:

Moody's Municipal Bond Ratings

Rating	Definition
Aaa	Best quality; carries the smallest degree of investment risk.
Aa	High quality; margins of protection not quite as large as the Aaa bonds.
A	Upper medium grade; security adequate but could be susceptible to impairment.
Baa	Medium grade; neither highly protected nor poorly secured—lacks outstanding investment characteristics and is sensitive to changes in economic circumstances.
Ba	Speculative; protection is very moderate.
B	Not desirable investment; sensitive to day-to-day economic circumstances.
Caa	Poor standing; may be in default but with a workout plan.
Ca	Highly speculative; may be in default with nominal workout plan.
C	Hopelessly in default.

Municipal bonds in the top four categories (Aaa, Aa, and A, and Baa) are considered to be of investment-grade quality. Additionally, bonds in the Aa through B categories that Moody's concludes have the strongest investment features within the respective categories are designated by the symbols Aa1, A1, Baa1, Ba1, and B1, respectively. Moody's also may use the prefix *Con.* before a credit rating to indicate that the bond security is dependent on (1) the completion of a construction project, (2) earnings of a project with little operating experience, (3) rentals being paid once the facility is constructed, or (4) some other limiting condition.[4]

---

[4]It should also be noted that, as of 1984, Moody's applies numerical modifiers 1, 2, and 3 in each generic rating classification from Aa through B to municipal bonds that are issued for industrial development and pollution control. The modifier 1 indicates that the security ranks in the higher end of its generic rating category; the modifier 2 indicates a midrange ranking, and the modifier 3 indicates that the bond ranks in the lower end of its generic rating category.

The municipal note ratings system used by Moody's is designated by four investment-grade categories of Moody's Investment Grade (MIG):

Moody's Municipal Note Ratings

Rating	Definition
MIG 1	Best quality
MIG 2	High quality
MIG 3	Favorable quality
MIG 4	Adequate quality

A short-term issue having a "demand" feature (i.e., payment relying on external liquidity and usually payable upon demand rather than fixed maturity dates) is differentiated by Moody's with the use of the symbols VMIG1 through VMIG4.

Moody's also provides credit ratings for tax-exempt commercial paper. These are promissory obligations (1) not having an original maturity in excess of nine months, and (2) backed by commercial banks. Moody's uses three designations, all considered to be of investment grade, for indicating the relative repayment capacity of the rated issues:

Moody's Tax-Exempt Commercial Paper Ratings

Rating	Definition
Prime 1 (P-1)	Superior capacity for repayment
Prime 2 (P-2)	Strong capacity for repayment
Prime 3 (P-3)	Acceptable capacity for repayment

Standard & Poor's

The municipal bond rating system used by Standard & Poor's grades the investment quality of municipal bonds in a 10-symbol system that ranges from the highest investment quality, which is AAA, to the lowest credit rating, which is D. Bonds within the four categories (AAA, AA, A, and BBB) are considered by Standard & Poor's as being of investment-grade quality. The respective 10 alphabetical ratings and definitions are the following:

Standard & Poor's Municipal Bond Ratings

Rating	Definition
AAA	Highest rating; extremely strong security.
AA	Very strong security; differs from AAA in only a small degree.
A	Strong capacity but more susceptible to adverse economic effects than two above categories.
BBB	Adequate capacity but adverse economic conditions more likely to weaken capacity.
BB	Lowest degree of speculation; risk exposure.
B	Speculative; risk exposure.
CCC	Speculative; major risk exposure.
CC	Highest degree of speculation; major risk exposure.
C	No interest is being paid.
D	Bonds in default with interest and/or repayment of principal in arrears.

Standard & Poor's also uses a plus (+) or minus (−) sign to show relative standing within the rating categories ranging from AA to BB., Additionally, Standard & Poor's uses the letter *p* to indicate a provisional rating that is intended to be removed upon the successful and timely completion of the construction project. A double dagger (‡) on a mortgaged-backed revenue bond rating indicates that the rating is contingent upon receipt by Standard & Poor's of closing documentation confirming investments and cash flows. An asterisk (*) following a credit rating indicates that the continuation of the rating is contingent upon receipt of an executed copy of the escrow agreement.

The municipal note-rating system used by Standard & Poor's grades the investment quality of municipal notes in a four-symbol system that ranges from highest investment quality, SP-1+, to the lowest credit rating, SP-3. Notes within the top three categories (i.e., SP-1+, SP-1, and SP-2) are considered by Standard & Poor's as being of investment-grade quality. The respective ratings and summarized definitions are:

Standard & Poor's Municipal Note Ratings

Rating	Definition
SP-1	Very strong or strong capacity to pay principal and interest. Those issues determined to possess overwhelming safety characteristics will be given a plus (+) designation.
SP-2	Satisfactory capacity to pay principal and interest.
SP-3	Speculative capacity to pay principal and interest.

Standard & Poors also rates tax-exempt commercial paper in the same four categories as taxable commercial paper. The four tax-exempt commercial paper rating categories are:

Standard & Poor's Tax-Exempt Commercial Paper Rating

Rating	Definition
A–1+	Highest degree of safety.
A–1	Very strong degree of safety.
A–2	Strong degree of safety.
A–3	Satisfactory degree of safety.

How the Rating Agencies Differ

Although there are many similarities in how Moody's and Standard & Poor's approach credit ratings, there are certain differences in their respective approaches as well. As examples we shall present below some of the differences in approach between Moody's and Standard & Poor's when they assign credit ratings to general obligation bonds.

The credit analysis of general obligation bonds issued by states, counties, school districts, and municipalities initially requires the collection and assessment of information in four basic categories. The first category includes obtaining information on the issuer's debt structure so that the overall debt burden can be determined. The debt burden usually is composed of (1) the respective direct and overlapping debts per capita as well as (2) the respective direct and overlapping debts as percentages of real estate valuations and personal incomes. The second category of needed information relates to the issuer's ability and political discipline for maintaining sound budgetary operations. The focus of attention here is usually on the issuer's general operating funds and whether or not it has maintained at least balanced budgets over the previous three to five years. The third category involves determining the specific local taxes and intergovernmental revenues available to the issuer, as well as obtaining historical information on both tax collection rates, which are important when looking at property tax levies, and on the dependency of local budgets on specific revenue sources, which is important when looking at the impact of federal revenue sharing monies. The fourth and last general category of information necessary to the credit analysis is an assessment of the issuer's overall socioeconomic environment. Questions that have to be answered here include determining the local employment distribution and composition, population growth, and real estate property valuation and personal income trends, among other economic indexes.

Although Moody's and Standard & Poor's rely on these same four informational categories in arriving at their respective credit ratings of general obligation bonds, what they emphasize among the categories can result at times in dramatically different credit ratings for the same issuer's bonds.

There are major differences between Moody's and Standard & Poor's in their respective approaches toward these four categories, and there are other differences in conceptual factors the two rating agencies bring to bear before assigning their respective general obligation credit ratings. There are very important differences between the rating agencies, and although there are some zigs and zags in their respective rating policies, there are also clear patterns of analysis that exist and that have resulted in split credit ratings for a given issuer. The objective here is to outline what these differences between Moody's and Standard & Poor's actually are. Furthermore, although the rating agencies have stated in their publications what criteria guide their respective credit-rating approaches, the conclusions here about how they go about rating general obligation bonds are not only derived from these sources, but also from reviewing their credit reports and rating decisions on individual bond issues.

How Do Moody's and Standard & Poor's Differ in Evaluating the Four Basic Informational Categories? Simply stated, Moody's tends to focus on the debt burden and budgetary operations of the issuer, and Standard & Poor's considers the issuer's economic environment as the most important element in its analysis. Although in most instances these differences of emphasis do not result in dramatically split credit ratings for a given issuer, there are at least two recent instances in which major differences in ratings on general obligation bonds have occurred.

The general obligation bonds of the Chicago School Finance Authority are rated only Baa1 by Moody's, but Standard & Poor's rates the same bonds AA−. In assigning the credit rating of Baa1, Moody's bases its rating on the following debt- and budget-related factors: (1) The deficit funding bonds are to be retired over a 30-year period, an unusually long time for such an obligation; (2) the overall debt burden is high; and (3) the school board faces long-term difficulties in balancing its operating budget because of reduced operating taxes, desegregation program requirements, and uncertain public employee union relations.

Standard & Poor's credit rating of AA– appears to be based primarily upon the following two factors: (1) Although Chicago's economy has been sluggish, it is still well diversified and fundamentally sound; and (2) the unique security provisions for the bonds in the opinion of the bond counsel insulate the pledged property taxes from the school board's creditors in the event of a school-system bankruptcy.

Another general obligation bond wherein split ratings have occurred is the bond issue of Allegheny County, Pennsylvania. Moody's rates the bonds A, whereas the Standard & Poor's rating is AA.

Moody's A credit rating is based primarily upon four budget-related factors: (1) above-average debt load with more bonds expected to be issued for transportation related projects and for the building of a new hospital, (2) continued unfunded pension liabilities, (3) past unorthodox budgetary practices of shifting tax revenues from the county tax levy to the county institution district levy, and (4) an archaic real estate property assessment system, which is in the process of being corrected.

Standard & Poor's higher credit rating of AA also appears to be based upon four factors: (1) an affluent, diverse, and stable economy with wealth variables above the national medians, (2) a good industrial mix with decreasing dependence on steel production, (3) improved budget operations having accounting procedures developed to conform to generally accepted accounting principles, and (4) a rapid debt retirement schedule that essentially matches anticipated future bond sales.

Are State General Obligation Bonds Fundamentally Different from Local Government General Obligation Bonds? There is also another difference between the credit rating agencies in how they apply their analytical tools to the rating of state general obligation bonds and local government general obligation bonds. Moody's basically believes that the state and local bonds are not fundamentally different. Moody's applies the same debt- and budget-related concerns to state general obligation bonds as they do to general obligation bonds issued by counties, school districts, towns, and cities. Moody's has even assigned ratings below A to state general obligation bonds. When the state of Delaware was having serious budgetary problems in the period beginning in 1975 and extending through 1978,

Moody's gradually downgraded its general obligation bonds from Aa to Baa1. It should be noted that when Moody's downgraded Delaware general obligation bonds to Baa1 and highlighted its budgetary problems, the state government promptly began to address its budgetary problems. By 1982 the bond rating was up to Aa. In May of 1982, Moody's downgraded the state of Michigan's general obligation bonds from A to Baa1 on the basis of a weak local economy and the state's budgetary problems. Another example of Moody's maintaining a state credit rating below A was in Alaska, where until 1974 the state general obligation bonds were rated Baa1. Here, Moody's cited the heavy debt load as a major reason for the rating.

Unlike Moody's, Standard & Poor's seems to make a distinction between state and local government general obligation bonds. Because states have broader legal powers in the areas of taxation and policy making that do not require home-rule approvals, broader revenue bases, and more diversified economies, Standard & Poor's seems to view state general obligation bonds as being significantly stronger than those of their respective underlying jurisdictions. Standard & Poor's has never given ratings below A to a state. Additionally, of the 38 state general obligation bonds that both Moody's and Standard & Poor's rated in mid-1986, the latter agency had given ratings of AA or better to 34 states and ratings of A to only four states. On the other hand, Moody's had given ratings of Aa or better to only 30 states, and ratings in the A range to eight states. On the whole for reasons just outlined, it seems that Standard & Poor's tends to have a higher credit assessment of state general obligation bonds than does Moody's. Furthermore, it should be noted that Moody's views these broader revenue resources as making states more vulnerable in difficult economic times to demands by local governments for increased financial aid.

How Do the Credit-Rating Agencies Differ in Assessing the Moral Obligation Bonds? In more than 20 states, state agencies have issued housing revenue bonds that carry a potential state liability for making up deficiencies in their one-year debt service reserve funds (backup funds), should any occur. In most cases if a drawdown of the debt reserve occurs, the state agency must report the amount used to its governor and the state budget director. The state legislature, in turn, may appropriate the requested amount, though there is no legally enforceable obligation to do so. Bonds with this makeup provision are the so-called moral obligation bonds.

Below is an example of the legal language in the bond indenture that explains this procedure.

> In order to further assure the maintenance of each such debt service reserve fund, there shall be annually apportioned and paid to the agency for deposit in each debt service reserve fund such sum, if any, as shall be certified by the chairman of the agency to the governor and director of the budget as necessary to restore such fund to an amount equal to the fund requirement. The chairman of the agency shall annually, on or before December first, make and deliver to the governor and director of the budget his certificate stating the sum or sums, if any, required to restore each such debt service reserve fund to the amount aforesaid, and the sum so certified, if any, shall be apportioned and paid to the agency during the then current state fiscal year.

Moody's views the moral obligation feature as being more literary than legal when applied to legislatively permissive debt service reserve makeup provisions. Therefore, it does not consider this procedure a credit strength. Standard & Poor's, to the contrary, does. It views moral obligation bonds as being no lower than one rating category below a state's own general obligation bonds. Its rationale is based upon the implied state support for the bonds and the market implications for that state's own general obligation bonds should it ever fail to honor its moral obligation.

As for the result of these two different opinions of the moral obligation, there are several municipal bonds that have split ratings. As examples, in mid-1986 the Nonprofit Housing Project Bonds of the New York State Housing Finance Agency, the General Purpose Bonds of the New York State Urban Development Corporation, and the Series A Bonds of the Battery Park City Authority have the Moody's credit rating of Ba, which is a speculative investment category. Standard & Poor's, because of the moral obligation pledge of the state of New York, gives the same bonds a credit rating of BBB+, which is an investment-grade category.

How Do the Credit-Rating Agencies Differ in Assessing the Importance of Withholding State Aid to Pay Debt Service?   Still another difference between Moody's and Standard & Poor's involves their respective attitudes toward state-aid security-related mechanisms. Since 1974 it has been the policy of Standard & Poor's to view as a very positive credit feature the automatic withholding and use of state aid to pay defaulted debt service on local government general obligation bonds. Usually the mechanism requires the respective state treasurer to pay debt service directly to the bondholder from monies due the local issuer from the state. Seven states have enacted security mechanisms that in one way or another allow certain local government general obligation bondholders to be paid debt service from the state-aid appropriations, if necessary. In most instances the state-aid withholding provisions apply to general obligation bonds issued by school districts.[5]

Although Standard & Poor's does review the budgetary operations of the local government issuer to be sure there are no serious budgetary problems, the assigned rating reflects the general obligation credit rating of the state involved, the legal base of the withholding mechanism, the historical background and long-term state legislature support for the pledged state aid program, and the specified coverage of the state-aid monies available to maximum debt-service requirements on the local general obligation bonds. Normally, Standard & Poor's applies a blanket rating to all local general obligation bonds covered by the specific state-aid withholding mechanism. The rating is one or two notches below the rating of that particular state's general obligation bonds. Whether the rating is either one notch below or two notches below depends on the coverage figure, the legal security, and the legislative history and political durability of the pledged state-aid monies involved. It should also be noted that, although Standard & Poor's stated policy is to give blanket ratings, a specified rating is only granted when an issuer or bondholder applies for it.

Although Moody's recognizes the state-aid withholding mechanisms in its credit reviews, it believes that its assigned rating must in the first instance reflect the underlying ability of the issuer to make timely debt-service payments. Standard & Poor's, to the contrary, considers a state-aid withholding mechanism that provides for the payment of debt service equally as important a credit factor as the underlying budget, economic, and debt-related characteristics of the bond issuer.

What Is the Difference in Attitudes toward Accounting Records? Another area of difference between Moody's and Standard & Poor's concerns their respective attitudes toward the accounting records kept by general obligation bond issuers. In May 1980 Standard & Poor's stated that if the bond issuer's financial reports are not prepared in accordance with

---

[5]The states involved are Indiana, Kentucky, New Jersey, New York, Pennsylvania, South Carolina, and West Virginia.

generally accepted accounting principles (GAAP) it will consider this a "negative factor" in its rating process. Standard & Poor's has not indicated how negative a factor it is in terms of credit rating changes but has indicated that issuers will not be rated at all if either the financial report is not timely (i.e, available no later than six months after the fiscal year-end) or is substantially deficient in terms of reporting. Moody's policy here is quite different. Because Moody's reviews the historical performance of an issuer over a three- to five-year period, requiring GAAP reporting is not necessary from Moody's point of view, although the timeliness of financial reports is of importance.

MUNICIPAL BOND INSURANCE

Municipal bond insurance is a contractual commitment by an insurance company to pay the bondholder any bond principal and/or coupon interest that is due on a stated maturity date, but has not been paid by the bond issuer. Once issued, this municipal bond default insurance usually extends for the term of the bond issue.

The bondholder or trustee who has not received payments for bond principal and/or coupon interest on the stated due dates for the insured bonds must notify the insurance company and surrender to it the unpaid bonds and coupons. Under the terms of the policy, the insurance company is usually obligated to pay the paying agent sufficient monies for the bondholders. These monies must be enough to cover the face value of the insured principal and coupon interest that was due but not paid. Once the insurance company pays the monies, the company becomes the owner of the surrendered bonds and coupons and can begin legal proceedings to recover the monies that are now due it from the bond issuer.

The Insurers

Municipal bond insurance has been available since 1971. Some of the largest and financially strongest insurance companies in the United States are participants in this industry, as well as smaller monoline insurance companies. By mid-1986, approximately 25 percent of all new municipals were insured. The following companies are some of the major municipal bond insurers as of 1986:

American Municipal Bond Assurance Corporation (AMBAC).
Bond Investors Guaranty Insurance Company (BIG).
Financial Guaranty Insurance Corporation (FGIC).
Municipal Bond Insurance Association (MBIA).

Market Pricing of Insured Municipal Bonds

In general, although insured municipal bonds sell at yields lower than they would without the insurance, they tend to have yields substantially higher than Aaa/AAA-rated noninsured municipal bonds.

EQUIVALENT TAXABLE YIELD

An investor interested in purchasing a municipal bond must be able to compare the promised yield on a municipal bond with that of a comparable taxable bond. The following general formula is used to approximate the equivalent taxable yield for a tax-exempt bond:[6]

$$\text{Equivalent taxable yield} = \frac{\text{Tax-exempt yield}}{(1 - \text{marginal tax rate})}$$

For example, suppose an investor in the 28 percent marginal tax bracket is considering the acquisition of a tax-exempt bond that offers a tax-exempt yield of 8 percent. The equivalent taxable yield is 11.11 percent, as shown below:

$$\text{Equivalent taxable yield} = \frac{.08}{(1 - .28)} = .1111$$

---

[6]For a more precise procedure for determining the equivalent taxable yield see Martin L. Leibowitz, "Total Aftertax Bond Performance and Yield Measures for Tax-Exempt Bonds Held in Taxable Portfolios," in *The Municipal Bond Handbook*, vol. I., ed. Frank J. Fabozzi, Sylvan G. Feldstein, Irving M. Pollack, and Frank G. Zarb (Homewood, Ill.: Dow Jones-Irwin, 1983), chap. 32.

When computing the equivalent taxable yield, the traditionally computed yield-to-maturity is not the tax-exempt yield if the issue is selling below par (i.e., selling at a discount) because only the coupon interest is exempt from federal income taxes.[7] Instead, the yield-to-maturity after an assumed tax on the capital gain is computed and used in the numerator of the formula. The yield-to-maturity after an assumed tax on the capital gain is calculated in the same manner as the traditional yield-to-maturity. However, instead of using the redemption value in the calculation, the net proceeds after an assumed tax on the capital gain is used.

There is a major drawback in employing the equivalent taxable yield formula to compare the relative investment merits of a taxable and tax-exempt bond. The yield-to-maturity measure assumes that the entire coupon interest can be reinvested at the computed yield. Consequently, taxable bonds with the same yield-to-maturity cannot be compared because the total dollar returns may differ from the computed yield. The same problem arises when attempting to compare taxable and tax-exempt bonds, especially since only a portion of the coupon interest on taxable bonds can be reinvested, although the entire coupon payment is available for reinvestment in the case of municipal bonds.

STATE AND LOCAL TAX TREATMENT[8]

The tax treatment of municipal bonds varies by state. There are three types of tax that can be imposed: (1) an income tax on coupon income, (2) a tax on realized capital gains, and (3) a personal property tax.

There are 43 states that levy an individual income tax, as does the District of Columbia. Six of these states exempt coupon interest on *all* municipal bonds, whether the issue is in state or out of state. Coupon interest from obligations by in-state issuers is exempt from the state individual income taxes in 32 states. Five state levy individual income taxes on coupon interest whether the issuer is in state or out of state.

---

[7]An investor who purchases a tax-exempt bond at a premium will not be entitled to a capital loss if the bond is held to maturity because the premium must be amortized.

[8]The source of information for this section is from Steven J. Hueglin, "State and Local Tax Treatment of Municipal Bonds," in *The Municipal Bond Handbook,* vol. I, ed. Frank J. Fabozzi, Sylvan G. Feldstein, Irving M. Pollack, and Frank G. Zarb (Homewood, Ill.: Dow Jones-Irwin, 1983), chap. 4.

State taxation of realized capital gains is often ignored by investors when making investment decisions. In 42 states, a tax is levied on a base that includes income from capital transactions (i.e, capital gains or losses). In many states where coupon interest is exempt if the issuer is in state, the same exemption will not apply to capital gains involving municipal bonds.

There are 20 states that levy a personal property tax. Of these 20 states, only 11 apply this tax to municipal bonds. The tax resembles more of an income tax than a personal property tax. For example, in several states, personal property taxes are measured on the annual income generated by a bond.

In determining the effective tax rate imposed by a particular state, an investor must consider the impact of the deductibility of state taxes on federal income taxes. Moreover, in 13 states, *federal* taxes are deductible in determining the state income taxes.

THE PRIMARY AND SECONDARY MARKETS

The Primary Market

A substantial number of municipal obligations are brought to market each week. A state or local government can market its new issue by offering them publicly to the investing community or by placing them privately with a small group of investors. When a public offering is selected, the issue is usually underwritten by investment bankers and municipal bond departments of commercial banks. Public offerings may be marketed by either competitive bidding or direct negotiations with underwriters. When an issue is marketed via competitive bidding, the issue is awarded to the bidder submitting the lowest best bid.

Most states mandate that general obligation issues be marketed via competitive bidding; however, this is generally not required for revenue bonds. Usually state and local governments require that a competitive sale be announced in a recognized financial publication, such as *The Bond Buyer*, which is the trade publication of the municipal bond industry. *The Bond Buyer* also provides information on upcoming competitive sales and most negotiated sales as well as the results of the sales of previous weeks.

When an underwriter purchases a new bond issue, it relieves the issuer of two obligations. First, the underwriter is responsible for the distribution of the issue. Second, the underwriter accepts the risk that investors might fail to purchase the issue at the expected prices within the planned time period. The second risk exists because the underwriter may have incorrectly priced the issue and/or because interest rates rise, resulting in a decline in the value of unsold issues held in inventory. The underwriter spread (that is, the difference between the price it paid the issuer for the issue and price it reoffered the issue to the public) is the underwriter's compensation for undertaking these risks as well as for other services it may have provided the issuer.[9]

An official statement describing the issue and issuer is prepared for new offerings.

The Secondary Market

Although municipal bonds are not listed and traded in formal institutions, as are certain common stocks and corporate bonds on the New York and American stock exchanges, there are very strong and active billion-dollar secondary markets for municipals that are supported by hundreds of municipal bond dealers across the country. Markets are maintained on local credits by regional brokerage firms, local banks, and by some of the larger Wall Street firms. General market names are supported by the larger brokerage firms and banks, many of whom have investment banking relationships with the issuers. Buying and selling decisions are often made over the phone and through municipal bond brokers. For a small fee these brokers serve as intermediaries in the sale of large blocks of municipal bonds among dealers and large institutional investors. These brokers are primarily located in New York City and include Chapdelaine & Company, Drake & Company, the J. J. Kenny Company, and Titus & Donnelly, Inc., among others.

In addition to these brokers and the daily offerings sent out over *The Bond Buyer's* "munifacts" teletype system, many dealers advertise their municipal bond offerings for the retail market in what is known as *The Blue List*. This is a 100+ -page booklet which is published every weekday by the Standard & Poor's Corporation. In it are listed state municipal bond and note offerings and prices.

---

[9]For example, in the case of negotiated offerings there is the value of the origination services provided by the underwriter. Origination services represent the structuring of the issue and planning activities surrounding the offering.

In the municipal bond market, an odd lot of bonds is $25,000 (five bonds) or less in par value for retail investors. For institutions, anything below $100,000 in par value is considered an odd lot. Dealer spreads—the difference between the dealer's bid and ask prices—depend on several factors. For the retail investor, the dealer spread can range from as low as one quarter of one point ($12.50 per $5,000 of par value) on large blocks of actively traded bonds to four points ($200 per $5,000 of par value) for odd lot sales of an inactive issue. The average spread for retail investors seems to be around two points ($100 per $5,000 of par value). For institutional investors, the dealer spread rarely exceeds one half of one point ($25 per $5,000 of par value).

REGULATION OF THE MUNICIPAL SECURITIES MARKET[10]

As an outgrowth of abusive stock market practices, Congress passed the Securities Act of 1933 and the Securities Exchange Act of 1934. The 1934 act created the Securities and Exchange Commission (SEC), granting it regulatory authority over the issuance and trading of *corporate* securities. Congress specifically exempted municipal securities from both the registration requirements of the 1933 act, and the periodic reporting requirements of the 1934 act. However, antifraud provisions did apply to offerings of or dealings in municipal securities.

The reasons for the exemption afforded municipal securities appear to have been due to (1) the desire for governmental comity, (2) the absence of recurrent abuses in transactions involving municipal securities (3) the greater level of sophistication of investors in this segment of the securities market (that is, institutional investors dominated the market), and (4) the fact that there were few defaults by municipal issuers. Consequently, from the enactment of the two federal securities acts in the early 1930s to the early 1970s, the municipal securities market can be characterized as relatively free from federal regulation.

In the early 1970s, however, circumstances changed. As incomes

---

[10]This discussion is drawn from Thomas F. Mitchell, "Disclosure and the Municipal Bond Industry," chap. 40, and Nancy H. Wojtas, "The SEC and Investor Safeguards," chap. 42, in *The Municipal Bond Handbook,* vol. I, ed. Frank J. Fabozzi et al.

rose, individuals participated in the municipal securities market to a much greater extent. As a result, public concern over selling practices occurred with greater frequency. For example, in the early 1970s, the SEC obtained seven injunctions against 72 defendants for fraudulent municipal trading practices. According to the SEC, the abusive practices involved both disregard by the defendants as to whether the particular municipal bond offered to individuals were in fact appropriate investment vehicles for the individuals to whom they were offered and misrepresentation or failure to disclose information necessary for individuals to assess the credit risk of the municipal user, especially in the case of revenue bonds. Moreover, the financial problems of some municipal users, notably New York City, made market participants aware that municipal users have the potential to experience severe and bankruptcy-type financial difficulties.

Congress passed the Securities Act Amendment of 1975 to broaden federal regulation in the municipals market. The legislation brought brokers and dealers in the municipal securities market, including banks that underwrite and trade municipal securities, within the regulatory scheme of the Securities Exchange Act of 1934. In addition, the legislation mandated that the SEC establish a 15-member Municipal Securities Rule Making Board (MSRB) as an independent, self-regulatory agency, whose primary responsibility is to develop rules governing the activities of banks, brokers, and dealers in municipal securities.[11] Rules adopted by the MSRB must be approved by the SEC. The MSRB has no enforcement or inspection authority. This authority is vested with the SEC, the National Association of Securities Dealers, and certain regulatory banking agencies such as the Federal Reserve Bank.

The Securities Act Amendment of 1975 does *not* require that municipal issuers comply with the registration requirement of the 1933 act or the periodic-reporting requirement of the 1934 act. There have been, however, several legislative proposals to mandate financial disclosure. Although none has been passed, there is clearly pressure to improve disclosure. Even in the absence of federal legislation dealing with the regulation of financial disclosure, underwriters began insisting upon greater disclosure as it became apparent that the SEC was exercising stricter application

---

[11]For a detailed discussion of the MSRB, see Frieda K. Wallison, "Self-Regulation of the Municipal Securities Industry," chap. 41 in *The Municipal Bond Handbook*, vol. I, ed. Frank Fabozzi, et al.

of the antifraud provisions. Moreover, underwriters recognized the need for improved disclosure to sell municipal securities to an investing public that has become much more concerned about credit risk by municipal issuers. Thus it is in the best interest of all parties—the issuer, the underwriter, and the investor—that meaningful disclosure requirements be established.

THE CHANGING NATURE OF THE MUNICIPAL BOND INDUSTRY

By the mid-1980s there were three characteristics of the municipal bond industry that distinguished it from what it was in 1960, 1970, and even as recently as 1980. First, municipal bond and note volume increased along with the volatility of interest rates—regardless of the maturity, credit quality, or type of financing structure involved. Second, new financing techniques emerged resulting in more diverse, complex, and changing bond and note security structures. Third, there was growing reliance on retail investors and on those institutional buyers such as bond funds which catered primarily to individuals.

Increased Volume and Interest-Rate Volatility

A characteristic of the municipal bond industry by the mid-1980s was that it had become a major capital market. As an example, according to *The Bond Buyer* tax-exempt state and local government long-term debt outstanding by year-end 1960 was only $66 billion, whereas by year-end 1985 it was over $700 billion.[12] This represented a 1,060 percent increase over 25 years. During this same period outstanding U.S. government direct and guaranteed debt increased from $237 billion in 1960 to $1,858 billion by year-end 1985, an increase of 784 percent.[13]

With this increased volume also has come a further expansion of the municipal bond industry. Numerous brokerage firms and commercial banks—both national and regional in scope—have entered the municipal bond business. By the 1980s many had extensive municipal securities trad-

---

[12]These data were derived from *The Bond Buyer*.
[13]These data were prepared by the Merrill Lynch Securities Research Division.

ing and syndicate departments, public finance, and new business specialists, as well as institutional and retail salesmen and credit analysts. Even
the traditional institutional buyers of municipal bonds, such as property
and casualty insurance companies, had begun to maintain quasi-trading
positions in municipals. An increasing number of investors also began to
"buy and trade" municipals, discarding the traditional "buy and hold"
investment strategy.

One corollary of this broadening base of market participation was that
there were more transitory and speculative forces in the marketplace than
in the past. These forces may help explain the volatility of interest rates that
characterize the municipal bond and note markets almost on a daily basis as
well as the relative lack of sustained trading patterns in many sectors of the
market. It should also be noted that the dramatic moves in the business
cycle and changing Federal Reserve Board monetary strategies have also
been overall contributing factors.

New Financing Techniques

Along with the increased municipal bond volume issuers and investment
bankers have been using new financing techniques and security structures.
Additionally, as inflation and U.S. government borrowing increased in the
early 1980s, many traditional private sector borrowers began to look to
tax-exempt securities—and particularly revenue bonds—as more economical financing vehicles. For instance, in 1970 only 33.5 percent, or $5.959
billion, of the total amount of municipal bonds issued in that year were
revenue bonds; in the first 11 months of 1984, 70.3 percent, or $56.859
billion, of all municipals issued were revenue bonds.[14] By 1984, revenue
bonds were being used to raise capital for hospitals, major corporations
with pollution control projects, airports, seaports, single-family home
mortgage lenders, electric utilities, and builders of multifamily housing,
among others. Revenue bonds have also been used to provide capital for
loans to students and small businesses.

Because of the availability of various federal aid and taxation benefits,
many municipal revenue bonds have elaborate bond security structures
which could be subject to future adverse congressional actions and IRS in-

---

[14]Data were derived from *The Bond Buyer*, December 6, 1984, p. 17.

terpretations.[15] Housing bonds backed by future federal "Section 8" appropriations and leveraged lease resource recovery revenue bonds incorporating certain tax benefits for the plant vendors are but two examples. Additionally, because of the dramatic changes that occurred in the early 1980s in the U.S. tax code and in specific federal aid programs as the results of Reaganomics, the "state of the art" in structuring revenue bonds has been undergoing constant change. Even state and local government general obligation bond issuers, because of their dependency on numerous intergovernmental aid and revenue sharing programs, developed more complex financial structures.

In addition to the greater reliance on revenue bonds, it should also be noted that investor fears of inflation have eroded confidence in long 20- to 30-year municipals regardless of the particular security structure used. Unlike the U.S. Treasury market where an invested yield curve existed for much of the late 1970s and early 1980s, the municipal bond market was characterized by having a very steep yield curve—where the yield differential between 1-year notes and 30-year bonds of equal creditworthiness was at times as wide as 500 basis points.

Because of the widespread investor resistance to buying long municipals, investment bankers introduced several new financing techniques. These included "put" bonds, variable coupon rate bonds, "super sinkers," and "zero" coupon bonds, all described earlier in this chapter. Commercial banks used tax-exempt commercial paper, lines of credit, and letters of credit in structuring new municipal bond and note financings. Government bond dealers and investment bankers incorporated "collateralized" repurchase agreements (repos) into several bond and note security structures. The goal of these various innovative structures was either to attract investors to long-term municipal debt instruments and/or to reduce the financing costs for the borrowers.

---

[15]As an example of the potential role of the IRS, in June of 1980 the Battery Park City Authority sold $97.315 million in construction loan notes which at the time received legal comfort from bond counsel that interest on the notes were exempt from federal income taxation. In November of 1980, however, the IRS held that interest on such notes was not exempt. The issue was not resolved until September 1981 when the Authority and the IRS signed a formal agreement by which the authority agreed to pay annually to the IRS the arbitrage gains and the IRS, in turn, agreed that the interest paid on the notes was not taxable.

Increased Importance of the Retail Investor

With the growth of confiscatory federal, state, and local government taxes on personal incomes in the 1960s and 1970s, individuals—particularly upper-income as well as middle-income wage earners—looked to municipal securities as a convenient way to shelter nonearned incomes. The increased bond volume and reduced commercial bank and casualty insurance company earnings which decreased their traditional robust appetites for tax-exempt bonds made municipal yields very attractive for retail investors. As an example, in September of 1982 short-term ready-access municipal note funds offered investors federal tax-free yields of over 6.5 percent compared to 5.5 percent in taxable passbook savings accounts.

Because of the strong demand by retail investors for tax-exemption, certain anomalies in yield relationships began to occur by the early 1980s. During one week in the spring of 1982, Dade County, Florida, sold general obligation bonds due in 25 years at a yield of 14 percent. The bonds were rated A-1 by Moody's and A by Standard & Poor's. During the same week New York City sold 25-year general obligations as well. Its bonds—at the time rated Ba-1 by Moody's and BBB by Standard—sold at a yield of only 14.5 percent. This narrow yield spread of 50 basis points resulted from the higher tax burden on individuals in New York. High personal income taxes created strong demands for local municipal bonds which are tax-exempt from state of New York, New York City, and federal income taxes.

Municipal bond funds, which sell primarily to individuals, also became major institutional forces in the marketplace. These institutional buyers, unlike many insurance companies and banks, were "yield" buyers who bought long-term A-rated revenue bonds for their relatively high yields. This preference by the bond funds for A-rated paper along with the weaker market for the high grades, i.e., AA- and AAA-rated bonds, brought about some other very unusual yield relationships. As an example, in 1982 the state of Florida sold 20-year high investment grade, AA-rated general obligations at a yield of 13.90 percent. At the same time the North Carolina Eastern Municipal Power Agency sold 20-year A-rated revenue bonds at a yield of 13.25 percent. As a result of the increased role of retail buyers and the weaker demand by banks and insurance companies for high grades, by the 1980s the market at times priced retail-type weaker credit quality bonds at comparable or lower yields than it did higher quality bonds.

READING 9

INVESTING IN MORTGAGE-BACKED SECURITIES

Worth Bruntjen
Paul Zoschke

Mortgage-backed securities have piqued the curiosity of many individual investors, particularly since they have fared so well in the most recent market environment. Yet, they are a source of confusion to many investors.

From an investor's point of view, mortgage-related securities offer a combination of investment quality, high yield, and liquidity. Many mortgage-related securities have U.S. agency or "quasi-agency" status, which lends some amount of security to the underlying instruments, and are generally triple-A rated.

On the other hand, the variety of mortgage investments available and the uncertain rate of principal repayment, which influences such considerations as yield to maturity, cause many individual investors to overlook an attractive investment opportunity.

WHAT IS A MORTGAGE-BACKED SECURITY?

Mortgage-backed securities were introduced in the 1970s and have grown into a $500 billion dollar industry, up more than ten-fold in the past six

Source: *AAII Journal*, February 1987. Used with permission.

years alone. It is estimated that the market has the potential to reach $1.5 trillion during the next decade.

Briefly, a mortgage-backed security is a portfolio of mortgages assembled by a master servicer who collects the monthly payments of principal and interest from the homeowner. The servicer passes the payments which are usually monthly, to the owner of the mortgage security, after an initial delay of 45 to 75 days; generally, the servicer will deduct a servicing fee from the payments. The securities are backed by either a government agency or a private organization, which guarantees the payments.

Currently, mortgage securities are issued by the Government National Mortgage Association (Ginnie Mae), the Federal National Mortgage Association (Fannie May), and the Federal Home Loan Mortgage Corporation (Freddie Mac) as well as the private sector.

Ginnie Mae is by far the largest participant in the mortgage security market, with over $250 billion outstanding in a variety of slightly different pooling programs. Ginnie Maes are "fully modified pass-through securities," meaning that the investor will be paid interest plus scheduled principal payments regardless of whether the original borrowers make their own mortgage payments. Beyond this, all Ginnie Mae issues are backed by the full faith and credit of the U.S. government.

In contrast, Freddie Mac issues, although quite safe, are backed not by government guarantees, but by the agency itself, which pledges "timely" payment of interest and "ultimate" payment of principal. The slightly lower credit status plus the possibility that an investor might have to wait for up to a year before the principal is repaid can result in a yield that is 0.10 percent to 0.20 percent more than that of a Ginnie Mae.

HOW DO THEY COMPARE?

Mortgage-backed securities are a form of fixed-income investment investment and thus carry risks similar to those of bonds. Primarily, this involves a volatility in return when interest rates fluctuate.

The total return on a mortgage-backed security is a combination of the gain or loss in the underlying value of the security, and the interest income the security holder receives from the underlying mortgages. If interest rates rise, the value of a mortgage-backed security will fall. Conversely, if interest rates fall, the value of a mortgage-backed security will rise. Thus, the total return of a mortgage-backed security will fluctuate.

The interest that the holder receives from the underlying mortgages is fixed; in this sense, mortgage-backed securities are similar to other fixed-income instruments such as bonds. However, unlike bonds, the periodic payments from mortgage-backed securities include both interest and a return of principal. This creates some accounting headaches for security holders, and it also increases the reinvestment risk: The periodic payments must be reinvested, and if interest rates have fallen, that money will be reinvested at lower rates, thus lowering future total return. Conversely, if interest rates rise, those larger payments (compared to other fixed-income investments) can be reinvested at higher rates, which will gradually boost the interest earned.

Mortgage-backed securities also carry the risk that the underlying mortgages will be paid off more quickly than anticipated, and thus the holder will receive the stated interest for a shorter time period than desired.

Mortgages are prepaid for a variety of reasons as homeowners relocate and refinance. The prepayment experiences of mortgage-backed securities vary depending on the underlying mortgages, and there is no way of accurately predicting an individual security's life. However, the general level of interest rates will affect prepayments, because refinancing becomes more or less economically advantageous. A new 30-year 9 percent mortgage would have an average life of 21.0 years based on the scheduled amortization included in the monthly payments. When a large group of these mortgages are aggregated, however, about 10 percent of these mortgages on average are prepaid when interest rates and housing conditions remain constant. If you assume a 10 percent prepayment rate, a mortgage pool's average life is reduced to about eight years. This average life could be shorter, though, if market interest rates decline substantially below the existing mortgage rates, leading more homeowners to refinance. Prepayment generally occurs when it is least desirable from the mortgage-backed security holder's point of view, forcing reinvestment of payments at lower yield levels; conversely, it is delayed when it is most desired, under conditions of higher interest rates.

Mortgage-backed securities compensate for the extra risk involved with prepayments with yields that are higher than other fixed-income instruments of comparable quality. For example, over time, Ginnie Maes have tended to yield 10 percent to 15 percent more than the yield on intermediate Treasuries. This is illustrated in Figure 1, which charts the yields offered by Ginnie Maes and 10-year Treasuries from 1980 through 1986. At year-end, Ginnie Maes yielded 8.3 percent, which is 17 percent higher than the 7.10 percent offered by 10-year Treasuries.

FIGURE 1
Ginnie Maes versus 10-Year Treasuries (Current Coupons 1/1/80 through 12/30/86)

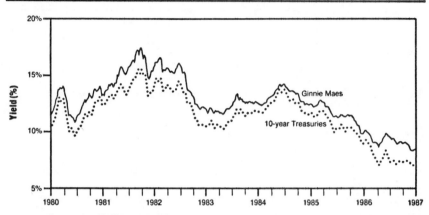

Source: The First Boston Corp. fixed-income research

Mortgage securities also pay interest monthly, compared to semi-annually with other fixed-income instruments. This provides for more frequent compounding of interest, which can boost the yield by as much as a quarter of a percent. For example, a mortgage security with a stated interest of 10.25 percent will yield 0.22 percent more than an equivalently priced Treasury issue that also has a 10.25 percent stated interest.

In addition, because the principal is partially repaid each month along with the interest, mortgage securities have, in effect, a ladder of maturities. Some portion of the principal investment will be due each month, but the investor receives the benefit of a long-term yield for the whole maturity curve.

One other characteristic of mortgage securities, which can be both a risk and an advantage, is a result of the different experiences each security may have with mortgage prepayments. Figure 2 shows the cash flow patterns for three mortgage securities where the underlying mortgages are prepaying at annual rates of 5 percent, 15 percent, and 25 percent. The mortgage securities with prepayments running at about 15 percent provide annual cash flows (both interest and principal) of 20 percent to 25 percent of one's initial investment in the first few years, with declining rates of cash flow as the years pass; in contrast, the mortgage security that is experiencing 5 percent in pre-payments has a much steadier cash flow, while the security experiencing 25 percent prepayments has even higher cash flows in the ini-

FIGURE 2
Ginnie Mae Cash Flow at Different Rates of Prepayment (10 Percent at Par)

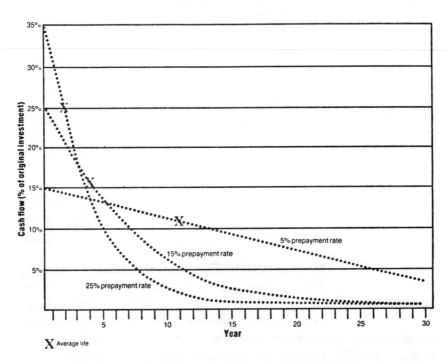

X Average life

tial years. As the chart illustrates, owning a portfolio of mortgage securities is like owning a substantial portion of bonds with a relatively short maturity, a moderate portion of bonds with an intermediate maturity, and a small portion of bonds with a long maturity. This helps explain why mortgage securities generally experience less dramatic interest-rate-related price changes than most 10-year or longer-maturity bonds.

ENTERING THE MORTGAGE SECURITY MARKET

Although private sector mortgage issues carry insurance, the public sector issues, such as Ginnie Mae, Freddie Mac, and Fannie Mae, actually guarantee the underlying securities. For this reason, it is advisable that individual investors stick with the public sector issues. There are three basic ways an individual can enter the market: directly, through a mutual fund, or through a unit investment trust.

Direct investment—Individual investors can purchase mortgage securities from their brokers, and, in most cases, from their banks. The minimum purchase for most mortgage securities is $25,000; this is measured in terms of "original face amount"—the amount outstanding when the mortgage pool was created. When the security is actually purchased, the amount outstanding can be materially lower.

The amount outstanding is indicated by a mortgage security's factor. For instance, if the pool is newly created, almost all of its principal balance will be outstanding, and it will sell close to $25,000 and have a factor close to 1.00000. If the pool is several years old, the combination of scheduled principal payments and prepayments due to refinancings or property sales may have reduced the principal balance to 80 percent, 60 percent, or 40 percent of its original face amount. With a factor of 0.60000, a $25,000 original face certificate will have $15,000 of principal still outstanding, to which the price will be applied. Thus, investments can be made for less than $25,000.

Since mortgage securities are sold in a dealer market over the counter, rather than on an exchange, the selling costs and brokers' commissions are generally buried in the price. Retail investors buying in $25,000 odd lot prices will not receive as good an execution as institutional investors buying in the millions. Still, a good broker-dealer firm that makes its own market in mortgage securities should, under today's favorable conditions, be able to provide executions within one-quarter to one-half point of the institutional market. This is not always the case. When the market weakens, the odd lot investor is hurt the most.

Mutual Funds—Mutual funds made up of diversified portfolios of securities have soared in popularity in recent years. And with good reason. First, you can invest in them for as little as $1,000 (some funds even have a $250 minimum for IRA accounts). Even more important, the fund's active management lessens the risk that changing market conditions will cause your yield to plummet. Active managers adjust the coupon level and type of underlying mortgage (for instance, fixed-payment mortgages versus graduated payment mortgages). Diversification is used to reduce prepayment uncertainty.

Mutual fund managers are also able to employ a number of important portfolio management techniques. For example, some fund managers will purchase Ginnie Mae options to limit the impact of prepayments. Prepayments become more of a problem when interest rates decline, but this causes the value of the options to increase, offsetting at least some of the loss from prepayments. The option purchase program then restores a better mix of risk and reward to the portfolio.

In contrast to an option purchase program, some funds write (i.e., sell) options against their portfolio holdings of mortgage securities. These programs earn extra income, but at the expense of forgoing even more of the mortgage securities' limited price appreciation potential. Meanwhile, those portfolios retain most of the risk of price loss when interest rates increase.

Not all funds use all of these techniques, and the combination used by a particular fund may affect its risk level.

Mutual funds are available in a variety of formats including front-end load, no-load, and back-end load.

Mutual funds will reinvest your principal and may reinvest your interest, saving considerable time and effort, as well. In addition, the accounting headaches involved with mortgage-backed security investing are handled by the mutual fund, and record keeping is simplified when dealing with one mutual fund versus several direct investments.

Unit trusts—Some advisers caution against investing in unit trusts, although they offer the same low minimum investments as mutual funds. Unit trusts offer an incremental degree of predictability over direct purchases because an investor can buy into a portfolio holding 20 or 30 securities; however, unlike a mutual fund, this same portfolio is retained throughout the life of the trust. Their main drawback is potentially poor liquidity; if you own small lots of a small trust, bids can be low and sales charges steep. Since unit trusts are unmanaged, they are subject to the same prepayment risks that plague individual mortgage securities. In addition, because the portfolio does not change, principal and interest payments cannot be reinvested in the unit trust, and the investor must reinvest the payments himself.

CMOs (collateralized mortgage obligations)—One other way investors can invest in mortgage-backed securities is through this hybrid security, which has been turned into an investment resembling a bond in that they typically make semiannual interest payments. Principal payments go first to those holding issues with the shortest maturity.

CMOs are worth looking into for an investor with a specific investment horizon. Here, the investor can usually get a good quality security at a yield comparable to that of a corporate bond of less quality.

On the other hand, a CMO splits off your cash flows and you no longer receive all the advantages inherent in a mortgage security, such as monthly interest and principal payments.

CONCLUSION

Mortgage-backed securities have caught the attention of many investors because of their recent high returns. Much of this has been caused by the drop in the overall level of interest rates—which, of course, may not continue. This illustrates both the risks and rewards of investing in mortgage-backed securities. There are a number of risks, including:

- The total return will vary with changes in the general level of interest rates: They are hurt by rising rates and helped by falling rates.
- The maturity of the securities is variable and unknown in advance, since it depends on the life of the underlying mortgages.
- Mortgage prepayments will increase with falling interest rates, which means that the security will have a shorter life than anticipated, and the holder will be faced with a greater amount of his monthly principal and interest payments that must be reinvested at lower rates.

In return, there are certain advantages:

- The yields are higher than other fixed-income investments with similar characteristics.
- They tend to be less sensitive to interest rate changes than other longer-term fixed-income instruments.

As with any investment, it is important to balance the risks against the rewards and to judge whether the investment will fit in with the needs of your overall portfolio. Mortgage-backed securities have their own unique set of risks and rewards and are simply another investment option open to individual investors.

READING 10

GINNIE MAES

Jade Wu

You may be one of the many investors who own a Government National Mortgage Association (GNMA) certificate, which goes by the Southern belle nickname of "Ginnie Mae." But if you understand how they actually work, you may be among the very few.

Ginnie Maes are mortgage-backed securities. Residential mortgages are packaged in pools and then resold to investors as certificates of at least $25,000.

Why are Ginnie Maes so popular? They provide a potent combination of safety and high yield. At least, that is what is used in a sales pitch.

Regular payments to investors are guaranteed by the GNMA, a government agency which is part of the Department of Housing and Urban Development, whether or not payments have been received by the lending institution servicing the loan. More important, the certificates are also backed by the full faith and credit of the federal government. This guarantee makes Ginnie Maes as risk-free as Treasury bonds.

On top of this prized safety feature, returns on Ginnie Maes are generally 1 percentage point higher than on comparable Treasury bonds.

That edge doesn't mean you should march right out and fill your portfolio with Ginnie Maes, however. Income from the securities is fully taxable, except in a few states. So they are perhaps best suited for an Individ-

---

Reprinted from *Personal Investor Magazine*, April 1985, pp.50–54. Published bimonthly by Plaza Communications, Inc., 4300 Campus Drive, Newport Beach, CA 92660. Used with permission.

ual Retirement Account or other tax-sheltered vehicle, or they can benefit someone already retired and in a lower tax bracket who is seeking maximum monthly income.

You may also be in for some surprises if you don't know the uniquely complex characteristics of Ginnie Maes.

This sophisticated investment instrument was created by the GNMA to help finance new housing by making real estate mortgage investments appealing to institutional and individual investors. To attract such investors, the association works with housing lenders—and with investment bankers, who pool existing mortgages and package them as collateral for securities, which are sold as Ginnie Maes. Each GNMA certificate gives an investor a share in a specific mortgage pool, which usually totals at least $1 million.

The mortgage bankers run the pools, which are made up of Federal Housing Administration (FHA) and Veterans Administration (VA) guaranteed mortgages. They collect the monthly payments and pass the interest and principal through directly to the GNMA holder. That's why Ginnie Maes are called "pass-through" securities.

The development of Ginnie Maes spawned a myriad of other mortgage-backed securities, from the Federal Home Loan Mortgage Corporation's similarly named Freddie Macs to "collateralized mortgage obligations," or CMOs, which are sponsored by banks and private financial firms. However, none approach Ginnie Maes in popularity. Since 1970, more than $224 billion in Ginnie Maes have been marketed to institutional and individual investors. In 1984, nearly $30 billion worth were sold.

Initially, Ginnie Mae certificates were offered in units of at least $100,000, putting them out of the reach of most individual investors. This minimum has since been reduced to $25,000 on newly issued certificates. Investment firms have meanwhile created products that permit investors with as little as $1,000 to purchase Ginnie Maes in other formats. There are unit investment trusts, or portfolios of Ginnie Mae securities, which are put together by brokerage firms like Merrill Lynch and then sold to individuals in $1,000 pieces. These mini-Ginnies have the same features as the $25,000 certificates. A secondary, or resale, market exists for these units as well, but purchase fees run from 2 to 5 percent of the investment; there is no fee for selling a unit.

Over the last 18 months, Ginnie Mae mutual funds have really taken off. There are also Ginnie Mae futures, which trade as commodity contracts on the Chicago Board of Trade; however, they have not proven popular.

Ginnie Mae pass-through certificates are highly complex securities. The main reason is that they combine features of both bonds and mortgages.

Like bonds, Ginnie Maes move up and down in market value as interest rates fluctuate. But unlike bonds, in which the owner receives interest income (usually twice a year) but does not get repaid the face value of the bond until it matures, the owner of a Ginnie Mae receives checks once a month which include both interest and a repayment of part of the principal, just like the monthly mortgage payments that are made to a lender. The initial monthly payments are almost entirely interest, but over time the principal component increases, until the final payments are almost entirely principal. (By the way, taxes are levied only on interest income, and not on the return of your original principal.)

When a Ginnie Mae expires, there is no final payment, since the entire principal has already come back to the owner of the certificate. In other words, Ginnie Maes are "self-liquidating" investments.

Let's suppose you purchase a certificate with a coupon rate of 12 percent for $100,000. Your certificate is 10 percent of a $1 million Ginnie Mae pool. Initially, you will be receiving $12,000 in annual income, or $1,000 a month. Actually, your check will be closer to $995, as some nominal management fees will be subtracted. But let's use $1,000 as a round number. Virtually all of this is interest at the beginning.

At some point, $100,000 of the $1 million gets paid off, and you receive 10 percent of this amount, or $10,000, back as a repayment of your share of the principal. Since the underlying mortgage pool is now reduced to $900,000, your 10 percent represents $90,000. And your monthly checks will drop to $900. As prepayments continue, the pool shrinks, as does the amount of principal on which you are earning a monthly return.

Some Ginnie Mae investors are unaware that their monthly payments include both interest income and principal, and wind up spending the entire amount. Only later do they learn that they've been exhausting their nest egg. Although you receive a single lump sum monthly, for record keeping and tax filings you get a record of how much is interest income and what is returned principal.

Even if an investor knows about this repayment feature, he or she still faces the problem of how to reinvest the returned principal so that it keeps compounding at a high rate. The problem is exacerbated by the fact that the principal is returned in unpredictable dribs and drabs or in unexpected chunks.

It's not hard to see why investors who have not anticipated these complications can be thrown for a loop. And the Securities and Exchange Commission has received an unusually high number of complaints from angry Ginnie Mae purchasers. Even some brokers, it seems, didn't quite know what they were selling.

If you look in the financial pages of a newspaper, you'll see that Ginnie Maes are available at coupons, or interest rates, between about 8 and 16 percent. Those being issued currently have around a 12 percent coupon; the rest were issued in the past when interest rates were either higher or lower than they are now. In the next two columns, to the right of the coupons, are the bid and ask prices of the certificates. The lower the coupon, or interest-based return on the certificate, the lower the price of the certificate; the higher the coupon, the higher the price. In this sense, Ginnie Maes are just like bonds.

The investor pays a market price for a low-coupon certificate that is considerably lower than the certificate's face value; the difference between the market price he pays and the face value, which is returned to him over time, compensates him for the low coupon. Note, however, that this difference is taxed as regular income. On the other hand, the market price of the high-coupon certificates is higher than their face value. The investor gets a high interest-based return but loses the difference between the face value and the market price.

The main difference between bonds and Ginnie Maes is that, unlike bonds, Ginnie Maes do not have a fixed maturity. Movements in interest rates affect the speed at which mortgages get repaid and this in turn has a dramatic effect on a Ginnie Mae's yield-to-maturity. For example, if an investor is holding a Ginnie Mae with a 14 percent coupon, which corresponds to some homeowner's 14 percent mortgage, and interest rates fall to 10 percent, the homeowner is likely to pay off his original 14 percent mortgage as soon as possible in order to refinance at the new lower rate. This means the investor's 14 percent return will end sooner than he suspected.

"There is never really a certain yield," warns Blaine Roberts, vice president and manager of mortgage-backed securities research at Merrill Lynch. "No one can predict a concrete figure." So, if you come across some advertisements promising Ginnie Mae annual yields of 13 percent or higher, you should understand these numbers do not represent returns you are certain to obtain.

For the sake of convenience—some might argue, confusion—newspapers assume a 12-year life span for all Ginnie Maes regardless of their coupon. Indeed, the average Ginnie Mae lasts 12 years. Thus, in the fourth column, newspapers list annual yields that range from about 11.3 percent for certificates with 8 percent coupons to 13.6 percent for those with 16 percent coupons. In reality, however, the 8 percent coupon Ginnie Maes are likely to last much longer than the 16 percent coupon ones—at least if interest rates remain where they are or fall even further. This means that the yields-to-maturity on all Ginnie Maes are actually expected to be quite similar.

As expectations about interest rates change, expectations about the life spans of the variously couponed certificates change. This, in turn, affects their prices; and the resulting price differential works to even out their yields-to-maturity.

The life span—and thus yield-to-maturity—of a Ginnie Mae is affected not only by interest rates. Any factor that might cause homeowners to pay off their mortgages early will shorten the life span of certificates and affect their yields-to-maturity. If a certificate has a low coupon, a speed-up in repayment is advantageous for the investor because he expects the lion's share of his return from the difference between the face value of the certificate and the market price he paid; the sooner he collects that sum, the better for him. It's the opposite with high-coupon Ginnie Maes: the sooner the principal gets returned, the less time the investor receives his high-interest return, whence he expects the lion's share of his income from interest payments. These days, homes are bought and sold with a lot more frequency, favoring the yields-to-maturity of the low-coupon certificates.

Working out a Ginnie Mae investment strategy is not terribly easy. Basically, you want to figure out where you think interest rates are going and act accordingly.

"If you think rates are coming down, buy a lower coupon Ginnie Mae that is trading at a discount," says Steven Hirsch, the head of mortgage-backed securities for Prudential-Bache. You do just the opposite if you think rates are going up, opting for the certificate trading at a premium. Reason: if rates are falling, the discounted, or low-coupon, Ginnie Maes will be repaid faster increasing their yields-to-maturity; if rates are rising, the premium-priced, or high-coupon, certificates, will be paid back more slowly, again increasing the yield-to-maturity.

For example, assume Ginnie Maes currently have a 12 percent coupon and you buy an old one with an 8 percent coupon at $0.79 on the dollar, expecting interest rates to fall. According to the newspaper, the annual yield of your certificate will be only 11.3 percent, while the current issues are yielding 12 percent annually. However, you believe that interest rates will fall and your certificate will be paid back faster than in 12 years. Let's suppose you're right and the interest rates do fall; and to make a point, let's assume they fall so low that both your certificate and the ones issued currently are repaid in exactly one year. You bought a $100,000 certificate for $79,000 and after a year have $29,000 in profits (the face value of the certificate plus 8 percent interest minus what you paid); meanwhile, the person who bought a $100,000 certificate for $100,000 with a 12 percent coupon has only $12,000 in profits (the face value of the certificate plus 12 percent minus what he paid). You're clearly ahead. One more point to remember: you are getting back principal monthly. To get the amounts cited above, you have to reinvest your monthly payments of principal at about the same rate.

On the other hand, let's say you expect interest rates to rise. So, you buy a $100,000 certificate with a 16 percent coupon at $1.12 on the dollar. The newspaper says your annual yield over 12 years will be 13.6 percent, which is, of course, higher than the 12 percent yield expected on current issues. Obviously, most people believe that interest rates will stay where they are or fall and that homeowners will refinance their 16 percent mortgages as soon as possible, bringing the yield-to-maturity of the 16 percent coupon certificates in line with that of current issues. However, let's suppose interest rates rise and they rise so much that the 16 percent coupon Ginnie Maes last all 12 years. At the end of the period, you're obviously ahead, as you've been receiving 16 percent annual interest on your $112,000 investment while the purchasers of what were current issues have been getting only 12 percent. True, you've lost $0.12 on the dollar, or $12,000 of principal, not paid back, but the interest-based return outweighs this premium you've had to pay.

As a means of comparing the two, consider two 12-year self-liquidating mortgages as approximation of the two Ginnie Mae certificates. When all the math is done, your 16 percent certificate generated $225,475 in payments, leaving a net proceed of $113,475 after subtraction of the $112,000 purchase price. By contrast, the 12 percent certificate generated $189,193 in payments for a net proceed of $89,183 after subtraction of the $100,000 purchase price. The proceeds from your 16 percent certificate equal 101.3 percent of its purchase price, as opposed to 89.2 percent in the case of the 12 percent certificate.

Playing on the twin appeals of high yield and safety, marketers such as Merrill Lynch, Shearson Lehman/American Express, Prudential-Bache, and others have packaged the high-yield investment for easier purchase. Until last year, the most saleable form was the unit investment trust. Unit trusts pool money from investors to buy the certificates through a broker. (Usually 80 percent of the portfolio is in Ginnie Maes, and the remaining portion is in other government securities.) An investor needs only $1,000 minimum to participate, and reinvestment plans for interest, principal, or both are offered.

Again, the investment is self-liquidating, and there are drawbacks. "A percentage of the investment goes toward marketing and servicing fees," says Christine Porco, senior analyst at Mabon, Nugent & Company, a New York brokerage firm. The yield winds up reduced by about one fifteenth. Note, too, that every time you want to reinvest in another unit you have to pay a purchase transaction fee, which can run 2 to 5 percent of the investment. Liquidating is free.

And because they are basically just little pieces of Ginnie Maes, these units also rise and fall in value when interest rates go up and down. Any investors who want to sell a Ginnie Mae unit purchased before a subsequent rise in interest rates would find the unit worth less than when it had been first bought. Conversely, a drop in rates like we've seen in the last eight months raises the market value of a Ginnie Mae unit. Many investors have been unprepared for this kind of price volatility, let alone the other complexities discussed above. Wall Street firms sold $4 billion in Ginnie Mae unit trusts in 1983, but last year sales totaled less than $250 million.

The current emphasis on Ginnie Mae mutual funds is an attempt to get around some of these problems. In 1984, the number of funds rose from 4 at the beginning of the year to 17 by year's end, and assets in 12 months sextupled, climbing to $6 billion by the end of the year. And on a total return basis—counting both interest income and gains in principal—Ginnie Mae mutual funds were up last year by an average of 13.18 percent, according to Lipper Analytical Services, which tracks fund performance.

These funds, unlike unit investment trusts, are actively managed. A professional does the tricky work of selecting the best Ginnie Maes at any time. Different GNMA securities are bought and sold to maximize the return on the funds, whereas, in a unit trust, the same holdings are maintained until maturity.

In addition, the Ginnie Mae mutual funds take care of reinvesting the irregular monthly principal payments, although they also offer automatic redemption plans through which you can have a fixed amount of your original principal returned to you monthly.

The minimum investment in a GNMA mutual fund varies: Pilgrim Group requires $1,500; Vanguard $3,000; Kemper Investments $1,000. As with all mutual funds, shares can be sold directly to the investor without a broker. The investor receives monthly dividend checks at a fixed interest, which is determined from conservative estimates of what the funds' performance will be over the year. Any positive difference between interest paid out and the sum of the total interest income earned and capital gains made is paid to the investor at the end of the fiscal year. If there is a negative difference—an event that most funds have yet to experience—the funds sell off certificates, lowering share value. As with all mutual funds, there is no guaranteed rate of return.

PART 3

STOCK MARKET INVESTING

READING 11

THE STOCK MARKET AND BUSINESS CYCLES

John Markese

Recently, financial headlines read: "Investors Selling Off Consumer Stocks and Moving into Basic Industries." Terms such as *consumer stocks, basic industries*, and *cyclical stocks* are frequently bandied about. But often these stock groupings are not completely understood by individual investors.

Stock groups have historically had varied performance at different point in the business cycle. The business cycle—referring to changes in the level of economic activity—is usually characterized with terms such as recession and expansion.

This reading will concentrate on an overview of the stock market and business cycles, highlighting the stock groups that have performed well at different points of the cycle.

THE OVERALL CYCLE

Common stocks in general have displayed an important relationship to the economy. The stock market is consistently a leading indicator of economic activity. What does this mean? Common stocks overall have hit a top, on average, about nine months before the economy has peaked, and common

---

Source: *AAII Journal*, November 1986. Used with permission.

FIGURE 1
The Business Cycle, Stock Market, and Stock Groups

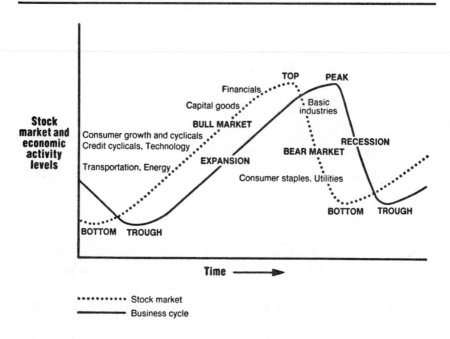

stocks, overall, have reached a bottom, on average, about four months before the economy has hit a trough. Investor expectations about future economic levels have usually been collectively correct. Investors acting upon those expectations by making stock transactions have made common stocks a leading indicator of the economy. One of the best sources on business-cycle activity is Business Conditions Digest, published by the U.S. Department of Commerce.

While common stocks, overall, have been a leading indicator of the economy, the stock groups that compose the market have had different relative performance over the business cycle. Figure 1 represents the relationship between the stock market and the economy over the business cycle. The curves are not meant to represent precise business-cycle and stock market movements but, instead, their generalized relationship. The upward slant of the curves reflects the long-term growth in stock values and the economy.

The stock groups positioned on the stock market curve represent the major categories of stocks, and the points on the curve represent where these stock groups have historically performed at their best over the market cycle. These groups are detailed in Table 1. Although these groups are very generalized, one good source of industry and stock group information is the Survey of Current Business, published by the U.S. Department of Commerce.

The performance of any group is inevitably linked to the economic cycle but generally leads, as do most stocks, the particular economic conditions. For example, the stocks of capital goods producers (machinery, equipment, industrial buildings, etc.) tend to do well during mid to late bull markets. As the economy starts moving and capacity utilization rises, the demand for capital goods rises and capital goods producers generate increased profitability. During bear market environments, after the economy has peaked, consumer staples are viewed as defensive stocks with stable earnings and low volatility—consequently performing well in a declining economic environment.

WHICH DOES BEST WHEN?

Of course, some stock groups perform well at more than one point of the business cycle due to changes in economic variables that impact the group significantly. Financials, for example, are primarily composed of banks and insurance companies and benefit dramatically when interest rates decline during the latter stages of an economic contraction due to their financial assets and activities. But these firms may also do well in early bull markets near economic troughs, when economic activity and loan demand may pick up without substantial increases in the cost of funds. The same, of course, is true of utility stocks. These stocks tend to do well in the trough of the economic cycle: When the economy heads down and rates are dropping, they do well because they are heavily leveraged and their profitability increases; when the economy picks up, energy demand rises and they also increase their profitability.

Energy is an example of a group that is primarily tied to one part of the business cycle: As the economy picks up, the demand for energy-related products increases, as does the profitability of energy-producing firms. This trend, however, has been significantly disrupted by the actions of OPEC.

Credit cyclicals are usually tied to the housing market and respond to interest rate developments as well as the housing demand, particularly new

TABLE 1
Stock Groups

Many stocks are difficult to categorize, and these groups are necessarily generalized. Below is a listing of the categories presented in Figure 1 and a description or examples of the types of firms falling within the group.

Basic industries: Firms manufacturing chemicals, plastics, or paper products, for example.

Capital goods: Firms that produce goods used to produce other goods, such as equipment and machinery manufacturers.

Consumer credit: Firms that are tied to the housing industry, such as savings and loans.

Consumer cyclicals: Manufacturers of consumer products that respond to changes in disposable income—automobile manufacturers, department stores, fast-food chains.

Consumer growth: Consumer products growing in demand and not sensitive to the business cycle—computer and video outlets, for example.

Consumer staples: Manufacturers of basic consumer products, such as foods, drugs, cosmetics, tobacco, and liquor.

Energy: The major oil companies, for example.

Financials: Banks and insurance companies.

Technology: Computer and computer-related firms; companies in the aerospace industry; semiconductor manufacturers.

Transportation: Trucking companies and the airlines, for instance.

Utilities: Electric utilities, primarily.

---

housing starts. Consumer growth refers to products that are not sensitive to business-cycle changes, while consumer cyclicals, such as automobile manufacturers and department stores, respond to changes in disposable income. The basic industries—paper and chemical producers, for example—might do well when stockpiles are diminished and inflation resurges.

CAUTIONS AND CONCLUSIONS

Not all stock groups, or for that matter, individual stocks, are easily categorized. And it should be remembered that both the categories and their positions on the stock market curve are very generalized.

But one important conclusion can be drawn that tends to mitigate the lack of relative performance recognition for detailed subsets of the stock groups. Stock groups aside, it should be of no great surprise that stocks with a high degree of risk, as measured by beta, do well during early bull markets, and stocks with lower risk do relatively well in latter phases of a bear market.

Beta is a measure of stock return volatility relative to the market's volatility. The market's beta is always 1; stocks and groups with a beta higher than 1 have returns that, on the average, are better than the market's in a bull market and worse than the market's in a bear market. Stocks and stock groups with betas significantly above 1 would be expected to do well in early bull markets, and stock groups with betas below 1 would be considered defensive and would do relatively well in late bear markets.

Unfortunately, investors do not know with certainty when a market or economic turning point is reached until after the event. But having some idea about how stock groups may be expected to perform at various points of the market and economic cycle should provide information useful in adjusting portfolio composition in anticipation of longer-term market and economic trends.

READING 12

A GUIDE TO THE MAJOR
STOCK MARKET INDEXES

John Markese

The bull market of the 1980s has been accompanied by an explosion in market indexes. While there are still many more common stocks than market indexes, picking up the financial section of your local newspaper may convince you otherwise. Rapid growth in the number of indexes reported has created rapid growth in investor confusion as to what the various indexes represent and how they should be used. Adding to the problems of sorting out the indexes are the indexes that have been created by options exchanges and futures markets to facilitate options and futures trading on a market or industry index.

WHAT IS A MARKET INDEX?

A market index is a statistical composite that measures the ups and downs of the market it is designed to follow. There are many indexes that follow numerous markets, including the stock markets, the bond markets, industry sectors, etc.

Investors use indexes in monitoring their own portfolios. It is important, however, to monitor an index that mirrors the investor's portfolio composition and diversity. Observing how financial, economic, and polit-

---

Source: *AAII Journal,* October 1987. Used with permission.

ical events affect an index with similar composition to an investor's portfolio enables the investor to not only monitor what causes current changes in a portfolio but to also formulate expectations of portfolio behavior in anticipated financial scenarios.

Additionally, an index serves as a benchmark for performance comparisons. How well your portfolio of stocks or mutual funds has done relative to the market is useful in judging your investment success or the success of the managers of your funds. Comparing performance of a portfolio to an inappropriate index may lead to less than optimal investment decisions.

The two primary variables for any market index are the sample and the construction used. This reading is focused on common stock and broad market indexes. For these indexes, the sample essentially means exchange. Are the stocks in the index listed on the New York Stock Exchange, the American Stock Exchange, the over-the-counter market, or some combination of all three? This is the important component that determines how the index will respond in various financial environments and how meaningful the index will be for the individual investor. The more American Stock Exchange-listed stocks and over-the-counter stocks, the more volatile the index. American and OTC stocks are smaller and have greater price variability than the larger stocks listed on the NYSE, although some very small stocks are listed on the NYSE and some very large stocks are traded over the counter.

Construction of a market index is less important than the stocks tracked but, nonetheless, an understanding of how the index is calculated can give some insights into the interpretation of the index. First, while the term index has been used and is by far the most common construction, averages also exist— most notably the Dow Jones Industrial Average.

An index calculates the value of the stocks in the sample at a certain point in time and sets this value as the base. All future values can be compared to this base. For example, an index with a base of 100 (other bases may be used) and a current value of 200 has doubled over the time period.

The second point of construction is the weights used for the stocks in the index. Almost all of the commonly quoted indexes are value-weighted. Value-weighted means that the price of each stock is multiplied by the number of common stock shares outstanding. Stocks with higher prices and more shares outstanding have a bigger impact on the index value.

One exception to this value-weighted approach is the Value Line Index, which is an unweighted (equal-weighted) index. In the case of Value

Line, the daily price change is calculated for each stock in the index and a compound average return for all stocks in the index is derived; the new index level is determined by applying this average return to the previous value of the index. This technique of calculation results in, effectively, an equal amount invested in each stock in the index at the start of each day—an impractical approach for investors and an index construction that renders the index less useful for comparisons to investment portfolios. Unweighted indexes, such as Value Line, tend to be more volatile, reflecting the movements of all stocks in the index without regard to the price and shares outstanding. Small stocks have just as much impact as large stocks.

THE DOW JONES AVERAGE

The Dow Jones Industrial Average deserves a special consideration because it represents a small sample (30 stocks), it is an average and not an index, and it is widely quoted.

Once upon a time, the Dow was reported by adding up the prices of all 30 stocks and dividing by 30. However, over the years, stock splits and stock dividends had to be taken into consideration, and this was done by changing the divisor. Currently, the divisor is at 0.784. So when you hear that the Dow is at 2700 it really means that the average share is worth $2,700 before all splits and stock dividends over the years. Beyond the restricted sample of only large stocks (high prices and many shares outstanding), the adjustment to the divisor has actually caused the growth in the average to be understated. Stocks that split have less future impact on the average, yet the stocks that split tend to be the ones experiencing growth.

USING AN INDEX

How do you make a simple comparison of how your portfolio has done relative to an index? Assuming your portfolio has the same composition (risk and diversification) as the index and ignoring cash dividends, just compare the percentage change. While this is not a total return calculation, the resulting numbers are useful. As an example, the Standard & Poor's index of 500 stocks (a value-weighted, broad sample of large stocks) closed 1986 with a value of about 242 and began the year at about 211. The percentage change would be calculated as follows:

$$\frac{242-211}{211} = 0.147 = 14.7\%$$

If your portfolio was composed of primarily large New York Stock Exchange-type stocks and you had not made substantial changes to your portfolio over the period, you could compare your ending portfolio value to your beginning portfolio value and the resulting percentage change could in turn be compared to the index change for a rough idea of relative performance.

As an easy reference guide, the accompanying table (see p. 158) gives brief descriptions of the key elements of the most reported indexes and the ones that may be useful to the individual investor. An example of the type of index that has not been included in the table is the NYSE Beta Index. As mentioned earlier, many indexes were created by exchanges as the underlying instrument for options and futures trading. The NYSE Beta Index is composed of the 100 most volatile issues traded on the NYSE. These stocks have recently averaged 70 percent greater volatility than the overall market—an interesting index to trade options against, but not an index that most individuals should monitor.

Use the table, particularly the composition column, to find an index that best reflects your own portfolio and monitor the index on a timely basis for both changes in the condition of financial markets and as a benchmark for comparison of performance. All of these indexes can be found in *The Wall Street Journal, Barron's Investor's Daily,* and some major newspapers, and they are often quoted on the news.

TABLE 1
The Major Stock Market Indexes

Index	*Composition*	*Construction*	*Sub-Indexes Available*
American Stock Exchange Market Value Index	All stocks listed on the American Stock Exchange.	Value-weighted	Series of sector indexes
Dow Jones Industrial Average*	Thirty large NYSE firms representing major industry sectors.	Average (price-weighted)	20 Transportation 15 Utilities 65 Stock Composite
NASDAQ OTC Composite Index	Over 2,000 stocks listed on the OTC market representing major industry sectors.	Value-weighted	Industrials Insurance Banks National Market Composite National Market Industrials
New York Stock Exchange Composite Index	All stocks listed on the New York Stock Exchange.	Value-weighted	Industrials Utilities Transportation Finance
Standard & Poor's 500 Index	500 stocks representing major industry sectors and all large NYSE stocks plus some major Amex and OTC stocks.	Value-weighted	400 Industrials 20 Transportation 40 Utilities 40 Financials
Value Line Composite	The close to 1,700 stocks followed by Value Line Investment Services.	Equal-weighted	Industrials Rails Utilities
Wilshire 5000 Index	Close to 6,000 stocks including all NYSE (82%), Amex (4%), and larger OTC stocks (16%).	Value-weighted	—

*Technically, an average is not an index.

READING 13

THE S&P 500

Albert S. Neubert

The Standard & Poor's 500 Composite Stock Price Index, which stood at 249.05 as of December 1, 1986, is one of the most widely followed indexes of stock market performance today. It is also one of the U.S. Commerce Department's 12 leading business indicators. Yet many investors are unfamiliar with its underlying concepts. This article is an introduction to the S&P 500 from an investor's viewpoint.

WHAT IS IT?

The S&P 500 was introduced in 1957 and is designed to provide investors with a truly representative measure of common stock price movement. Until 1976, the index was limited to issues traded on the New York Stock Exchange. However, coverage was then expanded to include the bank and insurance sectors and to make certain other improvements, including the introduction of some over-the-counter issues. Currently, the S&P 500 tracks 500 companies traded on the New York Stock Exchange, the American Stock Exchange, and the over-the-counter market.

Component stocks are chosen with the aim of achieving a distribution of broad industry groupings that approximates the distribution of these groupings in the New York Stock Exchange common stock population,

---

Source: *AAII Journal*, January 1987. Used with permission.

which is taken as the assumed model for the composition of the total market. (See Table 1 on the next page.)

The S&P 500 is a market-weighted index, which means that each company's stock influences the index in proportion to its importance in the stock market; the weighting is achieved by multiplying a stock's market price by the number of common shares outstanding. The level of the index at any time represents the quotient of the aggregate market value of the component stocks divided by their aggregate market value as of the base period 1941 to 1943; the average aggregate market value for that period has been assigned a value of 10.

The S&P 500 was not the first market gauge to be used by investors. In fact, the Dow Jones Industrial Average is the oldest and probably the most familiar to individual investors. Many investing professionals, however, believe it is not as accurate as the S&P 500 in reflecting overall stock market performance. There are several reasons for this.

First, the Dow is not an index but rather an arithmetic average of the price of 30 stocks. Thus, higher-priced stocks tend to carry more weight in the Dow than do less expensive ones. In addition, if one of the 30 stocks that comprise the Dow is a merger or acquisition target that rises substantially in price, this in itself is sufficient to cause dramatic moves in the average, regardless of overall stock market activity.

Second, many of the 30 stocks that comprise the Dow have industrial or cyclical characteristics and may not be reflective of the broader market. Such stocks have become less significant to many investors as smaller, high-growth companies in the service and high-technology sectors have gained in prominence.

Although the S&P 500 and the Dow tend to track each other fairly closely over the short run, their performance over a longer period diverges because of their different characteristics. The Dow measures the performance of a small sector of the market, notably large-capitalization, blue-chip stocks. The S&P 500, on the other hand, reflects broader sectors of the market and, therefore, measures the performance of smaller-capitalization stocks along with the blue chips. Because investor interest can shift from blue chips to smaller or "second-tier" stocks (or vice versa), this difference is significant in terms of index performance.

In addition, the Dow experiences more dramatic swings than does the S&P 500, and these may not correspond to broad market activity. In a broad market move, the S&P 500 should move one point for every seven points gained or lost by the Dow. If the S&P 500 does not move in this

TABLE 1
S&P 500 Group Composition*

400 industrials: 77.3%
Aerospace/defense
Aluminum
Automobile
Auto parts (after market)
Auto parts (original market)
Auto, trucks and parts
Bev. (brewers)
Bev. (distillers)
Bev. (soft drinks)
Broadcast media
Building materials
Chemicals
Chemicals (diversified)
Coal
Communication—
  equipment/mfrs.
Computer & business
  equipment
Computer service
Conglomerates
Cont. (metal & glass)
Cont. (paper)
Copper
Cosmetics
Drugs

Electrical equipment
Electronics (defense)
Electrical (elec. major cos.)
Elec. (instrumentation)
Elec. (semiconductors/
  components)
Entertainment
Foods
Forest products
Gold
Hardware & tools
Homebuilding
Hospital management cos.
Hospital supplies
Hotel/motel
Household furnishings &
  appliances
Leisure time
Machine tools
Machinery (diversified)
Manufactured housing
Manufacturing (divers. inds.)

Metals—miscellaneous
Miscellaneous
Miscellaneous (high
  technology)
Offshore drilling
Oil composite
Oil well equipment & service
Paper
Pollution control
Publishing
Publishing (newspapers)
Restaurants
Retail stores (composite)
Retail specialty
Shoes
Soaps
Steel
Textile (apparel mfrs.)
Textile (textile products)
Tire & rubber goods
Tobacco
Toys

20 transportation: 2.6%
Air freight
Airlines
Railroads
Truckers
Transportation
  (miscellaneous)

40 utilities: 12.9%
Electric companies
Natural gas (distributors &
  pipelines
Telephone (new)

40 financial: 7.2%
N.Y.C. banks
Banks (outside N.Y.C.)
Life insurance
Multi-line insurance
Property-casualty
Savings & loans hold. cos.
Personal loans
Financial (miscellaneous)

S&P 500 Index (12/1/86):249.05

*As of August 29, 1986

corresponding fashion, the Dow's movement is probably not reflective of broader market activity.

HOW THE INDEX CHANGES OVER TIME

The S&P 500 index is designed to represent the market as a whole. Because the market is constantly changing, the index is constantly reviewed by the S&P Index Committee. This group consists of seven Standard & Poor's managers and executives, who are responsible for ensuring that the S&P 500 index is an accurate gauge of market performance. The committee determines the overall policy and objectives of the S&P 500 and establishes guidelines and criteria for adding or dropping a company from the index. Judgments concerning the investment merits of stocks *do not* enter into decision making. The committee strives to maintain a consistency in the composition of the S&P over time, with every effort made to avoid excessive turnover. However, additions and deletions do occur.

There are several reasons for removing a company from the S&P 500. The most common is a merger or acquisition. A less common cause for removal is bankruptcy, while the least frequent reason is lack of representativeness.

In the case of a merger or acquisition, the committee will not remove a company from the S&P 500 unless it is a certainty that the stock will halt trading. In cases of bankruptcy or industry group representativeness, the committee never anticipates an event but, instead, allows actions to become clearly defined with regard to the ultimate fate of a company. In any event, a vote is taken on the stock in question, and the result must be a unanimous decision.

In recent years, there has been an increase in the number of index changes due to takeovers and leveraged buyouts. During the 1970s, one or two changes a year in the composition of the index was common, while during the last few years as many as 25 to 30 changes per year have been required. In addition, the wave of mergers and buy-outs has resulted in fewer relatively large companies that remain to be considered for inclusion in the S&P 500. The index committee has therefore been forced to reach out to smaller companies.

Changes and additions to the index are carefully analyzed by the committee. At a typical index committee meeting, a detailed report on pending corporate actions is reviewed. The report, prepared by S&P's index services group, is organized by priority, with companies requiring immediate action slated for consideration first. The report includes a comprehensive statistical and analytical summary of each corporate action.

An essential element in the report presented to the index committee is the alternative replacement scenarios available to the committee. The committee evaluates the recommendations for replacement by using the following criteria:

- Industry classification:
  Majority of sales related to the industry.
  Profitability within industry.
- Size as measured by market value (common shares outstanding times price per share).
- Capitalization:
  Total common shares outstanding.
  Controlling interests.
  Institutional holdings.
  Float.
- Trading volume/turnover, measured by average daily volume divided by average shares outstanding, both for a reasonable period of time.
- Emerging companies/industries.
- Stock price—movements must in general be responsive to changes in industry affairs.

Because admission to the S&P 500 tends to be a positive factor for a stock, strict confidentiality is maintained regarding the selection of a stock for inclusion in the index. Once the decision has been reached, a date for implementation is established. In general, changes in the composition of the S&P 500 are made at the close of trading on Wednesdays, with exceptions handled on a case-by-case basis.

Changes in the S&P 500 index are disseminated rapidly. ADP, the primary calculator and disseminator of the index, and Bridge Data and the S&P Index System, both back-up disseminators, are updated first to allow for accurate calculation of the index on the following day. The company being added and the news media are also notified. In addition, S&P has a notification service that informs subscribers of changes after the close of the day's trading. Clients include index funds, arbitrageurs, money managers, and big trading firms.

Over time, the S&P 500 index has, to some extent, been reshaped by the increasing number of new, rapidly growing companies that have become part of it. The S&P 500 now includes representatives of such industries as telecommunications equipment manufacturers, high-tech electronics firms, biotechnology companies, and health care concerns. Because responsiveness to economic changes is key to the S&P 500's respect among investors, the S&P 500 Index Committee constantly monitors emerging industries for possible inclusion in the index.

The individual changes in the composition of the index tend to have little effect on the overall index, however. It takes a move of approximately $70 million of market capitalization to move the S&P 500 index one basis point, or 0.01.

USING THE S&P 500

The S&P 500 is useful to individual investors as a representative picture of stock market performance. *The Wall Street Journal,* local newspapers, investment publications, and most TV and radio business programs provide investors with daily high, low, and closing figures for the S&P 500. Many also report the S&P 500's best- and worst-performing groups, data which S&P supplies to news organizations on a monthly basis.

Investors would do well to compare the performance of the S&P 500 with that of the Dow before drawing conclusions about broad-based market moves. In addition, the S&P 500 is a good comparative measure to judge portfolio performance, be it a mutual fund or an individual stock portfolio. Performance can be measured against the overall performance of the index, and the performance of a stock which an investor owns can be compared against the performance of the S&P 500's representative industry group. For example, Coleco's performance can be measured against that of the toy industry group index, while the performance of Kellogg Company could be compared with that of the food industry group index. Sector mutual funds can be compared with the S&P industry group, as well.

Astute investors also keep track of the changing composition of the S&P 500. Changes in the index may reflect changing economic conditions and a growth in relative importance of various industries. In addition, changes in the composition of the index are indicative of changes in the composition of the stock market.

It is also interesting to note that stocks enjoy market gains and substantial increases in trading volume the day after their inclusion in the S&P 500, as many studies have shown. Professionally managed index funds are the cause of this boost in performance. These portfolios are designed for large institutional players to mirror the market and thereby equal its performance; currently, there is over $121 billion invested in these funds, of which approximately $70 billion is invested in index funds based on the S&P 500. When a new firm is added to the S&P 500, these funds must purchase significant amounts of the added stock to reflect the new composition of the index.

There are also financial instruments available to individual investors that are based on the S&P 500 index. Several mutual funds offer individuals index funds, which, like the institutional funds mentioned above, mirror the S&P 500. These funds offer investors a portfolio that follows the overall market; since there are few active investment decisions that must be made, the expenses of these funds tend to be much lower than other mutual funds. Another newer financial instrument being offered to investors are "SPINS," which are debt securities that offer payments indexed to the performance of the S&P 500, with downside protection in the form of guaranteed repayment of principal. Such new securities will join S&P 500 index futures and options as investment and hedging opportunities for both individual and professional investors.

And, of course, the S&P 500 index offers investors a standard to beat—a goal that many professional advisers frequently fall short of.

PART 4

INVESTING IN FUNDS

READING 14

INVESTING IN INVESTMENT COMPANIES

Wilbur W. Widicus
Thomas E. Stitzel

INTRODUCTION

An *investment company* is any of several types of companies that are formed to acquire and manage a portfolio of investment securities. Owners of the investment companies provide the capital to purchase these securities and receive the benefit of their ownership. There are two main types of investment companies in the United States. By any measure, the more important of these is the *open-end investment company,* or *mutual fund* as they are usually called. Developed earlier, but a distant second in size since World War II, are the *closed-end investment companies.* These more nearly resemble the standard business corporation and for this reason will be examined first. Other kinds of investment companies exist, but compared with these two they are relatively unimportant. Figure 1 shows the growth in assets of investment companies from 1940 to the beginning of 1984.

Money market mutual funds first appeared in 1971. Their incredible growth is pictured in Figure 1. While money market funds are true mutual funds, their investment policies set them apart from traditional investment companies.

Source: From Wilbur W. Widicus and Thomas E. Stitzel, *Personal Investing*, 4th ed. (Homewood, Ill.: Richard D. Irwin, 1985). Used with permission.

FIGURE 1
Growth in Investment Company Assets

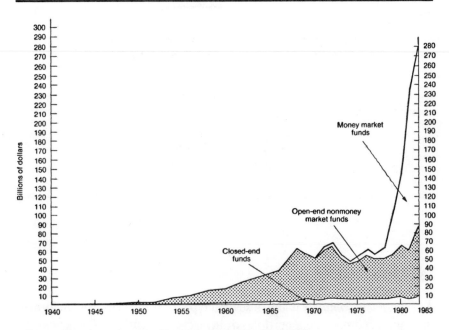

Source: Wiesenberger Investment Companies Service, New York, 1983.

CLOSED-END INVESTMENT COMPANIES

Closed-end investment companies first appeared on the American investment scene in the 1920s. They differed from mutual funds and from the modern closed-end investment companies in that their capital structures often contained bonds and preferred stock. Use of these senior securities provided great financial leverage and created an investment that was potentially very risky.

The term *closed-end* refers to the fact that, like a regular corporation, once the company's capital structure was set, it could only be changed by issuing or retiring securities, or retaining earnings. While it was legal to change the size of these companies through these methods, in practice this was rarely done. Consequently, these funds were closed ended in that they were not expected to increase the amount of their capital stock from what it was when the company was organized. Figure 2 presents the 1983 statement

FIGURE 2
Lehman Corporation Statement of Assets and Liabilities

	December 31,	
	1983	*1982*
Assets		
Investments in stocks (average cost 1983—$483,855,277; 1982—$321,964,438) (Note 2)	$722,270,700	$536,623,250
U.S. government obligation	—	5,812,500
Corporate short-term notes (Note 2)	48,805,535	131,672,200
Cash	1,599,156	366,509
Receivable for securities sold	5,445,249	425,866
Dividends and interest receivable	1,466,000	1,204,305
Total assets	779,586,640	676,104,630
Liabilities		
Payable for securities purchased	2,758,432	2,758,917
Management fee payable	682,541	610,549
Accrued expenses	68,700	57,185
Total liabilities	3,533,673	3,426,651
Net assets	$776,052,967	$672,677,979
Shares of capital stock $1.00 par value, authorized 50,000,000; outstanding	42,527,653	40,433,959
Net asset value per share	$18.25	$16.64

Source: Lehman Corporation *1983 Annual Report,* February 8, 1984, p. 17.

of assets and liabilities of Lehman Corporation, a large closed-end investment company representative of the type first organized in this country.

In a conventional company, profits come from the difference between sales revenue and the costs incurred to obtain these revenues. Investment company profits are generated in a somewhat different manner. Revenue takes the form of interest and dividends received and capital gains obtained on the securities owned by the company. Expenses are the costs of buying and selling the company's investment securities and the costs of administering the company. Nearly all the assets of investment companies are investments in other companies. Management consists of buying securities that will, hopefully, give owners of investment company shares a higher return for an amount of risk that they could obtain by investing an equal amount of money on their own. The typical investment company pays no income taxes.

One notices immediately that Figure 2 is arranged differently from the conventional balance sheet. The emphasis of this accounting statement is on *net asset value per share,* which is the amount of assets "owned" by each share of outstanding capital stock. To obtain net asset value per share, the company's liabilities are deducted from the current market or fair value of its assets. The difference is *net assets,* a term that has the same meaning as *liquidating value.* Dividing net assets by the number of shares outstanding provides the measure of net asset value per share.

Valuing Closed-End Shares

The market price of a closed-end investment company share (like that of any other corporation) is set by supply and demand. Supply and demand is in turn influenced by several factors. Expected future earnings and dividends are of great importance, but net asset value per share is also a determinant of market price.

Because closed-end investment company shares are not continuously redeemed, shareholders cannot obtain the net asset value of their shares from the company. Nevertheless, increases and decreases in this value have an effect on the market prices of all closed-end shares. Over the long run, market prices tend to increase when net asset value increases, and vice versa. At any given time, market prices may be above or below net asset value. These premiums and discounts are caused by current security market conditions, including investor favor or disfavor toward the major industries represented in the portfolio, expected future earnings of the company, and many other things that affect stock values.

The number of closed-end funds has increased in recent years. Most of the older funds are invested in diversified portfolios of common stocks. The majority of the newer companies invest in bonds and specialized investments of one type or another.

OPEN-END INVESTMENT COMPANIES

While open-end companies closely resemble closed-end funds, there are definite differences that readily explain why the open-end type has become so much more important. Figure 3 shows the statement of assets and liabilities of Eaton Vance Investors Fund, a large, well-known open-end investment company. One can see that this statement looks much like that of the Lehman Corporation.

FIGURE 3
Eaton Vance Investors Fund Statement of Assets and Liabilities

---

Financial Statements

Statement of Assets and Liabilities—January 31, 1984

Assets

Investments in securities, at value (Note 1A) (average cost $123,587,012)	$150,211,303
Cash	182,845
Receivable for investment securities sold	191,494
Receivable for capital stock sold	1,776
Interest and dividends receivable	1,629,053
Total assets	$152,216,471

Liabilities

Distributions payable February 29, 1984 on shares requesting payment in cash—		
Dividend from income ($0.15 a share)	$2,012,741	
Capital gain distribution ($0.52 a share)	3,315,498	
Payable for investment securities purchased ...	1,481,780	
Payable for capital stock repurchased	141,763	
Accrued expenses and taxes	25,924	
Total liabilities		6,977,706
Net assets for 19,055,151 shares of capital stock outstanding ..		$145,238,765
Net asset value per share		$7.62

Source: Eaton Vance Investors Fund, *Annual Report* 1984, p. 12.

The most important difference in these companies is the way they are capitalized. The closed-end investment company is essentially restricted in the amount of its capital stock to the initial amount authorized and sold. The open-end company may increase its capitalization at any time simply by selling more shares of its capital stock. Large numbers of authorized but unissued shares make this possible. This is the key difference because it enables the company to become larger as more people purchase shares.

Valuing Mutual Fund Shares

The net asset value of a share of stock in a mutual fund is of far more importance to the investor than is the net asset value of a share in a closed-end company. This is because these companies offer to sell or buy their shares on the basis of current net asset values.

On the date of the Eaton Vance statement, this company offered to sell its shares on the basis of the net asset value per share—$7.62 plus commissions—or to buy its shares at $7.62.

It is *net asset value* rather than supply and demand factors that determines the market price of mutual fund shares. In fact, shares of mutual funds are not traded on the securities exchanges. These firms sell new shares through underwriters and brokers or directly to investors. They repurchase all shares offered for sale.

Open-end investment companies often provide share owners with a wide variety of services and accounts not provided by the closed-end companies. This is one reason for the rapid growth of these funds. Another important reason is that there is incentive for these companies to continue to market their securities aggressively. As will be explained later, the managers of mutual funds, like those of closed-end funds, receive management fees based on the dollar volume of the company's assets. Larger assets mean larger fees.

Regulation of Investment Companies

Most investment companies are organized as corporations or business trusts. The laws of the state of incorporation determine the mechanics by which the companies conduct affairs such as organization, transfer of shares, election of directors, etc. These laws affect all corporations and are not specific to investment companies. State "blue sky" laws encompass the sale of investment company shares as well as other securities. They may provide some protection for shareholders, but the main regulation of investment companies is through federal laws.

Investment companies that have chosen to be regulated under the terms of the Investment Company Act of 1940 and the Investment Company Amendments Act of 1970 are known as *regulated investment companies*. These firms are also regulated under the Securities Act of 1933 and the Securities Exchange Act of 1934, as are all corporations that sell securities publicly to residents of at least two states. These laws affect investment companies mainly in that they require them to register issues of their stock with the SEC. The SEC may block the registration of these securities if it is determined that the company has made erroneous, misleading, or incomplete statements about itself. Investment companies, like other corporations, must provide prospectuses to people interested in purchasing new issues of their shares.

The Investment Company Act of 1940 was designed specifically to change the way investment companies were managed. Companies were required to include outside (presumably independent) people on their boards of directors. Each board was then required to approve contracts the company made with other businesses or individuals. The purpose of this legislation was to keep the investment companies from giving management, brokerage, or other contracts to people or firms that did not fully warrant receiving the contracts. The regulation also forced companies to provide a certain minimum amount of asset diversification. At least 75 percent of a company's total assets must be invested so that no more than 5 percent of this amount is in the securities of one company. No more than 10 percent of the outstanding voting securities of any company may be owned.

Finally, the act restricted the maximum amount of leverage that a regulated investment company could have in its capital structure. Open-end companies could have no financial leverage. Closed-end companies were allowed to issue only limited amounts of bonds or preferred stock.

Most investment companies choose to become regulated under the 1940 act because of the special tax advantages offered to regulated companies. While the law is complex, the theory it follows is simple. Regulated investment companies are seen as being *conduits* through which income passes to their shareholders. As long as the investment company meets certain minimum tests as stated in the act, it pays no income taxes. However, dividends and interest received by investment company shareholders are taxed as income.

The Investment Company Amendments Act of 1970 imposed a fiduciary duty standard on investment company managers, directors, and officers. The act has made it easier for shareholders to protest excessive management fees, sales charges and other expenses.

A regulated investment company is not necessarily a "safe" or a "good" company. The regulation, like other security laws, is designed to provide investors with enough facts to make intelligent decisions and to protect them from fraud. Managers of investment companies can still make poor investment decisions and shareholders can and do lose money on these investments. There is no doubt, however, that investment company shares are much safer now than they were before federal regulation was passed.

Figure 4 is a copy of a mutual fund share. Note how closely it resembles a regular common stock certificate.

HOW MUTUAL FUNDS OPERATE

Figure 5 pictures all the participants of a mutual fund organization. It shows how these groups are related and how mutual fund shares are sold. This is an illustration of a large company that sells its securities through an underwriter and other selling groups. There is always a sales commission when shares are sold this way. Companies may also sell directly to investors, performing the underwriting function themselves and bypassing the selling groups. These companies may require no sales commission.

The Mutual Fund

The fund itself is the corporation in which the purchaser of mutual fund shares invests money.[1] This corporation is the legal owner of the investment securities and other assets that are purchased through the sale of its shares to the public. Managers of mutual funds spend much time marketing their company's securities. This effort includes preparation of promotional literature, hiring and instructing sales personnel, making sales agreements with brokerage companies, and devising mutual fund plans that have appeal for large numbers of investors.

Custodian, Transfer Agent, and Registrar

These institutions perform the same services for the mutual fund as they do for closed-end investment companies or other corporations. The *custodian* holds the company's assets, which are mainly in the form of investment securities, and guards them against physical loss.

The *transfer agent* accounts for the changes of ownership in the company's shares and makes certain that the shares it transfers are genuine. The transfer agent's certification appears on the face of all shares. (See Figure 4.)

---

[1]Some mutual funds are organized in the legal form known as a Massachusetts trust. From the investor's viewpoint, there is no significant difference between this and the corporate form.

FIGURE 4
A Share of Mutual Fund Stock

Courtesy of Columbia Growth Fund, Inc.

FIGURE 5
Organization of a Typical Large Mutual Fund

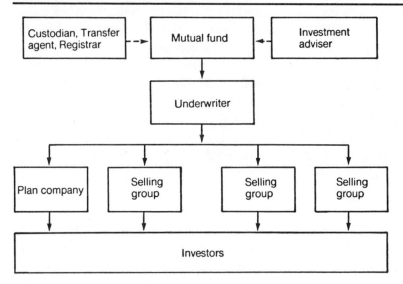

The *registrar* is an officer of a trust company or commercial bank that is independent of the investment company and the transfer agent. This person's job is to make certain that the transfer agent's efforts have been diligent and that the investment company issues no unauthorized stock.

Investment Adviser

For an investment company to be successful over the long run, it must be able to invest its owners' money in a more productive fashion than they themselves could do. Excellent investment management can do this, or so we are told by the managements of all mutual funds. Mutual fund managers set investment policy. The *investment adviser* provides the advice that determines which securities the mutual fund will purchase and sell to carry out this policy. The adviser is paid a fee for this service.

Underwriter

Underwriters of mutual fund shares perform the same service for those companies as underwriters perform for other corporations. That is, they purchase securities from the issuing company for resale to brokers or other selling groups or for direct sales to investors. But because mutual fund shares are continuously issued and repurchased, the underwriter of these securities has a continuous relationship with the mutual fund company. From earlier discussions about the underwriting of corporate securities, it will be remembered that the agreement between underwriter and issuer lasted only as long as necessary to sell the securities that were being issued.

In some cases, the underwriter sells directly to investors, taking the entire commission from the sale. At other times, the underwriter acts as a wholesaler, purchasing securities from the mutual fund for resale to brokers and others who in turn sell them to investors. Under this arrangement, the wholesaler and other sellers share the commissions.

Selling Groups

A substantial number of underwriters employ *selling groups* of brokers to give wider sales distribution to their products. These people serve as agents of the underwriter. In some cases, they have exclusive sales agreements with a single company. Under other arrangements, a selling group may market securities of several different mutual funds. Large mutual funds may market their securities through many different selling groups.

Plan Companies

Most large mutual funds sell their securities under a variety of sales plans. Some programs obligate customers to buy securities periodically, others require the mutual fund to sell securities and make periodic payments to account holders. When mutual fund shares are sold this way, some group must be responsible for holding contributions, making certain that the correct number of securities are credited to each account, and performing the accounting for plan investors. A normal way of providing these services is by organizing a separate *plan company*.

This group markets the same securities that would be sold by the underwriter or by other selling groups. In fact, they typically obtain the securities from the underwriter as needed to meet sales demand. The plan company employs its own sales force and, like the other selling groups, splits commissions with the underwriter. No commissions go to the mutual fund itself. The company receives only the net asset value of the shares sold.

PURCHASES AND SALES OF INVESTMENT COMPANY SHARES

Closed-End Companies

Recall that closed-end shares are publicly traded. Their prices are set by supply and demand, with some regard to the net asset value of the stock. *The Wall Street Journal* reports the weekly closing price of these securities each Monday in the format shown in Figure 6. On Wednesday, prices of closed-end bond funds are reported. Other financial news services carry the same information.

The *net asset value* ("N.A. Value") of these companies is always published but the price at which stock is traded is listed in the third column under the abbreviation "Stk Price." Commission charges would be added to this amount if one were buying these securities and deducted if one were selling. Commissions are computed in the same way that they are com-

FIGURE 6
Closed-End Fund Prices

Publicly Traded Funds

Friday, February 24, 198⁻.
Following is a weekly listing of unaudited net asset values of publicly traded investment fund shares, reported by the companies as of Friday's close. Also shown is the closing listed market price or a dealer-to-dealer asked price of each fund's shares, with the percentage of difference.

	N.A. Value	Stk Price	% Diff		N.A. Value	Stk Price	% Diff
Diversified Common Stock Funds				BancrftCv	24.48	23⅛–	5.5
				Castle	29.90	31⅞–	6.6
AdmExp	16.81	15¾–	6.3	CentSec	13.41	12¼–	8.7
BakerFen	38.40	33 –	14.1	Claremont	34.54	29 –	16.0
bEqStrat	z	z	z	CLAS	.11	1¼	z
GenAInv	15.94	16⅞+	5.9	CLAS Pfd	19.56	z	z
Lehman	14.23	15½+	8.9	Cyprus	.52	3⅜–	597.1
NiagaraSh	17.15	18¼+	6.4	Engex	22.36	17½–	21.7
OceasSec	6.41	7⅛+	11.2	Japan	12.92	13¼+	2.6
Source	31.40	29⅝–	5.7	Mexico	b3.58	3⅜–	5.7
Tri-Contl	23.68	23⅜–	1.3	Nautilus	31.36	33½+	6.8
US&For	22.82	22⅜–	5.2	NewAnFd	36.77	31½–	16.7
Specialized Equity and Convertible Funds				Pete&Res	29.13	28¾–	1.3
AmCapCv	30.10	30⅜+	0.9	a-Ex-dividend. b-As of Thursday's close. z-Not available.			
bASA	68.81	68 –	1.2				

puted for other common stock because these securities are sold through brokers like any other stock. The percent-difference column tells the percentage that the stock price differs from the stock's net asset value.

Mutual Funds

Mutual fund shares are not sold like other securities. The mutual fund company agrees to redeem shares in the company on any business day. At least twice each business day, the net asset value of the company's shares is computed. It is at this net asset value that the shares are redeemed. Some mutual funds charge a modest amount for the privilege of redemption but this is unusual.

Mutual fund share prices are quoted by nearly every newspaper in the United States because so many people own these investments. The list in Figure 7 contains only a part of the several hundred funds reported on a daily basis in *The Wall Street Journal.*

Mutual Fund Commissions. The *net asset value* (NAV) listed in Figure 7 is the value per share at the close of trading. The *offering price* is the price at which the company offers shares for sale. The difference be-

FIGURE 7
Mutual Fund Prices

Mutual Funds

Friday, February 24, 1984
Price ranges for investment companies, as quoted by the National Association of Securities Dealers. NAV stands for net asset value per share; the offering includes net asset value plus maximum sales charge, if any.

	Offer NAV	NAV Price Chg.			Offer NAV	NAV Price Chg
ABT Family Funds:				**Eaton Vance Funds:**		
Arbitrg	10.87	11.88+ .22		EH Bal	7.30	7.87+ .08
A Birthrt	11.39	12.45+ .27		EH Stk	10.74	11.58+ .22
Emrg Gr	10.04	10.97+ .14		Growth	6.39	6.98+ .19
Tax Mgt	12.80	13.99+ .17		High Yld	4.67	5.10 .03
Acorn Fnd	27.61	N.L.+ .44		Inc Bost	8.68	9.49 ...
ADV Fund	18.84	N.L.+ .36		Invests	7.41	8.10+ .09
Afuture Fd	12.17	N.L.+ .35		Spc Eqty	17.45	18.81+ .57
AIM Funds:				Tax Mge	12.55	13.72+ .13
Conv Yld	12.25	13.10+ .08		VS Specl	13.90	15.19+ .36
Grnway	7.71	8.25+ .16		**Eberstadt Group:**		
HiYld Sc	10.24	10.95 ...		Chem Fd	9.29	10.15+ .22
Summit	4.75	(z) + .13		Enrgv R	11.83	12.93+ .22
Alli Mtge	9.50	10.00 ...		Surveyr	13.11	14.33+ .36
Alli Techn	17.34	18.95+1.42		Energy Utl	19.42	N.L.+ .19
Alpha Fd	19.19	20.20+ .50		Evergrn r	36.29	N.L.+ .58
American Capital Group:				Evrgrn TR	15.07	N.L.+ .10
Comstk	13.98	15.28+ .25		Farm B Gr	12.91	N.L.+ .31
Corp Bd	6.82	7.45- .02		**Federated Group:**		
Enterpr	14.28	15.61+ .35		Am Lead	11.14	11.91+ .14
Exch Fd	44.22	N.L.+1.13		Exch Fd	32.26	N.L.+ .68
Fd Amer	14.41	15.75+ .17		GNMA	10.52	N.L.+ .04
Growth	25.31	N.L.+ .65		Hi Incm	11.89	12.72+ .01
Harbor	12.86	14.05+ .26		Incm Tr	10.26	N.L.- .03
High Yld	9.90	10.62- .03		Intrmd	9.44	N.L. ...
Muni Bd	17.31	18.17- .03		SIMT	10.11	N.L.- .02
O T C	9.30	10.16+ .19		Stock Tr	14.40	N.L.+ .24
Pace Fd	19.48	21.29+ .41		Tax Free	9.15	9.58- .03
Prov Inc	5.65	6.09+ .05		US Gvt S	8.43	8.83- .02
Venture	13.75	15.03+ .25		**Fidelity Group Funds:**		
AE Growth	14.05	N.L.+ .22		Bd Corp	6.63	N.L.+ .01
American Funds Group:				Congr St	49.79	N.L.+ .92
Am Bal	9.41	10.28+ .14		Contra	9.68	N.L.+ .17
Amcap F	8.01	8.75+ .15		Discovr	17.85	N.L.+ .31
Am Mutl	13.72	14.99+ .25		Eq Incm	25.39	25.91+ .31
Bnd FdA	12.59	13.76 ...		Exch Fd	40.62	N.L.+1.11
Fund Inv	10.73	11.73+ .30		Fidel Fd	14.15	N.L.+ .23
Gth FdA	12.39	13.54+ .27		Freedm	11.28	N.L.+ .24
Inc FdA	10.05	10.98+ .10		Govt Sec	9.23	N.L.+ .02
I C A	10.17	11.11+ .23		Hi Incm	8.89	N.L. ...
Nw Econ	12.86	14.05+ .25		High Yld	11.33	N.L. .04
Nw Prsp	8.29	9.06+ .13		Ltd Muni	8.23	N.L.- .02
Tax Ex	9.51	9.98- .02		Mageln	34.56	35.63+ .72
Wash Mt	9.52	10.40+ .20				

tween the NAV and the offering price is the amount of the maximum commission. It is usually between 7½ and 8½ percent of the NAV.

Looking back at Figure 3 reveals that the net asset value of the Eaton Vance Investors Fund was $7.62. Its offering price was $8.27. The difference of $0.65 represents a sales commission of 8.5 percent of the net asset value.

The mutual fund industry has come under criticism for these seemingly high commissions. While most funds have a scale of commission charges that is graduated down from the maximum rates, the graduation usually begins with purchases of $10,000 or $15,000.

Some mutual funds charge lower commissions to people who sign a letter of intent to buy a substantial dollar amount of securities over a specified period of time. These purchasers pay commissions at the rate they would have paid if they had purchased the total amount of securities all at one time. This way, the total commission on the purchase may be lower than it would have been if the securities had been purchased piecemeal. These and other features of mutual fund purchase plans may serve to lower the commission charge for some purchasers, but on the whole, these charges remain substantial.

For many years, the Securities and Exchange Commission has sponsored legislation that would lower mutual fund commissions. Suggestions have been made for a maximum commission of 5 percent, with lower rates on larger purchases. While no legislation has been passed that limits mutual fund commissions, more funds are being sold that charge no commissions. Recent changes in the commission structure of common stock purchases and sales have generally acted to increase the commissions on small trades. For example, the typical major brokerage house now charges about $40, or 4 percent, to buy or sell $1,000 of common stock. Narrowing of the difference between commission charges on mutual fund shares and small purchases of common stock will probably cause some people to shift from direct stock investments to mutual funds.

No-Load Funds

Many mutual funds charge no sales commissions—Acorn and Afuture, for example (see Figure 7). These are *no-load funds,* and the bid and ask prices of these securities are identical. No-load funds are usually sold directly to the purchaser by the fund. The sales effort of these companies is not at all aggressive.

At the beginning of 1984, more than 60 percent of all mutual funds were no-load. Ten years ago, less than 25 percent were of this type.

To purchase no-load securities, the investor must usually use some personal initiative. The best sources of information on these companies are *Investment Companies, Forbes,* various market letters, and the financial press.

Few no-load funds offer the wide variety of purchase options and accounts commonly available at other funds. They all allow an investor to start off with 100 percent of his or her money invested, which should result in a larger return on the total amount invested—all other things being equal. A few no-load funds charge a small fee to redeem shares.

ADVANTAGES AND DISADVANTAGES OF
PURCHASING INVESTMENT COMPANY SHARES

Professional Investment Management

At the time of this writing, over 800 mutual funds and about 50 actively traded closed-end funds are in operation. All these companies are supposedly operated to attain a specific goal or goals for their owners, and all companies list professional investment management as one of their strengths.

Professional management implies that the investment company can manage the investor's money better than the individual, assuming the goals of each are similar. Making any sort of scientific test of whether investment companies are in fact more successful investors than individuals is very difficult. An investment company having successful investment performance in the past will not necessarily have the same success in the future, and one that has done poorly in the past may become profitable. The topic of performance measurement will be examined in detail later in this reading. At this point, it is sufficient to state that for the person who knows little about investments, or has limited time or little inclination to manage them, the professional management offered by the investment company is probably valuable.

Diversification

A *diversified investment company* spreads the risk associated with the purchase of investments among many different holdings. It is difficult for an individual to do this unless substantial money is available to invest. If a person had $10,000 and wanted to invest it in a way to obtain the same amount of diversification as a regulated investment company would provide, nearly 20 different securities would have to be purchased. A maximum dollar amount of $500 would be invested in each security, as no more than 5 percent of the total investment could be in any one form. These purchases would probably be of odd lots of securities, and commission charges would be high. Perhaps of more importance is the problem of managing 20 different investments. This large number of different securities would take a great deal of time if they were adequately managed. Few people have or want to devote the necessary time to this task.

Diversification may take many forms. Bonds, preferred stocks, and common stocks may be purchased to provide different types of securities. Diversification may be by industry or by geographical location. It may be performed by purchasing securities of many different companies that are in the same type of business.

The purpose of diversification is to spread risk over a large number of different investments so that it becomes nearly impossible for the investor to have exceptionally poor investment results. But while it protects against loss, it also "protects" the investor against better-than-average profits. Because of this, a well-diversified investment company has great difficulty in performing much better than the stock market averages, even though the company has professional investment management.

In the late 1960s, a new concept of investment company appeared. These companies were formed to provide investment *performance,* not diversification and safety. The strategy was not to diversify but to concentrate investments in relatively few companies that have great growth potential. The professional management of these companies supposedly offsets the risk that one takes when investments are not diversified. More will be said about this type of fund when we discuss some of the different types of investment policies followed by various investment companies.

Low Cost Shifting of Investments

All the larger mutual fund companies offer *families of funds.* These are funds having different investment goals that are organized and sold by the same company. For example, in 1983 the Eaton and Howard, Vance Sanders group of investment companies included nine different funds. Shareholders may transfer the net asset value of their investment from one fund to another at a maximum cost of $5. Because the objectives of all nine funds are different, the thrust of an investment program may be changed quickly and at practically no cost.

How valuable is this privilege? An investor wishing to shift from $10,000 market value of common stock to an equal amount of bonds would pay a commission of up to 3 percent to sell the stock and a smaller commission to buy the bonds. The shift would probably cost at least $400, an expense that would be repeated if the investment were shifted back to common stock. The usual $5 or $10 charge for shifting within a family of funds provides a significant cost saving.

Many funds allow accounts to be shifted over the phone—the ultimate in convenience. Others shift only after written notification. Some restrict switching privileges to a maximum number of changes per period or to a minimum dollar amount. Shifting between unrelated no-load funds can be accomplished easily and at little or no cost by selling out of one fund and buying into another. However, all shifts, even those between securities in a family of funds where no cash changes hands, are recorded as sales and purchases of new securities for income tax purposes.

TYPES OF MUTUAL FUND ACCOUNTS

In marketing their products, managers of mutual funds have followed the examples set by the life insurance industry. They offer prospective buyers many different payment plans and several choices of dividend distributions. In sharp contrast to this, purchasers of closed-end investment company shares normally pay cash for their shares and have limited options on dividend distributions.

The Regular Account

This is the most popular and least complicated account sold by the mutual fund industry. In early 1984, more than 92 percent of all mutual fund accounts (exclusive of money market funds) were of this type.

Purchasers of these shares invest a certain amount of money (some funds have a minimum dollar amount of shares that will sell) and receive a certain number of shares of stock in the fund. Investors make no agreement to purchase more shares of the fund, and dividends are disbursed periodically as they are realized. Income dividends are usually paid quarterly, and capital gains dividends annually. Most accounts allow automatic reinvestment of dividends.

Accumulation Plans

These plans are of two types—voluntary and contractual. Under a *voluntary accumulation plan,* the investor begins by purchasing some modest dollar amount of investment company shares. This may be as low at $100; the minimum amount varies among mutual funds. At the time of this purchase, the investor declares an intent to make future periodic purchases of a minimum amount. The regular commission is charged on each future purchase, and the number of shares purchased is credited to the investor's account. These are known as *level-loaded plans* because sales commissions are a constant percentage of each payment. Such plans allow people to acquire shares in small amounts as money becomes available. Many plans allow the purchase of fractional shares. The investor has no legal liability to continue to make the agreed-upon purchases, and the account may be canceled and shares may be redeemed at their net asset value at any time.

The *contractual plan* differs from the voluntary in that the agreement between the buyer and the fund is much more formalized. When opening one of these plans, the purchaser agrees to buy a certain dollar amount of mutual fund securities over a specified period of time. Most of these plans run at least two years, often much longer. Purchasers are allowed to miss payments or to make larger than agreed-upon payments. Most plans allow early withdrawal of funds and reinvestment of the withdrawn amount at no additional cost. This feature allows investors to use fund proceeds to meet temporary financial needs. Most of the plans allow the purchaser to have all dividends reinvested in additional shares of stock in the fund.

These investments are often sold through the plan companies discussed earlier. Commissions are commonly at the highest rate allowed under law and would typically be close to 9 percent of the total invested. But the commission is not usually deducted evenly as shares are purchased. Rather, most of the commission is deducted from early payments, a practice known as a *front-end load*.

The 1970 amendments to the Investment Company Act of 1940 created protections for contractual plan purchasers. Front-end loading of commissions is allowed, but maximum charges are specified. Investors may cancel out of a contractual plan within 45 days of its inception and receive the current net asset value of their shares plus all commissions and other charges. Investors canceling within 18 months receive the net asset value of their shares and may receive a portion of sales charges. The 18-month cancellation privilege may or may not be available, depending on how the commissions have been assessed. Information about commission payments and refunds is contained in the offering prospectus. This document should be carefully studied by all people buying mutual fund securities, but it is especially important for those entering into contractual purchase plans.

Some companies sell insurance that is used to complete a plan if the plan owner dies prior to this time. This is simply term insurance that declines in amount as the investment goal is approached. A medical examination to prove insurability is often required if the amount of insurance exceeds $10,000. Insurance premiums are usually paid monthly along with plan contributions.

Accounts with Automatic Dividend Reinvestment

Automatic dividend reinvestment means that the income or capital gain dividends of the fund, or both, are reinvested immediately in additional shares of stock of the mutual fund. No dividends are received currently, but the new shares that are purchased with the reinvested dividends in turn receive dividends. The effect is similar to interest compounding.

Reinvestment of dividends may allow the investor to acquire more shares without paying the normal commissions. Reinvested income dividends are applied to the purchase of additional shares at the current *offering price*. This price includes commission charges. Capital gains dividends are often reinvested at the current *net asset value* of the company's shares. This price includes no commission. The procedure varies from fund to fund. Although all dividends are reinvested, they are taxed as income in the period in which they are declared. Later, when the investor redeems the account and takes possession of these securities, no tax is levied on the amount that has been reinvested. Automatic dividend reinvestment is a feature of most mutual funds. Several closed-end investment companies offer similar services.

Withdrawal Accounts

These plans appeal to those who wish to receive a certain sum of cash regularly from their investments. Variable annuities sold by life insurance companies most nearly resemble this investment. In 1982, less than 2 percent of all mutual fund accounts, excluding money markets, were of this type.

The usual withdrawal plan begins when an investor purchases a minimum dollar amount (usually $10,000) of mutual fund shares. These are normally purchased in a single transaction, although most mutual funds allow other types of accounts to be changed into withdrawal plans if they are large enough. The mutual fund agrees to make periodic payments from the account to its owner or to other designated people.

Payments will be made as long as the account has value. If the beginning amount of the account was large and the withdrawals small, or if the investment experience of the fund were exceptional, payments could be made indefinitely. This is usually not the case. Withdrawal payments are first made from dividend income, and if the dividends do not cover the withdrawal, the additional amount is obtained by redeeming fund shares. If a mutual fund has a very poor investment experience, and if withdrawal payments are large relative to the size of the investment, the principal of the investment might be rapidly used up.

INVESTMENT POLICIES OF INVESTMENT COMPANIES

Investment company shares are purchased for a variety of reasons, including convenience of purchase, ability to sell shares immediately, diversification of investments, and professional management. It is probably professional management that attracts most people to these investments.

Investment companies, like individual investors, have different goals. The investor must first determine his or her own investment objectives. Then, if the purchase of investment company shares is desired, the shares of a company having an investment goal similar to that of the investor should be purchased.

Every investment company makes a statement of its policies and goals in its offering prospectus, a document easily obtained from the company or a broker. Most investment companies may be classified as one of the following types, although many of them have unique features. Table 1 shows the importance of these different types of funds.

Balanced Funds

The investment objective of these funds is long-term growth of both capital and income through purchase of bonds, preferred stocks, and common stocks. The term *balanced* comes from the policy followed by some of these companies of trying to "balance" portions of their investment portfolios among these different securities in some fairly constant proportions. While

TABLE 1
Investment Companies Classified by Investment Objective (As of December 31, 1982)

Type of Fund	No. of Funds	Combined Assets (000)	Percent of Total
Common stock:			
Maximum capital gain	92	$ 11,068,600	4.1
Growth	157	22,794,400	8.4
Growth and income	108	20,382,800	7.5
Specialized	22	880,400	0.3
Balanced	24	3,070,900	1.2
Income	126	12,914,400	4.8
Bond and preferred stock	13	2,284,600	0.8
Money market	214	180,458,800	66.6
Tax-exempt municipal bonds	53	8,213,800	3.0
Tax-free money markets	25	8,811,300	3.3
	834	$270,880,000	100.0

Source: *Investment Companies,* 1963 ed. (New York: Wiesenberger Investment Companies Service), p. 41.

there is wide diversity in the performance of these funds, they are usually managed so that they offer shareholders both capital gains and dividend income. Price fluctuations of the net asset values, or market values in the case of closed-end companies, are usually less than most other types of funds.

Bond and Preferred Stock Funds

As the name implies, investments of such funds are all senior securities. The specific investment objective of these companies varies mainly in its emphasis on income and price stability. One could not reasonably expect anything but very modest capital gains distributions from this type of fund. Share value should be fairly constant, except when changes in market interest rates cause changes in prices of senior securities.

Money Market Funds

The funds are of two types: the regular money market fund and the tax-free money market fund. Both funds invest exclusively in the short-term liquid debt instruments known as money market investments. They differ in that the regular fund buys taxable securities—Treasury bills, certificates of deposit, banker's acceptances, commercial paper—while the tax-free funds invest in short-term municipal debt. Interest on the first group of securities is taxed as ordinary income by the federal government, while interest on municipal securities is not.

Growth in the number of money market funds and total money market fund assets has been phenomenal. No such funds existed before 1971. In the 11-year period following, they have become by far the most popular funds sold. Nearly 30 percent of all mutual funds were money market funds in 1982. Almost 70 percent of all mutual fund assets were represented by money market funds.

Money market funds provide investors with a return that may be very high in periods when short-term interest rates are high. During such times, these investments are much more attractive than savings accounts because they pay higher yields. Of course, as short-term interest rates decline, returns to these funds will also decline. Many of these investments are more liquid than savings accounts because they allow owners to write checks against their accounts, and they provide other ways to quickly obtain funds.

In the typical money market fund, the net asset value is held constant at $1 per share. As interest is earned, it is automatically used to purchase more shares. Money market funds seldom generate capital gains or losses. All dividends are typically taxed as interest income.

Income Funds

These funds emphasize liberal current income. The objective may be realized through purchase of bonds, preferred stock, or common stock. Most of these companies hold a variety of investments. They offer greater-than-average price stability, high yearly income dividends, and low capital gains distributions. Many withdrawal plans are income funds.

Tax-Exempt Municipal Bond Funds

The earliest of these companies were organized as *unit trusts,* and some still are. Under this arrangement, a portfolio of municipal securities is purchased and "units" or interests in the portfolio are sold. Units are not redeemed until the trust is wound up, but periodic distributions of tax-free interest are made to unit owners based on the number of units owned. There is no continuous offering of these securities, but units may be sold to other investors.

Municipal bond mutual funds have been offered since 1976. These resemble other mutual funds in that offering and redemption of securities is continuous. Management of the funds is provided by the mutual fund company, and income is passed through to shareholders in the usual manner. Both load and no-load funds are available. Growth of these funds has been rapid. Their appeal is tax-exempt income, safety of principal, and a fairly high yield for people in the high-income tax brackets.

Common Stock Funds

These funds invest primarily in common stocks or securities that are convertible into common stocks. This general classification includes the largest number of funds in existence today. The objectives of these firms vary in the degree to which they seek dividend income or capital gains growth and in the way they go about attaining their investment objectives. Their shares would typically have less price stability than the shares of balanced funds, income funds, money market funds, or those holding senior securities.

Specialized Common Stock Funds. These funds were organized with the objective of purchasing common stocks of firms engaged in a certain industry. They are offered as a way for investors to participate in the growth and profits of industries such as electronics, air travel, oceanography, and chemicals. What diversification there is in the investment company's portfolio comes from purchasing the shares of different companies in a given industry.

Several funds invest only in the shares of companies located in certain countries, for example, the Japan Fund. They diversify investments among different types of companies, but all companies are located in the same country. The philosophy of this type of investment is to participate in the economic growth of a certain country. Investments may be in bonds or stock, although stock investments are emphasized.

Growth, Growth Income, and Capital Gains Funds. These titles serve to indicate that the investment objective of the fund is capital growth. The usual vehicle for this growth is investment in common stocks of smaller, less well-known companies. Some of these investment companies seek modest financial leverage by borrowing money to increase their ability to purchase securities. Some of the funds diversify their investments, and some do not. It is very difficult to draw a line between this class of funds and the even more speculative ones discussed next. One should expect little price stability in the shares of these companies and few income dividends. Some of these funds have performed very well in rising markets. Most of them have suffered substantial losses in share values in declining markets.

Many of these companies were first organized as private investment trusts and were unregulated by the SEC or the 1940 Investment Company Act as amended. Some are regulated investment companies but they have chosen to be nondiversified companies.[2] They vary greatly in their investment objectives and in the way they are operated.

Index Funds.   Only a few publicly traded *index funds* exist at this time, and for this reason they are not identified as a separate mutual fund category. However, they are unique investments that will probably grow in importance.

Many research studies have pointed out the difficulties of any well-diversified fund in consistently outperforming the stock market. Actually, most investment companies and investment managers historically have underperformed the market because of the cost of managing their portfolios and aggressively trading securities. Index funds are designed to duplicate the performance of one of the stock market indexes while keeping costs to a minimum. Some are modeled after the Standard & Poor's 500 Composite Index. Others attempt to match the performance of the Value Line on some other broad stock index.

Index funds invest in the same securities that make up the index that they hope to duplicate. Trading of securities is limited to keeping the proportions of each security the same as they are in the index. Management and brokerage costs are, therefore, minimal.

Because of the large number of different securities involved, the individual investor cannot hope to create a portfolio of securities that will

---

[2]Nondiversified companies must register as such and notify potential shareholders of their status. Nondiversified means that the company may have as few as 50 percent of its assets in diversified investments. No more than 25 percent of its assets may be invested in the securities of a single company.

"match the market." Index funds provide an easy and inexpensive way to do this.

ANALYSIS OF INVESTMENT COMPANY SHARES: MEASURING PERFORMANCE

The performance of a given investment company should be measured against the company's stated objectives. If the fund's goal is to produce maximum current income, then this is the main factor to be measured. If the objective is to obtain capital gains with little or no emphasis on dividend income, then this is the important thing to measure. Unfortunately, mutual fund sales representatives often emphasize the growth performance of their funds to the exclusion of other investment characteristics that, in the long run, may be more important.

The performance of a mutual fund—and most closed-end funds—has traditionally been measured by summing the effect of the following: (1) changes in the net asset value of mutual fund shares, or the market value of shares of closed-end companies, (2) the amount of income dividends paid, and (3) the amount of capital gain dividends paid. This information is compiled as an annual percentage return and presented by yearly periods as an index of performance. This index may be compared with the Dow Jones or other stock averages, or with a performance index of other investment companies.

Lipper Analytical Distributors, Inc., provides weekly information on fund performance. Figure 8 is a reproduction of the Lipper performance information that appears in *Barron's*. Investment companies are divided into more categories than were presented in Table 1, but the category titles are descriptive of the funds' investment goals. Wiesenberger Investment Companies Service publishes *Management Results*, a monthly publication that updates and supplements information contained in their annual publication, *Investment Companies*. *Barron's* publishes a quarterly summary of mutual fund performance titled "Quarterly Mutual Fund Record." Donoghue's "Money Fund Report," published weekly in *Barron's*, provides performance information on money market funds. *Forbes* publishes an annual study of mutual fund performance each August.

Several companies present individual investment company performance information in varying degrees of detail. Figure 9 is a portion of the information of the Eaton Vance Investors Fund shown in *Investment Companies*. The data are given in a form that makes it easy to see how this

FIGURE 8
Mutual Fund Performance Averages

LIPPER MUTUAL FUND INVESTMENT PERFORMANCE AVERAGES							
		February 24, 1984					
LIPPER FUND INDICES				**AVERAGE FUND PERFORMANCES**			
		Percentage Change Year to				Percentage Change Year to	
	Close	Date	Weekly	No. Type of Fund		Date	Weekly
Growth Funds	196.24	− 10.85	− 2.23	76	Capital Appreciation	− 11.32	− 1.91
				170	Growth Funds	− 9.96	− 1.99
Growth Income	305.88	− 7.25	− 2.47	24	Small Co. Growth Fds	− 11.38	− 1.83
				92	Growth & Income	− 6.55	− 1.46
Balanced Funds	254.45	− 5.85	− 2.01	31	Equity Income	− 4.33	− 1.22
				393	Average Performance	− 9.07	− 1.78
				24	Balanced Funds	− 4.21	− 1.30
				24	Income Funds	− 0.58	− 0.61
OTHER MARKET INDICATORS				7	Natural Resources	− 0.81	+ 1.22
D. J. Industrial	1,134.62	− 9.85	− 1.76	14	Specialty Funds	− 6.67	− 1.83
				17	Global Funds	− 3.45	− 0.64
S. & P. 500	154.29	− 6.45	− 1.18	9	International	+ 1.13	− 0.06
				10	Gold Oriented	+ 11.26	+ 7.88
S. & P. 400	174.39	− 6.36	− 0.87	5	Option Growth	− 5.80	− 0.96
				10	Option Income	− 4.71	− 1.13
N.Y.S.E. Comp.	88.69	− 6.82	− 1.27	132	Fixed Income	+ 1.12	− 0.52
				645	Average Performance	− 5.64	− 1.21
Amex Index	203.35	− 8.82	− 1.37	645	Median Performance	− 5.64	− 1.28

Data supplied by Lipper Analytical Services. Year to date and weekly percentage changes on Thursday for mutual funds include reinvestment of income dividends and capital gains distributions, other market indicators do not. Only funds in existence for the entire period covered are included. Total number of funds, by objective, may include funds with net asset values unavailable at compilation time.

company has performed over a 10-year period. This is but a part of the information that *Investment Companies* provides on this and other funds. Investment company annual reports and prospectuses present similar information.

Risk Adjusted Performance

The recent trend in the measurement of mutual fund performance is toward *risk adjusted performance*. In general, average investment returns increase as risk increases. Average yields on common stocks are higher than yields on bonds because stocks are riskier. A mutual fund portfolio of common stocks should outperform (yield more than) one of bonds for the same reason.

Portfolio risk may be measured by the average beta and alpha of the portfolio. Beta measures how much the price of a given security is expected to rise and decline when security markets rise and decline. Alpha

FIGURE 9
Mutual Fund Performance Information

EATON VANCE INVESTORS FUND, INC.
(Formerly Vance, Sanders Investors Fund, Inc.)

The fund's investment objectives are to provide current income and long-term growth of capital. Management places emphasis on equity securities considered to be of high or improving quality. Investments will also be made in fixed-income securities such as preferred stocks, bonds, debentures, notes or money market instruments in order to maintain a reasonable level of current income, preserve capital, or create a buying reserve.

At the end of 1982, the fund had 61.9% of its assets in common stocks, of which the major proportion was concentrated in five industry groups: petroleum (9.8% of assets), insurance (8.6%), drugs (6%), electric utilities (4.9%), and office equipment (4.7%). The five largest individual common stock investments were IBM (4.1% of assets), Squibb Corp. (4%), Phillips Petroleum (3%), and Farmers Group and Atlantic Richfield (each 2.9%). The rate of portfolio turnover during the latest fiscal year was 28% of average assets. Unrealized appreciation was 19.4% of calendar year-end assets.

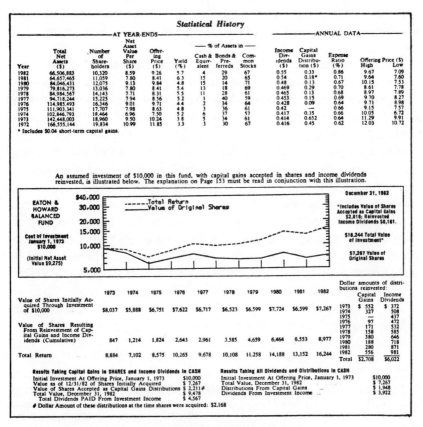

Source: Wiesenberger Investment Companies Services, New York, 1983.

measures whether the returns on the security are expected to be better or worse than the average security. Portfolio beta and alpha values are calculated by all portfolio managers who seek to measure portfolio performance on a risk adjusted basis. Then, a theoretical portfolio having beta and alpha characteristics equal to those of the real portfolio is created. The performance of the real portfolio is compared with the theoretical portfolio. Risk characteristics of both are the same, so if the real portfolio returns exceed those of the theoretical portfolio, it can be said that the fund achieved superior performance relative to its risk level.

Quite a number of risk adjusted performance studies of mutual funds have been done during the past decade. They indicate that bond funds are indeed less risky than common stock funds and that funds with aggressive investment policies are more risky than others. This was to be expected, of course. The studies also indicate that on the basis of risk adjusted performance, the average mutual fund performs no better than an unmanaged (securities chosen randomly) portfolio having the same risk characteristics.

Similar conclusions can be drawn by looking at the performance records of funds having the same investment objectives. Reports of performance, current as well as historical, are published by a number of financial services. There are very few companies that consistently outperform others having similar investment objectives.

The task of choosing a mutual fund can be made easier by (1) purchasing shares in companies having investment goals that are the same as yours. Don't try to increase returns by buying into excessively risky funds, (2) whenever possible, buying no-load funds. Historically there has been little difference in the performance of load and no-load funds. Because no commission is charged, investing in no-load funds puts your entire investment to work immediately, (3) selecting funds that have relatively low operating costs. A study by the SEC concluded that on average, the higher costs associated with "aggressive" portfolio management and with large management fees did not increase portfolio returns, and (4) avoiding funds that have poor performance records.[3]

---

[3]U.S. Securities and Exchange Commission, *Institutional Investors Study* Report (March 10, 1971), Washington, D.C.: U.S. Government Printing Office. Also see Irwin Friend et al., *A Study of Mutual Funds*. Prepared for the SEC by the Wharton School of Finance and Commerce (Washington, D.C.: U.S. Government Printing Office, 1962).

INVESTMENT CHARACTERISTICS OF INVESTMENT COMPANIES

Because of the wide variety of investment companies, it is usually possible to select an investment having acceptable risk and return characteristics. But, as with all investments, it is not possible to avoid all types of investment risks. Bond funds will generally have low financial risk, but they will also have high interest rate and purchasing power risk. Common stock funds offer long-run protection against erosion of purchasing power, but share price fluctuations may be high. Index funds offer performance nearly identical to the stock market averages. Except for some funds invested heavily in foreign securities, political and social risk is low. Marketability for all fund shares is excellent.

Money market funds offer an investment that has very little financial or interest rate risk, and that is highly liquid. However, if interest rates return to historical levels, these funds will yield little more than savings accounts.

Marketability has not been a problem for mutual funds, to date. Marketability for closed-end companies is provided by the security markets, and for most of these firms it is fairly good. Marketability for open-end fund shares comes from the fund's ability and willingness to repurchase any shares offered to it for redemption. There are no recent examples of mutual funds that have had to resort to panic selling of portfolio securities to meet redemption requests. Consequently, marketability of shares in these companies may also be seen as good.

SUMMARY

An *investment company* is a company formed for the purpose of purchasing and managing a portfolio of investment securities for its shareholders. These companies are of two main types: *open-end,* or *mutual funds,* and *closed-end* funds. Shares of open-end companies are sold and redeemed by the mutual fund on a continuous basis. Shares of closed-end companies are sold like those of any other corporation. Except in the case of some unit trusts organized for a specific time period, shares of closed-end companies remain outstanding indefinitely. Mutual funds are of far more importance than closed-end funds or unit trusts.

Mutual fund shares are sold on the basis of *net asset value per share.*

Commissions vary from nothing on no-load funds to 8.5 percent of net asset value.

Most investment companies are regulated under the Investment Company Act of 1940 as amended, and various rules of the Securities and Exchange Commission and certain state agencies. Regulation has been directed toward providing investors with information they may use to make informed decisions and controlling some of management's actions. Investment companies regulated under the 1940 act pay no taxes themselves, passing income through to their shareholders.

Investment companies offer shareholders two important things—*diversification* of investments and *professional investment management.* Diversification is the spreading out of investment risks by purchasing a large number of different kinds of investments. Diversification reduces investment risk; a well-diversified investment portfolio should not experience exceptionally large losses. However, diversification also keeps the portfolio from experiencing above average profits. Really aggressive investment portfolios are seldom diversified. Studies of mutual fund performance indicate that the average mutual fund performs about as well as a randomly chosen selection of securities having the same risk characteristics.

Balanced funds invest in both common stock and fixed-income securities. These funds do not usually show great changes in market value over time.

Bond, preferred stock, and income funds are similar in that they seek high current returns and offer relative price stability.

Money market funds invest in short-term, highly liquid debt securities. These investments allow the small investor to obtain the high interest returns that are normally available only to individuals or companies able to purchase large amounts of Treasury bills, commercial paper, and other high-yield debt instruments. Money market funds offer higher yields, nearly as much safety, and greater liquidity than savings accounts.

Municipal bond funds provide investors with the opportunity for a tax-free income from a diversified portfolio of debt securities.

Common stock funds having growth and income objectives are probably the least risky, as far as financial risk is concerned, while those emphasizing maximum capital gains are probably most risky.

Investment characteristics vary greatly from fund to fund. In general, the performance-oriented funds usually offer the most financial risk, while those invested in fixed-income securities offer the least. Marketability of all fund shares has remained good.

READING 15

HOW TO SELECT
MONEY MARKET FUNDS

Donald D. Rugg
Norman B. Hale

INTRODUCTION

If you know about the struggle between the bulls and the bears, then you know that the bear is a beast you inevitably will encounter. When confronted with a prolonged bear market, it is advisable for most investors to reduce their equity investments. Under these circumstances you must ask yourself the following questions: How can I best employ my idle cash? Shall I put it in a bank? U.S. Treasury bills? Bonds? Certificates of deposit? or where?

Finding the best method of employing idle cash is a problem that has long perplexed investors. This problem grows even more complex during periods of high inflation. Why? Because rates of return must keep pace with inflation in order to maintain purchasing power. Thus, what is needed is an investment that is *high yielding*. But high yields alone do not satisfy all our needs—for as we await the next bull market we also need *safety of principal* and *liquidity*. In addition, the investment must be within the reach of the small investor—thus, the *minimum investment* must be *small*.

Source: From Donald D. Rugg and Norman B. Hale, *The Dow Jones-Irwin Guide to Mutual Funds* (Homewood, Ill.: Dow Jones-Irwin, 1983).

Let's see how some traditional investments fare in terms of safety, liquidity, high yields, and the size of the minimum investment.

Let's first examine *banks*. The rate of return on bank accounts during inflationary periods is typically less than the rate of inflation. What about long-term deposits? Although long-term deposits pay higher rates, they lack liquidity. Obviously banks don't satisfy our needs—for although they are generally safe and the minimum investment is small, they do not have adequate liquidity or sufficiently high yields.

What about *bonds*? Although rates of return on bonds may be attractive, you will be exposing yourself to considerable money market risk. Since bonds are long-term investments and have a fixed yield, you leave yourself open to potentially large capital losses. Thus, bonds fall short of our requirements in terms of safety.

How about *U.S. Treasury bills*?[1] Treasury bills may be attractive in terms of rates of return, liquidity, and safety—but you are faced with a problem. To purchase a Treasury bill you must have at least $10,000 (as of the writing of this book). Thus, Treasury bills may have an excessively large capital requirement for many investors.

What about *negotiable certificates of deposit*?[2] Although the yields, liquidity, and safety of this instrument are usually quite high, negotiable certificates of deposit fall short of our needs in one main respect—the minimum investment is $100,000 which is far beyond the reach of most investors.

At this point you may be disillusioned—but don't despair. There is a solution to the problem of employing your idle cash—simply place your cash in a no-load mutual fund that invests solely in short-term money market instruments. This type of mutual fund is commonly called a money market fund or liquid asset fund.

Why are money market funds the solution? Because they meet *all* our needs in terms of safety of principal, liquidity, high yields, and minimum investments.[3] Although these four factors (plus others) are discussed in detail later in this chapter, let's now briefly discuss how money market funds

---

[1]Treasury bills will be discussed in detail in the section entitled "Types of Money Market Instruments."

[2]Certificates of deposit will be discussed in the section entitled "Types of Money Market Instruments."

[3]The degree of safety of principal may vary from fund to fund. The risks involved in each type of money market instrument and categorizing each fund by risk are presented later in this chapter.

FIGURE 1
Assets of Money Market Funds

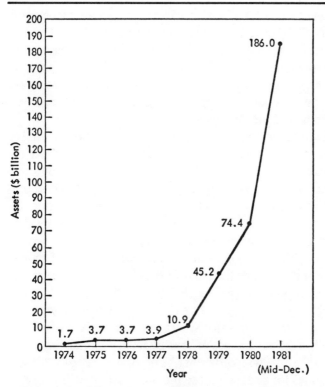

satisfy each of these factors. First, money market funds typically have diversified portfolios of high-quality, short-term money market instruments; therefore, these funds offer safety of principal. Second, since money market funds allow investors to purchase or redeem their shares at their discretion, they are highly liquid. Third, due to the large assets and professional management of money market funds, you are able to own an interest in the highest yielding money market instruments currently available in the marketplace. Finally, since the minimum investment of money-market funds generally ranges from $100 to $5,000, they are within the reach of most investors.

The increased popularity of money market funds is illustrated in Figure 1 which shows the total assets held by money market funds since they were first introduced in 1973. Notice that by the middle of July 1981 the total assets held by all such funds were $186 billion! The enormity of this number is revealed by the fact that cumulative investment in all equity mutual funds is now close to $40 billion, or less than one quarter of the amount held by money market funds.

This phenomenal growth is attributable in part to the fact that money market funds best satisfy all the criteria outlined above, namely, safety, liquidity, high yields, and a small minimum investment. The importance of these attributes has been increasingly realized by the public as it has sought shelter from the turbulent financial markets of the past decade. In addition, the corrosive impact of inflation on low-yielding deposits in banks and savings and loan associations has also helped fuel this expansion.

The popularity of money market funds is likely to increase as long as yields remain high relative to competing financial instruments. At the present time the government is deregulating other financial (and nonfinancial) institutions and easing its crusade against the merger of *large* corporations. This should ultimately enable other institutions to compete more favorably with money market funds, a development that may some day slow the rapid growth rates experienced in recent years.

The remainder of this reading is devoted to a discussion of money market funds and how they fit into the mutual fund program. There are five major sections within the reading. The first two sections provide background material which describes the nature of the money market and identifies the main types of instruments that are traded within this market. The third section describes the advantages offered by money market funds and their suitability for investors with different risk objectives. The fourth section presents guidelines for selecting those funds consistent with your risk objectives that are likely to perform best in the future. The final section is a summary of the key ideas presented in the reading.

WHAT IS THE MONEY MARKET?

Prior to discussing money market funds, it is first necessary to explain the meaning and importance of the *money market*. The money market is the marketplace where short-term credit instruments are bought and sold. This market, like the stock market, is an auction market for most instruments. That is, it is a market in which competitive forces determine both price and yield. One the other hand, the money market differs from the stock market in that it has no specific location but rather is comprised of various institutions throughout the nation where money market transactions take place. These institutions, many of which are located in New York City, include the following: banks, government securities dealers, commercial paper dealers, bankers' acceptance dealers, and money market brokers.

The money market plays a significant role in our economy for three main reasons. First, it offers borrowers a marketplace where short-term financing may be obtained. Many borrowers, such as the U.S. government, banks, and corporations, find that issuing short-term credit instruments is a desirable method of satisfying some of their debt needs. For instance, borrowers like General Motors Acceptance Corporation need the flexibility of short-term financing due to the cyclical nature of the auto industry and their continuously changing financial needs. Therefore, they tap the money market by issuing commercial paper.

Second, the money market is significant because it offers lenders a place to invest their funds. Due to the normally high degree of liquidity and low risk of principal, many lenders find money market instruments suitable for their investment needs. For instance, if an oil company accumulates cash reserves, it will normally prefer to put this money to work by purchasing money market instruments. Individual investors are also participants on the lending side of the money market.

The third reason why the money market plays a significant role in our economy concerns the Federal Reserve Board. The purchase and sales of U.S. government securities by the Federal Reserve Board, which is frequently referred to as *open-market operations*, is an important tool for implementing monetary policy. When the Federal Reserve Board wants to *ease* monetary policy, it *buys* U.S. government securities; and when it wishes to *tighten* monetary conditions, it *sells* these securities. The successful implementation of sound monetary policy is, of course, a very important factor in successfully controlling inflation and providing the environment for a prosperous economy.

As you can see, the money market meets a real need in our society. Through the money market the short-term credit requirements of both borrowers and lenders are satisfied. Thus, the money market offers a means by which capital that might otherwise sit idle can be used productively. Let's now turn to a discussion of the instruments that comprise the money market.

TYPES OF MONEY MARKET INSTRUMENTS

Although there are many different types of money market instruments, our interests lie solely with those which are held most frequently by money market funds. Prior to discussing each of these instruments we must point out that there are trade-offs, involving risk and rewards, between the different alternatives. Those instruments that have the highest yields also have the highest risks, while those with the lowest yields have the lowest risk. It is important to first understand the risks and rewards of each money market instrument before selecting the money market fund most suitable for yourself.

There are eight types of money market instruments that we shall discuss. First, we shall look at those instruments that are issued and backed by the U.S. government and by federal agencies. Instruments issued by the U.S. government and the federal agencies are the least risky instruments; hence, their yields tend to be below those of all other instruments. Second, we shall examine those instruments that are issued and backed by domestic commercial banks. These instruments include the following: repurchase agreements, certificates of deposit, bankers' acceptances, and documented discount notes. Bank-issued instruments are higher in risk and yield than government and federal agency instruments. Third, we shall examine commercial paper. Commercial paper is an unsecured money market instrument issued by corporations. The yields and risks on commercial paper are among the highest of all money market instruments. Finally we shall discuss Eurodollar instruments. Eurodollar instruments, U.S. short-term assets in *foreign* banks, are typically riskier than any of the above-mentioned money market instruments; hence, yields tend to be higher relative to the other instruments. Each of these eight money market securities will, in the following section, be categorized according to our four risk categories (aggressive, moderate, conservative, and extremely conservative).

Before entering into a discussion of money market instruments we wish to inform you that this section is highly technical; if you only desire to learn how our money market fund program is carried out, you may want to skip this section entirely and begin reading the next section entitled "What Is a Money Market Fund?" Those of you who are interested in obtaining an understanding of each money market instrument are advised to go ahead and read this section.

U.S. Government Securities

These are securities that are both issued and backed by the U.S. government. Government securities are issued by the U.S. Treasury for the purpose of financing the federal debt. The principal and interest on these securities are backed by the taxing power of the federal government; therefore, these securities are rated highest of all the money market instruments in terms of safety. Since these securities are quite safe, their yields are typically the lowest of all money market instruments.

There are three main types of U.S. government securities—Treasury bills, notes, and bonds.

Treasury bills are issued with the shortest maturities of all government securities—the maturities are three months, six months, or one year. Treasury bills maturing in three months or six months are sold on a weekly basis, while those maturing in one year are sold monthly. Treasury bills require an initial investment of $10,000, but additional purchases may be made in multiples of $5,000. Treasury bills account for the largest portion of all securities issued by the government and, in fact, are the most widely held liquid investment in the world. They are highly desirable investments for money market funds, as well as many other individuals and institutions, due to their short maturities and high liquidity. As a result they are actively traded in the secondary market.[4]

Treasury notes are the intermediate-term government securities with maturities ranging from one to seven years. Unlike Treasury bills, these securities are not issued on a periodic basis but rather are issued whenever the Treasury finds its debt needs dictate their issuance. Treasury notes require an initial investment of $1,000, and additional purchases may be made in multiples of $1,000. Although Treasury notes are highly liquid (due to an active secondary market), these securities are not as widely held by money market funds as are Treasury bills, due to the greater interest rate risk.

Treasury bonds are long-term government securities having maturities of about 20 to 25 years. Treasury bonds, like Treasury notes, are issued whenever the Treasury deems it necessary. The initial investment is also $1,000 with additional purchases in multiples of $1,000. Treasury

---

[4]The secondary market is where instruments may be bought and sold after the initial purchase and before the date of maturity.

bonds are never purchased by money market funds due to the high risk caused by their long period to maturity.

All of these government securities have two things in common. First, they are all initially sold on an *auction* basis. Thus, the initial yields of these securities are determined by competitive bids in the auction market. Second, all government securities may be sold in the *secondary market* prior to maturity.

Since government securities are very safe (if held to maturity) and highly liquid, they are popular with conservative investors. However, all classes of investors may find refuge in government securities during periods of great economic uncertainty.

Federal Agency Securities

Federal agency securities are securities issued by various federal agencies for the purpose of financing their lending program. The federal agencies that issue securities include the following: The Federal House Loan Bank, Bank for Cooperatives, Federal Intermediate Credit Banks, Federal Land Banks, the Export-Import Bank, Farmers Home Administration, Federal Housing Administration, Small Business Administration, Tennessee Valley Authority, Federal Home Loan Mortgage Corporation, the Commodity Credit Corporation, and the U.S. Postal Service. Federal agency securities, as opposed to government securities, are generally not sold on an auction basis. Instead the issuing agency consults with various institutions (such as the Federal Reserve and the Treasury) in order to determine the yield for the issue. The vast majority of securities issued by federal agencies have maturities of one year or less. The minimum initial purchase price of these securities varies from agency to agency.

Since most of these securities are backed indirectly by the taxing power of the U.S. government, they are very safe investments. In fact, there never has been a default on any of these securities.

Although the *risks* of investment in federal agency securities are not substantially different from U.S. government securities (in some cases they are the same), the *yields* on federal agency securities are typically higher. Therefore, many investors prefer to purchase federal agency securities rather than U.S. government securities.

The liquidity of these securities varies from agency to agency depending upon the activity in the secondary markets. Securities issued by the Federal Land Banks, the Federal Intermediate Credit Banks, and the Federal National Mortgage Association have active secondary markets and are highly liquid. The secondary market for the rest of the federal agency securities is not as well established; hence, they may lack liquidity.

Extremely conservative investors should invest only in U.S. government securities or federal agency securities.

Repurchase Agreements

A repurchase agreement involves the sale of any money market instrument with the provision that this instrument be resold to the seller on an agreed-upon future date. For the use of the borrowed funds, the issuer of the repurchase agreement agrees to pay the lender a fixed amount of interest. Although repurchase agreements can theoretically be established for any money market instrument, U.S. government and federal agency securities are the principal types of securities traded in this manner.

Repurchase agreements are issued primarily as a means of raising temporary funds by commercial banks and U.S. government securities dealers. For instance, if a government securities dealer needs to raise funds for purposes of financing its inventory position, it might sell some of its government securities under a repurchase agreement. The attractiveness of issuing a repurchase agreement is that the issuer can tailor the instrument to his own special needs and be assured that the underlying securities will be returned when desired.

Maturities on repurchase agreements are usually seven days or less, and vary according to one of the following three types of repurchase transactions: overnight transactions, open transactions, and fixed-date transactions.

Overnight repurchase transactions constitute the shortest maturity of any money market instrument, having a maturity of one business day, and they are the most widely used type of repurchase agreement. An *open repurchase transaction* is a means by which an overnight transaction may be extended on an indefinite basis; such agreements are effective until one of the parties decides to terminate it. Repurchase agreements may also be bought under a *fixed-date repurchase transaction* for periods longer than one day. Under this type of agreement the length of maturity is agreed upon when the instrument is issued. All three types of repurchase transactions offer both issuers and purchasers a means of adjusting their short-term liquidity needs.

Since the issuer of a repurchase agreement must surrender underlying securities as collateral, repurchase agreements are as safe as the underlying securities. However, there is some risk that the issuing party will be unable to make its interest payment (the interest that is paid by the issuer in addition to the interest of the underlying securities) to the lending party. For example, if a bank sells Treasury bills to a money market fund under a repurchase agreement and the bank subsequently fails, then the money market fund may never receive any interest on the repurchase agreement from the bank (though it would receive both the principal and interest from the underlying Treasury bill).

Due to the interest paid by the issuer, yields on repurchase agreements are higher than yields on the underlying securities being traded. The main factors that influence the size of these yields are the interest rates on federal funds, the interest rates on all money, and the maturity of the agreement. Since repurchase agreements are a means of raising the effective yield of an instrument, these vehicles are frequently utilized by money market funds.

Certificates of Deposit

A certificate of deposit (commonly called a CD) is a receipt for having deposited funds at either a bank or a savings and loan. In return for depositing funds the issuer of the CD agrees to repay the amount of the deposit plus interest on a specified date. Yields on CDs tend to be higher than for government agency securities, but competitive with other bank-issued money market instruments (such as bankers' acceptances) and commercial paper of similar maturities. Maturities on CDs range from 30 days to several years.

There are two main types of CDs, *negotiable* CDs and *ordinary* CDs. Negotiable certificates of deposit differ from ordinary certificates in two main respects. First, negotiable certificates of deposit can usually be sold prior to maturity in the secondary market, whereas ordinary certificates of deposit must be held to maturity (or penalties are involved). Second, negotiable certificates are sold in denominations of $100,000, whereas ordinary certificates of deposit are sold in amounts less than $100,000.

In terms of safety of principal and interest, CDs are as safe as the soundness of the issuing institution. Therefore, as long as the issuing bank is liquid, there should be no problems with safety.

The liquidity of CDs boils down to the following question: Can the CDs be sold in the secondary market on short notice and at a fair market price? The liquidity or marketability of CDs is dependent primarily upon the identity of the issuing bank and the denomination of the CD. The identity of the issuing bank is typically the most important factor influencing marketability. CDs of large, well-known banks are normally far more marketable than those issued by smaller, lesser known banks. Since yields are inversely related to marketability, it follows that the CDs of small institutions provide yields above those offered by larger institutions.

A second factor influencing marketability is the denomination of the CD. Since dealers like to trade in units of $1 million, certificates with smaller denominations are less marketable and, as a consequence, must offer higher yields.

Depending upon the marketability of the instrument, CDs may be purchased by investors in the aggressive, moderate, or conservative risk categories.

Bankers' Acceptances

A bankers' acceptance is defined as a draft or bill of exchange which is accepted by a bank or trust company. Before we continue, let's first explain what is meant by a bill of exchange. A bill of exchange is defined as a promissory note used in international trade in which the drawer unconditionally guarantees to pay to the drawee a sum of money at a given date. For instance, if an American business needed short-term financing in order to import a large quantity of television sets from a Japanese exporter, it might establish this financing by means of a bill of exchange. But, as we pointed out, a bill of exchange is only a promissory note; if the American importer and Japanese exporter have never done business before, then the Japanese exporter will demand some guarantee that he will be paid. So, the American importer will go to a bank to seek an "acceptance." When a bill of exchange is "accepted" (which means it is unconditionally guaranteed) by the bank, it is then known as a bankers' acceptance. With the bankers' acceptance the Japanese exporter can rest assured that he will receive payment.

Bankers' acceptances are negotiable and may be traded in the secondary market. The issuing bank therefore has the option of keeping acceptance for its own account or selling the acceptance in the secondary market at a discount. Maturities on bankers' acceptances range from 30 to 270 days, but most expire within 180 days.

What are the risks involved in the ownership of bankers' acceptances?

The risks are limited to the ability of the issuing bank to fulfill its guarantee. Therefore, as long as the issuing bank is sound, there should be no problems in terms of safety.

How about the yields and liquidity of bankers' acceptances? The yields on bankers' acceptances are competitive with other bank-issued instruments and commercial paper. Similarly, the liquidity of bankers' acceptances is dependent upon the same factors as for CDs (i.e., the identity of the issuing bank and the size of the denomination). Instruments issued by large, well-known banks are normally highly liquid.

As with CDs, the suitability of bankers' acceptances to different types of investors is primarily dependent upon the quality of the issuing bank.

Documented Discount Notes

Documented discount notes, which may also be called *bank guaranteed letters of credit*, are a means by which businesses raise funds through the sale of notes which are guaranteed by a bank. Let's focus upon an example of how a documented discount note arises. If a business needs to raise funds and finds that its bank has no money to lend, the business may decide to generate funds by selling a documented discount note. In order to obtain the bank guarantee (to support the notes), the business must have a letter of credit from a bank. With the letter of credit, the notes are guaranteed and are therefore more attractive to investors (assuming the issuing bank is sound). The investor, such as a money market fund, may purchase these documented discount notes from the guaranteeing bank.

Since there is no secondary market for these notes, they lack liquidity. However, as these notes are usually of short maturity—usually about 30 to 35 days—this compensates somewhat for the lack of a secondary market. Yet, if a money market fund with an almost exclusive portfolio of documented discount notes were faced with massive investor redemption, serious problems could result.

These notes normally have higher yields than other bank-issued instruments. Therefore, money market funds that purchase documented discount notes are often among the highest yielding funds.

These notes, like CDs and bankers' acceptances, are as safe as the soundness of the guaranteeing bank. Yet, there is an additional source of safety in that banks are required to use the same standards of financial strength that ordinary borrowers must meet when qualifying a business for a letter of credit. Therefore, the business selling the notes must be financially sound before the bank will issue the required letter of credit.

Documented discount notes, just like the other bank-issued instruments, are suitable for aggressive, moderate, and conservative investors depending upon the size of the issuing bank.

Commercial Paper

Commercial paper is a short-term promissory note issued by a business. Commercial paper is usually unsecured; therefore, only the largest, most creditworthy companies are able to tap this market. Participants on the borrowing side of this market include both sales finance companies (such as Ford Credit Corporation) and nonfinancial companies (such as Xerox Corporation). Participants on the lending side of the commercial paper market include financial and nonfinancial corporations and individuals.

There are two major types of commercial paper—*directly placed paper* and *dealer's paper*. Directly placed paper is sold to buyers by a large sales finance company, such as General Motors Acceptance Corporation or Sears Roebuck Acceptance Corporation, *without* the user of a dealer. Only those firms that have large sales finance companies normally find it economically feasible to maintain the necessary staff to directly place their paper. Directly placed paper accounts for the largest portion of all outstanding commercial paper and normally exhibits a maturity of between 3 and 270 days.

Dealer's paper is commercial paper sold by corporations to specialized dealers who, in turn, sell this paper to other investors. The dealer's paper market is used by corporations that find the cost of directly placing their paper prohibitive. Maturities on dealer's commercial paper range from 30 to 180 days.

Yields on commercial paper are competitive with bank-issued instruments (such as CDs and bankers' acceptances) of similar maturities, and liquidity is normally quite high. Prime commercial paper is also reasonably safe despite the fact that such paper is usually unsecured. However, even prime rated paper can turn sour—as was demonstrated by the famous Penn Central bankruptcy.

Commercial paper is, in the authors' opinion, suitable only for investors in the aggressive and moderate risk categories (see section entitled "Types of Money Market Funds").

Eurodollar Instruments

Eurodollars are simply U.S. dollar deposits placed with banks outside the United States. Eurodollars are no different from any other U.S. dollars except that the dollars are in the hands of a foreign bank. Eurodollars make up the major part of the international money market known as the Euromoney market. The Euromoney market is where the world's major currencies are traded—the most notable currencies include Swiss francs, British pounds, German marks, Canadian dollars, and Japanese yen.

Participants in the Eurodollar market include central banks, commercial banks, corporations, and individuals. Banks are the primary participants in this market, and the Eurodollar market serves as "an international pool of bank liquidity."[5] That is, liquidity shortages and surpluses of banks may be smoothed out by using this market. Corporations are also important participants in the Eurodollar market, as they frequently use this market to deposit surplus funds or to borrow for short-run financing purposes. Individuals also participate in the Eurodollar market for purposes of borrowing and lending—though they are relatively unimportant.

The Eurodollar market, like the money market in the United States, has no specific location. This market is comprised of dealers in the major financial centers of Europe—especially in London. London is the center of the Eurodollar market for two reasons. First, London has traditionally been an international finance center. Second, and more importantly, London Eurobanks are "treated as a sort of extraterritorial market" (which means they are not subject to British banking regulation—such as reserve requirements).[6] This freedom from regulation has attracted many bankers.

Purchasing Eurodollar instruments involves greater risk than the purchase of U.S. money market instruments for several reasons. First, as we just pointed out, many Eurobanks (like in London) are unregulated—this opens the door to potential problems. Second, in some instances short-term deposits at Eurobanks are lent out for medium-term loans—obviously this is a risky practice. Third, sometimes the final use of the money in a Eurodollar loan is unknown to the lender—certainly this violates sound banking procedure. Fourth, the viability of the Eurodollar market is dependent upon confidence in the U.S. dollar.

---

[5] Herbert V. Prochnow, ed., *The Eurodollar* (Skokie, Ill.: Rand McNally, 1970), p. 106.
[6] Ibid., p. 110.

Due to the high degree of risk with Eurodollar instruments, yields on these instruments are usually substantially higher than instruments issued by domestic banks. These instruments are suitable only to those investors in the aggressive category.

What Is a Money Market Fund?

A money market fund is a mutual fund that invests its assets only in highly liquid money market instruments. The choice of money market instruments depends upon the investment policies and restrictions of the fund. To illustrate, let's examine the portfolio of the Scudder Cash Investment Trust shown in Table 1. Notice that this portfolio is diversified among four types of money market instruments—repurchase agreements, commercial paper, certificates of deposit, and bankers' acceptances. Notice also that holdings in the last three categories are widely diversified among different issuers to further reduce risks.

Money market funds differ from mutual funds holding stocks in that these funds generally sell at a fixed price, such as $1 per share. Your return from a money market fund is represented by the accumulation of additional shares—not by changes in the net asset value. For example, if you were to invest $10,000 in a money market fund that had a net asset value (NAV) of $1, you would have 10,000 shares; and if over a year's time your return was equal to 10 percent, you would have accumulated another 1,000 shares.

The yield of a money market fund is the method by which performance can be measured. These yields are reported on a weekly basis in *The Wall Street Journal*, *Barron's*, and many local newspapers. In general, the yields on most money market funds have far exceeded those available from other financial institutions with similar maturities and the same degree of liquidity. This, in turn, has been a major impetus behind their phenomenal growth during recent years.

There are three major categories of no-load money market mutual funds based upon the clientele to which they are oriented. The largest category in terms of total assets are the funds sponsored by broker-dealers such as Merrill Lynch or E.F. Hutton. As of December 1981, there were 37 such funds with a combined asset value of over $95 billion. The next largest category consists of the 93 funds oriented to individual investors. These funds, which are often sponsored by large mutual fund organizations such as the Dreyfus Corporation or T. Rowe Price Associates, had a combined

TABLE 1
Scudder Cash Investment Trust

Schedule of Investments, June 30, 1980

	Maturity	Principal Amount	Cost	Market Value (Note A)
SECURITIES HELD UNDER REPURCHASE AGREEMENT—2.4%				
Repurchase Agreement with State Street Bank at 8.00%, collateralized by Federal National Mortgage Association Discount Notes due 8/1/80	7/1/80	$ 4,810,000	$ 4,811,068	$ 4,811,068
COMMERCIAL PAPER—59.5%				
CONSUMER—8.2%				
DRUGS & TOILETRIES—8.2%				
Warner-Lambert Co. 9.625%	7/11/80	$ 8,000,000	$ 7,978,611	$ 7,978,611
Pfizer, Inc. 9.875%	7/18/80	7,000,000	6,967,358	6,967,357
Warner-Lambert Co. 8.125%	7/31/80	2,000,000	1,986,458	1,986,458
			$ 16,932,427	$ 16,932,426
FINANCIAL—26.1%				
CREDIT & FINANCE—26.1%				
General Electric Credit Co. 11.0%	7/3/80	$ 6,000,000	$ 5,996,333	$ 5,996,332
U.S. Steel Credit Corp. 13.125%	7/3/80	5,000,000	4,996,354	4,996,354
General Motors Acceptance Corp. 11.0%	7/7/80	2,000,000	1,996,333	1,996,333
Sears Roebuck Acceptance Corp. 10.25%	7/16/80	3,000,000	2,987,188	2,988,437
Shell Oil Credit Corp. 10.25%	7/17/80	5,000,000	4,977,222	4,978,536
Mobil Oil Credit Corp. 9.5%	7/18/80	5,000,000	4,977,569	4,977,569

TABLE 1—Continued

Schedule of Investments, June 30, 1980

	Maturity	Principal Amount	Cost	Market Value (Note A)
Ingersoll-Rand Financial Co. 8.25%	7/25/80	3,000,000	2,983,500	2,983,500
Amoco Credit Corp. 7.9%	7/28/80	7,000,000	6,958,524	6,958,524
U.S. Steel Credit Corp. 9.125%	7/29/80	5,000,000	4,964,514	4,964,513
Mobil Oil Credit Corp. 8.125%	8/1/80	2,800,000	2,780,410	2,780,409
ARCO Credit Corp. 8.35%	8/11/80	10,000,000	9,904,903	9,904,902
			$ 53,522,850	$ 53,525,409
MANUFACTURING—9.1%				
CHEMICAL—4.3%				
Dow Chemical Co. 8.25%	8/4/80	$ 4,000,000	3,968,833	3,968,833
Union Carbide Corp. 8.125%	8/26/80	5,000,000	4,936,806	4,936,805
			$ 8,905,639	$ 8,905,638
PETROLEUM-SERVICE & EQUIPMENT—4.8%				
Halliburton Co. 8.375%	7/24/80	$ 10,000,000	9,946,493	9,946,493
UTILITIES—16.5%				
PUBLIC UTILITIES—COMMUNICATIONS—10.2%				
Pacific Telephone & Telegraph Co. 8.75%	7/10/80	$ 4,000,000	3,991,250	3,991,250
Pacific Telephone & Telegraph Co. 8.875%	7/11/80	5,000,000	4,987,674	4,987,673
Ohio Bell Telephone Co. 8.4%	7/29/80	7,000,000	6,954,266	6,954,266
Indiana Bell Telephone Co. 8.875%	7/30/80	5,000,000	4,964,253	4,964,253
			$ 20,897,443	$ 20,897,442

TABLE 1—Continued

Schedule of Investments, June 30, 1980

	Maturity	Principal Amount	Cost	Market Value (Note A)
PUBLIC UTILITIES—ELECTRIC—6.3%				
Northern Indiana Public Service 8.375%.	7/7/80	$ 5,000,000	$ 4,993,020	$ 4,993,020
Florida Power Corp. 8.8%.	7/21/80	5,000,000	4,975,555	4,975,555
Oklahoma Gas & Electric Co. 8.75%.	8/1/80	3,000,000	2,977,395	2,977,395
			$ 12,945,970	$ 12,945,970
Total commercial paper.		$123,800,000	$123,150,822	$123,153,378
CERTIFICATES OF DEPOSIT—9.2%				
Northern Trust Co. 9.375%.	7/11/80	$ 5,000,000	$ 5,000,000	$ 5,000,000
First Nat'l Bank of Minneapolis 8.375%.	7/28/80	5,000,000	5,000,000	4,999,264
First Nat'l Bank of Minneapolis 8.2%.	8/8/80	4,000,000	4,000,000	4,000,000
Philadelphia Savings Fund Society 8.25%	8/25/80	5,000,000	5,000,000	4,995,468
Total certificates of deposit		$ 19,000,000	$ 19,000,000	$ 18,994,732
BANKERS' ACCEPTANCES—29.0%				
Morgan Guaranty Trust 9.6%	7/7/80	$ 3,000,000	$ 2,995,200	$ 2,995,200
Seattle First Nat'l Bank 8.14%.	7/15/80	4,000,000	3,999,409	3,999,409
Valley Nat'l Bank 12.45%	7/16/80	3,000,000	2,984,438	2,987,274
Nat'l City Bank of Cleveland 9.4%.	7/21/80	5,000,000	4,973,889	4,974,277
Pittsburgh Nat'l Bank 8.25%.	7/21/80	9,000,000	8,958,750	8,958,750
U.S. Nat'l Bank of Oregon 9.85%	7/22/80	4,000,000	3,977,017	3,979,233
Riggs Nat'l Bank 9.45%	7/31/80	5,000,000	4,960,625	4,960,625
Continental Illinois Nat'l Bank 8.25%.	8/1/80	6,000,000	5,957,374	5,947,945

TABLE 1—Concluded

Schedule of Investments, June 30, 1980

	Maturity	Principal Amount	Cost	Market Value (Note A)
Bank of America 8.45%............	8/1/80	3,000,000	2,978,170	2,978,170
Bank of New York 8.45%..........	8/5/80	3,000,000	2,975,354	2,975,354
Continental Illinois Nat'l Bank 8.15%......	8/11/80	3,000,000	2,972,154	2,972,154
Nat'l Bank of Detroit 8.3%.........	8/22/80	3,000,000	2,964,033	2,964,033
Republic Nat'l Bank—Dallas 8.3%.......	8/25/80	9,000,000	8,885,875	8,885,875
Total bankers' acceptances...........		$ 60,000,000	$ 59,582,288	$ 59,578,299
TOTAL INVESTMENTS		$207,610,000	$206,544,178*	$206,537,477
SUMMARY:				
Investments as shown above........		100.5%		$206,537,477
Other assets and liabilities (net)		(.5%)		(1,004,723)
Net assets		100.0%		$205,532,754

*Cost for federal income tax purposes.

asset value of approximately $55 billion. The smallest group of funds are those oriented to institutional investors such as bank trust departments and trust companies. At the present time there are 29 of these funds with a combined asset value of about $33 billion.

Money market funds within any of the above categories are suitable for purposes of our investment program.

During recent years, an entirely new type of money market fund has also emerged—namely, tax-free money funds. These funds combine the features of a municipal bond fund and a money market fund. Municipal bond funds provide income which is free from *federal* income tax, a feature which appeals to investors in high income tax brackets. However, most outstanding municipal bonds have long-term maturities and are therefore far more risky and volatile than a money market fund.

To overcome this problem the tax-free money funds invest exclusively in municipal bonds which are close to maturity, typically having two to four months of remaining life or in various types of short-term municipal notes. By doing so the risks associated with fluctuating interest rates are greatly reduced and are similar to those associated with regular money market funds. While these funds may appeal to certain investors, we do not recommend them for our investment program for several important reasons.

First, there are a limited number of municipal bonds in existence at any one time that are due to mature within three or four months. As more and more tax-free money funds are introduced, there is a distinct possibility that there won't be enough suitable bonds to go around. Thus, these funds will be forced to depend more and more on an increased supply of short-term municipal notes. However, since municipalities use revenues from these bonds to finance *long-term* projects, such as water pipelines and sewers, they may not accommodate the tax-free funds by issuing *short-term* money market instruments as this would necessitate continual refinancing. This short-term refinancing would, in turn, greatly increase the financial risk to the issuing municipality which, we believe, will be unacceptable to many of them in the long run. However, thus far the municipalities have responded to the increased demand by issuing more short-term paper.

This scarcity of maturing municipal bonds is presently causing several adverse side effects for investors in tax-free money funds. First, due to the intense competition for these expiring bonds, their prices have been bid up and, as a result, their yields have been kept at relatively low levels. At the present time the yields on tax-free money funds average about 50 to 60 percent of those available from traditional money market funds. In addition, any fixed-dollar expense has a more adverse relative impact upon yields for a low-yielding fund than for a high-yielding fund. For example, assume that funds A and B each have $100 million in assets and that each fund has $1 million in legal, accounting, printing, and management fees. Let's also assume that fund A, a money market fund, earns $14 million on its investments, whereas fund B, a tax-free fund, earns $7 million. The $1 million in expenses will reduce the dividend payout of fund A from $14 to $13 million, or by about 7.1 percent. However, the payout of fund B will fall from $7.0 million to $6.0 million or by 14.3 percent. Obviously, fixed expenses have a more negative impact on the lower yielding tax-free fund.

Another disadvantage to tax-free fund investors is that tax-free funds have had to extend their maturities to purchase an adequate amount of suitable bonds. For example, at the present time the average maturity of the tax-free money market funds reported in the Wiesenberger Investment Company Service is 85 days, whereas the maturity for money market funds is about 22 days. This longer maturity increases the risk of owing tax-free funds and is definitely an undesirable feature.

Another feature which increases risk is the higher default risk for municipal bonds compared with money market instruments (many of which are backed directly or indirectly by the federal government). Many municipal bonds defaulted during the Great Depression which occurred in the United States during the 1930s, whereas no paper backed directly or indirectly by the federal government experienced a similar fate.

Given the reduced desirability of these funds and their increased risks, we believe that you will be well advised to avoid them entirely and to focus upon regular money market funds.

ADVANTAGES TO INVESTING IN A MONEY MARKET FUND

There are numerous advantages of money market fund investments. In particular, there are six which the authors believe merit special attention. The first four were briefly mentioned at the beginning of this chapter, namely, *safety of principal, high liquidity, high yields*, and *small minimum investment*. In addition to these four, *low-cost professional management* and *low purchase or redemption fees* must also be discussed. Let's now examine each of these advantages.

Safety of Principal

One of the primary objectives of a money market fund is safety of principal. When we speak of safety of principal we don't mean absolute safety (as there is no investment that is absolutely safe), but rather we are referring to the low risk of loss of principal. If you compare money market funds to other investments such as stocks and bonds, you will find that money market funds are usually far safer. What makes money market funds so safe in terms of preserving capital? The answer is simple—diversification and short-term maturity.

Diversification. Diversification is an important element in any portfolio of money market instruments because it reduces business risk. Just as it is unwise to commit all of your investment capital to one common stock, it is also foolish to commit all your liquid capital to one money market issue (excluding U.S. government and government agency securities).

Money market funds typically diversify their assets among several types of money market instruments and, within each type of instrument, they diversify among issuers. For instance, a money market fund may purchase commercial paper from a variety of corporations, certificates of deposit from a variety of banks, and U.S. government agency securities from several agencies. Thus, if one asset were to fail, the adverse impact on the portfolio would be greatly reduced.

In addition to the advantages of owning several different types of assets which are issued by many different issuers, money market funds also offer a *diversification* of maturities. For example, focus upon the portfolio of the Reserve Fund as shown on Table 2. Notice that under the "Days to Maturity" column several instruments mature in 1 day, another in 4 days, and so on down to an instrument that may mature in as many as 84 days. With various instruments maturing every few days the portfolio can be "rolled over" and kept current with changes in money market rates. This reduces the risk of abnormally large changes in the value caused by changes in the value of assets of a given maturity.

TABLE 2
The Reserve Fund, Inc.

Statement of Investments, May 31, 1979

CERTIFICATES OF DEPOSIT (92.1%)
(95% in Foreign Branches of U.S. Banks)

	% Face Rate	Days to Maturity	Cost	Value* (Note 1)
Bank of America.	10.00–11.00	5–76	$ 71,472,882	$ 72,560,668
Bankers Trust Co., New York	10.19–10.31	1–32	69,053,702	69,192,620
Manufacturers Hanover Trust Co.	10.00–12.15	27–75	67,765,606	68,367,384
Citibank, N.A., New York	10.23–10.77	12–61	61,137,152	61,485,761
First National Bank, Chicago	10.26–10.80	11–70	60,189,555	60,799,544
Chase Manhattan Bank	6.40–11.70	1–60	59,140,047	59,926,718
Morgan Guaranty Trust Co.	10.17–12.20	4–75	58,320,950	58,976,250
Chemical Bank, New York	10.25–11.69	19–55	55,137,188	55,916,473
Continental Illinois N.B.	10.35–10.55	5–84	55,030,806	55,622,143
Mellon Bank, N.W., Pittsburgh	10.39–12.08	5–67	53,667,545	54,398,876
First National Bank, Boston.	10.40–10.85	7–70	40,020,839	40,541,904
Crocker National Bank	10.41	91	40,000,985	40,000,985
Bank of New York.	10.25–10.85	4–62	39,076,013	39,583,786
Wells Fargo Bank	10.30–11.20	26–62	39,081,282	39,533,536
Security Pacific N.B.	10.31–10.47	6–13	35,000,000	35,301,997
Republic N.B., Dallas	10.22–10.45	7–63	32,035,535	32,078,532
United California Bank	10.31–11.45	7–82	25,526,948	25,779,086
Texas Commerce Bank	10.50–11.64	11–69	21,156,329	21,465,895
Detroit Bank & Trust Co.	10.35–10.82	21–63	21,023,991	21,165,593
Bank of Tokyo Trust Co. N.Y.	10.30–10.80	27–49	20,000,000	20,303,435
Rainier National Bank, Seattle	10.40–10.56	20–60	20,011,496	20,293,272
Harris Trust & Savings Bank	9.13–10.65	40–77	20,064,233	20,248,652
Seattle First National Bank	10.30–10.60	20–61	20,004,582	20,195,412
First City N.B., Houston	10.37–12.20	7–54	16,224,649	16,420,921
Irving Trust Co., New York	10.52–11.80	4–67	16,191,143	16,391,984
United States Trust Co., N.Y.	10.31–10.37	14–28	12,000,000	12,002,859
Equitable Trust Co., Baltimore	10.30	60	10,000,000	10,000,000

TABLE 2—Continued

Statement of Investments, May 31, 1979

CERTIFICATES OF DEPOSIT (92.1%) (95% in Foreign Branches of U.S. Banks)	% Face Rate	Days to Maturity	Cost	Value* (Note 1)
First National Bank, Dallas	10.65	47	9,000,000	9,121,471
National Community Bank of N.J.	10.40	6	6,000,000	6,041,647
Winters Natl. Bank and Trust Co., Dayton. ...	10.31	25	6,000,000	6,010,278
Rhode Island Hospital Trust N.B.	10.30	32	6,000,000	6,003,502
American Savings & Loan Assn., Cal. ...	10.35	14	5,018,254	5,110,085
National Bank of Detroit	10.43	39	5,002,997	5,077,605
The Northern Trust Bank, Chicago	10.65	42	5,004,026	5,067,308
J. Henry Schroder Bank & Trust Co., N.Y. ...	10.44	4	5,000,000	5,040,600
The First N.B. & T. Co. of Tulsa.	10.35	6	5,000,000	5,034,539
Old Stone Bank, Providence.	10.65	69	5,000,000	5,034,047
The Sumitomo Bank of California	10.45	7	4,000,000	4,096,634
The First National Bank of Atlanta.	10.35	54	4,000,000	4,042,923
Birmingham Trust National Bank	11.13	55	3,092,043	3,118,297
American Bank and Trust Co., Baton Rouge	10.50	1	3,000,000	3,042,890
Central Bank of Birmingham.	10.20	25	3,000,000	3,005,948
California First Bank, San Francisco	12.0	33	1,047,743	1,050,539
Total certificates of deposit.			1,113,498,521	1,124,452,599
SECURITIES HELD UNDER REPURCHASE AGREEMENTS (4.6%) With Lehman Government Securities, Inc., collateralized by:				
Fed. Home Loan Corp.	10.0	1	16,200,000	16,205,220
Fed. Natl. Mtg. Assn. discount notes ...	10.0	1	13,650,000	13,672,864
With Ehrlich-Bober Government Securities, Inc. collateralized by:				
Fed. Home Loan Corp. discount notes ...	10.0	1	9,350,000	9,365,662
Fed. Natl. Mtg. Assn. discount notes ...	10.0	1	9,465,000	9,471,433

TABLE 2—Concluded

Statement of Investments, May 31, 1979

	% Face Rate	Days to Maturity	Cost	Value* (Note 1)
SECURITIES HELD UNDER REPURCHASE AGREEMENTS (4.6%)				
With Discount Corp. collateralized by:				
Manufacturers Hanover bankers' acceptances, due 147–176 days..........	10.0	1	8,000,000	8,000,000
Total securities held under repurchase agreements........			56,665,000	56,715,179
U.S. Government Obligations (2.0%)				
Fed. Natl. Mtg. Assn. discount notes		53–54	24,379,250	24,653,076
Documented Discount Notes (1.3%)				
First National Bank of Atlanta		1–5	5,898,890	5,997,265
Fidelity Union Trust Company, Newark......		20–46	4,883,292	4,954,721
State Street Bank & Trust Co., Boston......		20–77	2,935,795	2,951,367
Security Pacific N.B.......		71	1,362,665	1,371,704
Total documented discount notes.....			15,080,642	15,275,057
TOTAL INVESTMENTS (100%)			$1,209,623,413	$1,221,095,911

*Investments are stated at fair value plus accrued interest receivable.

Aggregate cost for federal income tax purposes was $1,209,623,413.

Gross portfolio yield—10.29 percent (annualized, not compounded, valuing securities at fair value). The dollar-weighted average maturity of the portfolio is 37 days; the longest maturity is 91 days.

Short-Term Maturity. Money market funds, like the Reserve Fund, generally purchase money market instruments with very *short-term maturities*. By holding only short-term maturities, these funds are able to virtually eliminate interest rate risk. Even though the prices of money market instruments may change (due to the inverse relationship between prices and interest rates), by holding the instrument to maturity any price changes are irrelevant because face value is paid at maturity. In contrast to bonds, which have long-term maturities, money market instruments are much lower in terms of the potential for capital losses due to changes in interest rates. We advise that you limit your investments in money market funds to funds with average maturities of less than 60 days. The Reserve Fund would have fallen within this guideline as its average maturity was just 37 days.

High Liquidity

When we speak of liquidity we are referring to the ease with which shares may be converted to and from cash. A high degree of liquidity means that shares may be easily converted to cash. Since money market funds strive to purchase only short-term money market instruments, which are easily bought and sold on short notice, they are highly liquid. What does this mean to you as an investor? It means that you may purchase or redeem shares at your discretion. Thus, you need not be concerned about the holding period of your investments. You can hold the fund for as short as one day or as long as several years—it's up to you! This high degree of liquidity means that you are not "locked into" your investment and that you can take advantage of any new investment opportunity that may suddenly develop.

Money market funds often offer several convenient means by which shares can be redeemed. Some funds allow you to redeem by telephone or by telegraph, and payments are normally issued within one day. Other funds offer a check-writing privilege where you may write a check against your money market investment, thereby redeeming your shares. This check-writing feature is especially attractive to our investment program as you can switch from a money market fund to a stock fund with your money working for you continuously until the check clears. Suffice it to say, the high degree of liquidity offered by money market funds may mean extra profits for you.

FIGURE 2
Reserve Fund Field History, 1980–1981

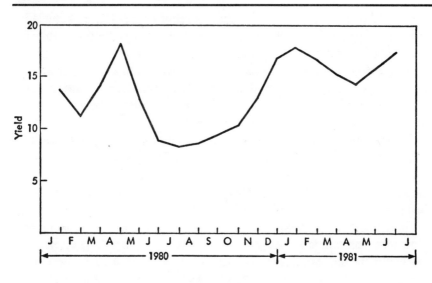

Average annualized net yield for the indicated months.

High Yields

Cash funds strive to maintain the highest possible yields while minimizing risk. What kind of yields can you expect from these funds? That is difficult to say because the yields of money market instruments constantly fluctuate with changes in inflation rates, loan demand, and other conditions affecting the money market. An example of the possible range of yields that may be encountered during a given period is shown in Figure 2 which documents the yield history of the Reserve Fund on a month-end basis during 1980 and the first part of 1981. During this period, the yield of the Reserve Fund ranged from a low of 8.3 percent to a high of 17.9 percent with an annual average yield of 13.5 percent.

Whatever the circumstances, these funds pick out the highest yielding short-term money market instruments consistent with their safety objectives. Thus you are assured of superior returns in addition to the other advantages mentioned earlier.

Low-Cost Professional Management

Successful investing in the money market requires specialized knowledge of the money market, money market instruments, economics, international finance, and many other subjects. Money market funds have professional portfolio managers who possess this specialized knowledge and are able to employ it to maximize fund performance. Another attractive aspect of this professional management is that it costs so little—management fees are usually less than one half of 1 percent.

Professional money fund managers can do many things that an individual investor normally cannot undertake. First, since money market portfolio managers are constantly in touch with conditions in the money market, they are able to adapt their portfolios quickly in anticipation of changing circumstances. For instance, if money market rates were rising, the portfolio managers could take advantage of this by purchasing very short-term instruments. Second, because these managers keep in close touch with the money market, they are able to search out the highest yielding securities. Indeed, they generally call several money market dealers to locate the most favorable terms by which to buy or sell money market instruments. Third, these portfolio managers have the background and resources necessary to thoroughly research the financial condition of institutions who issue money market instruments; therefore, the ownership of poor-quality instruments is generally avoided. Fourth, money market portfolio managers work full time to provide high-quality management. All four of the reasons suggest that money market portfolio managers are generally better able to manage money market investments than are individual investors.

Low Purchase or Redemption Fees

Most money market funds are no-load funds—that is, there are no fees whatsoever for purchasing or redeeming shares. Yet, you should be aware that there are a few money market funds that do charge either a purchase or redemption fee; we advise that you steer clear of these funds. The negative effect of load fees is far more severe on a money market fund than on a stock fund because a load fee adversely affects liquidity.

Small Minimum Investment

The minimum initial investments required to open an account at a money market fund are typically from $1,000 to $5,000, but some funds require as little as $100. At first glance this may not seem like an important advantage of the money market funds, but it most certainly is. Why? Because most money market instruments have much higher minimum investments. Remember that negotiable CDs are sold in denominations of $100,000 and Treasury bills require a minimum investment of $10,000. The fact is that the money market is geared to large institutions dealing with millions of dollars. Money market funds offer smaller investors a means to indirectly purchase these desirable large denomination instruments.

DETERMINING THE RISKINESS OF MONEY MARKET FUNDS

In our discussion of money market instruments we indicated there are differences in risks between alternate types of instruments. We also explained that the quality of the institution issuing the instrument is an important factor influencing risk. We would now like to indicate that there are considerable risk differences in the portfolios of different money market funds. Thus, a money market fund, just like a stock fund, may be classified according to risks. The objective of this section is to present guidelines for the classification of these funds.

We have constructed Table 3, which contains our four risk categories—aggressive (1), moderate (2), conservative, (3) and extremely conservative (4). This table shows whether or not a given money market instrument is *allowed* in the portfolio of a fund in each category and, in addition, if there are any additional limitations such as the size of the issuing bank or the rating of commercial paper.

Let's first focus upon risk category 1, the aggressive category. Any of the eight money market instruments are allowable investments, and in addition, there are no restrictions in terms of the quality of instruments. Investors in category 1 seek the highest possible yield with little regard to risk.

Category 2, the moderate risk category, is similar to category 1 in terms of the types of instruments that are allowable investments with one

TABLE 3
Risk Categorization of Money Market Instruments

Type of Instrument	Risk Category			
	(1)	(2)	(3)	(4)
Eurodollar	Yes	No	No	No
Commercial paper.............	Yes	Rated P-1 or A-1	No	No
Documented discount notes	Yes	At least $1 billion assets or $75 million net worth	At least $2 billion assets or $100 million net worth	No
Bankers' acceptances	Yes	Same as above	Same as above	No
Certificates of deposit...........	Yes	Same as above	Same as above	No
Federal agency securities	Yes	Yes	Yes	Yes
U.S. government securities	Yes	Yes	Yes	Yes
Repurchase agreements of federal agency and U.S. government securities	Yes	Yes	Yes	Yes

major difference—Eurodollars are no longer an allowance investment. In addition, there are some minor differences between categories 1 and 2 in terms of restrictions regarding the quality of the instruments. First, note that there is now a restriction involving commercial paper—it must be rated A-1 by Standard & Poor's or Prime-1 by Moody's Investors Service. Due to this restriction, category 2 funds avoid lower quality commercial paper. Second, observe that all bank-issued instruments, which include documented discount notes, bankers' acceptances, repurchase agreements, and CDs, must be purchased from banks that either have total assets of at least $1 billion or a net worth (capital, capital surplus, and undivided profits) of $75 million. In addition, these banks must be a member of the Federal Deposit Insurance Corporation (FDIC). In summary, those investors in risk category 2 are looking for high yields but are striving to avoid exceptionally high risks.

Risk category 3, the conservative risk category, is somewhat more restrictive than category 2. Notice that commercial paper (which is unsecured) is not an allowable investment in category 3. Also notice that all bank-issued instruments must be purchased from banks with either total assets of at least $2 billion or $100 million net worth. These banks must also be members of the FDIC. In summary, those investors in risk category 3 are desirous of avoiding any unsecured instruments and of seeking out only high-quality bank-issued instruments.

Risk category 4, the very conservative category, differs markedly from categories 1, 2, and 3 in that only federal agency securities, U.S. government securities, and repurchase agreements of these instruments are allowable investments. Those investors in risk category 4 are seeking to minimize risk.

At this point we must caution that the categories on Table 3 are intended only as a guideline. For example, you may find that although you are a moderate investor in stock funds, you are a more aggressive investor in money market funds because of the inherent safety of these vehicles.

In addition, you may want to switch risk categories in response to economic conditions. For instance, if the banking system appears to be particularly weak, then investors in categories 1, 2, and 3 might find it advisable to retreat to risk category 4. On the other hand, when economic conditions are strong, then some investors may desire to switch to a higher risk category. The important thing is that you choose a risk category that is suitable for yourself. If you find yourself losing sleep because of your money market fund investment, you may wish, just as with stock funds, to switch to a lower risk category. Alternatively, if you feel constrained, then it's advisable that you switch to a higher risk category. Nevertheless, we strongly recommend that you closely follow our procedures when beginning your fund program.

Now that you know how to categorize money market funds according to risk exposure levels, you must assemble the prospectus of suitable funds and select those which are consistent with your desired risk exposure level. To simplify this task we recommend that you consider only those funds that have been in existence for more than four years and that have at least $1 billion under management. These funds not only have experienced portfolio managers but also have usually been quite competitive with other funds in terms of yield and customer services. We also advise that you limit your investments to those funds that have average maturities of less than 60 days as was mentioned above.

The next section will show you how to select from this list of suitable alternatives the best individual money market fund.

SELECTION OF MONEY MARKET FUNDS

Once you have obtained a list of candidate funds that are suitable for your risk category, you are ready to select the one fund that is best suited to your individual needs. To help facilitate this selection process, we have constructed Table 4. Note first of all the funds that fall into your risk category are listed in the left-hand column. The next three columns list the most recent average *30-day yield* produced by each fund, the *minimum allowable investment*, and *the method of redemption*. The extreme right-hand column is left open for miscellaneous comments. For instance, if the distribution of dividends is an important factor for you, then you should enter dividend distribution data in this column.

Let's now consider a hypothetical example of how an investor might use this table in the selection process. Let's say that our investor intends to place $3,000 in a money market fund that offers a check-writing privilege. The first step that must be taken is to examine the minimum investment column to see if the required minimum investment can be met. Notice that fund D must be eliminated due to its $5,000 minimum investment. Next, column 3 must be examined to see if the fund offers a check-writing privilege. Since only funds B and C offer such a privilege, funds A, E, and F must also be eliminated. Thus, our investor is left with two funds, B and C. Since this investor has no preferences in column 4, the "other column," the only task is to choose the highest yielding fund. Since fund C yields more than fund B (9.50 percent versus 9 percent), the $3,000 should be placed in fund C.

Let's take another example. Assume that an individual with $4,000 to invest desires only a one-day redemption and has no other preferences. Which fund is most desirable for this investor? The answer is fund A because it is the highest yielding fund that meets this individual's minimum investment and redemption preferences.

The above procedures should enable you to find the best possible fund consistent with your desired risk level. However, since most money market funds maintain high-quality diversified portfolios of money market instruments with suitable average maturities and services, and since the risk levels for such funds are extremely low, many investors may wish a simplified selection procedure. We first recommend that you obtain prospectuses from any five no-load money market funds. In selecting a fund, simply eliminate those that (1) have average maturities over 60 days, (2) have been in existence for less than 4 years, and (3) have less than $1 billion

TABLE 4

	(1) Rate of Return (percent)	(2) Minimum Investment	(3) Method of Redemption	(4) Other
Fund A..........	9.75%	$1,000	One-day wire	
Fund B..........	9.00	2,000	Checking	
Fund C..........	9.50	1,000	Checking	
Fund D..........	10.00	5,000	One-day phone	
Fund E..........	8.50	1,000	One-day wire	
Fund F..........	8.00	2,000	One-day phone	

under management. Select the fund with the highest yield, and you will probably do almost as well as those who undertake a complete analysis.

SUMMARY

This reading presented a background study of the money market, the characteristics of eight money market instruments, and a detailed discussion of money market funds. In addition, we classified these funds by risk and showed you how to select the best fund that meets your own personal needs.

READING 16

VARIATIONS ON A THEME: CLOSED-END FUNDS

John Markese

Along with the dramatic growth of mutual funds has been a parallel growth of closed-end funds. There are now over 100 in number. And, in fact, many investors often confuse closed-end funds with mutual funds.

Yet, although they share some similarities, there are very distinct differences. Both use pooled money to make their investments. But the primary difference is the way in which shares are priced and traded.

A mutual fund, also known as an open-end fund, can issue an unlimited number of fund shares. When an investor puts money into the fund, new shares are issued, and the money is used to purchase more securities for the fund; if an investor withdraws from the fund, the shares are redeemed by the fund, which must draw down on existing cash balances or possibly sell securities. The purchase price of a mutual fund share is based on the net asset value of the fund, plus any sales commission (load) if there is one; net asset value is simply total fund assets divided by the number of shares outstanding. Investors can purchase shares either directly from the fund (in the case of all no-load funds and many low-load funds), or from a distributor, usually a broker or financial planner (in the case of load funds).

In contrast, a closed-end fund issues a limited number of fund shares to raise money for its investments. Once those shares are sold, they are

---

Source: *AAII Journal*, July 1987. Used with permission.

traded on an exchange in the same manner that occurs when a corporation issues shares; money from the purchase of a share goes to the owner of the share, rather than to the fund, and shares that are sold are bought by other investors, not the fund. To purchase shares in a closed-end fund, an investor must go through a brokerage firm and pay the attendant brokerage costs, the way he would if purchasing a corporate security.

Since closed-end fund shares are traded, their price depends on supply and demand market factors, rather than on net asset value. In fact, closed-end funds rarely sell at net asset value; they usually sell at a discount to net asset value and occasionally at a premium.

The discount or premium for a closed-end fund is calculated as follows:

$$\text{Premium (Discount)} = \frac{\text{Fund share price} - \text{N.A.V.}}{\text{N.A.V.}}$$

where: N.A.V. = Net asset value

A negative result implies a discount, which occurs when the share price is less than net asset value; a positive result implies a premium, which occurs when the share price is greater than net asset value. For example, suppose the Adams Express Company, a closed-end diversified common stock fund that is listed on the NYSE (ticker symbol ADX), was selling for $21.125 per share and had a net asset value of $21.80 per share. The discount (since it is selling below net asset value) is determined as follows:

$$-3.1\% = \frac{\$21.125 - \$21.80}{\$21.80}$$

There is a tendency for new closed-end funds to initially sell at a premium and then slip to a discount. If sell orders exceed buy orders in the market for a closed-end fund, the fund's price will decline until the orders are in balance without regard to the net asset value of the fund.

Explanations for the persistent discounts have been given as built-up tax liability due to paper profits; illiquid assets held by the fund; and the expenses and management fees charged by the closed-end fund.

Some closed-end funds have consistently sold at premiums—sometimes very high premiums—for specific reasons. The shares of a few single-country funds have exclusive licenses to deal in the common stock of the country's firms. This exclusivity has produced premiums over net asset value of nearly 100 percent. The Taiwan Fund and Korea Fund are two examples.

Generally, closed-end funds are divided into three categories: diversified common stock funds, bond funds, and specialized equity and convertible funds. These funds, from a portfolio composition standpoint, are indistinguishable from their open-end counterparts. Specialty funds, for example, include funds investing in specific market sectors such as utilities, gold, oil, real estate, and venture capital; convertible funds usually hold both convertible bonds and convertible preferred stocks. These latter portfolios provide a steady income stream with the potential for capital gains and losses due both to changing interest rates and changing underlying common stock values.

Probably the most unusual closed-end fund investment objective is the dual-purpose objective. In this case, investors holding income shares have a claim on all of the income generated by the fund, while investors holding capital shares receive all of the capital gains generated.

Closed-end funds, like their mutual fund counter-parts, pay dividends from investment income and make capital gains distributions. These distributions are subject to the same tax treatment as mutual fund distributions. However, in the past, many closed-end funds were not set up to allow shareholders to reinvest these distributions into new shares. This was always easy for open-end companies and was a somewhat unique and very attractive service. Many closed-end companies, particularly the newer ones, are trying to be more competitive with mutual funds and have structured their share authorizations to accommodate reinvestments of income and gains distributions. The fund's prospectus will detail all available services, such as reinvestment and withdrawal programs, as well as set forth the fund's investment objectives.

The discounts and premiums on closed-end funds provide an additional dimension of fund selection and investment strategy. With new fund offerings, the trend of initial premiums dissolving into eventual discounts argues against purchasing new funds at the initial offering. However, if these new funds do well or have a financial monopoly, the fund performance may overshadow the evaporation of the premium, or in the case of the single-country monopolies, the premium may escalate along with a rise in share price due to positive performance.

One closed-end investment strategy argues for purchasing funds selling at a substantial discount—a 30 percent or 40 percent discount is not unusual. This is a defensive strategy that assumes that if the market declines, shares of deeply discounted closed-end funds will fall less, with the discount providing a cushion. There is, of course, nothing to prevent the fund from maintaining the same discount or falling to an even greater percentage discount. Another reason for buying discounted funds is the income effect. A fund selling for only 70 percent of net asset value still has 100 percent of its assets potentially generating income. This gives a built-in boost to yield without raising the risk level of the portfolio's investments. Under this strategy, income-oriented investors would seek out closed-end funds that emphasize income in their investment objective statement and that are selling at a discount.

Where can an investor get information on closed-end funds? Because they are listed and traded on the exchanges, you must deal with a broker. Requests for annual, semi-annual, or quarterly reports can be directed to your broker or to the fund itself.

There are some publications that cover the larger closed-end funds. Moody's, Value Line, and the Wiesenberger Investment Companies Service are all usually found in libraries and contain detailed presentations, with addresses of selected funds. *Barron's,* in each issue, and *The Wall Street Journal,* each Monday, publish a table devoted to closed-end funds showing stock price, net asset value, and discount or premium. These tables, however, only cover the well-known funds. The daily high, low, and close price; the 52-week high-low range; and the dividend yield are quoted daily on the exchange where the shares are listed. Shares of small funds traded over-the-counter may not be listed on a daily basis.

Table 1 provides a summary of sources of information on closed-end funds.

TABLE 1
Sources of Information on Closed-End Funds

Barron's: Dow Jones & Co., 200 Burnett Rd., Chicopee, Mass. 01020; Weekly; Separate listing of selected funds and listing of prices by exchange.

The Wall Street Journal: Dow Jones & Co., 200 Liberty Street, New York, N.Y. 10281; Daily; Monday issue has a separate listing of selected funds and listing of prices by exchange.

Moody's Bank and Finance Manual: Moody's Investors Service, 99 Church St., New York, N.Y. 10007; Annual; Financial details and summaries of selected funds.

The Value Line Investment Service: Arnold Bernhard & Co., 711 Third Ave., New York, N.Y. 10017; Closed-end fund industry summary and evaluation of selected funds.

Wiesenberger Investment Companies Service: Warren, Gorham & Lamont, Inc., 210 South St., Boston, Mass. 02111; Annual; Financial details and summaries of selected funds with historical performance comparisons of the active funds.

For a directory of closed-end funds, write to: Directory of Closed-End Funds, Association of Publicly Traded Funds, 70 Niagara St., Buffalo, N.Y. 14202.

PART 5

INSURANCE PRODUCTS AS INVESTMENTS

READING 17

A PRODUCT UPDATE: CASH-VALUE LIFE INSURANCE

Glenn Daily

In previous articles, I have suggested that you won't be missing out on anything if you limit yourself to term insurance and universal life. I have also suggested that you should use the handful of no-load products as points of reference to evaluate commissionable products. With these suggestions in mind, let's take another look at some of the cash-value products in the marketplace.

TRADITIONAL WHOLE LIFE

No insurance product tells you less about itself than traditional whole life does, but some companies are now revealing the interest rate used to determine current dividends—when it suits their purposes. One New York company is "proud to announce" that its dividend rate is 13.25 percent. The story behind this is that they bought a lot of long-term bonds several years ago when interest rates were high, and now they're inviting everyone to share in the bonanza. (They can do this because they use the "portfolio average" method of allocating investment earnings among their policyholders. If they used the "investment year" method, the high yields would only be paid to the policyholders whose money was used to buy the bonds,

---

Source: *AAII Journal,* January 1987. Used with permission.

and newcomers would receive much less, reflecting the decline in current market rates. In effect, the old policyholders are financing the company's campaign to increase its market share.) Naturally, this company is happy to send you 50-year illustrations based on 13.25 percent interest, even though they have good reason to believe that this rate cannot be sustained indefinitely.

Insurance products like this put financial advisers in a bind. What can one say against a product with such wonderful illustrations, even if it is a black box?

Well, two can play the illustration game. As an experiment, I constructed an alternative with the same annual outlay and the same death benefit, using a no-load universal life product with a gross interest rate of 9.9 percent. The result? The no-load alternative had a higher cash surrender value until the 19th year. Apparently, the full-load product's higher investment yield is more than offset by its undisclosed expenses and its undisclosed cost of insurance.

A lot can happen in 19 years, and of course there's no guarantee that the breakeven point won't recede even further, like a mirage in the desert. No one can predict the future, so here's a suggestion: Tell the agent that you'd be glad to buy his "high-yielding" policy if the insurance company agrees to hold his commissions in escrow for 20 years, to give you a chance to verify that his product really is a better deal. That's fair, isn't it?

Interestingly, many agents complain bitterly whenever an insurance company proposes "level commissions"—a schedule in which the high first-year commission is spread out over the first few years—but they seem to have no qualms about recommending products whose benefits may not materialize for decades.

FIXED-PREMIUM UNIVERSAL LIFE

This is also called "interest-sensitive whole life" or "current assumption whole life." You can think of it as a way station between traditional whole life and flexible-premium universal life. The interest, insurance, and expense components of the policy are displayed separately—or "unbundled"—but premiums must be paid according to a pre-arranged schedule, additional deposits and partial withdrawals are usually not allowed, and death benefit adjustments are limited.

Despite its relative inflexibility, fixed-premium universal life has one important advantage over a flexible-premium product: It can offer greater benefits to the buyer because it reduces the company's uncertainty about its future cash flow and its future profits.

Based on current interest, mortality, and expense assumptions, a 25-year-old male non-smoker who puts $2,000 a year into a $300,000 no-load fixed-premium policy would have about $108,000 at age 45, versus $101,400 with the flexible-premium version. Using a no-load annual renewable term policy for comparison and assuming a 30 percent rate at surrender, the internal rates of return (see the November 1986 *Journal* for a detailed explanation of the calculation) would be 8.3 percent and 7.9 percent, respectively. At higher issue ages, such as 35, the difference would be smaller.

Most people probably do not need *all* of the flexibility of "pure" universal life, so it might make sense to give up *some* control over premiums, cash values, and death benefits. This is an area of product design that is likely to receive more attention in the future.

SINGLE-PREMIUM WHOLE LIFE

By making efficient use of every available tax advantage, single-premium whole life attempts to turn life insurance into an attractive investment vehicle. Most sales presentations focus on one feature in particular: the ability to generate "tax-free income" by taking out loans against the policy's cash value. The result is a purportedly unique combination of living and death benefits.

For example, suppose at age 55 you put $50,000 into a single-premium whole life policy with a net interest rate (after insurance expenses, and profit) of 8 percent and an initial death benefit of $140,000. If you let the cash value accumulate for 10 years, you would be able to borrow about $8,000 a year to supplement your other sources of retirement income. And, salesmen like to point out, this "income" does not enter into the calculations for determining how much of your Social Security benefits are taxable.

Scenarios like this have made single-premium whole life a big hit, but there are a few questions that need to be asked.

What happens if better opportunities come along and, after you've been borrowing for a while, you want to extricate yourself from the policy?

Here are three answers. First, you can die. That solves the whole problem. One company's sales brochure puts it more delicately, of course, but that's their answer. (Tax planning tip: Make sure you die before the policy matures, usually at age 95. More on this shortly.)

Second, you can borrow almost all of the cash value and reinvest it somewhere else. However, if you borrow too much, the policy will eventually lapse, triggering an unpleasantly large tax bill. How much is too much? That's hard to say, because some contracts give the company the right to change the "net cost" of borrowing (the spread between what the company pays and what it charges for the loan).

A recent IRS private letter ruling has suggested a third escape route: Exchange your policy for another life insurance policy by assigning it to the second insurer. But this won't help you if you want something other than life insurance.

What happens if Congress perceives that single-premium whole life is abusive?

Many people focus only on current tax laws, and then they think it's unfair when the rules are changed "in the middle of the game." But after five years of major tax code revisions, it's obvious that one of the rules of the game is that the rules of the game can change. With that in mind, it seems prudent to consider the possibility that policy loans might someday be treated as taxable distributions,[1] with one of the following transition rules for existing policies, in order of decreasing "unfairness":

- No grandfathering of existing loans (i.e., they would have to be paid back by a certain date to avoid tax).
- Grandfathering of existing, but not future, loans.
- Grandfathering of all loans on existing policies.

Clearly, the first two transition rules would reduce the future benefits of the policies that are being sold today.

What happens if you live until the policy matures? Although you probably don't expect to live until age 95, there's a chance that you will. The probability that a 65-year old man will live another 30 years is somewhere between 2 percent and 11 percent, depending on the mortality table that you use. When the policy matures, the difference between the account bal-

---

[1] *Editor's note:* The 1988 Technical Corrections Act makes withdrawals or loans from a single-premium life policy taxable as ordinary income, to the extent the distribution exceeds the policy-holder's basis. This affects policies purchased or materially changed after June 21, 1988.

ance and the single premium will be considered taxable income, and it is quite possible that the net surrender proceeds will not be sufficient to pay the tax.

But here's the most interesting question: Is it really true that single-premium whole life offers an unmatched combination of benefits?

As an experiment, I constructed an alternative with a single $50,000 premium and a death benefit of over $150,000, using a no-load universal life policy. Instead of tax-free loans, I assumed that, starting at age 65, the policyholder would make a taxable withdrawal each year in an amount that would leave about $8,000 after tax. The result? If the difference between the *gross* interest rate (before deducting expenses and the cost of insurance) on the universal life policy and the *net* interest rate on the single-premium whole life policy was 2 percent or greater, the universal life policy would provide the same after-tax "income" and a higher death benefit, with less risk. If the difference was only 1 percent—which is probably the minimum spread that one might expect over the long run—the universal life policy would provide an after-tax "income" of $6,600. In other words, your compensation for the additional risk would be, at most, $1,400 a year.

I consider the purchasers of single-premium whole life to be speculators. They are speculating that favorable tax treatment will continue or that existing policies will be fully shielded from future tax law changes. They are speculating that the difference between the net interest rate on the single-premium policy and the gross interest rate on universal life will be relatively small. And finally, they are speculating that they will die before the policy matures.

UNIVERSAL LIFE

Unlike traditional products, universal life shows you the interest credits and the insurance and expense deductions, but this structural simplicity hides the fact that only the insurance company knows what is *really* going on.

It's no secret that many companies are currently offering higher interest than their own portfolio yield would justify. They can do this by reducing their profit margins, drawing upon the surplus accumulated from previous generations of policyholders, and offsetting the investment losses with gains from the insurance charges. Although it is possible to obtain a list of the investments in the company's "general account," there is no way of knowing how the investment earnings are being allocated among the various product lines. Without this and other information, you must simply have faith that the company will keep the interest rate "competitive."

It's also no secret that some companies are projecting future improvements in mortality that may or may not materialize. Information about the company's mortality assumptions is even more difficult to obtain than information about its investments. This is one more reason to be extremely cautious in using long-term illustrations to compare universal life (or, for that matter, any cash-value) products.

You will sometimes hear that universal life offers fewer guarantees than traditional whole life does. This is not true. Every universal life policy has a guaranteed interest rate (usually 4 percent to 6 percent, a guaranteed cost of insurance (usually based on a standard mortality table), and guaranteed expenses. With traditional whole life, the difference between actual and guaranteed performance is reflected in the dividends; with universal life, it is reflected in the current (nonguaranteed) interest rate, mortality charges, and expenses. Universal life offers the same level of safety as traditional whole life if you base your annual premium payments on conservative—rather than current—assumptions.

VARIABLE PRODUCTS

Variable and variable universal life are attracting considerable attention as a result of recent tax law changes, especially the elimination of the favorable treatment of long-term capital gains. These products typically allow the buyer to allocate the premiums and cash value among several types of investments, including stocks, bonds, real estate, gold, and the money market. With variable life, you generally have no control over the relationship between the cash value and the death benefit; variable universal life is more flexible in this respect.

From a marketing point of view, variable insurance products hold out the possibility of attractive investment returns with no income tax. But there's another explanation for the enthusiasm with which some companies are embracing the concept: It offers an escape from the highly competitive universal life market. Here's a recent comment by one company president: "We propose to improve our profitability picture by marketing variable products where we place the investment risk and the investment opportunity with the purchaser with a markup of adequate basis points to cover our mortality risk and profit.'' Naturally, the companies that are adopting this strategy want everyone to believe that variable products are the ''wave of the future,'' in the hope that this will become a self-fulfilling prophesy.

As with all cash-value products, the performance of variable products will depend upon investment earnings, the cost of insurance, and expenses. The investment earnings will be determined by the performance of the funds within the policy and by your own allocation decisions. In this respect, variable insurance products are similar to families of mutual funds.

Information about the various charges and the cost of insurance is scattered throughout the prospectus. Incredibly, both the state insurance departments and the SEC allow companies to ''disclose'' the cost of insurance in technical language rather than in easy-to-understand rates per $1,000 of protection. The variable universal life prospectus prepared by one well-known company contains this paragraph:

> [The company] deducts a mortality charge on each Monthly Date to cover anticipated mortality costs. This charge is based upon the net amount at risk under a Contract (the amount by which the Contract's death benefit, computed as if there were neither riders nor Contract debt, exceeds the contract fund), the insured's risk classification, sex, and current attained age, and the *1980 Commissioner's Standard Ordinary Mortality Table* (the ''1980 CSO Table''). If [the company] determines that a lesser amount than that called for by this mortality table will be adequate to defray anticipated mortality cost, a lesser deduction may be made. [The company] has determined to charge less than the full mortality charges specified in the 1980 CSO Table for Contracts on insured males *of attained age 36 and above* and for Contracts of insured females *of attained age 41 and above,* but reserves the right to make full mortality charges based on the 1980 CSO Table. (Emphasis added.)

For those insurance buyers who do not happen to be familiar with the 1980 CSO Table, Table 1 shows the cost per $1,000 of protection at various ages. The 1958 CSO Table is also shown, because—believe it or not—at least one company is actually using this table to compute its insurance charges.

Based on 1980 CSO rates, a 35-year-old man, would pay $211 during the year ($17.58 each month) for $100,000 of insurance within the vari-

TABLE 1
Cost per $1,000 of Insurance

Age	1958 CSO	1980 CSO†	
	Male*	Male	Female
25	1.93	1.77	1.16
30	2.13	1.73	1.35
35	2.51	2.11	1.65
40	3.53	3.02	2.42
45	5.35	4.55	3.56
50	8.32	6.71	4.96
55	13.00	10.47	7.09
60	20.34	16.08	9.47
65	31.75	25.42	14.59

*Female rates are obtained by using an "age setback" of up to six years.
†A smoker/nonsmoker version of the 1980 CSO table was developed several years ago. The rates shown here are from the aggregate table, which is in wider use.

able universal policy, versus $132 for a no-load term insurance policy. As indicated in the prospectus (and confirmed by the company), this *maximum* rate is *currently* being charged to men under age 36 and women under age 41. Here's an interesting fact: As of June 1986, two-thirds of the buyers of this product were under 35. How many of these people read—and more importantly, understood—the prospectus?

Obviously, if the cost of insurance and the expenses are high, the policy cannot possibly be attractive unless the investment funds are stellar performers. This is what many buyers must be counting on, although it is not clear what basis they have for their optimism.

Even if the cost of insurance and the expenses are reasonable, variable universal life may still be less attractive than a combination of taxable mutual funds and term insurance or universal life. Table 2 shows internal rates of return for a no-load variable universal product, assuming a 12 percent gross (before management and other fees) rate of return. This represents the after-tax rate of return that you would have to earn on taxable mutual funds if you bought the same company's term insurance and "invested the difference." Although these results are relatively good, are they good enough to justify restricting yourself to a handful of investment choices?

TABLE 2
Internal Rate of Return: No-Load Variable Universal Life
(Male, Age 40, Nonsmoker, $100,000 Face Amount, 12% Gross Return)

Holding Period	Tax Rate at Surrender	
	0%	*30%*
5 years	4.6%	4.6%
10 years	8.4	7.0
20 years	9.9	8.4

I believe that it is possible to design a variable universal life policy that would be attractive to informed insurance buyers, but no one has done it yet.

CONCLUSIONS

No financial product is more difficult to buy with confidence than cash-value life insurance. The financial planning community is becoming increasingly aware of this, and consumers are likely to benefit as more questions are asked. In the meantime, keep in mind that you have an alternative to cash-value products: You can buy convertible, guaranteed-renewable term insurance and wait.

READING 18

INCOME STREAMERS

Russ Wiles

The Babylonians had annuities, and so did the Romans. But it took a while before Americans showed much interest. In fact, annuities didn't make much headway in the United States until the Great Depression hit. By then, shell-shocked investors flocked to them out of a desire for safety and steady income.

Recent stock market declines have again renewed interest in annuities. Yet in many ways these investments have changed considerably over the years. Today, annuities appeal to both conservative and aggressive investors. What these people have in common is a desire for substantial tax savings.

Annuities can be among the simplest financial instruments. Stripped down, they represent little more than an agreement to make a contribution now or in installments, in return for a series of payments later—for a fixed number of years or life. Pensions are a type of annuity. But when people speak of annuities, usually they're referring to various contracts offered by insurance companies.

All insurance annuities revolve around the basic "pay-now, receive-later" concept. They allow investors to prepare for future cash needs, such as planning for retirement or educating children, while granting significant tax benefits. Annuities come in several varieties. The frequency and amount of investor contributions vary, as do the payout options. Some contracts pay safe, fixed rates guaranteed by the insurance company, while

---

Source: *Personal Investor*, March 1988. Used with permission.

others offer more volatile returns that fluctuate according to the underlying stock, bond, or money-market investments.

With an annuity, the first question to consider is how soon you need to receive money. Shortly after you sign the contract and pay a lump-sum premium to the insurance company, immediate annuities begin returning on your principal, plus interest, at regular intervals—semimonthly, monthly, quarterly, semiannually, or annually.

The main advantage of annuities is that they allow interest or earnings to accumulate tax-free until you withdraw the money. Over a long accumulation phase, this can represent a sizable savings. Because immediate annuities don't make much use of this tax advantage, they aren't too popular. As a result, most annuities are deferred—meaning they start paying off after a lengthy period, usually many years.

Once you decide when to receive money, you must determine the method for making contributions. Deferred annuities may be purchased either with a single, up-front premium of at least $2,500 to $5,000, or in installments, starting as low as $100. Immediate annuities require a single premium. But other plans, under the "flexible-premium" heading, let you add money as desired.

The most important consideration with annuities concerns the amount of risk you wish to assume. On fixed annuities, the insurance company safeguards your principal and contracts to pay a guaranteed interest rate, thereby assuming the investment risk. On variable annuities, you bear this risk.

F. L. Kirby, senior vice president with brokerage Rodman & Renshaw, Inc., in Chicago, recommends only the fixed-rate variety. These conservative products have enjoyed a rush of renewed interest following the wild gyrations of the stock market. In terms of safety, Kirby considers fixed annuities to be in the same league as bank certificates of deposit and even Treasury bills. Of the three. annuities alone pay tax-deferred interest, even though their rates often surpass those of CDs and T-bills.

Fixed-rate annuities really aren't as rigid as their name implies. Most insurance companies guarantee the yield only for a specific period—typically one to five years. After that, the new rate reflects the current yield on one-year Treasury notes or other benchmarks. Investors generally must accept the going rate or surrender the policy.

Surrender can be painful, however, because insurance companies usually slap a penalty on any withdrawals that represent more than 10 percent of an account's yearly balance. These "surrender fees" typically last several years, phasing out much like a back-end load on a mutual fund. For example, many insurers charge 7 percent on excess withdrawals during the first year, 6 percent the second year and so on, until the fee lapses in year eight.

To sidestep this dilemma, many contracts offer "bailout" safeguards. Should the renewal rate drop more than one percentage point below the rate you initially signed up for, the insurance company will waive the surrender fee on any withdrawals you make. You still might face taxes on the proceeds, however, unless you transfer the funds into another annuity through what's known as a "1035 exchange." With this transfer and a bailout provision, you can move from a relatively low-yielding contract to a more attractive one at little or no cost.

With or without bailout clauses, fixed-rate contracts guarantee a minimum payment—usually around 4 percent or so—regardless of how low interest rates drop.

COMPARING CONTRACTS

When shopping among fixed-rate policies, don't be seduced by the numbers alone. Some companies offer above-market rates as a short-term gimmick, perhaps for a few months. After that, the yield typically drops back down.

More important, the insurer might find itself hard-pressed to support especially attractive rates. Insurance companies have maintained a virtually flawless record of meeting their annuity obligations, and they regularly contribute to state funds designed to indemnify troubled firms. Yet the failure of Baldwin-United Corporation in the early 1980s pointed out the risks involved. Holders of Baldwin-United's annuities have just recently recouped their principal with interest. Even so, those unlucky investors had to wait years for their money, and they didn't receive the double-digit rates originally promised.

In short, chasing the highest yield might require settling for an inferior firm. A. M. Best Company of Oldwick, N. J., rates insurers according to financial strength, dispensing grades from A+ down to C. These ratings aren't foolproof, but they do provide a relatively easy and reliable way to screen companies.

Sometimes, you can have your cake and eat it, too. A strong insurer might pay a rate equal to that offered by a weaker company, simply because the two firms disagree over the future direction of interest rates, the size of their expected assets and liabilities, and other uncertainties. In short, it pays to shop around.

ASSUMING INVESTMENT ONUS

Imagine a mutual fund that lets you make switches and accumulate profits tax-free. That, in a nutshell, represents a variable annuity. Because the performance of these securities depends on the fate of the stock, bond, or money markets, the size of future payments isn't certain. In fact, the payout amount will vary even after you "annuitize," or start receiving regular payments.

As a result, a variable annuity will only be as safe as the underlying fund. Insurance companies typically offer five or six stock and bond funds to choose from, in addition to a money-market alternative for short-term safety. Some companies have a relatively exotic fleet of funds focusing on zero-coupon bonds, health- or natural-resources stocks, real estate or foreign securities, for instance. Annuity holders generally enjoy four or more yearly opportunities to switch from one fund to the next, with no tax consequences.

Selecting a variable-annuity investment involves essentially the same research as choosing a traditional mutual fund: Look for superior past performance, proven management, moderate expenses and similar factors. Usually, the variable alternative is a "clone" of a regular mutual fund, run by the same managers and holding a similar portfolio. In many cases, outside investment-advisory companies manage variable-annuity funds for insurers.

With variable annuities, there isn't the same need to select an especially strong insurer, because investor funds are segregated in a separate custodial account, away from the company's general assets. Fixed annuities enjoy no such safeguard.

LONG-TERM ORIENTATION

Unfortunately, the favorable treatment that allows interest and capital gains to accrue tax-free on variable annuities works against these investments during down markets, because losses can't be deducted until the money is withdrawn, payments begin, or the policy is surrendered. Many annuity holders learned this lesson the hard way—while watching their funds slide lockstep with the market during the October crash.

Even so, variable-annuity contracts are for the long term, which suggests that most people holding these investments will likely show profits eventually. In a sense, the steep surrender fees charged in early years could prove a blessing in disguise by discouraging investors from cashing out at market bottoms.

PAYOUT POSSIBILITIES

Whether you opt for a fixed rate or a variable return, the payout method you select will influence the amount received. In other words, the fewer years the insurer expects to make disbursements, the bigger each check will be. So if you seek relatively large payments, consider the "life annuity" option, which guarantees income for the rest of your life only.

However, because the balance of the account would revert to the insurance company upon the insured's death, this option tends not to be too popular, says Alecia Oberg, a consultant in annuity marketing for The New England in Boston. "It involves gambling on your life expectancy," she says.

Under the "joint and last survivor" method, the annuity payments would go to your spouse or other survivor upon your death. Unless the two of you die simultaneously, the insurance company will have to make payments for a longer period. So, expect each check received to be proportionately smaller than under the life-annuity option.

This latter arrangement can be modified so that your survivor receives money for only a certain number of years, not life. For instance, you could set up a life annuity for yourself with a 20-year payment plan for your spouse. The annuity would guarantee income for as long as you live, and your survivor would receive payments until year 20 should you die before then.

Under all these plans, however, a good chunk of the account could revert to the insurance company if you and/or your survivor died relatively soon. One way to get around this danger is to add an option that would refund the account's balance to your beneficiary. This way, the bulk of the money wouldn't be lost if you died relatively early. You pay for this protection, however, in the form of smaller periodic disbursements.

Another way to safeguard your money involves basing the annuity payments not on your life expectancy but on a certain number of years, after which payments cease. The danger here is outliving your annuity payments.

Yet there are advantages with this latter method, too. Because the in-

Key Terms

Annuitize: To begin receiving payments from an annuity at regular intervals, usually following an accumulation phase during which interest and other earnings compound tax-deferred. The Internal Revenue Service taxes annuitized payments differently than withdrawals.

Annuity: A payment at regular intervals for several years or life. Fixed-rate annuities pay a constant amount each period, while on variable-rate contracts the amount fluctuates according to the performance of the underlying investment portfolios.

Bailout: A feature of fixed-rate annuities that lets investors redeem their contracts, free of surrender charges, should the renewal rate fall by a certain amount, typically one percentage point below the rate initially offered.

Premium: The payment, either lump-sum or in installments, needed to buy an annuity.

Surrender fee: Charge levied by insurance companies against annuity investors who withdraw more than 10 percent of their account's balance in a year. The fee, which is used to compensate brokers and insurance agents for selling annuities, typically declines from 7 percent or so in the first year down to nothing in year eight.

Withdrawal: Money taken from an annuity account other than through a regular annuitized payment.

surance company can estimate more precisely its total obligation, the size of each payment tends to be larger.

DEALING WITH TAXES

Instead of accepting regular payments, there's another way to get at money in an annuity contract: simply withdraw the funds, as needed or in a lump sum. Unfortunately, you would likely face a larger tax bill on withdrawals, because the Internal Revenue Service gives favorable treatment to annuitized payments. The IRS considers each such payment to be composed of both investment earnings and a return of principal. You pay taxes on the earnings component only.

By contrast, the IRS treats withdrawals entirely as taxable income (except in cases of total disability) until the account balance falls to the principal amount. After that, withdrawals would be tax-free. For example, suppose you invested $22,000 in an annuity that's now worth $39,500. The first $17,500 withdrawn would be taxed as ordinary income, while the remaining $22,000 would pass tax-free. (Up until 1982, annuity holders enjoyed preferential IRS treatment because the procedure was reversed: Initial withdrawals didn't incur taxes until investors took out all their accumulated interest and earnings.)

Besides this ordinary-income tax hurdle, the IRS treats annuity withdrawals like withdrawals from an individual retirement account. That is, anybody who takes money out before age 59½ generally incurs a 10 percent penalty. To tap your account penalty-free before that age, you must annuitize rather than withdraw money. Unfortunately, the annuity payments must be spread out over your estimated remaining life span, which means the size of each disbursement won't be large.

Whether annuities will reach new heights of popularity remains to be seen. A depressed stock market might convince more people to seek the relative safety of a fixed-rate contract. And both fixed- and variable-rate annuities would likely come into vogue if tax rates increase.

In the meantime, annuities offer enough flexibility to satisfy most types of investors. The size and timing of premiums, the frequency and method of payouts, and other considerations can all be tailored to suit individual needs. Perhaps most important, each person enjoys the option of assuming the investment risk or passing it along to the insurance company.

THE MEANING OF LIFE

The Tax Reform Act of 1986 left a smaller selection of investments offering shelter from Uncle Sam. Most municipal bonds retained the bulk of their tax benefits, as did real estate and certain types of limited partnerships. The insurance industry fared even better in protecting two broad classes of investments—annuities and the single-premium life policies.

In some ways, the two types of insurance products are remarkably similar. Annuities allow interest and other investment earnings to compound tax-free for many years. So do single-premium life policies. In addition, annuity holders can opt for either a fixed rate of return, guaranteed by the insurance company, or a variable rate that fluctuates according to the underlying stock, bond, and money-market funds. Investors in the life-insurance alternatives also enjoy this choice, through what are known as single-premium whole life and variable-life policies.

Yet when it comes to getting at the money in an account, the similarities end. Sizable surrender fees discourage early withdrawals from annuities, as do Internal Revenue Service penalties slapped on investors below age 59½. Individuals who annuitize, or start receiving regular payments (as opposed to withdrawals), bypass these obstacles. But the portion of their annuity payments that represent investment earnings still face taxation as ordinary income.

Single-premium life avoids these liquidity problems. While investors who pull out of life policies prematurely also face hefty surrender fees, they can gain access to their money by borrowing it at highly favorable rates.

Provided enough money is left in the account to maintain the insurance coverage, the principal part of a policy loan can generally be borrowed[1] for as little as 1 percent or 2 percent or so, while the earnings component might carry no interest charge at all, depending on the insurer. These loans don't have to be repaid either—the charges are simply deducted from the amount going to beneficiaries upon the insured's death.

Single-premium life enjoys other advantages, too. As insurance, these policies come with a "free-look" period, during which investors can back out and recoup their money. Depending on each state's insurance laws, this grace period can extend from 10 to 45 days for variable life, and up to a year for single-premium whole life. Annuities don't offer this feature.

Perhaps more important, life policies also provide death benefits, which pass to survivors free of income taxes and probate (although estate taxes may apply). Every dollar of investment return increases the death benefit, with the amount of additional coverage depending on the insured's age, health, and other factors, says Andrew D. Westhem, chairman of Western Capital Financial Companies in Los Angeles.

Despite these many benefits, single-premium life also comes with a few problems, both real and potential. Of greatest concern is the possibility that Congress could repeal the favorable borrowing privileges in upcoming tax legislation. The nation's lawmakers would probably grandfather these provisions so that current investors could still take out low-interest policy loans, but there's no guarantee this would be the case.

Another potential drawback deals with the insurance coverage on variable-life policies, in that a string of investment losses could start drying up the death-benefits coverage. "Theoretically, it's possible that poor performance could cause the contract to lapse if the person didn't or

---

[1] Editor's note: The 1988 Technical Corrections Act makes withdrawals on loans from a single-premium life contract taxable as ordinary income, to the extent the distribution is earnings above basis.

couldn't put more money in," says Westhem. For this reason, he recommends sticking with those policies that guarantee a minimum death benefit.

The cost of insurance, moreover, can be a detriment to both variable and whole-life policies, by making less money available for investment.

According to Westhem, a single-premium whole-life policy might carry costs of about 2.25 percent a year compared with 1.75 percent annually for a single-premium fixed-rate annuity—a difference of about half a percentage point (50 basis points) a year. After 20 years earning 12 percent (before fees) on a one-time $50,000 contribution, the annuity would be worth $352,000 compared with about $321,400 for the life policy, says Westhem. This underscores the basic difference between the two types of insurance products. "You have to ask yourself whether the additional tax, liquidity, insurance, and other advantages of the life policy would be worth 50 basis points a year," he says.

READING 19

VARIABLE ANNUITIES:
A PRODUCT UPDATE

Glenn Daily

A lot has happened since I looked at variable annuities in the September 1985 *AAII Journal*. The Tax Reform Act of 1986 eliminated the favorable tax treatment of long-term capital gains as well as the deductibility of certain investment-related expenses. As a result of these and other changes, the insurance industry is congratulating itself on having one of the new remaining tax shelters, and mutual fund investment advisers are exploring ways to tap this potentially lucrative market.

But before you reach for your checkbook, let's take another look at this hot product of the moment.

HOW IT WORKS

A variable annuity allows the contractholder to invest in a family of mutual funds on a tax-deferred basis. The choices usually include a money market fund and one or more stock and bond funds. A few contracts offer a real estate fund; some also offer a fixed-interest option, which is similar to investing in a tax-deferred CD. Most contracts permit several switches between funds each year without charge; however, the exact provisions vary greatly among contracts.

Source: *AAII Journal*, March 1987. Used with permission.

During retirement, the accumulated account balance can be converted into a series of monthly payments. Most variable annuities provide for variable payments that are based on the insurer's mortality assumptions and the investment performance of the underlying funds. Variable annuities may also provide for fixed payments, based on the insurer's current rates at the time of distribution. Note, too, that you have the options of exchanging one annuity for another or of surrendering it and receiving a lump-sum payment.

Like fixed annuities, variable annuities should be thought of as relatively illiquid, long-term savings vehicles. There are three limitations on your ability to get at your money:

- Loans against annuity balances are considered to be taxable distributions.
- With only a few exceptions, there is a 10 percent penalty tax on amounts withdrawn before age 59½.
- Most variable annuities hit you with a declining surrender charge that can last as long as 12 years.

Note also that annuity balances receive unfavorable tax treatment at death. Stocks, bonds, real estate, and life insurance pass income-tax-free to your beneficiaries; annuities do not.

SHOULD YOU BUY IT?

Table 1 summarizes the important features of four investment choices; variable annuities, no-load mutual funds, self-directed non-deductible IRAs, and variable life insurance. The Tax Reform Act of 1986 has added a few new wrinkles to comparisons of investments. Investors now have to inquire about the deductibility of investment advisory fees and the procedure for calculating taxable income on withdrawals.

Gathering the information in Table 1 is only a first step in comparing variable annuities with other investments. The real goal is to figure out which choice is likely to produce the greatest aftertax wealth, measured either as a lump sum or as an aftertax retirement income. Let's focus on one decision in particular: Should you buy a variable annuity or invest in taxable no-load mutual funds?

Once you've made the necessary assumptions about the rate of return, expenses, and taxes, it's fairly easy to calculate the future value of a variable

TABLE 1
A Comparison of Several Investment Alternatives

Variable Annuity	No-Load Mutual Funds	Nondeductible IRA	Variable Life Insurance
All investment earnings grow tax-deferred.	Appreciation is tax-deferred. Income and capital-gain distributions are taxable.	All investment earnings grow tax-deferred.	All investment earnings grow tax-deferred.
Limited number of investment choices. However, permits access to load fund advisers without the normal load.	Large number of investment choices.	Large number of investment choices.	Limited number of investment choices. However, permits access to load fund advisers without the normal load.
Transfer between funds is not a taxable event. Exchange of contracts is not a taxable event if done properly.	Transfer between funds is a taxable event.	Transfer between funds is not a taxable event if done properly.	Transfer between funds is not a taxable event. Exchange of contracts is not a taxable event if done properly.
Total expenses are typically about 2% per year.	Total expenses are typically about 1% per year.	Total expenses are typically about 1% per year.	Total expenses depend upon policy design. Minimum is about 1.5% per year, plus cost of insurance.
Usually has a declining surrender charge.	In most cases, no surrender charge.	In most cases, no surrender charge.	Has a declining surrender charge or a front-end load.
In most cases, 10% penalty tax for withdrawals before age 59½.	No penalty tax.	In most cases, 10% penalty tax for withdrawals before age 59½.	No penalty tax.

TABLE 1—Concluded

	Variable Annuity	No-Load Mutual Funds	Nondeductible IRA	Variable Life Insurance
	Loans are treated as taxable distributions.	May be margined or used as collateral.	Loans are treated as taxable distributions.	Loans are permitted; offsetting cash value is shifted to fixed-interest account.
	Distribution requirements vary by contract.	No minimum distribution requirements.	Distributions must begin shortly after age 70.	No minimum distribution requirements.
	Investment advisory fees are not added back to taxable income and are, in effect, tax-deductible.	Investment advisory fees are not tax-deductible unless misc. deductions exceed 2% of adjusted gross income.	Treatment of investment advisory fees is unclear as of January 1987.	Investment advisory fees are not added back to taxable income and are, in effect, tax-deductible.
	No aggregation with other investments to determine taxable income. Withdrawals are from interest first, then principal. Annuity payments are part interest, part principal.	No aggregation with other investments to determine taxable income. Withdrawals are part appreciation, part principal, with flexibility to determine proportions.	Aggregated with deductible IRAs to determine taxable income upon distribution. Withdrawals are part interest, part principal, in same proportions as total balance.	No aggregation with other investments to determine taxable income. Treatment of withdrawals depends upon pre- and post-change policy values.
	Appreciation is taxed as ordinary income at death.	Appreciation escapes income tax at death, because fund shares receive a "stepped-up basis."	Appreciation is taxed as ordinary income at death.	All proceeds pass income-tax-free to the beneficiary. Death benefit will exceed the cash value, due to insurance.

annuity. Suppose the gross annual rate of return on the funds within the annuity is 12 percent, the total expenses (investment advisory fee, fund operating expenses, the insurer's "mortality and expense risk charge," and the annual maintenance fee) are 2 percent, and the combined tax rate (federal, state, and local) is 35 percent. If you invest $10,000, you'll have $67,275 in 20 years, or $47,229 after taxes if you surrender the annuity. Your average annual aftertax rate of return will be 8.07 percent; that's what you would have to earn each year on an initial investment of $10,000 in order to have $47,229 at the end of 20 years. On the other hand, if you decide to convert the annuity balance into annual payments lasting for 20 years, you'll get $5,311 each year after taxes. That's equivalent to an aftertax rate of return of 8.43 percent on the same initial investment of $10,000. This increase in the effective rate of return is a measure of the advantage to be gained from spreading taxes over a long distribution period.

Doing a parallel calculation for no-load mutual funds is much more difficult, however, because you have to account for taxes each year. Taxes depend upon portfolio turnover, and portfolio turnover takes place at two levels: at the mutual fund level (fund managers buy and sell securities) and at the individual investor level (individuals buy and sell mutual fund shares).

Suppose the total return of a growth-and-income fund, before expenses and taxes, is 12 percent a year, consisting of 3.6 percent dividends, 3.6 percent realized capital gains, and 4.8 percent unrealized capital gains. The fund has nondeductible expenses of 1 percent a year. Also, suppose the investor's tax rate is 35 percent and his annual portfolio turnover is 75 percent, defined to mean that each year he realizes 75 percent of his accumulated unrealized gains (including the current year's gains). If he invests $10,000 in the mutual fund, he'll have $10,722 at the end of the first year ($10,000 + $360 dividends + $720 realized capital gains + $120 unrealized capital gains − $100 expenses − $378 taxes), and $37,699 at the end of the twentieth year. After liquidating his fund shares and paying taxes he'd be left with $37,505, and his average annual aftertax rate of return would be 6.83 percent. In this example, the effective rate of return would increase only slightly if he gradually redeemed his shares over a 20-year period, because most of his capital gains are realized each year.

By performing similar calculations for various sets of assumptions, you can get some idea of what is to be gained—or lost—by buying a variable annuity. The top half of Table 2 shows the difference in the average annual aftertax rate of return for an investor in the 35 percent tax bracket,

TABLE 2   Variable Annuities versus Taxable Mutual Funds: The Difference In Annual Aftertax Rates of Return*

Under Current Tax Laws—
Tax on ordinary income: 35%
Tax on capital gains: 35%

Holding Period (Years)	Money Market, Bonds: 8%	Growth and Income: 12%		Aggressive Growth: 15%	
		25% Turnover	*75% Turnover*	*25% Turnover*	*75% Turnover*
5	(0.15)%	(0.01)%	0.09%	0.04%	0.31%
10	0.04	0.38	0.54	0.58	1.01
15	0.20	0.74	0.92	1.07	1.57
20	0.35	1.04	1.24	1.46	2.00
25	0.48	1.29	1.50	1.77	2.34
30	0.60	1.50	1.71	2.02	2.60

A "What-if" Scenario—
Tax on ordinary income: 40%
Tax on capital gains: 24%

Holding Period (Years)	Money Market, Bonds: 8%	Growth and Income: 12%		Aggressive Growth: 15%	
		25% Turnover	*75% Turnover*	*25% Turnover*	*75% Turnover*
5	(0.04)%	(1.19)%	(1.12)%	(1.89)%	(1.69)%
10	0.16	(0.74)	(0.63)	(1.23)	(0.91)
15	0.34	(0.33)	(0.20)	(0.65)	(0.27)
20	0.51	0.02	0.17	(0.17)	0.23
25	0.66	0.31	0.46	0.20	0.62
30	0.79	0.55	0.71	0.49	0.92

*A positive difference means the variable annuity is better. All comparisons assume an expense ratio of 1% for the taxable mutual funds and 2% for the variable annuity. Mutual fund expenses are assumed to be nondeductible. Investment returns for growth-and-income funds are assumed to be 30% dividends, 30% realized capital gains, and 40% unrealized capital gains. Investment returns for growth funds are assumed to be 10% dividends, 20% realized capital gains, and 70% unrealized capital gains.

assuming both investments are liquidated at the end of the holding period. A positive difference favors the annuity, while a negative difference favors taxable mutual funds. Money market and bond funds are assumed to have an 8 percent gross annual return, consisting entirely of dividends. For growth-and-income funds, the annual return is assumed to be 12 percent, consisting of 30 percent dividends, 30 percent realized capital gains, and 40 percent unrealized gains; for aggressive growth funds, the annual return is 15 percent, consisting of 10 percent dividends, 20 percent realized gains, and 70 percent unrealized gains. (These proportions are based upon historical results for a representative sample of funds.)

The results suggest that variable annuities can have a significant long-term advantage over taxable funds, especially for investors who buy and sell frequently. Note, however, that the comparison may be biased in favor of annuities, because it ignores surrender charges and the penalty tax on withdrawals. In addition, it assumes a high tax rate, a high gross rate of return, and the non-deductibility of fund expenses. If different assumptions were made in these areas, the 1.24 percent advantage in the earlier example (8.07 percent − 6.83 percent) could easily be erased, even if you assume an extended distribution period rather than liquidation.

Here are two questions to ponder as you examine the comparisons in Table 2:

- Do you have a reasonable chance of finding taxable mutual funds that will outperform the funds within the annuity by 2 percent to 3 percent annually?
- By giving you the opportunity to time the market painlessly, will the variable annuity actually make it more difficult for you to achieve superior performance?

The results presented so far were based on the assumption that ordinary income and capital gains would both be taxed at 35 percent. But what happens if Congress decides to raise tax rates and reinstate preferential treatment for long-term capital gains?

The bottom half of Table 2 shows the result. What a difference a little change in the tax law makes! If the tax rate on ordinary income is raised to 40 percent and capital gains are taxed at 24 percent (in other words, a 40 percent exclusion), many equity investors would have to hold the annuity for at least 15 years just to break even.

Given the risks involved, the products that are currently on the market are probably most appropriate for people who are obsessed with saving money on taxes, at any price.

Under prudent assumptions about future tax rates, portfolio turnover, and rates of return, a variable annuity would have to have a total expense ratio of about 1 percent in order to match the performance of similar no-load mutual funds. Such a product would still suffer, however, from the unfavorable tax treatment that annuities receive. A consumer-oriented variable life insurance policy might be even more attractive.

If insurance companies are unable to manufacture a variable annuity that meets more demanding specifications, then perhaps they should just forget the whole idea and come up with something else for us to buy. For example . . .

MARKET-VALUE-ADJUSTED PRODUCTS

You haven't seen market-value-adjusted annuities and life insurance yet, but you will. The necessary regulations are being put into place in New York, and other states are sure to follow. Market-value-adjusted products address a problem that has plagued the insurance industry since the 1970s: When surrender values for non-variable products (such as traditional and interest-sensitive whole life, universal life, and fixed annuities) are based on the *book* value of the company's assets rather than on their *market* value, an insurer's financial stability can be seriously threatened during periods of volatile interest rates. (For a more detailed discussion of this problem, see the March 1986 *AAII Journal*.) According to some studies, it might cost a company about 1 percent in portfolio yield to fully hedge against the risk of surrender. In the current highly competitive environment, few companies are able to price this surrender option into their products. Instead, many try to lessen their exposure by investing in securities of a shorter maturity—and, therefore, a lower yield.

Market-value-adjusted products offer a solution to this problem by shifting some of the investment risk onto the policyholder. If interest rates rise, the surrender value will be reduced according to a prescribed formula; conversely, the surrender value will increase if interest rates fall. One hope is that market-value adjustments will enable companies to offer a higher return over the long run to policyholders who do not surrender.

Will the additional return be adequate compensation for the additional risk that you will bear? That remains to be seen, but there's an important lesson here. The insurance industry wants your money—"asset-gathering," one prominent executive calls it—so you can be sure that product-development actuaries are busy designing new enticements. You don't have to throw money at today's hot product; tomorrow's will be along shortly.

READING 20

HOW DO SINGLE PREMIUM DEFERRED ANNUITIES STACK UP?

Glenn Daily

The popularity of single premium deferred annuities is on the rise as investors search for alternatives to volatile stock and bond markets. In this reading, we'll look at the product's strengths and weaknesses, and suggest some questions to ask.

The most attractive feature of SPDAs is the tax-deferred accumulation of interest within the contract. Table 1 shows the value of tax deferral to an investor in the 30 percent tax bracket, for various holding periods and credited interest rates. As an example, an 8 percent before-tax certificate of deposit yield is equivalent to 5.6 percent after tax, whereas the same 8 percent interest results in a 6.6 percent annual aftertax return if it accumulates within an SPDA for 20 years. This results in a 1 percent difference favoring the SPDA. The difference would be even greater with a longer holding period, a higher interest rate, or a higher tax rate.

All SPDAs have a minimum guaranteed interest rate—usually 3 percent to 6 percent —but current rates are structured in a variety of ways. As with CDs, there are different guarantee periods, ranging from less than 1 year to as many as 10 years. Some companies pay higher interest on larger account balances. And there are two different approaches to apportioning invest-

Source: *AAII Journal,* January 1988. Used with permission.

TABLE 1
Tax-Deferred SPDAs versus Taxable Bonds and CDs: Annual Aftertax Return Differences*

Investment Period (Years)	Interest Rate			
	6.0%	8.0%	10.0%	12.0%
5	0.1%	0.2%	0.4%	0.5%
10	0.3	0.5	0.8	1.1
15	0.5	0.8	1.1	1.5
20	0.6	1.0	1.4	1.9
30	0.8	1.3	1.8	2.3

*Assumes a 30% tax rate.

ment income among policyholders: portfolio-average and investment-year. Under the portfolio-average approach, the same rate is paid on all contracts, regardless of when the premium was received. Under the investment-year method, contracts are grouped by the year (or some other selected period) of issue, and the credited rate for each group of contracts is determined separately.

Table 2 shows the actual performance history of several SPDAs. Note that the performance history of an investment-year product is itself a table; each column shows the initial and renewal rates for contracts issued in that year. For example, people who purchased Company G's SPDA in 1981 received 10.5 percent the first year, 13.5 percent the next year, 9.0 percent in 1983, and so on.

Although this is a small sample of the available products, you can still make a few useful observations. First, no single product consistently outperforms all of the others; in fact, only one of the six portfolio-average products is consistently in the top half of the sample. Second, today's SPDA rates are generally above current CD yields, but no company matched the high interest rates of the early 1980s. This suggests that it is important to find out what the company plans to do if interest rates rise again.

Finally, information about past performance can raise questions that might shed some light on future performance. For example, why did Company G lower the interest rate so quickly for contracts issued in 1980 and

TABLE 2
Historical Performance of Selected SPDAs (1979–1987)

	1979	1980	1981	1982	1983	1984	1985	1986	1987
Yields on Taxable Alternatives*									
One-year CDs	11.1%	13.1%	15.5%	15.0%	9.4%	10.0%	9.1%	7.9%	6.2%
Long-term corporate bonds	9.3	12.4	13.4	15.3	12.0	12.1	12.1	9.7	8.4
Selected SPDAs†									
Portfolio-Average Method—									
Company A	—	—	11.5%	12.8%	10.0%	10.0%	10.0%	10.5%	8.5%
Company B	—	8.8%	10.5	13.0	11.3	11.0	11.3	10.0	9.0
Company C	6.3%	6.3	6.3	6.3	6.3	10.5	9.5	8.3	6.3
Company D	—	9.3	12.0	13.5	9.5	11.0	10.5	9.3	8.3
Company E	—	8.0	12.3	12.8	10.8	11.3	10.8	8.6	7.3
Company F	—	7.1	7.2	13.5	10.8	11.5	11.0	9.3	8.0
Investment-Year Method—									
Company G	1979	1980	1981	1982	1983	1984	1985	1986	1987
Issued in: 1979	9.00%								
1980	9.25	10.50%							
1981	9.25	10.50	10.50%						
1982	9.50	12.50	13.50	14.50%					
1983	9.00	9.00	9.00	12.00	13.00%				
Paid in: 1984	9.00	9.00	9.00	12.00	13.00	12.00%			
1985	9.00	9.00	9.00	10.00	10.00	11.00	12.25%		
1986	9.00	9.00	9.00	9.00	9.00	9.75	10.00	10.50%	
1987	7.00	7.00	7.00	7.00	7.00	7.00	8.00	8.00	9.50%

*As of February 1.
†Rates as of February 1, guaranteed for one year.

1981? Why was Company C so slow to raise its credited rate to competitive levels?

Here are some other features of SPDAs that you should be aware of:

- No interest rate risk: With most SPDAs, the surrender value is based on the book value of the company's assets; the company bears the investment risk if interest rates go up and the market value of its portfolio drops. A few SPDAs have a "market value adjustment"; the surrender value is adjusted up or down according to a predetermined formula if you surrender before the end of the guarantee period.
- Most SPDAs have no front-end load or annual maintenance fees, but they do have a surrender charge. This ranges from 4 percent to 10 percent of either the initial premium or the account balance, and it often declines by 1 percent a year. The surrender charge is usually waived in the event of death or annuitization, and it will be limited to the amount of accumulated interest if the contract has a money-back guarantee.
- Penalty-free withdrawals: Some contracts allow you to withdraw up to 10 percent of the account balance each year without charge. This provision effectively reduces the surrender charge, if you remember to make a withdrawal before the full surrender.
- Bailout provision: Some companies waive the surrender charge if the credited rate drops below some threshold; for example, 1 percent below the initial rate. This provision eliminates the possibility of a bait-and-switch—that is, the company lures you in with a high rate and then lowers it the following year—but it doesn't address a more important question: Will the company's rate keep pace if interest rates rise?
- Guaranteed and current settlement options: Most policyholders choose a lump-sum payment, but you do have other options, including monthly payments for life. Annuitization should be viewed as a separate investment decision, and you should shop around for the best rates when you're ready. Note that many SPDAs require that you annuitize the balance, or surrender the contract, by age 85.
- Tax-free exchanges: An annuity contract can be exchanged for another annuity contract without creating a taxable event, if the transaction is handled properly
- Avoidance of probate: Annuity proceeds pass directly to the named

beneficiary, without going through the expense, delays, and publicity of probate.
- Protection from creditors: In some states, annuity account balances are not available to satisfy creditors' claims.

The most unattractive feature of SPDAs is the lack of liquidity. Loans are treated as taxable distributions; distributions (loans, withdrawals, and surrenders) are deemed to be from interest first, rather than principal; and distributions of interest before age 59½ are subject to a 10 percent penalty tax, with only a few exceptions. This penalty tax significantly reduces or eliminates the tax-deferral advantages shown in Table 1.

Another drawback of annuities is that the accumulated interest is taxed to your beneficiaries if you die, whereas there is no income tax liability for life insurance, stocks, or real estate.

SHOULD YOU BUY IT?

The attractiveness of SPDAs depends to a large extent on future tax rates. If the tax rate when you redeem the policy is the same or lower than the tax rates during the accumulation period, a competitively-priced SPDA should outperform other fixed-income investments.

On the other hand, an increase in tax rates of 10 percent toward the end of the holding period would have the same effect as the current 10 percent penalty tax: The gain from tax deferral would be reduced or eliminated, and relative performance would depend on many factors, including gross investment yields, the spread between the earned and credited rates for banks and insurance companies, and the expense ratios and transaction costs associated with mutual funds and direct purchases of bonds.

HOW TO CHOOSE ONE

You cannot predict which insurance company will pay the highest interest over the next 5, 10, or 20 years. Nevertheless, there are some actions that you can take to increase your chances of being satisfied with your investment decision.

- To get a feel for what's available, look at Best's Retirement Income Guide. This contains contract descriptions and current rates for

SPDAs and other types of annuities. Copies are available in some libraries or directly from A. M. Best Company (Ambest Road, Oldwick, New Jersey 08858; $44 for two semiannual reports).

- Choose a financially-sound company and do not rely on state guaranty funds to protect you. There is no foolproof way to determine a company's financial health, but Best's safety rating offers some practical guidance. A consistent A+ rating is a good sign. (Safety ratings can be found in Best's Insurance Reports, available in many libraries.) Standard & Poor's and Moody's have recently begun to evaluate the claims-paying ability of a small number of insurers. Standard & Poor's highest rating is AAA; Moody's is Aaa.

  Although state guaranty funds may provide an additional measure of safety, it's a mistake to count on them. In most states, coverage is limited to $100,000, and unreasonably high guaranteed interest rates may not be honored. It's not always clear whether a product is covered—in 1984 at least one state fund argued that Baldwin-United annuities were securities rather than insurance products—or how bad things have to get before the system is triggered. Your money can be tied up for months or even years while regulators and other interested parties negotiate.

- Find out whatever you can about the company's investment and interest-crediting strategies. In particular, how does it plan to keep the credited rate attractive throughout future business cycles? The insurance industry does not yet operate at the same level of accountability that mutual funds do, so you'll have to get this information through personal correspondence with the company, rather than through regular published reports.

- Find out what the creditd rate has been in the past on the company's annuity products. If the company uses an investment-year method to allocate interest among policyholders, get the initial and renewal rates for each group of investors.

- Avoid products with unique features. An SPDA is a simple product, and complications should be viewed with suspicion. Several SPDAs have a dual interest rate; you get the higher rate if you annuitize the account balance and the lower rate if you surrender. This approach requires the company to maintain two parallel series of account balances, one for each payment option. Another company uses a "unique" index to determine "bonus" interest.

  When faced with a complicated product, try this: Tell the agent that you'll be happy to consider buying his SPDA—if he agrees to reimburse you for the cost of hiring a consulting actuary to evaluate it.

- Avoid products with commissions higher than 5 percent. High commissions do not mean better service or a better product; they mean higher surrender charges for you and a weakened financial position for the company. One Kansas company offers high interest and 7 percent commissions. How do they do it? Junk bonds.

   There are at least two commissionless products on the market: USAA's SPDA (800/531-8000) and Lincoln Benefit's Futurist II (800/525-9287).

- Avoid companies that have profit-sharing arrangements with agents. Profit-sharing can be accomplished through an "agent-owned reinsurance company"—the insurer sets up a reinsurer owned by the agents and then passes a portion of its business to them—or by other means, including direct ownership of the insurance company. Profit-sharing creates a disturbing conflict of interest between investors and agents. I know of at least one case where agents asked the company to lower the interest rate on its SPDA because the high rate was cutting into their profits.

- Give stock (as opposed to mutual) companies an extra measure of scrutiny. Agents will sometimes stress that the company they represent is backed by a hugh financial organization with vast resources. That should give you peace of mind, the salesman tells you. Then two weeks later you read in the newspaper that the company is up for sale, and no one knows who the new parent will be. This is not a rare occurrence; it has happened to me four times during the past year. One solution: Ask the company for a "poison pill bailout provision" that waives all surrender charges if there is a change in corporate ownership.

CONCLUSION

For investors with a long-term horizon and little need for liquidity, single premium deferred annuities can be an attractive alternative to taxable bonds and CDs. You can avoid the most serious pitfalls by asking a few reasonable questions and listening for reasonable answers.

PART 6

INVESTING IN REAL ASSETS

READING 21

WHAT IS A MORTGAGE?

Sherman J. Maisel

Mortgages and deeds of trust are central to real estate finance. In order to understand how they work, we must examine the concept of secured loans and their special features. Because the terminology of mortgage lending is important, much of this chapter is devoted to explaining the main terms as they appear in the standard fixed-rate mortgage. Mortgages are legal contracts covering individual loans involving large sums of money and long periods; therefore, they must be drafted carefully to cover many unique contingencies. Recently, however, the trend has been to use more and more standardized features in order to cut costs. Thus, home mortgages tend increasingly to be similar to one another. Mortgages on income properties, however, remain more individualized.

MORTGAGES, NOTES, AND MORTGAGE BONDS

A favorite story among mortgage bankers tells of a builder who tried to buy a $300 suit on credit and was turned down. He then went next door to the bank, where he was quickly granted a $200,000 loan to build a house. The story illustrates the difference in the ability to borrow money on a secured

---

Source: From Sherman J. Maisel, *Real Estate Finance* (New York: Harcourt Brace Jovanovich, 1986). Used with permission.

as opposed to an unsecured debt. The bank assumed that it could collect because it held a mortgage secured by real property.

A **mortgage** is a contract that pledges a specific property as collateral to insure the repayment of a debt. The property serves as a **security**, or promise that the borrower will meet the terms agreed upon. If the borrower fails to do so, the lender has the right to have the property sold to satisfy the debt. The ability to mortgage property means that borrowers obtain larger loans at lower interest and for longer periods. If they cannot pay, lenders expect that the mortgaged buildings will sell for enough to allow them to recover their money.

The amount of money borrowed and the terms of repayment for a real estate loan are described in a **promissory note** or in a *mortgage bond*. The notes and bonds are negotiable instruments. If not paid, the owner can sue to collect. A mortgage or deed of trust serves as an additional instrument to pledge a property as security for the repayment of the debt.

A typical promissory note, used when money is borrowed on real estate, contains the borrower's promise to pay and the terms of the loan. The note lists the interest rate, when and where the payments are due, prepayment rights or charges, and other pertinent information. In Figure 1, for example, prepayment is allowed without penalty; see clause 4. In the note, the borrower agrees to keep payments current and to accept the conditions that will cause the note to default.

Clause 8 makes clear that the note is a personal obligation and liability. In case of failure to repay, the borrower can be sued, as with any other debt. In addition, however, as clause 10 points out, the debt is secured by an accompanying contract—a mortgage, deed of trust, or security deed—which can also be used to protect the lender from loss.

Personal **liability** means that if the property is sold but it does not yield enough to satisfy the lender's claim, the lender may seek a **deficiency judgment** or writ to collect the difference from the borrower. For example, if the lender receives $150,000 after costs from the sale of a foreclosed property on which the debt is $200,000, the lender may seek a judgment of $50,000, which the debtor would have to pay from other assets or from income.

States place many restrictions on deficiency judgments. In some states, they cannot be obtained if the mortgage was taken out in the course of a purchase (a **purchase-money mortgage**). In others, the value of the property must be determined separately, whatever the amount received in the foreclosure sale. Many states require that deficiency judgments will be granted only after costly court procedures and long delays. As a result,

FIGURE 1
A Note to Accompany a Mortgage Contract

NOTE

...., 19............   ...., ...
                                                                    [City]   [State]

....
                                    [Property Address]

1. BORROWER'S PROMISE TO PAY

In return for a loan that I have received, I promise to pay U.S. $.. (this amount is called "principal"), plus interest, to the order of the Lender. The Lender is .... I understand that the Lender may transfer this Note. The Lender or anyone who takes this Note by transfer and who is entitled to receive payments under this Note is called the "Note Holder."

2. INTEREST

Interest will be charged on unpaid principal until the full amount of principal has been paid. I will pay interest at a yearly rate of ....%.

The interest rate required by this Section 2 is the rate I will pay both before and after any default described in Section 6(B) of this Note.

3. PAYMENTS

(A) Time and Place of Payments

I will pay principal and interest by making payments every month.

I will make my monthly payments on the .... day of each month beginning on ...., 19.......... I will make these payments every month until I have paid all of the principal and interest and any other charges described below that I may owe under this Note. My monthly payments will be applied to interest before principal. If, on ...., ..., I still owe amounts under this Note, I will pay those amounts in full on that date, which is called the "maturity date."

I will make my monthly payments at .... or at a different place if required by the Note Holder.

(B) Amount of Monthly Payments

My monthly payment will be in the amount of U.S. $..

4. BORROWER'S RIGHT TO PREPAY

I have the right to make payments of principal at any time before they are due. A payment of principal only is known as a "prepayment." When I make a prepayment, I will tell the Note Holder in writing that I am doing so.

I may make a full prepayment or partial prepayments without paying any prepayment charge. The Note Holder will use all of my prepayments to reduce the amount of principal that I owe under this Note. If I make a partial prepayment, there will be no changes in the due date or in the amount of my monthly payment unless the Note Holder agrees in writing to those changes.

5. LOAN CHARGES

If a law, which applies to this loan and which sets maximum loan charges, is finally interpreted so that the interest or other loan charges collected or to be collected in connection with this loan exceed the permitted limits, then: (i) any such loan charge shall be reduced by the amount necessary to reduce the charge to the permitted limit, and (ii) any sums already collected from me which exceeded permitted limits will be refunded to me. The Note Holder may choose to make this refund by reducing the principal I owe under this Note or by making a direct payment to me. If a refund reduces principal, the reduction will be treated as a partial prepayment.

6. BORROWER'S FAILURE TO PAY AS REQUIRED

(A) Late Charge for Overdue Payments

If the Note Holder has not received the full amount of any monthly payment by the end of .... calendar days after the date it is due, I will pay a late charge to the Note Holder. The amount of the charge will be ....% of my overdue payment of principal and interest. I will pay this late charge promptly but only once on each late payment.

(B) Default

If I do not pay the full amount of each monthly payment on the date it is due, I will be in default.

(C) Notice of Default

If I am in default, the Note Holder may send me a written notice telling me that if I do not pay the overdue amount by a certain date, the Note Holder may require me to pay immediately the full amount of principal which has not been paid and all the interest that I owe on that amount. That date must be at least 30 days after the date on which the notice is delivered or mailed to me.

(D) No Waiver By Note Holder

Even if, at a time when I am in default, the Note Holder does not require me to pay immediately in full as described above, the Note Holder will still have the right to do so if I am in default at a later time.

Continued

FIGURE 1—*Concluded*

(E) Payment of Note Holder's Costs and Expenses
If the Note Holder has required me to pay immediately in full as described above, the Note Holder will have the right to be paid back by me for all of its costs and expenses in enforcing this Note to the extent not prohibited by applicable law. Those expenses include, for example, reasonable attorneys' fees.

7. GIVING OF NOTICES
Unless applicable law requires a different method, any notice that must be given to me under this Note will be given by delivering it or by mailing it by first class mail to me at the Property Address above or at a different address if I give the Note Holder a notice of my different address.

Any notice that must be given to the Note Holder under this Note will be given by mailing it by first class mail to the Note Holder at the address stated in Section 3(A) above or at a different address if I am given a notice of that different address.

8. OBLIGATIONS OF PERSONS UNDER THIS NOTE
If more than one person signs this Note, each person is fully and personally obligated to keep all of the promises made in this Note, including the promise to pay the full amount owed. Any person who is a guarantor, surety or endorser of this Note is also obligated to do these things. Any person who takes over these obligations, including the obligations of a guarantor, surety or endorser of this Note, is also obligated to keep all of the promises made in this Note. The Note Holder may enforce its rights under this Note against each person individually or against all of us together. This means that any one of us may be required to pay all of the amounts owed under this Note.

9. WAIVERS
I and any other person who has obligations under this Note waive the rights of presentment and notice of dishonor. "Presentment" means the right to require the Note Holder to demand payment of amounts due. "Notice of dishonor" means the right to require the Note Holder to give notice to other persons that amounts due have not been paid.

10. UNIFORM SECURED NOTE
This Note is a uniform instrument with limited variations in some jurisdictions. In addition to the protections given to the Note Holder under this Note, a Mortgage, Deed of Trust or Security Deed (the "Security Instrument"), dated the same date as this Note, protects the Note Holder from possible losses which might result if I do not keep the promises which I make in this Note. That Security Instrument describes how and under what conditions I may be required to make immediate payment in full of all amounts I owe under this Note. Some of those conditions are described as follows:

Transfer of the Property or a Beneficial Interest in Borrower. If all or any part of the Property or any interest in it is sold or transferred (or if a beneficial interest in Borrower is sold or transferred and Borrower is not a natural person) without Lender's prior written consent, Lender may, at its option, require immediate payment in full of all sums secured by this Security Instrument. However, this option shall not be exercised by Lender if exercise is prohibited by federal law as of the date of this Security Instrument.

If Lender exercises this option, Lender shall give Borrower notice of acceleration. The notice shall provide a period of not less than 30 days from the date the notice is delivered or mailed within which Borrower must pay all sums secured by this Security Instrument. If Borrower fails to pay these sums prior to the expiration of this period, Lender may invoke any remedies permitted by this Security Instrument without further notice or demand on Borrower.

WITNESS THE HAND(S) AND SEAL(S) OF THE UNDERSIGNED.

....(Seal)
Borrower

....(Seal)
Borrower

....(Seal)
Borrower

[Sign Original Only]

deficiency judgments have become rare, particularly for owner-occupied houses. However, the threat that they might be obtained must be taken into account in proper investment planning.

The last section of the note repeats a very important condition contained in the mortgage. It is a promise called a **due-on-sale clause**. If the borrower sells or transfers the property being used as a security, the lender has the option of requiring immediate payment of all sums still owed. When lenders make a loan, they consider the borrower's credit and reason for borrowing. The due-on-sale clause gives the lender a chance to refuse credit to a poor risk. What is more important is that it allows the lender to renegotiate the terms of the loan. If interest rates have risen, the lender can demand the new, higher market rate.

THE MORTGAGE AND THE DEED OF TRUST

The Mortgage Relationships

As has been noted, a mortgage is a contract that pledges rights in a specific property to insure repayment of a debt. A deed of trust serves the same purpose, but it introduces a trustee between the borrower and the lender. Both mortgages and deeds of trust require a note and a pledge of security for them to fulfill their purpose. Except in a legal context, the term *mortgage* is used generally to describe the many ways in which money can be borrowed with property as security. If also refers to the amount borrowed through a secured loan on real estate. Thus it encompasses deeds of trust as well.

The mortgage part of Figure 2 illustrates a typical mortgage situation. A borrower—also called a debtor or **mortgagor**—gives a note and a mortgage to the lender—also known as the creditor or **mortgagee**—as security for the money lent. Lenders usually *record* the mortgage instrument, for reasons to be discussed later. That is, they file it with the proper official to place it on the public record. When or if the debt is repaid, the mortgagee-lender returns a release for the mortgage.

Title and Lien Theories. Two different theories of the nature of real estate mortgages are found among the states. They are called the title theory and the lien theory. Under the **title theory**, a mortgage transfers legal title to the mortgaged property from the mortgagor-borrower to the mortgagee-lender as a security for the loan. In theory, possession is also

FIGURE 2
The Difference between a Mortgage and a Deed of Trust

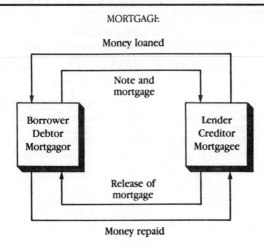

MORTGAGE

Money loaned

Note and
mortgage

Borrower
Debtor
Mortgagor

Lender
Creditor
Mortgagee

Release of
mortgage

Money repaid

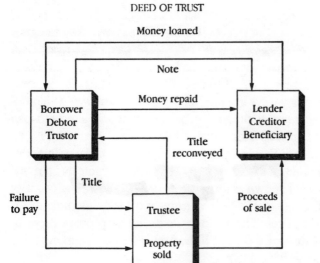

DEED OF TRUST

Money loaned

Note

Borrower
Debtor
Trustor

Money repaid

Lender
Creditor
Beneficiary

Title
reconveyed

Failure
to pay

Title

Trustee

Proceeds
of sale

Property
sold

transferred, but most mortgages in title theory states carry provisions that allow borrowers to keep possession as long as they do not default on their obligation. In case of default, the borrower's rights are terminated and the lender retains title and gains possession.

Most states use the **lien theory**, under which the mortgage creates a **lien**—a claim on the property as security—in favor of the lender. If the borrower fails to pay, the lender can go to court to enforce the lien in order to have the property sold for his benefit. In many states, the mortgage may include a *power of sale* clause, which allows the property to be sold in settlement of a debt without a judicial procedure.

The Deed of Trust

More complex relationships exist in a deed of trust than in a mortgage. Trust deeds introduce a third party at some additional expense, but they cut the cost of obtaining repayment when a security must be sold. The **deed of trust** involves three parties (refer again to Figure 2). The borrower signs a note to the lender—also known as the **beneficiary**—listing the conditions of the loan. The borrower also signs a trust deed that conveys the bare legal title of the property to a **trustee**. Such a deed contains a power of sale that the trustee can exercise if the borrower fails to meet the conditions of the loan. If the property is sold, the proceeds go to the lender-beneficiary. If no default arises, the trustee's title lies dormant. The grantor of the trust retains all normal ownership rights. When the debt is paid off, the trustee reconveys the title.

Although on the surface the deed of trust looks quite different from the mortgage, they serve the same function. Courts tend to treat them similarly. In practice, the variations among states in the ways in which they treat mortgages are greater than the differences between mortgages and trust deeds.

Deeds of trust are not allowed in all states. Where they exist, they are advantageous to lenders because they facilitate the foreclosure process. They tend to reduce slightly the interest rates compared to a standard mortgage.

THE STANDARD FIXED-RATE MORTGAGE

Many types of agreements can be entered into and secured by mortgages. These days, fewer contracts are of the kind traditionally considered standard. The number of payment patterns has been proliferating. However, an examination of the standard or **fixed-rate mortgage (FRM)** remains a good starting point. By first understanding the features of the standard mortgage, we gain a better grasp of why and how other types of agreement have evolved.

Mortgage Payments

How much a borrower must pay monthly, quarterly, or in total depends on the amount of the loan, on the interest and fees charged, and on the rate at which the debt is paid off or decreased.

1. The amount of money owed as debt is called the **principal**. In the usual case, lenders furnish cash. However, buyers often take over debts already in existence, and sellers often accept debt for part of their payment.
2. Lenders may charge a **loan fee**—typically from 1 percent to 3 percent of the amount lent. The fee may have to be paid at the time of the loan, or it may be included in the principal.
3. **Interest** is the charge for the use of money. It is usually expressed as a given percent per year of the principal. For example, a charge of $10 (the interest) for one year on a loan of $100 (the principal) yields a simple interest rate of 10 percent a year.
4. Loans must be repaid in a certain period. The length of this period is called the **term** of the loan—for example, 5, 15, or 30 years. The date of the final payment is the **maturity date** for the loan.
5. Most loans require repayment of part of the principal on an installment basis. In a standard mortgage, each monthly payment pays off some of the principal. The process of periodic repayment is called **amortization**.
6. The amount of each payment stated as a percent of the total loan is called the **mortgage constant**, or K. If the monthly payment on a $100,000 loan is $1,000, the monthly mortgage constant is 1 percent. In annual terms, if the annual payment is $12,000, the annual mortgage constant is 12 percent.

   The amount of each payment is determined by the principal, interest rates, the term, and the form of amortization. Lenders set quite firm limits on the relationship between a borrower's or a property's income and payments. Amortization agreements must often be adjusted to arrive at periodic payments low enough to meet the lender's standards.

TABLE 1

Annual Summary of Monthly Payments (On a $50,000 30-Year Mortgage at 12 Percent Interest)

Year	Annual Debt Service	Interest	Principal	Cumulative Principal Payments	End-of-Year Principal Balance
1	$6,171.60	$5,990.20	$ 181.40	$ 181.40	$49,818.60
2	6,171.60	5,967.20	204.40	385.80	49,614.20
10	6,171.60	5,640.20	531.40	3,291.00	46,709.00
20	6,171.60	4,417.70	1,753.90	14,152.60	35,847.40
28	6,171.60	1,612.80	4,558.80	39,074.40	10,925.60
29	6,171.60	1,034.60	5,137.00	44,211.40	5,788.60
30	6,171.60	383.10	5,788.50	50,000.00	0.00

Equal Level Payments

The standard fixed-rate mortgage calls for equal monthly payments. Some of each payment goes to pay the required interest and some pays off part of the principal. Because the outstanding balance declines each month, the amount owed for interest on the outstanding principal also declines. This allows the sum applied to reducing the principal to increase each month.

Example. Suppose that you borrow $50,000 on a mortgage at 12 percent interest and a term of 30 years. Table 1 contains an exerpt from a standard compound interest table summarizing the division of each payment between interest and principal. We note from column 2 that such a mortgage requires a monthly payment of $514.30 or $6,171.60 per year for each of the 30 years. Columns 3 and 4 demonstrate that in the first year most of your loan payments would be applied to cover the interest due, with the total reduction in principal being only $181.40, or less than .5 percent of the amount outstanding. However, the share going to interest declines every month because the interest rate applies against a smaller principal. Still, since so little has been paid off in the first year, most of your payments in the second year also go to interest, with the principal repayment rising only slightly. While the balance has shifted somewhat by the tenth year, 90 percent of the payment still covers interest.

In the final column, note that even after you have made payments for 10 years, less than 7 percent of the debt is paid off. By year 20, principal payments are more significant, but they still remain below one-third of the annual payment. Very few people stay in one house and make mortgage payments on it for 30 years, but it is only toward the end of the life of the loan that the amount going to principal increases sharply.

Figure 3 illustrates more completely how the standard FRM works. Part A shows the gradual drop in the share of the payment going to interest. The decline in interest on the amount owed becomes rapid only in the last one third of the loan period. Part B shows that even though the interest requirements decrease steadily, only after half the life of the loan does the gradual increase in monthly amortization have much effect on the amount outstanding.

Prepayments

The standard FRM usually lets the borrower pay off the loan faster than agreed to in the mortgage. The ability of borrowers to prepay either part or all of the principal is a **prepayment privilege**. A **closed mortgage** does not allow prepayment; an **open mortgage** does. Most single-family home mortgages are open, but they usually specify a prepayment penalty if more than some share—perhaps 20 percent—is paid off in any of the first five years. Such penalties are set by agreement. A common penalty might be six months' interest, or the penalty might be between 1 percent and 5 percent of the amount paid off.

This penalty is assessed because lenders may lose money when a mortgage is prepaid. Loan fees do not cover the entire cost of making a mortgage. If interest rates have dropped, the lender will receive less income because the amount repaid must be reloaned at a lower interest rate. In recent years, many mortgages on income properties have been closed for five to seven years, with penalties charged on prepayments that occur after the mortgage becomes open.

Loan Terms and Monthly Payments

Since payments depend on both the interest rate and the term, altering either will modify the amount required to be paid monthly. The lower the amount of payment required per dollar of loan, the larger the loan a borrower can afford, since less income is required to qualify for a loan of a given size.

Standard payment tables, such as Table 2, summarize the relationships between the required payments, interest rates, and the term of a loan.

FIGURE 3
Amortization of a Loan

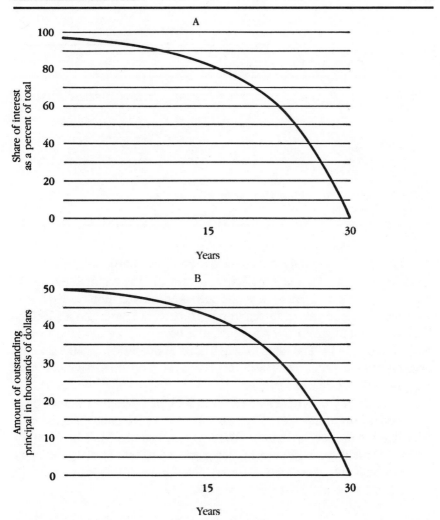

Amortization slowly decreases the share of a fixed mortgage payment going to interest and raises the share going to principal. In this example of a $50,000 12 percent loan for 30 years, the percent of each payment going to interest declines year by year (A), while the amount of principal still owed remains high until near the end of the loan period (B).

TABLE 2
Monthly Payments to Amortize a $10,000 Loan in a Given Period

Terms in Years	Monthly Payments	Interest Rates					
		6%	8%	10%	12%	14%	16%
5	60	$193.33	$202.76	$212.47	$222.44	$232.68	$243.18
10	120	111.02	121.33	132.15	143.47	155.27	167.51
15	180	84.39	95.57	107.46	120.02	133.17	146.87
20	240	71.64	83.64	96.50	110.11	124.35	139.13
25	300	64.43	77.18	90.87	105.32	120.38	135.89
30	360	59.96	73.38	87.76	102.86	118.49	134.48
35	420	57.02	71.03	85.97	101.55	117.57	133.85
40	480	55.02	69.53	84.91	100.85	117.11	133.56

To amortize a $10,000 loan at 12 percent interest in 30 years, a borrower must pay $102.86 per month for 360 months.

The table lists the monthly installments to amortize a $10,000 mortgage at different interest rates and a variety of maturities. The required payments rise with interest rates and fall as the period of amortization extends. For example, if the borrower agrees to pay 16 percent interest on a $10,000 loan and to amortize it over 5 years, the borrower would have to pay $243.13 per month. The same loan at 6 percent interest and a 40-year amortization would require only $55.02 per month. Of course, payments also increase with the size of the loan.

Standard payment tables enable us to find the monthly or annual payments on a loan of any size. For example, to find the annual payment of $6,171.60 in the second column of Table 2-1, take the $102.86 monthly payment on a 30-year 12 percent mortgage of $10,000 from Table 2 and multiply by 5 to find the amount of payment for a $50,000 loan. Multiply again by 12 to obtain the annual payment.

AFFORDABILITY

Lenders normally restrict the amount they will lend so that the monthly payment to cover principal, interest, and (frequently) property taxes and insurance (P.I.T.I.) does not exceed a certain percentage either of a family's income or of the cash flow on an income property. Thus, both income and the size of the required payment determine how much can be borrowed. This concept, under which income and the required payment limit the ability to borrow enough to purchase a property, is called **affordability**. It plays a central role in all real estate financing.

Income Limits

Example.　Assume that a lender restricts the amount of a mortgage payment to 25 percent of a family's income. How much could a family with a monthly income of $1,755 afford to borrow for a house? Three separate factors are involved in setting the maximum mortgage the family could obtain:

1. The amount of the family's income.
2. The limit on the share of the family income that lenders will permit to be allocated to the mortgage payment.
3. The amount of the mortgage payment, which depends on the interest rate and term to maturity.

If the family's income is $1,755 per month and lenders limit the mortgage payment of 25 percent of family income, the family could borrow as much as could be paid for with a payment of $438 per month. By dividing this sum by the required payments for a loan like that shown in Table 2, we can find the maximum loan amount allowed.

If interest rates were 10 percent, dividing the amount the family could afford by the payment per $10,000 ($438 ÷ $212), the family could borrow only about $20,000 if the loan had to be amortized over 5 years. In contrast, over $50,000 ($438 ÷ $85) could be borrowed if the amortization period was 40 years. Similarly, the table shows that the amounts that could be borrowed rise from under $20,000 ($438 ÷ $243) for a 5-year loan at 16 percent to almost $80,000 ($438 ÷ $55) for a 40-year loan at 6 percent interest—all for a family with $1,755 per month income. Note that the lower the interest, the more important the amortization period is in determining the size of the loan.

The Amount of Amortization

In order to increase the amount of a loan obtainable with a given income level, nonstandard mortgages have become more common. They have been especially prevalent in mortgages on income properties and in cases where sellers have financed a sale themselves. In many cases, for example, loans may be made without any amortization requirement. In an **interest-only loan**, the monthly payments cover the required interest. After a set period—say, five years—the entire principal must be repaid. In some cases **negative amortization**, in which payments are less than the interest owed, is permitted. The difference between the interest charge and the payment is added (or *accrues*) to the principal. When the mortgage becomes due, all the principal and accrued interest must be paid off.

Other agreements allow the amount of the payments to vary over time; either the interest charges or the rate of amortization may shift. A common method bases the amount of amortization on a period extending beyond the maturity date of the mortgage. For example, the level of monthly payments may be set at a rate that would amortize a loan over 30 years. In addition, the note requires that at the end of five years a payment must be made sufficient to repay all remaining principal. In these and similar examples, the final larger installment is called a **balloon payment**.

Loan-to-Value Ratio

Affordability can also be affected by the required down payment. To protect the safety of deposit institutions and insurance companies, laws and regulations commonly restrict the amount most lenders can lend to a maximum percent of the appraised value of a property (or the selling price, if it is less). This maximum is usually expressed as a percentage of the value and is called the **loan-to-value ratio (LTV)**. For example, a $50,000 mortgage on a house valued at $62,500 is said to have a loan-to-value ratio of 80 percent, or to be an 80 percent mortgage. This is typical, but the LTV may go up to 90 or 95 percent if mortgage insurance is obtained.

RIGHTS AND RESPONSIBILITIES OF BORROWERS AND LENDERS

Figure 4 is a uniform deed of trust. The Federal National Mortgage Association (Fannie Mae) and the Federal Home Loan Mortgage Corporation (Freddie Mac) require that this form be used for deeds of trust to be sold to them. There are only minor differences between this form and that which they require for mortgages. Both contain typical conditions outlining the rights and responsibilities of the lender and the borrower. This first page specifies the borrower, the lender, the trustee, and the property. It also

FIGURE 4
A Deed of Trust

--------------------------------- [Space Above This Line For Recording Data] ---------------------------------

DEED OF TRUST

THIS DEED OF TRUST ("Security Instrument") is made on ....,
19............ The trustor is ....
.... ("Borrower"). The trustee is ....
.... ("Trustee"). The beneficiary is
...., which is organized and existing
under the laws of ...., and whose address is ....
.... ("Lender").
Borrower owes Lender the principal sum of ....
.... Dollars (U.S. $................................). This debt is evidenced by Borrower's note
dated the same date as this Security Instrument ("Note"), which provides for monthly payments, with the full debt, if not
paid earlier, due and payable on .... This Security Instrument
secures to Lender: (a) the repayment of the debt evidenced by the Note, with interest, and all renewals, extensions and
modifications; (b) the payment of all other sums, with interest, advanced under paragraph 7 to protect the security of this
Security Instrument; and (c) the performance of Borrower's covenants and agreements under this Security Instrument and
the Note. For this purpose, Borrower irrevocably grants and conveys to Trustee, in trust, with power of sale, the following
described property located in .... County, California:

which has the address of ....
                                      [Street]   [City]
California .... ("Property Address");
             [Zip Code]

TOGETHER WITH all the improvements now or hereafter erected on the property, and all easements, rights,
appurtenances, rents, royalties, mineral, oil and gas rights and profits, water rights and stock and all fixtures now or
hereafter a part of the property. All replacements and additions shall also be covered by this Security Instrument. All of the
foregoing is referred to in this Security Instrument as the "Property."

BORROWER COVENANTS that Borrower is lawfully seised of the estate hereby conveyed and has the right to grant
and convey the Property and that the Property is unencumbered, except for encumbrances of record. Borrower warrants
and will defend generally the title to the Property against all claims and demands, subject to any encumbrances of record.

THIS SECURITY INSTRUMENT combines uniform covenants for national use and non-uniform covenants with
limited variations by jurisdiction to constitute a uniform security instrument covering real property.

CALIFORNIA—Single Family—**FNMA/FHLMC UNIFORM INSTRUMENT**   **Form 3005 12/83**

FIGURE 4—*Continued*

UNIFORM COVENANTS. Borrower and Lender covenant and agree as follows:

1. Payment of Principal and Interest; Prepayment and Late Charges. Borrower shall promptly pay when due the principal of and interest on the debt evidenced by the Note and any prepayment and late charges due under the Note.

2. Funds for Taxes and Insurance. Subject to applicable law or to a written waiver by Lender, Borrower shall pay to Lender on the day monthly payments are due under the Note, until the Note is paid in full, a sum ("Funds") equal to one-twelfth of: (a) yearly taxes and assessments which may attain priority over this Security Instrument; (b) yearly leasehold payments or ground rents on the Property, if any; (c) yearly hazard insurance premiums; and (d) yearly mortgage insurance premiums, if any. These items are called "escrow items." Lender may estimate the Funds due on the basis of current data and reasonable estimates of future escrow items.

The Funds shall be held in an institution the deposits or accounts of which are insured or guaranteed by a federal or state agency (including Lender if Lender is such an institution). Lender shall apply the Funds to pay the escrow items. Lender may not charge for holding and applying the Funds, analyzing the account or verifying the escrow items, unless Lender pays Borrower interest on the Funds and applicable law permits Lender to make such a charge. Borrower and Lender may agree in writing that interest shall be paid on the Funds. Unless an agreement is made or applicable law requires interest to be paid, Lender shall not be required to pay Borrower any interest or earnings on the Funds. Lender shall give to Borrower, without charge, an annual accounting of the Funds showing credits and debits to the Funds and the purpose for which each debit to the Funds was made. The Funds are pledged as additional security for the sums secured by this Security Instrument.

If the amount of the Funds held by Lender, together with the future monthly payments of Funds payable prior to the due dates of the escrow items, shall exceed the amount required to pay the escrow items when due, the excess shall be, at Borrower's option, either promptly repaid to Borrower or credited to Borrower on monthly payments of Funds. If the amount of the Funds held by Lender is not sufficient to pay the escrow items when due, Borrower shall pay to Lender any amount necessary to make up the deficiency in one or more payments as required by Lender.

Upon payment in full of all sums secured by this Security Instrument, Lender shall promptly refund to Borrower any Funds held by Lender. If under paragraph 19 the Property is sold or acquired by Lender, Lender shall apply, no later than immediately prior to the sale of the Property or its acquisition by Lender, any Funds held by Lender at the time of application as a credit against the sums secured by this Security Instrument.

3. Application of Payments. Unless applicable law provides otherwise, all payments received by Lender under paragraphs 1 and 2 shall be applied: first, to late charges due under the Note; second, to prepayment charges due under the Note; third, to amounts payable under paragraph 2; fourth, to interest due; and last, to principal due.

4. Charges; Liens. Borrower shall pay all taxes, assessments, charges, fines and impositions attributable to the Property which may attain priority over this Security Instrument, and leasehold payments or ground rents, if any. Borrower shall pay these obligations in the manner provided in paragraph 2, or if not paid in that manner, Borrower shall pay them on time directly to the person owed payment. Borrower shall promptly furnish to Lender all notices of amounts to be paid under this paragraph. If Borrower makes these payments directly, Borrower shall promptly furnish to Lender receipts evidencing the payments.

Borrower shall promptly discharge any lien which has priority over this Security Instrument unless Borrower: (a) agrees in writing to the payment of the obligation secured by the lien in a manner acceptable to Lender; (b) contests in good faith the lien by, or defends against enforcement of the lien in, legal proceedings which in the Lender's opinion operate to prevent the enforcement of the lien or forfeiture of any part of the Property; or (c) secures from the holder of the lien an agreement satisfactory to Lender subordinating the lien to this Security Instrument. If Lender determines that any part of the Property is subject to a lien which may attain priority over this Security Instrument, Lender may give Borrower a notice identifying the lien. Borrower shall satisfy the lien or take one or more of the actions set forth above within 10 days of the giving of notice.

5. Hazard Insurance. Borrower shall keep the improvements now existing or hereafter erected on the Property insured against loss by fire, hazards included within the term "extended coverage" and any other hazards for which Lender requires insurance. This insurance shall be maintained in the amounts and for the periods that Lender requires. The insurance carrier providing the insurance shall be chosen by Borrower subject to Lender's approval which shall not be unreasonably withheld.

All insurance policies and renewals shall be acceptable to Lender and shall include a standard mortgage clause. Lender shall have the right to hold the policies and renewals. If Lender requires, Borrower shall promptly give to Lender all receipts of paid premiums and renewal notices. In the event of loss, Borrower shall give prompt notice to the insurance carrier and Lender. Lender may make proof of loss if not made promptly by Borrower.

Unless Lender and Borrower otherwise agree in writing, insurance proceeds shall be applied to restoration or repair of the Property damaged, if the restoration or repair is economically feasible and Lender's security is not lessened. If the restoration or repair is not economically feasible or Lender's security would be lessened, the insurance proceeds shall be applied to the sums secured by this Security Instrument, whether or not then due, with any excess paid to Borrower. If Borrower abandons the Property, or does not answer within 30 days a notice from Lender that the insurance carrier has offered to settle a claim, then Lender may collect the insurance proceeds. Lender may use the proceeds to repair or restore the Property or to pay sums secured by this Security Instrument, whether or not then due. The 30-day period will begin when the notice is given.

Unless Lender and Borrower otherwise agree in writing, any application of proceeds to principal shall not extend or postpone the due date of the monthly payments referred to in paragraphs 1 and 2 or change the amount of the payments. If under paragraph 19 the Property is acquired by Lender, Borrower's right to any insurance policies and proceeds resulting from damage to the Property prior to the acquisition shall pass to Lender to the extent of the sums secured by this Security Instrument immediately prior to the acquisition.

6. Preservation and Maintenance of Property; Leaseholds. Borrower shall not destroy, damage or substantially change the Property, allow the Property to deteriorate or commit waste. If this Security Instrument is on a leasehold, Borrower shall comply with the provisions of the lease, and if Borrower acquires fee title to the Property, the leasehold and fee title shall not merge unless Lender agrees to the merger in writing.

7. Protection of Lender's Rights in the Property; Mortgage Insurance. If Borrower fails to perform the covenants and agreements contained in this Security Instrument, or there is a legal proceeding that may significantly affect Lender's rights in the Property (such as a proceeding in bankruptcy, probate, for condemnation or to enforce laws or

Continued

FIGURE 4—*Continued*

regulations), then Lender may do and pay for whatever is necessary to protect the value of the Property and Lender's rights in the Property. Lender's actions may include paying any sums secured by a lien which has priority over this Security Instrument, appearing in court, paying reasonable attorneys' fees and entering on the Property to make repairs. Although Lender may take action under this paragraph 7, Lender does not have to do so.

Any amounts disbursed by Lender under this paragraph 7 shall become additional debt of Borrower secured by this Security Instrument. Unless Borrower and Lender agree to other terms of payment, these amounts shall bear interest from the date of disbursement at the Note rate and shall be payable, with interest, upon notice from Lender to Borrower requesting payment.

If Lender required mortgage insurance as a condition of making the loan secured by this Security Instrument, Borrower shall pay the premiums required to maintain the insurance in effect until such time as the requirement for the insurance terminates in accordance with Borrower's and Lender's written agreement or applicable law.

8. Inspection. Lender or its agent may make reasonable entries upon and inspections of the Property. Lender shall give Borrower notice at the time of or prior to an inspection specifying reasonable cause for the inspection.

9. Condemnation. The proceeds of any award or claim for damages, direct or consequential, in connection with any condemnation or other taking of any part of the Property, or for conveyance in lieu of condemnation, are hereby assigned and shall be paid to Lender.

In the event of a total taking of the Property, the proceeds shall be applied to the sums secured by this Security Instrument, whether or not then due, with any excess paid to Borrower. In the event of a partial taking of the Property, unless Borrower and Lender otherwise agree in writing, the sums secured by this Security Instrument shall be reduced by the amount of the proceeds multiplied by the following fraction: (a) the total amount of the sums secured immediately before the taking, divided by (b) the fair market value of the Property immediately before the taking. Any balance shall be paid to Borrower.

If the Property is abandoned by Borrower, or if, after notice by Lender to Borrower that the condemnor offers to make an award or settle a claim for damages, Borrower fails to respond to Lender within 30 days after the date the notice is given, Lender is authorized to collect and apply the proceeds, at its option, either to restoration or repair of the Property or to the sums secured by this Security Instrument, whether or not then due.

Unless Lender and Borrower otherwise agree in writing, any application of proceeds to principal shall not extend or postpone the due date of the monthly payments referred to in paragraphs 1 and 2 or change the amount of such payments.

10. Borrower Not Released; Forbearance By Lender Not a Waiver. Extension of the time for payment or modification of amortization of the sums secured by this Security Instrument granted by Lender to any successor in interest of Borrower shall not operate to release the liability of the original Borrower or Borrower's successors in interest. Lender shall not be required to commence proceedings against any successor in interest or refuse to extend time for payment or otherwise modify amortization of the sums secured by this Security Instrument by reason of any demand made by the original Borrower or Borrower's successors in interest. Any forbearance by Lender in exercising any right or remedy shall not be a waiver of or preclude the exercise of any right or remedy.

11. Successors and Assigns Bound; Joint and Several Liability; Co-signers. The covenants and agreements of this Security Instrument shall bind and benefit the successors and assigns of Lender and Borrower, subject to the provisions of paragraph 17. Borrower's covenants and agreements shall be joint and several. Any Borrower who co-signs this Security Instrument but does not execute the Note: (a) is co-signing this Security Instrument only to mortgage, grant and convey that Borrower's interest in the Property under the terms of this Security Instrument; (b) is not personally obligated to pay the sums secured by this Security Instrument; and (c) agrees that Lender and any other Borrower may agree to extend, modify, forbear or make any accommodations with regard to the terms of this Security Instrument or the Note without that Borrower's consent.

12. Loan Charges. If the loan secured by this Security Instrument is subject to a law which sets maximum loan charges, and that law is finally interpreted so that the interest or other loan charges collected or to be collected in connection with the loan exceed the permitted limits, then: (a) any such loan charge shall be reduced by the amount necessary to reduce the charge to the permitted limit; and (b) any sums already collected from Borrower which exceeded permitted limits will be refunded to Borrower. Lender may choose to make this refund by reducing the principal owed under the Note or by making a direct payment to Borrower. If a refund reduces principal, the reduction will be treated as a partial prepayment without any prepayment charge under the Note.

13. Legislation Affecting Lender's Rights. If enactment or expiration of applicable laws has the effect of rendering any provision of the Note or this Security Instrument unenforceable according to its terms, Lender, at its option, may require immediate payment in full of all sums secured by this Security Instrument and may invoke any remedies permitted by paragraph 19. If Lender exercises this option, Lender shall take the steps specified in the second paragraph of paragraph 17.

14. Notices. Any notice to Borrower provided for in this Security Instrument shall be given by delivering it or by mailing it by first class mail unless applicable law requires use of another method. The notice shall be directed to the Property Address or any other address Borrower designates by notice to Lender. Any notice to Lender shall be given by first class mail to Lender's address stated herein or any other address Lender designates by notice to Borrower. Any notice provided for in this Security Instrument shall be deemed to have been given to Borrower or Lender when given as provided in this paragraph.

15. Governing Law; Severability. This Security Instrument shall be governed by federal law and the law of the jurisdiction in which the Property is located. In the event that any provision or clause of this Security Instrument or the Note conflicts with applicable law, such conflict shall not affect other provisions of this Security Instrument or the Note which can be given effect without the conflicting provision. To this end the provisions of this Security Instrument and the Note are declared to be severable.

16. Borrower's Copy. Borrower shall be given one conformed copy of the Note and of this Security Instrument.

17. Transfer of the Property or a Beneficial Interest in Borrower. If all or any part of the Property or any interest in it is sold or transferred (or if a beneficial interest in Borrower is sold or transferred and Borrower is not a natural person) without Lender's prior written consent, Lender may, at its option, require immediate payment in full of all sums secured by this Security Instrument. However, this option shall not be exercised by Lender if exercise is prohibited by federal law as of the date of this Security Instrument.

FIGURE 4—*Continued*

If Lender exercises this option, Lender shall give Borrower notice of acceleration. The notice shall provide a period of not less than 30 days from the date the notice is delivered or mailed within which Borrower must pay all sums secured by this Security Instrument. If Borrower fails to pay these sums prior to the expiration of this period, Lender may invoke any remedies permitted by this Security Instrument without further notice or demand on Borrower.

18. Borrower's Right to Reinstate. If Borrower meets certain conditions, Borrower shall have the right to have enforcement of this Security Instrument discontinued at any time prior to the earlier of: (a) 5 days (or such other period as applicable law may specify for reinstatement) before sale of the Property pursuant to any power of sale contained in this Security Instrument; or (b) entry of a judgment enforcing this Security Instrument. Those conditions are that Borrower: (a) pays Lender all sums which then would be due under this Security Instrument and the Note had no acceleration occurred; (b) cures any default of any other covenants or agreements; (c) pays all expenses incurred in enforcing this Security Instrument, including, but not limited to, reasonable attorneys' fees; and (d) takes such action as Lender may reasonably require to assure that the lien of this Security Instrument, Lender's rights in the Property and Borrower's obligation to pay the sums secured by this Security Instrument shall continue unchanged. Upon reinstatement by Borrower, this Security Instrument and the obligations secured hereby shall remain fully effective as if no acceleration had occurred. However, this right to reinstate shall not apply in the case of acceleration under paragraphs 13 or 17.

NON-UNIFORM COVENANTS Borrower and Lender further covenant and agree as follows:

19. Acceleration; Remedies. Lender shall give notice to Borrower prior to acceleration following Borrower's breach of any covenant or agreement in this Security Instrument (but not prior to acceleration under paragraphs 13 and 17 unless applicable law provides otherwise). The notice shall specify: (a) the default; (b) the action required to cure the default; (c) a date, not less than 30 days from the date the notice is given to Borrower, by which the default must be cured; and (d) that failure to cure the default on or before the date specified in the notice may result in acceleration of the sums secured by this Security Instrument and sale of the Property. The notice shall further inform Borrower of the right to reinstate after acceleration and the right to bring a court action to assert the non-existence of a default or any other defense of Borrower to acceleration and sale. If the default is not cured on or before the date specified in the notice, Lender at its option may require immediate payment in full of all sums secured by this Security Instrument without further demand and may invoke the power of sale and any other remedies permitted by applicable law. Lender shall be entitled to collect all expenses incurred in pursuing the remedies provided in this paragraph 19, including, but not limited to, reasonable attorneys' fees and costs of title evidence.

If Lender invokes the power of sale, Lender shall execute or cause Trustee to execute a written notice of the occurrence of an event of default and of Lender's election to cause the Property to be sold. Trustee shall cause this notice to be recorded in each county in which any part of the Property is located. Lender or Trustee shall mail copies of the notice as prescribed by applicable law to Borrower and to the other persons prescribed by applicable law. Trustee shall give public notice of sale to the persons and in the manner prescribed by applicable law. After the time required by applicable law, Trustee, without demand on Borrower, shall sell the Property at public auction to the highest bidder at the time and place and under the terms designated in the notice of sale in one or more parcels and in any order Trustee determines. Trustee may postpone sale of all or any parcel of the Property by public announcement at the time and place of any previously scheduled sale. Lender or its designee may purchase the Property at any sale.

Trustee shall deliver to the purchaser Trustee's deed conveying the Property without any covenant or warranty, expressed or implied. The recitals in the Trustee's deed shall be prima facie evidence of the truth of the statements made therein. Trustee shall apply the proceeds of the sale in the following order: (a) to all expenses of the sale, including, but not limited to, reasonable Trustee's and attorneys' fees; (b) to all sums secured by this Security Instrument; and (c) any excess to the person or persons legally entitled to it.

20. Lender in Possession. Upon acceleration under paragraph 19 or abandonment of the Property, Lender (in person, by agent or by judicially appointed receiver) shall be entitled to enter upon, take possession of and manage the Property and to collect the rents of the Property including those past due. Any rents collected by Lender or the receiver shall be applied first to payment of the costs of management of the Property and collection of rents, including, but not limited to, receiver's fees, premiums on receiver's bonds and reasonable attorneys' fees, and then to the sums secured by this Security Instrument.

21. Reconveyance. Upon payment of all sums secured by this Security Instrument, Lender shall request Trustee to reconvey the Property and shall surrender this Security Instrument and all notes evidencing debt secured by this Security Instrument to Trustee. Trustee shall reconvey the Property without warranty and without charge to the person or persons legally entitled to it. Such person or persons shall pay any recordation costs.

22. Substitute Trustee. Lender, at its option, may from time to time appoint a successor trustee to any Trustee appointed hereunder by an instrument executed and acknowledged by Lender and recorded in the office of the Recorder of the county in which the Property is located. The instrument shall contain the name of the original Lender, Trustee and Borrower, the book and page where this Security Instrument is recorded and the name and address of the successor trustee. Without conveyance of the Property, the successor trustee shall succeed to all the title, powers and duties conferred upon the Trustee herein and by applicable law. This procedure for substitution of trustee shall govern to the exclusion of all other provisions for substitution.

23. Request for Notices. Borrower requests that copies of the notices of default and sale be sent to Borrower's address which is the Property Address.

24. Riders to this Security Instrument. If one or more riders are executed by Borrower and recorded together with this Security Instrument, the covenants and agreements of each such rider shall be incorporated into and shall amend and supplement the covenants and agreements of this Security Instrument as if the rider(s) were a part of this Security Instrument. [Check applicable box(es)]

☐ Adjustable Rate Rider	☐ Condominium Rider	☐ 2–4 Family Rider
☐ Graduated Payment Rider	☐ Planned Unit Development Rider	
☐ Other(s) [specify]		

Continued

FIGURE 4—Concluded

BY SIGNING BELOW. Borrower accepts and agrees to the terms and covenants contained in this Security Instrument and in any rider(s) executed by Borrower and recorded with it.

....(Seal)
—Borrower

....(Seal)
—Borrower

———————————————— [Space Below This Line For Acknowledgment] ————————————————

refers to the underlying note and states that the borrower has the right to pledge the security.

The Covenants

The following sections outline agreements about the specific rights and duties of borrower and lender, called **covenants**. They enumerate special fees and charges as well as action to be taken if certain legal eventualities occur. They also require the borrower to keep adequate hazard insurance and to maintain the condition of the property. The lender can inspect the property to see that no waste is occurring. The covenants give the lender other rights, such as to take possession and manage the property under certain conditions and to substitute trustees. The lender agrees to request a reconveyance when all debts are paid.

Other clauses tend to be less uniform from one document to another, differing in accordance with agreements between the parties. Mortgages on income properties will have many more clauses which may require detailed individual bargaining.

Escrows.   Clause 2 of the deed of trust provides that the borrower will pay with the monthly mortgage payment the amount needed to cover taxes and insurance. The lender will hold these sums in *escrow* (in trust) until they are needed to pay these items. Such arrangements reduce the risk to the lender that insurance will lapse or that unpaid taxes will become a lien prior to the debt. Many mortgages, however, do not require escrows.

Assumptions. Clauses 10 and 17 deal with the question of **assumptions,** which are agreements that shift the duty to repay the debt to the buyer, and the right to sell the property *subject to a mortgage.*

If not prohibited by a clause such as 17, owners of properties may sell them subject to an existing mortgage. If the mortgage has an interest rate below the current market, continuing the mortgage will be advantageous to the borrower. Also, fees or costs that might be demanded if a new mortgage loan were made can be avoided by selling subject to the existing mortgage.

If a property is sold in this manner, the new buyer usually agrees to assume and become responsible for the mortgage payments and to make them directly to the lender. In the example, because a due-on-sale clause (17) is included, the debt will become due in full if the transfer occurs without the permission of the lender. Lenders usually grant permission for a new buyer to assume the loan if they are paid a fee or if an agreement is reached for a higher interest rate.

Releases. Clause 10 provides that even if a lender agrees to an assumption by a new purchaser, the lender need not **release** the original borrower from any obligation. In case of default, the original borrower still remains responsible for the debt. However, if the buyer has a good credit rating, the lender may be willing to substitute a new note and release the original borrower.

Many borrowers do not worry about the lack of a release, particularly on individual houses. The lender's first claim is against the new buyer. Furthermore, in most states deficiency judgments against the original borrower would be difficult or impossible to obtain. In addition, sellers may feel that, having received some payment for the sale from the new buyer, they would not mind getting the property back, since it is worth more than the loan. However, if the amount they received was low or most of it went to cover selling costs, they might find that the debt owed exceeded the value of the property.

Acceleration. Clause 19 is a general acceleration clause in addition to the specific one that applies if a sale occurs. The lender has the right to claim the trust deed to be in default if the borrower fails to live up to any of the agreements or covenants. Upon **acceleration,** all amounts owed, including the entire debt, become due and payable immediately. Clause 19 also spells out the steps the borrower can take to halt acceleration and clear the default and the duties of the trustee if this clause is invoked.

The Right to Reinstate.   Clause 18 outlines the conditions under which the borrower can reinstate the loan with its original terms. Even after the acceleration clause is invoked because of the failure to meet a covenant, the borrower has a limited period in which to correct any default.

DEFAULTS AND FORECLOSURES

Defaults

Probably more than two million deficiencies occur on mortgages every year. Borrowers are late in making payments (especially at Christmastime); tax or insurance bills get mislaid; properties are sold without notifying the lender. Each of these lapses creates a **default**, or failure by the borrower to perform according to agreement. A breach of any covenant is a default. It gives the lender the right to **foreclose**—that is, to force the sale of the property pledged as security in order to obtain funds to pay off the debt.

For most deficiencies and certain defaults, the lender takes no legal action; instead, a late payment penalty may be assessed. In more serious cases, where the ability to pay declines because of loss of a job, divorce, or death, the lender may extend the period of payment or recast the loan by altering the terms of payment. These are examples of **forbearance**, or the taking of more lenient action than allowed by law.

If the default cannot be cured, lenders may seek a **deed in lieu of foreclosure** in order to avoid costs and delays. If a borrower voluntarily grants a deed and possession, the lender will reconvey the mortgage. The borrower may simply want out of the agreement and may also want to avoid the stigma of foreclosure. Both sides save time and money by avoiding legal and court costs.

The Time to Gain Possession

The length of time required to foreclose a mortgage varies from one month to over two years. Three to four months is most typical. In recent years, many foreclosures have taken far longer, up to three or four years, because owners have declared themselves bankrupt to forestall foreclosure. Further, bankruptcy judges have wide powers and often delay foreclosure proceedings in an effort to make additional amounts available to other creditors.

In all states, there is some minimum period within which those who would lose by a foreclosure may reinstate their rights to the property by paying off the debt. This right existing prior to foreclosure is called an **equity of redemption**. In addition, about half the states grant a **statutory right of redemption** *after* foreclosure, which may result in further delays. This right gives borrowers a period after foreclosure in which to regain their property by paying off all debts owed. This period may be as long as a year, depending on the state. During this time the creditor and the property remain in a suspended state.

Foreclosure by Judicial Sale

If all else fails, the lender will foreclose. In most states this can be accomplished either by a judicial sale or by power of sale. Under the procedure of a **judicial sale**, the lender requests the court to sell the mortgaged property in order to obtain funds to repay the debt. A court hearing is required to determine that all rights have been respected and to make sure that all obligations, such as informing interested parties, have been carried out. Next, the court orders a public sale. The time and conditions of such sales differ depending on the law of each state.

Sales are conducted by a sheriff or a court officer. The results of the bidding are reported to the court, which confirms the sale if it appears reasonable. After a statutory period of redemption, the successful bidder receives a deed from the court. All junior liens named in the foreclosure proceedings are wiped out. (Junior liens are discussed in the next section.)

Usually the highest bid is made by the lender on the first mortgage in an amount equal to the debt. By bidding the amount owed, he obtains the property without having to put up more money and insures that no other bidder gets it for less than the outstanding loan. If any higher bids are received funds from the sale go first to pay the cost of the sale and then to repay the foreclosing creditor. In the usual case of a surplus, it is used to pay off junior liens in the order of their priority. If there are none or if they are more than covered, the debtor receives any amount left over.

Foreclosure by Power of Sale

Most deeds of trust and many mortgages contain a **power of sale** clause. In case of default, the lender can request the trustee to foreclose and to sell the property at a public action without a judicial decree. The steps required for such a sale differ from state to state. Depending on the state, the sale may be conducted by a trustee or by a public officer or by the lender. California statutes, which are quite typical, outline the following procedures:

1. If a default occurs, the beneficiary requests the trustee to record a notice of default in the county recorder's office. The debtor and all others on record as requesting a notice must be informed.

2. The debtor or any other lienholder has 90 days in which to clear the default. He may reinstate the loan by meeting late payments plus penalties, by paying taxes, or by correcting any other fault.

3. After 90 days, if no reinstatement has occurred, the lender has the right to collect the entire debt plus costs. The trustee will record a notice of sale. In addition, public notice of the proposed sale is required for 20 days. The notice must be posted conspicuously on the property and in a public place, such as the courthouse. During this period, the notice must also appear at least weekly in a newspaper of general circulation.

4. After the notice period, the trustee conducts a public sale, usually on the steps of the courthouse. Typically, the amounts bid and the distribution of the proceeds are similar to those described under judicial sale.

5. The trustee gives a deed covering all the rights of the debtor to the high bidder. Junior liens are wiped out, but all higher-order rights remain in effect.

The power of sale saves court costs and is faster than foreclosure by judicial sale. Either the redemption period is reduced, or there is none at all. Some states forbid deficiency judgments if the power of sale is used; in others, they can be obtained only through a court proceeding. Still, when the contract allows a public sale without requiring a court action, this faster, cheaper technique will normally be used even though no deficiency judgment is possible. The saving of time and costs usually exceeds any possible claim.

THE ORDER OF JUNIOR MORTGAGES AND RECORDING

Although it is not a legal requirement, most mortgages are recorded, or filed with the proper official (usually at the county courthouse) to place it on the public record. **Recording** is necessary so that ownership of a property or claims against it become public information. Recording gives **constructive notice**—that is, notice available to all who search the public record—of the existing interest in the property. Lenders give such notice in order to protect the priority of their claims. In most cases, priority depends on being the first to have the record accepted by the public official. A *first mortgage* is one that is recorded first; other recorded later are *junior mortgages*. While priority is usually granted in the order of recording, other liens may have preference. For example, tax liens or assessments come before the first mortgage.

Junior Mortgages

Mortgages whose priority follows the first mortgages are called **junior mortgages**. It is not uncommon to find second, third, or fourth mortgages. Each is *junior* to those carrying a lower number. If a foreclosure sale occurs, the receipts are used first to pay off the first mortgage; then if any funds are left over, they are used to pay off the second mortgage, and so on in order. When funds run out, the more junior mortgages receive nothing.

Because the order of recording is so crucial, in many states the process of closing the loan and examining the record to ascertain the order of priority is an extremely important ritual. In other states, the process of **escrow** is used. In this procedure, a neutral party is given the mortgage and the funds to be lent. Escrow agents are instructed to pay the money to the borrower only after they have assured themselves that the mortgage has been recorded with the agreed-upon priority.

Junior mortgages often carry special agreements or covenants. If the borrower defaults on a more senior mortgage, the total debt of the junior lien may be accelerated and become due. When foreclosing on a junior mortgage, in order to keep intact their claim to the property, lenders may have the right to clear defaults on higher-order mortgages by making the necessary payments. To ensure timely action, borrowers promise to give the junior lenders any notices received from prior lienholders.

Borrowers often demand a **subordination clause** that allows them to alter or substitute a new first mortgage. This clause keeps the junior mortgage from moving up to first if the borrower is able to get better terms by paying off the first mortgage and substituting a new one. Usually the clause will not permit the borrower to increase the amount owed on a prior lien.

Use of Junior Mortgages

Second mortgages are frequently used in at least three situations:

• Sellers make a sale possible by accepting a junior mortgage. Some sales are feasible only if the seller does not demand all cash, but instead raises the price and accepts partial payment in the form of a junior mortgage. Such situations arise constantly. An existing mortgage that can be assumed may carry a below-market interest rate. In other cases, borrowers may not be able to meet the payments required by a larger first mortgage. The seller can agree that only the interest or some part of it due on the second mortgage need be paid, while the rest accrues as part of the principal to be paid off as a balloon in three or five years. For example, a house worth $80,000 may have an existing $65,000 loan with an interest rate 2 percent below the current market. The buyers might be willing to pay $85,000 if they could assume the existing loan and pay the additional $20,000 with $10,000 in cash and $10,000 from a second mortgage. They might find this preferable to paying $80,000 made up of $65,000 from a new higher-rate first mortgage and $15,000 in cash.

• Owners of land or buildings may allow their claims to be subordinated so that a builder can obtain the financing needed for developing or rehabilitating a property. Typically, someone may have been trying to sell a lot for a long time. A builder offers to buy it and perhaps pay somewhat above the market price. He explains, however, that he will pay for the land with some cash and a mortgage payable when the house to be built is finally sold. Furthermore, he will have to borrow construction money from a bank, which will lend only on a first mortgage. Looking at such an offer, the seller of the lot may agree to accept a mortgage that will be subordinated to and have second priority behind the bank's claim.

• Many owners borrow against their equity, using a second mortgage, to obtain money for other needs. Risks and interest rates on second mortgages are usually lower than on personal or installment loans. For example, a group of doctors owns an office building whose value has gone up, and the doctors want to buy another property. Rather than selling the first building or refinancing it, they may be able to borrow against it on a second mortgage in order to obtain the down payment needed for their new purchase.

Wraparound Mortgages

The **wraparound mortgage** (or "wrap") is one of the most important types of junior mortgages, particularly in the sale of existing income properties. On a wrap, a second lender (frequently a seller) lends an amount over and above the existng first mortgage. The face amount of a wraparound mortgage equals the balance of the existing mortgage loan or loans plus the amount of the new loan. The borrower pays the wrap lender the interest and amortization on the face amount. The lender is responsible for making the necessary payments to the existing mortgage holders, retaining the difference between the amounts collected and paid out to cover the additional sums advanced.

Wraparounds are used for a variety of reasons such as the following:

• Many recent income property loans are closed for up to 5 or 10 years. Original borrowers wanting to sell the property cannot pay off the loan. In other cases, heavy prepayment penalties make paying off the loan undesirable. Furthermore, the purchaser may want a larger loan than the outstanding closed loan. The seller advances additional financing through the wraparound procedure.

• The interest rate on the existing mortgage may be below the current market rate. Both buyer and seller want to retain the existing loan to save having to pay the higher current rate.

• The buyer wants a higher loan-to-value ratio or more extended terms than will be granted by a conventional lender. The seller is willing to furnish the desired terms, or finds another lender who will do so, because the wrap mortgage yields a higher return. It also provides more protection than a simple junior mortgage.

Table 3 shows how a wraparound mortgage works. A buyer offers $1.2 million for a property but has only $200,000 for the down payment. The property has an existing $800,000 mortgage at 12 percent interest. The seller agrees to accept a $1 million wraparound mortgage from the buyer at 14 percent and to continue to make the payments on the existing mortgage. The buyer receives an additional $200,000 in financing. The buyer has issued a mortgage for $1 million to the seller, but the existing mortgage for $800,000 has the first claim on the property and the seller's claim is junior to it.

The wrap lender collects $140,000 in interest and pays $96,000 in interest to the holder of the first mortgage. The remaining $44,000 is re-

TABLE 3
The Return on a Wraparound Mortgage

	Amount	Interest	Lender's Interest Rate
Wraparound mortgage	$1,000,000	$140,000	14%
Existing first mortgage	800,000	96,000	12
Wraparound lender lends	200,000	44,000	22
Wraparound lender receives 14% on	200,000	28,000	14
plus 2% (14−12) on	800,000	16,000	2
for a total return of 22%			

tained for a 22 percent return on the additional $200,000 advanced. The final two lines of Table 3 show that the high return results from the fact that the 14 percent interest applies to the entire wraparound mortgage. Thus, the wrap lender is able to retain 2 percent on the $800,000 of the original lender's loan. The yield will vary if the amortization—and, therefore, the remaining principal—on the two loans differs.

The wrap can run into problems similar to those of other junior mortgages. It may be harder for the borrower to be sure that payments are made promptly by the wrap lender and that a clear title can be obtained when the borrower has made all the payments. In some states, returns above the usury ceilings may be allowed; in others they are not. (The usury ceiling is the maximum rate of interest that may legally be charged.) Expected returns can differ from actual returns as a result of prepayments.

SUMMARY

A mortgage is a contract pledging property as security for repayment of a debt. If the debtor fails to meet his or her obligations, foreclosure may occur. The lender can have the property sold so that the funds obtained can be used to repay the debt.

The conditions contained in mortgages are becoming more diverse and complex. The terms of the fixed-rate mortgage form a standard of comparison. The FRM calls for equal-level payments, each of which goes partly for interest and partly for some repayment of principal. The share going to principal increases steadily, initially at a slow rate but accelerating rapidly near the loan's maturity.

The amount of payment required rises with the rate of interest and with the amount borrowed, but it falls as the payment period lengthens. Because lenders limit the amount of income that can be committed to mortgage payments, the affordability of a loan and, therefore, of a property falls when interest rates rise and when the term is short.

The rights of borrowers and lenders vary depending on the law of each state and on the agreement or covenants they sign in the note and mortgage contract. Some states require a judicial procedure for foreclosure. Others allow a public auction under the terms of a deed of trust or of a mortgage with a power of sale. The length of time lenders have in which to declare a default or for borrowers to reinstate their loans also differs considerably, as does the ability to obtain a deficiency judgment.

Some mortgages allow a new owner to assume a debt. Others specify that the loan will accelerate so that the total outstanding amount will be due if a sale occurs. Similarly, some loans may be prepaid without penalty, while others may not. In closed mortgages, prepayments may not be made for a fixed period, if at all.

Junior mortgages have rights subordinate to other liens. They can be wiped out if the higher-order mortgagee forecloses. Usually the holders of junior mortgages can avoid such losses by foreclosing themselves and assuming the duties and covenants of the prior liens.

READING 22

REAL ESTATE INTERESTS AND FORMS OF OWNERSHIP

Charles H. Wurtzebach
Mike E. Miles

Real estate has value because of the uses to which it can be put, and its location is the critical element in determining those uses.

The question of use is approached from the perspective of inquiring into the mechanics by which interests in land can be created and transferred. These are the formal rules of the game and, consequently, an important part of the framework for decision analysis.

Real estate law is discussed not from the point of view of the attorney, but rather with two other objectives in mind:

- To explain basic legal concepts relating to land ownership and transfer that should be understood by a business person or investor who is negotiating a real estate transaction or facing a decision about how to use or dispose of real estate.
- To illustrate some of the unique investment advantages of real estate—in particular, the ability to divide a parcel of real estate into a number of separate physical and legal interests, each attractive to a different participant in the investment process.

Source: From Charles H. Wurtzebach and Mike E. Miles, *Modern Real Estate*, 3rd ed. (New York: John Wiley & Sons, 1987). Used with permission.

The features that make real estate a unique asset—its fixed location and its long life—also are the critical elements in determining its legal characteristics.

This reading is divided into three parts. First, real estate itself is examined to determine what precisely is owned in a physical sense. Next the different types of legal interests that can exist in a parcel of real estate are identified. Finally, we discuss the kinds of entities that are utilized in the ownership of real estate interests.

PHYSICAL INTERESTS IN REAL ESTATE

First to be examined is real estate itself, that is, the physical asset. A parcel of real estate consists of land plus whatever grows on the land (e.g., crops) plus whatever is permanently attached to the land (e.g., a building). In addition, a parcel of real estate includes all the space *above* and *below* the surface of the earth.

In legal parlance, property is the collection of jural relations that exists among people with regard to things. In our language, it is the set of rules that deals with ownership.

It is important to distinguish between **real property** and **personal property.** Real property, as noted earlier, is the land and all things attached to the land in a manner indicating that the intent was to make the attachment permanent. Personal property, on the other hand, is everything else that can be owned. Therefore, your car is personal property. When personal property (such as a roll of carpet) is permanently attached to a building (wall-to-wall carpeting is installed), it is called a **fixture** and becomes part of the real property.

So a parcel of real estate really consists of three different physical levels (see Figure 1):

- A designated portion of the earth's surface with its crops and attachments. When the land borders natural waters, certain water rights may be acquired.
- Above-surface space (i.e., **air space**) extending from the surface of the earth to some distance in space.
- Subsurface space within an area circumscribed by lines drawn from the surface boundaries of the land to the center of the earth (the subsurface space forming an inverted cone).

Each of these physical interests may be utilized or possessed sepa-

FIGURE 1
The Three Levels of Real Estate

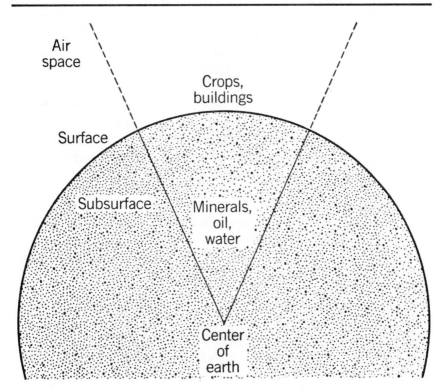

rately from the others. For example, X owns all the physical interests in a parcel of real estate called Blackacre. He may transfer to Y certain rights to possess or use the space beneath the surface of Blackacre (i.e., the subsurface rights), and he may transfer to Z ownership of the space above the surface of Blackacre (i.e., the air space). (See the two boxed features, Subsurface Rights and Using Air Space.)

Water Rights

Ownership of land bordering natural waters (lakes, rivers, or oceans) may or may not extend to land under the waters and may or may not include the right to use the waters. The rules are complicated and vary in different parts of the country, summarized as follows:

Subsurface Rights

Why would a person want **subsurface rights** in real estate that are separate and distinct from the surface rights? One reason would be to remove minerals such as coal, oil, or gas. Another would be to put something such as a pipeline or subway under the ground. The general rule is that the owner of subsurface rights in land may remove anything from it that he wishes, subject to the following restrictions:

- Any limits imposed under an agreement with the owner of the surface rights.
- Government regulations with respect to zoning and mining practices (e.g., laws barring strip mining).
- Limitations imposed by the common law (e.g., the rule that land may not be excavated to the point of depriving adjacent properties of their natural support, which might cause buildings on those properties to collapse).

Riparian Rights. The rights of an owner whose land borders a river, stream, or lake are governed in some states by the common-law doctrine of **riparian rights.** The doctrine of riparian rights permits the owner to use the water as he sees fit, subject only to the limitation that the owner may not interrupt or change the flow of the water or contaminate it. If the river, stream, or lake is nonnavigable, the owner of bordering land has title to the land under the water to the center of the waterway. However, in the case of navigable waters, the landowner's title runs only to the water's edge, with the state holding title to the land under the water. The reason for the distinction is that a navigable waterway is considered the same as a public highway.

Prior Appropriation. On the Pacific coast and in western states where water is scarce, the common law doctrine of riparian rights has been replaced by legislative law establishing the rule of **prior appropriation.** Under this rule, the right to use natural water is controlled by the state rather than by a landowner (except for normal domestic use). In prior appropriation states, the first user has priority but must obtain a permit from the state on showing of a need for the water. Title to the land under the water is generally subject to the same rules as in riparian rights states.

Using Air Space

The right to use air space (air rights) is especially valuable in prime downtown locations where space is very expensive. In such areas, air rights may be available above railroad rights-of-way, highways, school buildings, post office buildings, and other low-rise structures. One of the most dramatic examples of the use of air space is the Pan Am Building in New York City. The Penn Central Railroad originally owned all the physical interests at that location; it utilized the subsurface to operate trains and the surface (plus a limited amount of air space) for Grand Central Terminal. It leased all the remaining air space for 99 years to a development company that built the Pan Am Building. A necessary part of the lease of the air space included "support rights," which permitted the developer to place columns on the surface and subsurface that support the building.

When a municipal zoning ordinance prohibits buildings above a designated height, air space above the zoning ceiling will have no economic value. However, in order to encourage construction, some municipalities permit a developer to "transfer" air rights from one location (where additional construction would be permitted) to another (where it would not). In this way, desirable space can be developed even though overall building density in the neighborhood or municipality remains within permitted levels. Air rights eligible for transfer are known as "transferable development rights" or TDRs.

Note that an owner of real estate does not have exclusive control of the air space above the land parcel. Airplanes, for example, are not "trespassing" when they cross air space sufficiently far above the earth. However, when air traffic causes damage to the surface, the landowner may be entitled to damages. Consider the following story reported by United Press International on March 26, 1982.

Jet's Boom Kills Pigs; $26,000 Is Awarded

DELANO, Tenn., March 26 (UPI)—Betty Davis reluctantly accepted a $26,000 settlement in her suit charging that a low-flying Air Force Phantom jet cracked a sonic boom over her farmhouse, hammering the fillings out of her teeth, killing 61 pigs, and blowing her home off its foundations.

Mrs. Davis, whose family had demanded $2 million in damages from the Air Force, accepted the out-of-court settlement Thursday but said that what she really wanted was never to see another low-flying Phantom jet again.

Littoral Rights.   A special doctrine applies to land that borders large lakes and the oceans. Referred to as **littoral rights,** ownership of such land permits use of the waters without restriction; however, title extends only to the mean (average) high-water mark. All land on the waterside of this mark is owned by the government.

LEGAL INTERESTS IN REAL ESTATE

Real property—that is, the physical entity itself—is comprised of the three separate facets of surface, subsurface, and air space. The individual may have an ownership interest in any of these, in two out of three, or in all three. But of just what does ownership consist?

Ownership as a Bundle of Rights

In Anglo-American law, real estate ownership is most often viewed as consisting of a "**bundle of rights.**" This includes the rights of (1) **possession,** (2) **control,** (3) **enjoyment,** and (4) **disposition.**

- The *right of possession* refers to occupancy and includes the right to keep out all others.
- The *right of control* deals with the right to alter the property physically.
- The *right of enjoyment* protects the current owner from interference by past owners or others.
- The *right of disposition* permits conveyance of all or part of one's bundle of rights to others.

All these rights are subject to limitations or restriction by governmental action. They also are subject to restrictions created or agreed to by prior owners that are binding on their successors. For example, owners in a residential community may desire that no parcel of land may be used in the future for a commercial enterprise. Provided they comply with the legal rules, they can restrict future use of the land within reasonable limits.

The bundle of rights that constitute real estate ownership can be divided in a surprising number of ways. In general, these ownership rights can be classified into three major categories: (1) freehold estates, (2) possessory estates, and (3) nonpossessory interests. In the paragraphs that follow, these three general categories are described.

FREEHOLD ESTATES

Freehold (ownership) **estates** represent the highest quality of rights associated with real property under our legal system. In general, the holder of such an estate may exercise the full bundle of rights that relate to real property, subject always to overriding public policy as expressed in statute law, court decisions, and governmental regulation. The freehold category includes three significant types of estates: (1) **fee simple,** (2) **defeasible fees,** and (3) **life estates.**

Fee Simple Absolute

The most straightforward estate in land is known as the *fee simple absolute,* or *fee simple,* and is often referred to simply as a *fee.* Fee simple ownership represents the most complete form of private property ownership recognized by our law. A fee simple interest creates an absolute and complete right of ownership for an unlimited duration of time with an unconditional right of disposition and use (i.e., the complete bundle of rights). Consequently, fee simple ownership is the most desirable interest in land. A fee simple interest may be transferred by using the words "to X, his heirs and assigns" in the instrument conveying the interest.

Defeasible Fees

A special kind of freehold interest, seen infrequently today, is the *defeasible fee,* that is, a fee simple subject to being defeated or terminated. This type of interest is also known as a *qualified fee.* In plain terms, this is a fee simple interest subject to certain conditions that, if not met, will cause the owner to lose his interest in the property. The conditions may be permanent, or they may continue for a specified number of years. The origin of defeasible fees goes back to the early English common law when land was virtually the sole significant source of wealth. By tying up land with defeasible fees (and other devices), large landholders sought to ensure that the land would remain in certain uses or "within the family" for generations to come—which, in fact, often has been the case.

Two kinds of defeasible fees are (1) **fee simple determinable** and (2) **fee on condition subsequent.**

Fee Simple Determinable. A fee simple determinable is fee simple ownership that automatically will terminate on the happening (or failure to

FIGURE 2
Estates in Land

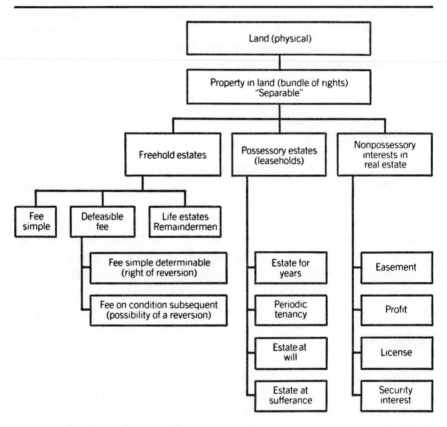

happen) of a stated condition. Such a fee is usually expressed by a convey-ance "to X, his heirs and assigns, *so long as they use the property for Y purpose.*" Provided that X does, in fact, use the property for Y purpose, he has all the bundle of rights associated with fee simple ownership (ex-cept, of course, the right to change the use). If the use is changed, X's title terminates, and the property reverts to the grantor, or to his heirs if he is no longer living. (Thus, the grantor has a possibility of a reversion.)

A few years ago, the New York courts were faced with a case in which land had been conveyed about 90 years earlier to a municipality "so long as the land is used as a railroad station." The grantor had desired to pro-vide a site for the commuter railroad and wished to ensure that the land would not be used for any other purpose. With changing times, the railroad discontinued service to the community, and the municipality sought to sell the land for another use. At that point, the heirs of the original grantor claimed that because the condition of use was no longer met, the land reverted to them. The court upheld their claim.

Fee on Condition Subsequent. Just as with a fee simple determinable, a fee on condition subsequent creates an ownership interest that can be lost on the happening of a stated event or condition in the future. The typical phrasing in a conveyance of such a fee from Y to X would be "to X, his heirs and assigns, *but if* the land is used for the purpose of selling alcoholic beverages, Y may enter upon the land and regain title."

As in the case of a fee simple determinable, it is clear from such a conveyance that the bundle of rights associated with fee ownership is limited in one particular respect—the use to which the property may be put.

What is the difference between the two types of defeasible fees? In essence, it is a matter of the precise manner whereby title will be lost by an owner failing to comply with the condition. In the case of a fee simple determinable, title is automatically terminated when the condition is violated; by comparison, the grantor of a fee on condition subsequent must exercise his right of reentry before title is lost by the grantee. (Thus, he has a **right of reentry.**) These highly technical distinctions are normally of interest only to a real estate attorney; they are mentioned here to show that real estate is subject to legal rules that sometimes are centuries old and yet may still have relevance today.

The primary objection to defeasible fees is that they are *restraints on alienability* (transferability). Defeasible fees limit the transferability of real estate because a prospective purchaser, knowing he would lose the title if the condition were to be violated, would be reluctant to buy. Courts and legislatures care about free transferability because both economic and social development would be hindered if many parcels of real estate were tied up with ancient restrictions that prevented the most productive use of the property in today's world. Consider the parcel of real estate, referred to earlier, that could be used only as a railroad station even though no railroad continued to serve that particular community.

As a result of the dislike of defeasible fees, many state legislatures have passed laws providing that a defeasible fee automatically will become a fee simple after a certain number of years (e.g., 25 years) if it has not been terminated by that time. A court of law, called on to interpret a conveyance as either a fee simple or a defeasible fee, will favor the former interpretation because of the public policy against restraints on alienability.[1]

Life Estates

The life estate is an extremely common form of freehold estate and has a long history. (See the boxed feature, Dower and Curtesy Rights.) In a life estate, the grantor conveys a fee simple interest to a grantee (usually a spouse or other family member) for a period measured by the lifetime of the grantee. A typical conveyance would be "to my wife X for her life and then to my son Y." In rare cases, the measuring lifetime may be that of a third party, for example, "to my son Y for the life of my wife X, and then to my daughter Z." As indicated by these conveyances, after the measuring lifetime has expired, title to the property automatically will to go another person. The subsequent interest is called a *remainder* (because it is what remains after the life interest expires), and the person who ultimately will receive it is called the **remainderman.** The person holding the life estate is the **life tenant,** a term that can be confusing since it has nothing to do with a lease.

The life tenant may treat the property in all respects as would an owner in fee simple, subject only to two restrictions:

The life tenant must maintain the property in reasonably good condition in order to protect the interests of the remainderman. The life tenant has a right to possess the property during the measuring lifetime but must act in a way to respect the future interests of the remainderman. For example, the family home that is left to the surviving spouse cannot be permitted to deteriorate to the point where it becomes uninhabitable and worthless to the remainder interest. Any act or omission by the life tenant that does permanent injury to the property or unreasonably changes its character or value constitutes *waste* and may be enjoined (prohibited) by a court as a result of a lawsuit brought by the remainderman.

Life tenants may convey the life interest to a third party but can convey

---

[1] In older books, the fee tail is also mentioned at this point. Under a fee tail, which has been abolished in the United States, the property was always inherited by the elder male child. This feudal concept clearly would be detrimental to a "market" economy because it prevents transfers to those who may be better able to utilize property (both in their own and in society's interests).

Dower and Curtesy Rights (Life Estates)

Life estates were an early form of social security. When a landowner died in feudal England, his wife automatically received a one-third interest in all his real estate, whether or not such an interest was specifically conveyed to her by will. In this way, widows would not become a burden on the community. The life estate in feudal England was known as the *dower interest*, and the widow holding such interest was known as a *dowager*, a term that has come to mean an elderly lady of means. Under certain circumstances, a widower also had certain rights in his wife's estate. This was known as the *right of curtesy*.

The traditional concept of dower and curtesy has been abolished in almost all the United States and has been replaced in some states by a *homestead right* and in other states by a *statutory interest* (or statutory share). Under a homestead right such as that created by Florida law, a surviving spouse is entitled to a life estate in the couple's residence if title was held by the deceased spouse at his or her death and regardless of any other disposition made by the will of the deceased spouse.

Under the statutory interest approach, the surviving spouse has the right to claim an interest in the deceased spouse's estate even though the surviving spouse was cut out of the will or given less than a certain percentage of the estate. For example, the surviving spouse may be entitled to receive a one-third interest in all the property (real and personal) owned by the deceased at his or her death, regardless of any contrary provision in the will.

---

no more than such interest. Because a life estate is a freehold interest, it includes the right of disposition. However, no person can convey more than he owns. Consequently, the life tenant can sell only the life estate. Since the duration of a life estate is always unknown (because it will terminate on the death of a named person), it is not likely that anyone would pay a great deal for such an estate. For this reason, life estates normally are not used in commercial transactions.

Life estates are frequently described as freehold estates but not estates of inheritance. This is obviously so whenever the measuring life is that of the life tenant. Such an estate cannot be inherited by another since it will terminate on the death of the life tenant. But in the rare case where the measuring life may be of another person, the life estate will be inherited by the heirs of the life tenant.

POSSESSORY ESTATES: LEASEHOLDS

The holder of a freehold estate has *ownership* of the property. By comparison, the holder of a **possessory or leasehold estate** has *possession* of the property. Since possession is merely one of the bundle of rights associated with ownership, it is clear that when a leasehold interest is created it represents a *separation* of the bundle of rights. The separation is into (1) a fee interest (the interest of the landlord, also called the *lessor*) and (2) a leasehold interest (the interest of the tenant, also called the *lessee*). The two interests in the property exist simultaneously.

- The tenant has the right to possession of the property, subject to the terms of the lease and for the duration specified in the lease.
- The landlord retains all the other ownership rights plus the right to regain possession when the lease expires (the *right of reversion*).

The ability to divide real estate into a fee and a leasehold interest offers enormous flexibility in putting together a transaction among several parties. Probably the greatest master of the technique of "slicing up" a parcel of real estate into various interests was the late William Zeckendorf, Sr. At different times, Zeckendorf referred to his technique as the *Hawaiian technique* (he claimed he thought of it while fishing in that state) or the *pineapple technique* (the initial single ownership interest in a parcel of land could be sliced up into a number of interests, just as a pineapple could be sliced into a number of sections). Whatever he called it, Zeckendorf was able to create complicated real estate interests that resulted in developments that otherwise might never have been built. A notable example is the United Nations Plaza building adjacent to the United Nations in New York City. In this development, three different fee interests plus a leasehold interest plus five mortgage interests were carved out of a single parcel of land. (The boxed feature, United Nations Plaza Building, describes how it was done.)

A *leasehold interest* is created by a **lease**, which is usually in writing but is sometimes oral. A lease is unique because it is both a *conveyance* (i.e., it transfers the right to possession of real estate) and a *contract* (i.e., it creates rights and duties between the landlord and the tenant).

United National Plaza Building—New York City

In midtown New York City, next to the United Nations, stands a single structure that consists of a six-story office building on top of which rise two 32-story residential towers. Begun in 1964, the project is a classic illustration of the late William Zeckendorf's *pineapple technique.* The project was originated by Zeckendorf's company, Webb & Knapp, but when it began its slide into bankruptcy, development was taken over by Alcoa Associates, a joint venture between Alcoa and Canadian interests.

The best way to visualize the various interests created in the building is to follow the transactions as they occurred.

Three fee interests.   The developer (Associates) originally owned the property in fee simple. The first step it took illustrates the fundamental operating principle that Zeckendorf followed, which was to minimize or eliminate entirely the need for any of his own cash in the transaction. Associates created two cooperative housing corporations, each to own one of the 32-story towers to be constructed above the office building. Associates then sold a fee simple interest in air space to each cooperative corporation. At that point, three separate fee interests had been created in the parcel of real estate. The price received for the two air space parcels was $38 million.

Leasehold interest.   To further reduce its cash requirements, Associates sold its fee interest (consisting of the land plus sufficient air space for the office building) to Equitable Life Assurance Society for $12 million. Simultaneously, Associates leased back the identical space from Equitable for a term of 999 years. This transaction is known as a *sale-leaseback.*

Leasehold mortgage.   Associates then obtained a loan of $3.5 million from Equitable secured by Associates' leasehold interest. This type of loan is called a *leasehold mortgage.* How could the leasehold interest be security for a loan? Associates anticipated making a substantial profit from the difference between the rent it would collect from office tenants and the rental (the *ground rent*) it would have to pay Equitable. This flow of income (anticipated for 999 years) was adequate security for a 27-year loan.

Four fee mortgages.   Since it was not likely that the cooperative apartment units could be sold without substantial financing, Equitable agreed to provide first mortgage financing to each of the cooperative corporations, and Associates agreed to provide financing secured by second mortgages.

> *Total of nine interests.* A total of nine different interests were created. Of these, three were fee interests, one was a leasehold interest, and five were security (mortgage) interests, consisting of a leasehold mortgage, two first fee mortgages, and two second fee mortgages (all of the fee mortgages covering the air space fee interests owned by the cooperative corporations). Associates raised a total of $53.5 million by selling off the two air space fee interests and mortgaging its leasehold interest. This probably came close to paying for the original land cost plus the cost of putting up the 6-story office building. Associates ended up (for very little cash investment) holding a 999-year leasehold of an office building in the heart of New York City.

A primary feature of leasehold interests is that they are never for a perpetual term. Consequently, it is convenient to categorize leasehold interests according to their duration. The four categories are:

- Estate for years.
- Estate from period to period (periodic tenancy).
- Estate at will.
- Estate at sufferance.

Estate for Years

By far the most common type of leasehold interest is the **estate for years.** This type includes all leases with a fixed term—whether a residential lease for one year or a ground lease for 99 years. An estate for years will expire automatically at the end of the period designated, at which time the tenant's right of possession ends and possession reverts to the landlord. The lease, however, may grant renewal options to the tenant that, if properly exercised, will continue the leasehold for another designated term.

Estate from Period to Period

This type of leasehold estate, also very common, is most often used for residential and small commercial properties. An **estate from period to period** is created whenever the lease specifies the amount of rent for a designated period but does not state a specified term for the lease.

For example, if a lease provides that rent shall be paid at the rate of $100 per month, a *month-to-month tenancy* is created. The tenant is entitled to possession and is obligated to pay rent until either landlord or tenant gives notice of intention to terminate the lease. The time of such notice and the form in which it must be given are usually determined by statute (e.g., either party may terminate the lease on 30 days' written notice, delivered personally or sent by certified mail to the other). Because this type of estate cannot assure the tenant of possession for any lengthy period, it is not normally used where a tenant, such as a retailer, must spend substantial sums to prepare the premises for use.

Estate at Will

An **estate at will** (or tenancy at will) is created by an oral agreement between landlord and tenant to the effect that the tenant may occupy the premises so long as it is convenient for both parties. Estates at will can create problems for both parties since no written instrument specifies the amount of rent or the rights or responsibilities of either party.

Estate at Sufferance

This rather unusual form of leasehold estate exists when a leasehold interest, whether for years, periodic, or at will, expires or terminates without the tenant vacating the property. In other words, the tenant continues to hold the premises at the sufferance of the landlord; this estate is called an **estate at sufferance.**

In theory, such a tenant may be dispossessed at any time by the landlord. However, as in the case of an estate will, a prior period of notice may have to be given by the landlord.

The Lease

As already noted, the lease instrument is both a conveyance of a real estate interest (a leasehold) and a contract between landlord and tenant. The lease should be in writing for several reasons. First, a written lease helps avoid misunderstandings. It is much easier to recall the specific understanding on a particular point when a lease is in writing. Commercial and office leases, which may extend for 25 or more years and involve cumulative rentals in the millions of dollars, may run to as much as 100 pages.

Types of Rental Payments

To a businessman or investor, the rent provisions of a lease are critical. Types and manner of rental payments are limited only by the ingenuity of real estate professionals. The most common types are these.

Gross rental (gross lease).   A gross rental is one that covers operating expenses as well as the landlord's profit. Under a gross lease, the landlord, not the tenant, pays the costs of operating the premises. An apartment house lease is an example.

Net rental (net lease).   A net rental is one that represents the landlord's return on his investment and does not include operating expenses, which are paid by the tenant separately. The net lease is typically used in commercial leases of freestanding premises (e.g., a building occupied by a single retail tenant such as a supermarket). The tenant pays all operating expenses, in addition to the net rental.

Flat (fixed) rental.   A flat rental is a rental that is fixed and unchanging throughout the lease term. At one time, flat rentals were common even for long-term commercial leases, but because of recent inflation, these are now rather uncommon. An apartment house lease typically calls for a fixed rental since the term is usually short.

Graduated rental.   A graduated rent is one that moves up or down in a series of steps during the lease term. A set-up rental involves an increase at each stage. A step-down rental involves a decrease in each stage.

Escalator (index) rental.   An escalator rental is a type of rental that moves up or down in accordance with an outside standard (e.g., the consumer price index) or an inside standard (e.g., operating costs of the particular property). Rental escalation has now become very common in office and commercial leases as a means of shielding the landlord against the effects of rapid inflation. Escalation clauses are also beginning to appear in apartment leases.

Percentage rental.   A percentage rental is an extremely common form of rental payment in retail store leases. The tenant normally pays a minimum fixed rent plus an additional rent equal to a percentage of sales over a fixed amount. The tenant's gross sales rather than net profits is almost always used as a standard in order to avoid disputes about how net profits are to be determined. In addition, gross sales are more likely to keep pace with inflation than are net profits. Consequently, a percentage rental based on sales is a better inflation hedge for the landlord than is one based on profits.

Second, a lease may have to be in writing to be legally enforceable. In most states, leases with terms exceeding a certain length will be enforced by the courts only if they are evidenced in writing.

The requirements of a valid lease include the following:

- Names and signatures of legally competent parties.
- Description of premises.
- Amount of rent.
- Term of the lease.
- Commencement and expiration dates.
- Rights and obligations of the parties during the lease term.

A typical lease will include provisions covering the following matters. What areas are to be maintained by the landlord and which by the tenant? Who will pay utilities? Who will pay for property insurance and property taxes? It is possible that, as costs increase, the tenant, pursuant to a lease clause, will bear the increase (an **escalation clause**). (See the box, Types of Rental Payments.) What improvements and alterations does the tenant have the right to make? What happens in the event that the tenant cannot pay? What happens if the property is condemned by the government under eminent domain? What happens at the end of the lease period? Does the tenant have the right to assign or sublease the premises? If so, at what price and under what terms?

Changing Concept of Leases

The concept of a lease has changed in an interesting and dramatic way in the past 20 years. For centuries, a lease was always regarded by the courts and legislatures as primarily a conveyance, with the contractual aspect purely secondary. As a result, a very dim view was taken of tenant efforts to hold back rent when landlords failed to carry out their obligations, such as providing heat in the wintertime.

The courts' view was that rent was the consideration for the conveyance of the right to possession. Consequently, the rent had to be paid regardless of the landlord's failure to perform his contractual duties. The reason for this seemingly harsh view was that leases originally were primarily for farmland, where the farmer operated as a totally independent businessman, putting up his own house and farming the land as an entreprenuer—quite a difference from a tenant who lives in a studio apartment in a 25-story apartment house.

However, in the past two decades, a very sharp shift has taken place toward emphasizing the contractual aspects of the lease. This is the legal rationale for such phenomena as *rent strikes,* where tenants hold back rent payments until landlords perform in accordance with the lease. In a broader context, this has been part of the consumer revolution that has seen the passage of a number of important statutes at both the federal and state level that seek to protect the rights of purchasers and users of property.

NONPOSSESSORY INTERESTS

The third category of interests that can be created in real estate are designated nonpossessory interests or rights—that is, none of these rises to the "dignity" of an interest that carries with it ownership or possession. The four common types are (1) easements, (2) profits, (3) licenses, (4) and security interests.

Easements

An **easement** is an interest in real estate that gives the holder the right to use but not to possess the real estate. A common form of an easement is a right-of-way—that is, the right to cross over the land of another. Another is the electric utility or telephone easement, which permits a utility company to place poles at designated points on the land and run wires between them. Because an easement involves some restriction or limitation of the right of ownership, land subject to an easement is said to be *burdened* with an easement, and, to some extent, its value may be diminished.

There are two general types of easements. The first is the **easement appurtenant,** which attaches to the land and is not a personal right. The second type of easement is an **easement in gross,** which does not benefit a property. Instead, it benefits the individual or institution that owns it.

There are several ways in which an easement may be created.

Express easement. An **express easement** is created by a writing executed by the owner of the *servient tenement* (the property subject to the easement). The writing may be called a *grant of easement* or similar title.

Consider two plots of land adjacent to one another. The deed, or document of title, to lot A gives its owner the right to cross over lot B in order to reach a public highway. In this situation, ownership of A (called the *dominant tenement*) includes as one of the bundle of rights of ownership an easement appurtenant (i.e., an easement that accompanies ownership). B, which is burdened by the right of way, is the *servient tenement;* it is subject to an obligation that may or may not reduce its value in any significant way, depending on the location of the right of way and the use to which B is being put.

Remember, an easement appurtenant, being part of the bundle of rights of ownership, is not a personal right but attaches to the land (the legal phrase is *runs with the land*) and so is conveyed to subsequent owners of the dominant tenement.

Real estate may be subject to an easement that is unconnected with any other parcel of land, that is, an easement personal to the individual or institution benefiting from it. Electric utility and telephone easements would be an example. Other types of commercial easements in gross are railroad and pipeline rights of way. Thus, both an easement appurtenant and an easement in gross may be expressively created.

Implied Easement.   An **implied easement** arises when the owner of a tract of land subjects one part of the tract to an easement (such as a right-of-way) that benefits the other part and then conveys one or both parts of the tract to other parties so that divided ownership results. In such a case, common law holds that an implied easement arises in favor of the *dominant tenement* and burdens the *servient tenement*.

Easement by necessity.   An **easement by necessity** is a special form of implied easement and arises when the owner of a tract subdivides or separates a part of the tract so that the severed part has no access to the outside world except across the balance of the tract. Under such circumstances and in order to permit the productive use of the isolated land, common law implies the right-of-way across the grantor's land to a public highway. Some states provide by statute that the owner of land lacking access to a public way may petition the courts to have a *cartway* condemned for this use. Again, the purpose is to encourage the development and use of land for the benefit of society in general. The concept is simple enough, but consider the problem raised in the box—Right-of-Way.

Easement by prescription.   An **easement by prescription** arises when a stranger (i.e., one without ownership or possessory right) makes use of land for a prescribed period of time (e.g., 10 years) and does so openly and without pretense of having the true owner's consent. Under such circumstances, the use that was originally adverse (against the interest of the owner) may ripen into an easement that is recognized by law. This is similar to the process of acquiring title to land by adverse possession (discussed on page 317). An example of a prescriptive easement would be extended use by one neighbor of another neighbor's driveway, with the first neighbor openly claiming the ''right'' to such use.

Right-of-Way Access Easement Destroyed when State Opens, Then Closes Road

When an easement is created for a specific purpose, the easement will last only as long as the purpose remains in existence. But what if a lapsed purpose for an easement is revived? Should the defunct easement then return to life?

Landlocked Lot

In 1949, Richard and Elizabeth Duffell owned a lot in Montgomery, Alabama, that had no street access. At the time, the nearest street was Ann Street, but an extension of Spruce Street was planned that would bring it closer to the Duffells' lot than Ann Street. Their neighbors, the Bonners, accommodated the Duffells by selling them a 25-foot-right-of-way easement across their property. The deed of easement stated that "it is the purpose and intention hereof to provide a means of ingress and egress and space for water line and sewage to and from Ann Street or to and from the proposed extension of Spruce Street. . . ." The Spruce Street extension was completed in 1951, and use of the easement lying between Spruce and Ann Streets was discontinued.

In the 1960s, Alabama began acquiring land in the area in connection with the construction of Interstate Highway 85. Spruce Street was closed to make way for an on-ramp. In order to regain local street access, Sasser, who now owned the Duffell property, sought the reactivation of the portion of the old easement running out to Ann Street.

Only One Easement

Unfortunately, Aronov, who now owned the Bonner property, had already leased the land over which the Ann Street portion of the easement ran. Aronov told Sasser to forget the easement, and litigation ensued. The trial court rejected Sasser's claim, and the matter went to the Alabama Supreme Court. There, the language of the easement was examined, particularly the stated purpose of providing ingress and egress "to and from Ann Street *or* to and from the proposed extension of Spruce Street." In the court's view, the use of the word "or" was evidence of an intent to create but one easement. These words plus the physical layout of the easement led the court to conclude that the easement was intended to provide access from the old Duffell property to the closest street.

Easement Extinguished by Halves

Sasser did not dispute the court's perceptions concerning the parties' intentions in creating the easement. He argued that there was nothing incompatible between these intentions and his claim that, when the Spruce Street extension was closed, an easement running out to Ann Street continued to exist. Against this argument, the court interposed the general rule to the effect that an easement given for a specific purpose terminates as soon as the purpose ceases to exist, is abandoned, or is rendered impossible of accomplishment. Upon completion of the Spruce Street extension, said the court, the purpose of the Ann Street portion of the easement ceased to exist, and that easement was forever extinguished. In like manner, once the Spruce Street extension was closed, the remaining portion of the easement was extinguished. [Sasser v. Spartan Food Sys., Inc., 452 So. 2d 475 (Ala. 1984)].

Observation

If the purpose for which an easement is required may be accomplished in either of two ways, it is important, from the standpoint of the grantee, to word the easement to preclude the kind of one-two punch destruction of the easement seen here.

Source: Real Estate Law Report, published by Warren, Gorham, and Lamont (New York), 14:6 (November 1984), p. 1.

Profits

A **profit** in land (technically known as *profit à prendre*) is the right to take a portion of the soil or timber or remove subsurface minerals, oil, or gas in land owned by someone else. A profit represents an interest in real property, and it must be in writing. The distinction between a profit and an easement is that the latter merely permits use of the property, whereas the former involves a removal of part of the land. A profit also is to be distinguished from a gas and oil or mineral *lease*. These require the lessee to pay a royalty to the landowner calculated on the amount of natural resource taken.

License

A **license** is the right to go on land owned by another for a specific purpose. A license in most cases is merely a revocable privilege granted by the owner to another and does not represent an interest in real estate. Almost everyone frequently is a licensee. Whenever a ticket is purchased to attend a sports or other event in a stadium or hall, the individual is purchasing a license. Similarly, if the privilege of hunting or fishing on the lands of another is given, whether or not for a consideration, the hunter or fisherman is a licensee.

Security Interests

A final type of nonpossessory interest in real estate is the **security interest** (i.e., the interest of one holding a mortgage). The holder of a mortgage has a legal interest in real estate, but it will not develop into possession or ownership unless a default occurs under the terms of the mortgage (e.g., nonpayment of an installment when due), at which point the mortgage holder can exercise its rights to foreclose against the property.

Liens and Deed Restrictions

In some sense, liens and deed restrictions also create nonpossessory interests. The lien holder (lender) has certain rights. Moreover, restrictions placed in a deed give certain rights to those who benefit from those restrictions.

FORMS OF OWNERSHIP

At this point, it should be clear that the following holds true:

- The physical entity that is real estate is really made up of three different elements: (1) *surface rights,* (2) *subsurface rights,* and (3) *air space* (called the *physical interests in real estate*).
- A variety of "shares" may be held in each of these physical interests in real estate, including (1) *ownership shares,* (2) *possessory shares,* and (3) *nonpossessory shares* (called the *legal interests in real estate*).

The manner of holding a legal interest in real estate—the third topic to be covered in this reading—is now introduced. There are five ways in which a legal interest in real estate may be held (the five simple *forms of ownership*).

- Single ownership.
- Tenancy in common.
- Joint tenancy with right of survivorship.
- Tenancy by the entirety.
- Community property.

FIGURE 3
Forms of Ownership

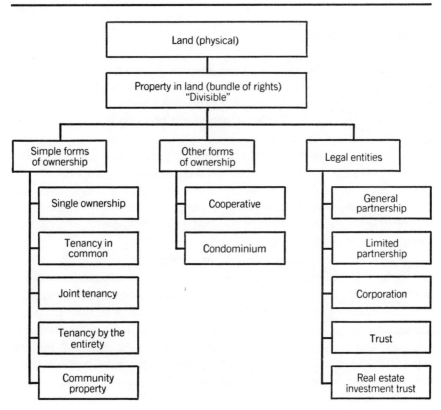

Note that all but the first are known generally by the term *concurrent ownership* (i.e., ownership by more than one person). Concurrent ownership can be created because the bundle of rights is divisible.

Single Ownership

Single ownership of an interest in real estate, is the simplest form of ownership, for no division of the bundle of rights is required. Residential properties and relatively small-scale business enterprises frequently are held by a single individual, whereas larger enterprises are frequently held by a single corporation or a single partnership. (Corporation, partnerships, and other vehicles for owning interests in real estate are discussed later in this reading.) Overall, most real estate interests in the United States are held in single ownership.

Tenancy in Common

The **tenancy in common** is the most frequently used form of concurrent ownership. When two or more persons hold as tenants in common (the term *tenants* as used here has nothing to do with a lease or leasehold interest), each has an undivided interest in the entire property to the extent of his ownership share.

For example, three tenants in common will each own a one-third undivided share in the entire property rather than each owning a specified one-third portion of the property. Although normally each tenant in common has the same share as his cotenants, this need not necessarily be the case; one of three cotenants may own a 40 percent undivided share, with each of the others owning 30 percent shares.

Each tenant in common may sell, mortgage, or give away his interest during his life and transfer it at death, just as though the entire property were owned in single ownership. The right of each tenant in common to possession of the property is subject to the right of his cotenants. Each has the right to an accounting of rents and profits (when the property produces income), and each is entitled to reimbursement by the others of monies expended by him for necessary maintenance, repair, property taxes, and other expenses.[2] Any such reimbursement will be proportionate to each tenant's interest.

Joint Tenancy

A **joint tenancy** is not the same as a tenancy in common; among other minor differences, one is very significant. The difference is the **right of survivorship,** which means that if any joint tenant dies, his interest automatically passes in equal shares to the remaining joint tenants.

---

[2]Because each tenant in common owns an undivided interest in the property, difficult problems may arise when they disagree among themselves and wish to go their separate ways. Any tenant in common is entitled to begin a legal proceeding called an *action for partition.* If the property cannot be equitably divided, the court will order it to be sold, with the proceeds to be divided among the cotenants according to their interests.

For example, if A and B are joint tenants and A dies, title to his one-half undivided share automatically goes to B, who thereby becomes the sole owner of the property. If three joint tenants had owned the property and one died, each of the two survivors would take one-half of the deceased joint tenant's interest.

Because the survivorship feature runs contrary to the traditional pattern of devise and descent (inheritance), those wishing to enter into a joint tenancy must clearly specify this intent at the time they take title. Otherwise, a tenancy in common is presumed.

Although a joint tenant cannot devise his interest by will (since it passes automatically on death), he can sell or give away his interest during his lifetime, thus changing the joint tenancy to a tenancy in common.

Tenancy by the Entirety

A **tenancy by the entirety** is a joint tenancy between husband and wife. The tenancy carries with it the same right of survivorship as a joint tenancy so that, on the death of either spouse, the survivor takes the entire estate. Unlike a joint tenancy, however, neither spouse can convey any part of the property during their joint lives unless the other spouse joins in the conveyance. In many states, any conveyance to a husband and wife is presumed to create a tenancy by the entirely. Thus, tenancy by the entirety acts to protect the rights of a surviving spouse in property owned during the marriage.

Property held under tenancy by the entirety is not subject to levy by creditors of only one of the owners. This feature was designed to protect the family from the business failures of one of the spouses. In the event the owners are divorced, the tenancy is destroyed and the divorced spouses become tenants in common.

Community Property

The three types of concurrent ownership just described—tenancy in common, joint tenancy, and tenancy by the entirety—are derivations of English common law. The type of ownership, known as **community property**, by contrast, derives from Spanish or French law and is now recognized by statute in eight states: Arizona, California, Idaho, Louisiana, Nevada, New Mexico, Texas, and Washington. In these states, each spouse is an equal coowner of all the property acquired during the existence of the marriage as a result of the joint efforts of the spouses, and there is a presumption that all the property of husband and wife is community property. However, the spouses can, by mutual consent, convert community property into the separate property of either spouse.

Property is not considered community property if it was owned by either spouse before the marriage or acquired by either spouse during the marriage by give, inheritance, or will. (Separate property must not be commingled, or it will lose its ownership identity and become community property.) Community property statutes sometimes also provide that one-half the earnings of either spouse during the existence of the marriage belongs to the other spouse. This rule has been the basis of some celebrated proceedings between both married and unmarried couples in recent years.

On the death of a spouse **intestate** (i.e., without leaving a will), the surviving spouse may or may not take all the community property, depending on the statute of the particular state. Divorce ordinarily destroys the community property status, and, pending a divorce, separation agreements involving property settlements and reservations with respect to the future earnings of one or both spouses, are usually made.

The effect of community property is similar (although the legal form is very different) to tenancy by the entirety. Both serve to protect the interest of the "uninformed" spouse. To ensure a good conveyance, both husband and wife must often sign the deed in community property state, and both signatures are always required when the selling interest is owned by a tenancy by the entirety.

TWO SPECIAL FORMS OF OWNERSHIP

In addition to the ownership forms just described, two special types of ownership interests exist in real estate, the condominium and the cooperative corporation.

Condominiums

As with community property, the **condominium** concept does not derive from English common law. Rather, it dates back over 2,000 years to Roman law, from which it has become a part of the civil law followed by most countries in Western Europe and South America. Although introduced into our country as recently as 1952 (in Puerto Rico), statutes authorizing condominium ownership now have been passed by every state and the District of Columbia.

Condominium (*codominion*) means joint ownership and control, as distinguished from sole ownership and control. In a condominium project, each unit (e.g., apartment) is individually owned, whereas the common elements of the building (e.g., lobby, corridors, exterior walls) are jointly owned. Although by far most condominium projects are residential, the concept has been extended to commercial, industrial, and recreational projects.

To create a condominium, the owners of the property must file a declaration of condominium (or master deed) with the local land records office. The declaration includes a detailed description of the individual units in the property and of the common areas that may be used by all of the owners. The declaration also sets forth the percentage of ownership that attaches to each individual unit. This percentage establishes the voting rights of each unit owner and each owner's contribution to the operating expenses of the property.

Each owner of a condominium unit may sell or mortgage his unit as he sees fit. Property taxes are levied on each unit rather than on the entire project. The condominium unit owners constitute an owners' association and elect a board of directors, which is responsible for the day-to-day running of the condominium project.

We will return several times in the text to the condominium concept. Its popularity in recent years has led to new financing techniques and complex property management questions.

Cooperative Housing Corporations

The essential element of a cooperative housing corporation (**cooperative**) is that ownership is in a corporation, the shares of which are divided among several persons, each of whom is entitled to lease a portion of the space by virtue of his ownership interest—that is, ownership and the right to lease and use the space are inseparable. Typically, a residential building is acquired by a corporation organized as a cooperative (as distinguished from a business corporation organized for profit). Each share (or specified group of shares) in the corporation carries with it the right to lease and use a designated apartment. Each shareholder executes a *proprietary lease* with the corporation, which is similar to a standard lease and pursuant to which the tenant-owner may occupy the designated unit.

Just as with a condominium, the cooperative project is run by a board of directors. Unlike a condominium, the project has a single owner—the cooperative corporation—which may mortgage the property (thus automatically providing financing for each apartment owner). The property is a single parcel for purposes of real estate taxation, and the taxes paid by the corporation are allocated among the various unit owners, as are all the common area and maintenance expenses of the building. Each owner then pays a monthly assessment (equivalent to rent) to cover the operation expenses and necessary repairs and replacements.

Difference between Condominiums and Cooperatives

A significant difference between a condominium and cooperative lies in the possible "snowball" effect if an individual owner defaults. In the case of a cooperative, default by a tenant-shareholder means that his portion of real estate taxes, mortgage debt service, and common area expense must be assumed by the remaining owners. If a number of tenant-shareholders default, the burden on the remaining owners becomes correspondingly heavier, and a snowball effect may be created, causing more and more tenants to default. Precisely this kind of situation happened during the depression of the 1930s, causing many cooperatives to fail.

By contrast, a condominium unit owner is responsible for his own mortgage financing and real estate taxes on the unit owned. Consequently, in the event of a default by a single-unit owner, only that owner's share of operating expenses (but not taxes or debt service) must be assumed by the remaining owners. As a result, a "snowball' is much less likely to occur in a condominium project—one obvious reason for the popularity of this form of ownership.

LEGAL ENTITIES FOR OWNING REAL ESTATE INTERESTS

The preceding section pointed out that a real estate interest may be held by one person (single ownership) or by several persons (concurrent ownership). This section considers what kinds of "persons," other than individuals, can own a real estate interest. The five types briefly discussed are

- The general partnership.
- The limited partnership.

- The corporation.
- The land trust.
- The real estate investment trust (REIT).

All these vehicles for ownership (except for the last) are not unique to real estate, being available for ownership of any kind of property. They are discussed here because they are commonly used by real estate investors to achieve additional flexibility in financing and managing real estate and in achieving the most desirable tax consequences.

Omitted from the list are two frequently used terms in real estate investing: **syndicate** and **joint venture**. The reason is that both terms merely refer to the general idea of group ownership. A syndicate may be made up of any number of investors from three to four to several hundred. Joint ventures generally describe a two-party relationship between a developer or operator and an institution that provides the financing (although sometimes more than two parties are involved).

Why Ownership Vehicles Are Used

Before discussing the various types of ownership vehicles, we should say a word about the reasons for utilizing them. The major advantage they offer is the ability to pool capital contributions from a number of individuals. Another significant advantage is that these vehicles (except for the general partnership) insulate the individual investors from any liability for losses beyond the capital contributions the investor agrees to make. In addition, these vehicles provide a way for individual investors inexperienced in real estate to benefit from the expertise of professional developers and investors who undertake (for a portion of the return) the management responsibilities of the investment. Finally, as described in Part VI, these different ownership vehicles have different tax characteristics, which are important in structuring the ideal vehicle to accomplish a particular investment objective.

General Partnership

The **general partnership** is a form of business organization in which two or more persons are associated as coowners in a continuing relationship for the purpose of carrying on a common enterprise or business for a profit. An agreement of partnership (also called *articles of partnership*) defines the rights and obligations of each partner and sets forth how profits and

losses are to be shared. Unlike a corporation, a general partnership requires no formal legal action or charter from the state in order to function.
Once organized, however, a partnership must operate in accordance with
legal rules that in most states follow a model known as the Uniform Partnership Act.

In the ownership or operation of real estate, a partnership has one
overriding advantage over the business corporation. The partnership is not
considered a tax entity apart from its members. Real estate investments
may generate "tax losses" that can be used to offset other investment income of the investor. Because a partnership is not a separate tax entity,
such tax losses on real estate owned by a partnership can be "passed
through" to the individual partners and used to offset their outside investment income. If a corporation is the owner, no pass-through can occur
since the corporation is treated as an independent tax entity.

Another important distinction between a general partnership and the
other forms of ownership entities is that each general partner is entitled to
an equal voice in partnership affairs, in the absence of a provision to the
contrary in the agreement of partnership. In the other ownership vehicles,
management is concentrated in the hands of a few of the participants.
Thus, the general partnership is appropriate when each participant wishes
to have the right to join in management decisions. On the other hand, because all (or sometimes a majority) of the partners must agree to decisions
in a general partnership, it is most suitable for relatively small and intimate
groups of investors who are confident of their ability to work together.

The general partnership format does have certain disadvantages. The
death of a general partner typically terminates the partnership and forces
reorganization. More important, each general partner is liable for his partner's acts on behalf of the enterprise. The risk of loss is not limited in
amount, and the liability may come as a result of a partner's actions completely independent of your own actions. If your partner signs a contract as
a general partner, you are bound to honor that contract.

Limited Partnership

A **limited partnership** is a special type of partnership. It is composed of
one or more general partners who manage the partnership affairs and one
or more limited partners who are passive investors, who do not actively
participate in the management of partnership affairs, and who, as a consequence, may legally limit their liability to the amount of cash actually in-

vested (or to the amount they specifically promise to provide in the event they are called upon to do so). By comparison, the general partner must assume full and unlimited personal liability for partnership debts.

The limited partnership is the most common form of organization used for real estate syndications since it combines for the limited partners the limited legal liability offered by the corporate form of organization with the tax advantages of the partnership form (i.e., the pass-through of losses). By using a limited partnership, a real estate professional may join the financial resources of outside investors with his own skills and resources and at the same time concentrate management in his own hands. Of course, there have been cases of a supposed "professional" fraudulently running away with the money. No ownership vehicle is foolproof, and personal ethics as well as the formal rules of the game are needed to ensure a game that benefits society.

A limited partnership is formed by a written agreement of partnership pursuant to a state statute. Most statutes are patterned after a model known as the Uniform Limited Partnership Act. Whereas a general partnership is an entity recognized by common law and can therefore come into existence independent of any statute, a limited partnership is a "creature of statute" and will not be given legal recognition unless an appropriate certificate of limited partnership has been filled with the appropriate state authority.

Corporation

A **corporation** is a separate legal entity—an artificial person—created in accordance with the laws of a particular state (the federal government not having the power to create business corporations). Thus, the corporation is an entity entirely distinct from its shareholders. Its charter may provide that it shall have a perpetual life, and it operates through a board of directors elected by the shareholders. The major advantage of, and the original purpose for, the corporate form was to limit each shareholder's liability to the amount of his capital investment; a secondary purpose was to make shareholder interests freely transferable by means of assignable corporate shares. Both of these features made corporation useful for aggregating investment capital.

The major disadvantage in using a corporation to own real estate is that the corporation is recognized as an independent entity for tax purposes. Thus, tax losses from corporately owned real estate may not be passed through to the individual shareholders but may be utilized only by the corporation itself. Because it may not have any other income against which the losses may be offset, the losses may be of no use. (Tax law changes may substantially lessen this problem.) On the other hand, if the corporate real estate produces net income, a problem of double taxation must be faced. The corporation first must pay a corporate income tax on its net income. Then, to the extent the income is distributed in the form of dividends, the shareholders must pay a personal income tax on such income. In the case of a small, closely owned corporation (known as a *close corporation*), the problem of double taxation often can be avoided by distributing corporate income to the shareholders in the form of salaries or other compensation. In this situation, the corporation may deduct the cost of such salaries and thus reduce its own income, although the shareholder-employees will be taxed on the income they receive.

In certain situations, it may be possible to use an **S Corporation**. This corporate election allows the shareholders to be taxed directly as in a partnership. Congress intended the S Corporation for small operating businesses, and in real estate it is most often used by active players, not by passive investors.

Trust

The **trust** is the least commonly used of the ownership vehicles, being somewhat cumbersome in its organization and operation. Nevertheless, it remains popular in some parts of the country (where it is often known as a *land trust*). A trust is a legal relationship among three persons, normally established by a written agreement, in which

- A *trustor* or *creator* transfers legal title to real estate to
- A *trustee,* who holds the legal title with the responsibility of administering it and distributing the income for the benefit of
- One or more *beneficiaries* who hold beneficial or equitable title to the real estate.

For example, a group of investors may organize a land trust, with themselves as beneficiaries, naming a trustee (such as a trust company) that utilizes funds provided by the beneficiaries to buy a parcel of real estate and administer it for their benefit.

The great advantage of the land trust, which it shares with the partnership, is its ability to act as a conduit for tax purposes. Thus, if the real estate generates tax losses, these can be passed through directly to the beneficiaries, but if the real estate produces taxable income, the trust avoids the double tax that results from use of the corporate form so long as it distributes the income.

Because legal title to the real estate owned by a trust is in the name of the trustee, transfers of title can be effected without disclosing the names of the beneficiaries or requiring their participation. In addition, any changes in the personal or business affairs of a beneficiary—such as business reverses or a divorce—have no effect on the title to the property owned by the trust (although the interest of the particular beneficiary may be affected).

To be distinguished from the land trust is the *personal trust,* which is a common means of holding property (real estate and otherwise) for the benefit of members of a family, particularly the spouse or children of a decedent. A trust may be set up by will (a testamentary trust) or may be set up during the lifetime of the trustor (an inter vivos trust, that is, one between living persons). In family estate planning, the trust is an extremely flexible instrument and for this reason is one of the most frequently used vehicles for controlling individual wealth.

Real Estate Investment Trust (REIT)

A special form of trust ownership is the **Real Estate Investment Trust** or **REIT,** which is wholly a creature of the Internal Revenue Code. REITs were set up as a parallel form of investment vehicle to common stock mutual funds, to permit small investors to invest in diversified portfolio of real estate just as they could in a portfolio of common stocks in a mutual fund.

The major tax benefit of a REIT is that, so long as it distributes at least 95 percent of its net income to its shareholder-beneficiaries, it need not pay any income tax (although the individual shareholders must pay a tax on the dividends received). Thus, the problem of double taxation is eliminated. REITs are strictly limited by statute to the types of operations they may conduct.

CURRENT TRENDS IN REAL ESTATE INTERESTS AND OWNERSHIP

Traditionally, the legal rules affecting rights in real property have changed very slowly. The major cause of this is the permanence of land and hence the long-term nature of interests in land. Courts and legislatures have hesitated to create new rules that might affect titles acquired many years ago or change the allocation of the bundle of rights created by long-standing leases or other agreements.

However, in the past quarter century, the pace of change in this area has speeded up a great deal. There are several reasons for this. One of the most important has been inflation, which has substantially changed the economic relationship between landlords and tenants and between developers and lenders. Another has been changes in the tax laws, which encourage new forms of investment techniques.

Here are several trends that can be expected to grow in importance in the future.

Growth of condominium ownership. The condominium has been called "the wave of the future" because it offers families and individuals a way to own their homes in an era of rising land costs and financing costs. The traditional detached one-family house in the suburbs has been priced beyond the reach of many families, but there is no doubt that most Americans still desire to own rather than rent the place in which they live. By combining the idea of ownership with that of multifamily housing, the condominium offers what seems to be the best solution to date. Unfortunately for investors, even the most obvious trends are not surefire ways to make money. Extensive condominium development has outpaced demand in many markets. In the mid-1980s, the thing not to have is a "stacked" (high-rise) condominium in the South.

Increase of real estate syndications. Real estate is now and is likely to remain the major store of national wealth. Consequently, public interest in real estate investment has become very great.

New lease relationships. Continuing concern over inflation is leading to significant changes in lease relationships. The traditional, long-term, fixed-rent lease is rapidly disappearing, to be replaced by shorter-term leases carrying rentals that are subject to periodic increases as outside costs rise and that impose on the tenant more and more of the responsibilities for maintaining his premises.

SUMMARY

The contents of this reading should have amply demonstrated that it is no simple matter to answer the question, "Who owns the parcel of real estate known as 150 Main Street?" Three parallel lines of investigation must be followed to provide an adequate answer.

First, one must determine if the physical real estate at 150 Main Street has been separated into different types of physical interests—that is, whether there has been a severance of air rights, surface rights, and subsurface rights or whether the physical interest remains a unified one.

Second, one must determine if there is a single legal interest in the real estate (i.e., a fee simple absolute) or whether there has been a separation of legal interests, between a present and future fee interest; a fee and leasehold interest, by creation of a nonpossessory interest such as an easement or license; or any possible combination of the foregoing.

Finally, one must determine whether each legal interest in each physical interest in the real estate is owned by a single person (*in severalty*) or divided through some concurrent ownership form. Additionally, different ownership vehicles are possible whether the real estate is owned by severalty or in some concurrent ownership form.

READING 23

REAL ESTATE INVESTING THROUGH MASTER LIMITED PARTNERSHIPS

Steven D. Kapplin
Arthur L. Schwartz, Jr.

Limited partnerships have been around for some time, providing individuals with the opportunity to invest in nonfinancial entities such as real estate.

Newer to the scene is the real estate master limited partnership, which is basically a publicly traded real estate limited partnership. The first real estate master limited partnership began operations in late 1981 when Ala Moana Hawaii Properties was spun off by Dillingham Corporation.

Real estate master limited partnerships offer certain advantages to investors over traditional limited partnerships—because the partnership units are traded in a public securities market, a real estate master limited partnership has significantly greater marketability. This article provides background information on these new instruments and an analysis of their recent rates of return.

A BRIEF DESCRIPTION

Master limited partnerships are not limited to real estate investments. Currently, there are master limited partnerships that invest in sports teams, restaurants, oil and gas, cable television, and farming.

Source: *AAII Journal*, September 1988. Used with permission.

Master limited partnerships are no different than ordinary limited partnership investments, except that they are openly traded on major stock exchanges. This latter feature makes the master limited partnership a significantly more liquid investment than the ordinary limited partnership. Investors may buy, sell, or obtain information on master limited partnerships by simply calling their stockbroker.

Trading in the securities of master limited partnerships is not restricted in any way, although there are restrictions on the percentage that can be traded in one year. Because of the general partnership rules, the percentage of ownership traded in any one year must be kept below 50 percent. If more than that is traded in one year, the partnership is considered terminated for tax purposes. Although this is certainly a legal concern, it is not a practical concern because the percentage of ownership available for public trade on most limited partnerships is much less than 50 percent of its total units.

Unlike limited partnerships, which usually make distributions on a quarterly basis, master limited partnerships may make distributions as frequently as management sees fit. Some make quarterly payments, while others make monthly payments. Distributions may consist of cash flows, taxable income, or capital returns.

Like limited partnerships, all income and capital losses or gains of a master limited partnership are passed through to the investor, where they are taxed at the investor's ordinary tax rate. Under the 1987 tax law changes, most master limited partnerships will continue to be taxed as partnerships. However, those that are actually operating companies rather than acting as passive investment companies will be taxes as corporations beginning in 1997. Unlike ordinary limited partnerships, the income or loss from a master limited partnership is considered as portfolio income or loss. It is no longer attractive as a tax shelter vehicle, although it retains the benefit of having only one level of taxation.

Liquidity is the primary benefit master limited partnerships bring to investors. Unlike ordinary limited partnerships whose interests have no organized market for exchange, the master limited partnership may be conveniently traded on either the New York Stock Exchange, the American Stock Exchange, or over the counter through the NASD automated system. Thus, investors may not only get the benefits of income and loss pass-throughs, but they may also benefit from unit appreciation.

They are not without certain risks, however. Like any security, the financial success of a master limited partnership is directly related to both the nature of its business and the capability of its management. Investors should take care to thoroughly investigate the financial potential of a master limited partnership's business. Investors should also carefully consider whether any underlying company's assets are fairly priced within the unit price of the partnership.

Control is also important. Most master limited partnerships require a larger percentage of unit holders' votes to change management than is required in many ordinary corporations. A master limited partnership's management may promise large distributions during the early years of the partnership's life, but may not continue those distribution levels for long. Unit holders may have little control over the distribution policies of many partnership managements.

Another risk is their lack of a performance history. While this article takes a look at their returns and risk versus the stock market, investors should note that these results are preliminary due to the rather short life of master limited partnerships. In addition, tax uncertainty during the latter part of 1985 and the first three quarters of 1986 make it difficult to interpret the results reported later in this paper.

TYPES OF PARTNERSHIPS

Real estate master limited partnerships can be categorized into three general types, based upon the origin of the partnership.

A "roll-up" master limited partnership is created by combining the partnership interests of several existing limited partnerships into a new master limited partnership. The first master limited partnership of any type was a roll-up—the Apache Oil and Gas MLP—put together by Apache Petroleum in 1981. It was created by converting 33 Apache oil and gas limited partnerships into one master limited partnership, and it provided unit holders of Apache limited partnerships with a tax deferred method of trading their low-marketability interests for a New York Stock Exchange–listed security.

An example of a roll-up real estate master limited partnership is Southwest Realty, Ltd., which was created in 1983. In this transaction, 25 existing real estate limited partnerships were combined. This particular master limited partnership has provided disappointing returns, probably due to the poor returns of its Texas and Oklahoma apartment properties. In general, the roll-up is the least common type of real estate master limited partnership. The number of new real estate roll-ups is not expected to in-

Types of Real Estate MLPs

Roll-up: MLP formed by combining the interests of several existing limited partnerships.

Roll-out: MLP formed through the sale or transfer of existing corporate real estate to a master partnership sponsored by the corporation.

Carve-out: A form of roll-out where the corporation sells its interests in the newly created MLP through an underwriting.

Spin-off: A form of roll-out where the corporation distributes its interests in the newly created MLP to its shareholders.

Roll-in: MLP formed to raise capital for the purchase of assets.

---

crease as rapidly as other types because of problems associated with valuing real estate assets and the difficult task of merging existing partnerships.

The "**roll-out**" is the most common type of real estate master limited partnership. It involves the sale or transfer of existing corporate real estate to a master partnership sponsored by the corporation, which receives either cash or units in the partnership in exchange for assets. If the corporation receives units in the partnership, it can sell them through an underwritten offering. This type of transaction is often called a "carve-out." If the corporation elects to distribute the units to its shareholders, this is often called a "spin-off."

The first real estate master limited partnership was a *roll-out spin-off*, created in late 1981 when Dillingham Corporation spun off Ala Moana Hawaii Properties to its shareholders. Ala Moana Properties' principal asset was the Ala Moana Shopping Center in Honolulu; it also owned land and other improved properties on Maui and Oahu. Dillingham's motivation for the spin-off was to allow shareholders to more fully realize the underlying value of its real estate assets. The value of Dillingham stock and Ala Moana was substantially greater after the spin-off occurred than was Dillingham's stock price prior to the distribution. Another example of a roll-out is Burger King Investors MLP. This partnership is also an example of a carve-out—it was sponsored by Pillsbury and involved the sale of 128 Burger King restaurants to the partnership. Pillsbury now leases the restaurant from the master limited partnership.

There are several benefits to the corporate roll-out master limited partnership's sponsor. First, the corporation may be able to realize better value for its real estate assets while retaining control of the assets. The roll-out could be used as a tactic for warding off corporate raiders. And the corporation earns substantial fees for sponsoring the partnership.

Investor benefits include the ownership of mature real estate assets with long-term leases. Many master limited partnership lease agreements provide for percentage of gross sales rents that could escalate if sales increase. However, the corporate sponsors typically extract hefty management fees. In addition, the purchase price paid by the partnership for the properties can be on the high side.

The third type of real estate master limited partnership is the **roll-in**. The term applies both to corporate conversions to master limited partnerships as well as new issues of master limited partnerships that are made to raise capital for the purchase of assets. For example, recently several home builders converted from publicly held corporations to master limited partnerships, including NV homes, UDC-Universal Development and Standard Pacific. The master limited partnership structure in this case is used to avoid corporate income taxes. An example of the other form of roll-in is the sponsorship by several leading syndicators of initial offerings in master limited partnerships to raise funds to invest in mortgages. These include partnerships sponsored by VMS Realty, Winthrop Financial Associates, America First Capital Associates, Angeles Funding Corporation, and Integrated Resources.

MASTER LIMITED PARTNERSHIP RETURNS

To date, there has been no research on master limited partnerships. The returns of real estate limited partnerships have been the subject of several studies (see, for instance, "Investing in Real Estate Limited Partnerships," by Messrs. Kapplin and Schwartz, in the September 1986 *AAII Journal*), although they are limited by data constraints since the secondary market for interests in these partnerships have only recently become organized. In general, the studies found that real estate limited partnerships that began in the 1973 to 1984 time period have provided fairly low returns to investors. It does not appear that these partnerships had rates of return in excess of the rate of inflation or that their returns exceeded that of the overall income property market.

Our study of master limited partnerships addressed several issues. First, returns were calculated for the entire period over which master limited partnership securities have existed: 1982 through 1987. Second, risk

TABLE 1
Year in Which Sample MLPs Began Operations

Year	Number of Sample MLPs
1987	6
1986	14
1985	3
1984	0
1983	4
1982	0
1981	3
Total	30

was measured by examining the relative volatility of master limited partnership returns and the relationship of those returns to the overall stock market.

The data in the study consisted of 30 master limited partnerships that began operations between 1981 and 1987. This sample contains the majority of real estate master limited partnerships that came into existence before 1988. Table 1 indicates the years in which these partnerships started operating; many of them began in 1986. Obviously, this is a fairly new type of security.

The sample includes all of the various types of partnerships: one roll-up, 12 roll-ins, and 17 roll-outs. The roll-outs typically were corporate spin-offs, and the roll-ins were typically corporate conversions.

Table 2 provides the returns for these partnerships, as well as returns for the Standard & Poor's 500 stock index. The returns are not adjusted for risk or market movements, and they are before taxes. Monthly returns are presented for 1986 and 1987, which provides a glimpse of how these returns fared during both the bear and bull market cycles of those two years. Because the sample size is so small prior to 1986, the monthly returns during 1982 through 1985 are aggregated to provide yearly returns.

It is clear from Table 2 that those master limited partnerships that began prior to 1986 provided, on average, fairly strong returns over the 1982 through 1985 time period. During 1985, for example, a portfolio of the seven to nine real estate master limited partnerships that were available at that time provided a yearly average return that was substantially greater than that of the S&P 500. In contrast, the previous study of real estate limited partnerships that began operations after 1981 found average rates of return in the range of 1 percent to 3 percent annually, after tax. While the small sample size of master limited partnerships hinders rigorous statistical comparisons, it appears that over the 1982 through 1985 time period, master limited partnership returns were driven by much different processes than the real estate limited partnerships. One possible explanation is that the early master limited partnerships consist of assets acquired by their sponsors much earlier than the master limited partnership itself began, and the returns reflect prior appreciation of the assets. Also during this time period, there was a moderately good investment climate, and master limited partnerships provided a greater degree of marketability. Furthermore, master limited partnerships were a novel product, and concern over tax reform didn't surface until 1985.

During 1986 and 1987, the number of master limited partnerships increased substantially. During 1986, the average monthly return for master limited partnerships was 1.77 percent, similar to the S&P's 1.68 percent. However during 1987, there was a noted divergence between partnership returns and the S&P: The average monthly return for the partnerships was − 1.88 percent, while the S&P had an average monthly return of 0.86 percent. On average, master limited partnerships did not participate in the strong bull market January through August of last year. Yet, their returns appear to have been negatively influenced by the substantial stock market correction last October and November. By any measure, master limited partnership returns substantially underperformed the overall stock market in 1987. A probable cause of this poor performance was proposals to tax master limited partnerships as corporations, which would have eliminated a substantial positive investment attribute. In early 1988, Congress decided not to tax them as corporations, although income and losses will be treated as portfolio income or loss for tax purposes. The uncertainty over this outcome could have held down returns in 1987.

A look at Table 2 would suggest that the returns of master limited partnerships do not closely parallel those of the stock market. But how much influence does the stock market have over these securities? To answer this question, statistical comparisons were made of the returns from master limited partnerships and the S&P 500. The results varied, depending on the time period studied, and are presented in Table 3.

During the 1982 to 1985 period, master limited partnership returns

TABLE 2
Master Limited Partnership (MLP) Returns versus the S&P 500

Time Period	No. of MLPs	Monthly Total Return (%)	
		MLPs	S&P 500
December 1987	30	− 1.54%	7.29%
November 1987	30	− 0.13	− 8.54
October 1987	30	−13.94	−21.76
September 1987	30	− 3.86	− 2.01
August 1987	30	− 0.12	3.91
July 1987	30	3.58	5.23
June 1987	30	− 2.54	5.21
May 1987	30	− 2.60	1.01
April 1987	28	− 4.89	− 0.74
March 1987	27	− 2.01	3.05
February 1987	25	1.27	4.10
January 1987	24	4.17	13.59
1987 monthly average	—	− 1.88	0.86
December 1986	20	− 2.39	− 2.42
November 1986	19	− 0.39	− 2.56
October 1986	15	0.31	5.88
September 1986	15	− 2.71	− 8.13
August 1986	13	3.56	7.53
July 1986	13	− 1.57	− 5.46
June 1986	13	7.53	1.82
May 1986	13	2.01	5.43
April 1986	13	− 0.13	− 1.01
March 1986	11	5.72	5.69
February 1986	10	5.79	7.56
January 1986	10	3.50	0.65
1986 monthly average	—	1.77	1.68

Time Period	No. of MLPs	Annual Compound Return (%)	
		MLPs	S&P 500
1987	24 to 30	−21.45	5.73
1986	10 to 20	22.65	18.77
1985	7 to 9	66.66	32.57
1984	7	28.76	6.5
1983	3 to 6	34.94	23.08
1982	3	17.13	21.11

TABLE 3
How Master Limited Partnership Returns Are Affected by the Stock Market

	Time Period				
	1982 through 1985	*1986 through 1987*	*1987*	*1982 through 1987*
Volatility of MLP returns versus the market*	1.3	0.45	0.44	0.80
Percentage of MLP return variations explained by movements in the stock market	61%	53%	69%	46%

*As measured by beta; the stock market's beta is 1. Beta measures movement relative to the market; a beta of 0.45 indicates the returns are 45 percent as volatile as the market; a beta of 1.3 indicates the returns are 30 percent more volatile than the market.

were about 30 percent more volatile than the overall stock market. In addition, it appears that about 61 percent of the variation in returns from master limited partnerships was related to movements in the stock market, which indicates fairly high influence.

For the two-year period 1986 through 1987, returns from master limited partnerships were much less volatile than the stock market, and the influence of the stock market on these returns also dropped, to 53 percent. It appears that nonstock market related factors, such as the uncertainty over taxation, may have affected returns during this time period.

During 1987, master limited partnership returns were less volatile than the stock market, yet the stock market's influence over those returns was high, accounting for nearly 69 percent of the variation.

What about the overall time period? Master limited partnership returns were less volatile than the stock market, and the influence of the market was relatively low—about 46 percent of the variation in returns from master limited partnerships was related to movements in the stock market. Thus, it appears that master limited partnership returns are generated by a process that is somewhat independent of the overall stock market. Of course, this is not an unexpected situation. Real estate master limited partnerships are portfolios of investment properties and real estate related businesses, and their returns would also be influenced by real estate related factors that probably are not highly affected by the stock market. On the other hand, we would have expected the market to have even less influence on the returns of master limited partnerships than was found in this study.

CONCLUSIONS

Investors can draw a number of conclusions from these results.

Real estate master limited partnerships do offer individuals the opportunity to invest in portfolios of real estate in a market that is more liquid than traditional limited partnerships.

In terms of return, real estate master limited partnerships had fairly high returns between 1982 through 1985. However, the sample size during that time period is fairly small, so any broad conclusions would be speculative. In 1986 and 1987, the number of partnerships rose substantially but returns were, on average, below that of the S&P 500. A longer time period will probably be necessary for a more accurate understanding of returns from these securities.

On the other hand, the results do have significant implications for portfolio diversification. The results of this study reinforce earlier studies that suggest that the real estate market is not significantly affected by movements in the stock market. This implies that real estate master limited partnerships offer an excellent means of diversifying a portfolio, bringing reduced risk without a significant loss in overall returns. Investors should note, however, that master limited partnership returns are not totally independent of movements in the stock market.

Where can investors get more information on master limited partnerships? If you are interested in a particular master limited partnership and know its name, you can get the address from the exchange on which it is listed. Since it is publicly traded, it must provide you with financial statements upon written request.

Coming up with a listing of master limited partnerships is more difficult. Although they are traded on the exchanges and over the counter, they are not easy to spot from a simple listing of exchange securities. Probably the most economical source is your broker. A more costly source is The Stanger Report ($345/year), published by Robert Stanger & Assoc., P.O. Box 7490, 1129 Broad St., Shrewsbury, N.J. 07702.

READING 24

DISASTER HEDGES

Kevin Ostier

You don't have to be a doom-sayer to own gold.

In fact, many financial advisers routinely recommend that investors place 5 percent to 20 percent of their portfolios in gold and other precious metals. For starters, bullion often moves counter to stocks, bonds and most other financial assets. In addition, gold serves as an inflation hedge, usually appreciating during periods when the purchasing power of paper money is declining. And for the doom and gloom crowed, gold stands as a universal currency whose value endures in the event of economic or political upheaval. "Call it disaster insurance," says Joseph C. Battaglia, chairman of the Gold & Silver Emporium in Encino, California.

Yet knowing that you want to hold gold isn't enough. You must still choose among several bullion coins, and even gold bars. Competing metals such as platinum and silver make the decision more complicated. Then there are precious metals storage accounts to consider. In addition, experts suggest shopping among dealers to get the best price and to ensure authenticity.

First, it's important to distinguish between the types of gold coins available. Bullion coins differ from numismatic, or rare coins in that they're not legal tender. Although some countries place a face value on bullion coins, their true worth depends on the "spot" or current cash price of the respective metal. Since gold can fluctuate widely on news about inflation, the dollar, interest rates, and the like, coins can be risky short-term investments.

Source: *Personal Investor*, May 1988. Used with permission.

Most of the leading bullion coins trade at roughly the same price, so buying decisions become largely a matter of personal preference. If you favor the high luster of pure gold, opt for Canadian Maple Leafs or Australian Nuggets.

However, some investors are turned off by the softness of 24-karat gold and favor the more durable U.S. Eagle, South African Krugerrand, and Mexican 50 Peso coins, along with Britain's new entry, the Britannia. Each of these coins contains an ounce of pure gold in addition to traces of copper and silver, used to reduce malleability. However, the inclusion of alloy metals doesn't affect the coins' resale values. "Both types are equally liquid," says Battaglia.

In general, expect to pay a premium of about 4 percent to 6 percent above the spot price for a coin containing one ounce of gold. Dealer commissions will add another 1 percent or so, but these expenses can vary.

Bullion coins also come in one-half, one-fourth, and one-tenth of an ounce, but these smaller sizes should be avoided whenever possible, experts say, because they carry proportionately higher premiums. With gold recently at $450, for example, a one-ounce American Eagle costs about $470, yet 10 one-tenth ounce Eagles would run around $525. The difference can be attributed largely to additional fabrication and handling costs.

Of the world's bullion coins, the Maple Leaf may well be the most popular, experts say. Its 99.99 percent gold content represents a strong marketing tool.

Austrailia's Nuggets, introduced early last year, already have challenged the Maple Leaf's lock on the "pure play" market. Nugget sales surpassed the 300,000-ounce level during the coin's first six months, and have continued strongly into early '88.

On the home front, the American Eagle gold coin has captured roughly 60 percent to 65 percent of a domestic market once dominated by Canada and South Africa. Eagle sales have surpassed three million ounces since the coin was introduced in late '86. Today's Eagles resemble the U.S. $20 Double Eagle, or St. Gaudens coin, minted from 1907 to 1933. Like most other bullion coins, Eagles, too, come in fractional sizes.

ADDITIONAL CHOICES

South Africa's Krugerrand pioneered the bullion coin industry more than two decades ago. In recent years, however, the coin has fallen from grace because of political sanctions—the United States and various other nations no longer import Krugerrands. As a result, public taste seems to have shifted away from the South African coin. Krugerrands shipped to America before the import ban took effect in October 1985 now carry the lowest premiums of any gold coins.

Other popular bullion coins include Mexico's 50 Peso, minted with 1.2 ounces of gold, and the Austrian 100 Corona, made with slightly less than an ounce of gold. The United Kingdom's Britannia series also has been selling well since it debut in late '87.

The Chinese Panda coins, first issued in 1982, technically fall into the bullion category, but their limited mintage and changing faces given them numismatic qualities. Pandas come in six sizes, including six-ounce and one-twentieth-ounce issues.

BARS AND OTHER METALS

The industrial precious metals, silver and platinum, also can be purchased as coins, With silver, investors can choose between the American Eagle and the Mexican Libertad. Some experts favor the latter because it's a tad cheaper. Mexico is the largest silver-producing nation and its labor costs are, of course, lower than in the United States.

Platinum enthusiasts have but one choice in the Isle of Man Noble. This coin hails from a small British island in the Irish Sea. It's 99.95 percent pure, and comes in sizes of one, one-fourth, and one-tenth ounces.

Prior to the coin rage, bullion's most prosaic forms were wafers, bars, and ingots weighing from a gram on up to 100 ounces and more. Investors can save money when buying in "bulk," since bars greater than 10 ounces generally carry lower premiums than those charged for smaller bars and coins.

However, because most bars are manufactured by private firms as opposed to governments, they must be assayed (at a cost of $25 or more per bar) each time they're sold to prove authenticity.

PHYSICAL CONCERNS

Whether buying coins or bars, investors face other costs when considering precious metals. Outlays to store and insure these assets start adding up, as do sales taxes. Yet such levies can be reduced or eliminated with gold storage, or accumulation, accounts.

These programs operate simply enough. Investors send their initial payments—ranging from $500 to $1,000 on up—to a depositary, which buys and stores the metals in bulk. Each account is then credited with coins or bars.

Additional purchases can be made for as little as $50. Many programs let investors make automatic monthly deposits, for dollar-cost averaging.

By contributing the same dollar amount on a regular basis, investors buy more ounces when prices are declining and fewer ounces when prices are rising.

Commissions on storage accounts range between 1 percent and 3 percent, depending on the program and the size of the purchases. Investors also pay a fee of roughly 1 percent when they sell. Insurance normally is included in the storage cost, which is figured on a per-ounce basis (up to $1.25 a year) or on the value of the metal held (usually one-half of 1 percent annually.)

Accumulation accounts can also benefit investors when it comes to taxes. Because most programs store metals in Delaware, a state free of sales taxes, buyers can skirt this expense.

But if you take delivery of your assets, you will be hit with a fabrication fee and any applicable home-state sales taxes. And unless you prefer a lumpy mattress or have deep pockets, you will have to rent a bank safety-deposit box or buy a safe.

CHECKING FOR TROUBLE

Counterfeiting rarely surfaces as a major concern in the bullion coin industry. Experts can spot fakes fairly easily, keying on size, weight, or design inconsistencies.

However, the business has had a few problems with unreliable sellers, so stick to the beaten path. For example, conduct business only with dealers who can document they've been trading metals for at least five years. Also check dealer accreditations. Reputable dealers belong to such organizations as the Industry Council for Tangible Assets, the Professional Numismatists Guild, and the Silver Dollar Round Table.

But by the same token, comparing coin prices and commissions can help you save money. One-ounce gold coins run about $20 to $30 above spot, while silver coins carry premiums of slightly under $1 to $4 or so. Also compare prices when you go to sell.

The same goes for storage programs, since commissions, fees, and reputations vary as well. One sure-fire way to verify the authenticity of a storage program is to call its depositary. In most cases, the Bank of Delaware or Wilmington Trust in Delaware serves in this capacity.

WHAT MAKES GOLD MOVE

For anyone doubting gold's role as a store of value during troubled times, think back to October's stock market crash. The metal rose nearly $16 an ounce in London on Black Monday, and finished the month up 3 percent.

Black Monday's shockwaves heightened investor awareness of precious metals. Sales of various coins rocketed roughly 400 percent worldwide during the two weeks following October 19 compared to the previous two weeks. As stocks crumpled, investors apparently eyed gold as an attractive way to preserve wealth.

Yet what seems to move the yellow metal even more than fears of the unknown are worries about higher inflation. In the early 1970s, gold nearly tripled as the consumer price index surged from 3.4 percent to 12.2 percent. Near the end of the decade, inflation shot up again, eventually pushing gold well above $800 an ounce. The correlation, of course, is not perfect. In 1986, inflation crept at its lowest rate since the mid-60s, yet the yellow metal gained 23 percent.

What also comes into play are inflationary expectations, not just the actual numbers. Gold's impressive performance over the past two years has been due in large part to inflationary fears generated by a falling dollar and rebounding energy prices.

In 1987, inflationary concerns pushed gold all over the place. In the spring and summer, for instance, gold climbed to $480 an ounce, backed off to $437, then rebounded to $450. For the year, the metal finished up 20 percent on the heels of a significant climb in the consumer price index to 4.4 percent, the highest level since 1981.

SOMETHING FOR EVERYONE

Whether or not the world is coming to an end, precious metals make sense for most investors. These assets provide a hedge against inflation and bear markets, and offer a safeguard against disaster.

Bullion coins, and to a lesser extent bars, represent an easy way to hold precious metals. They're easy to price, liquid, portable, and aesthetically pleasing. They can be stored and insured for a relatively low price, and they're nearly immune to counterfeiting.

In fact, the minting of bullion coins by the United States, Canada, Australia, and other governments seems to have increased public interest in civilization's oldest currency. The relatively new Eagle coins in particular have altered investor sentiment about precious metals, says Dick Ryan, former portfolio manager of the Midas Gold Shares & Bullion mutual fund in Minneapolis. "They have legitimized gold in the minds of many Americans."

READING 25

COLLECTIBLES: ARE THEY REALLY INFLATION-PROOF?

Stephen P. Ferris
Anil K. Makhija

The numerous market newsletters and massive media exposure given to stocks and bonds may lead the individual investor to conclude that promising investment opportunities are limited to these vehicles. Such a conclusion would be erroneous. There is an entire class of investments, commonly referred to as "real" or "tangible" assets, that are available for investor consideration in a diversified portfolio. This article will present evidence relating to the investment performance of three different collectibles: gold, diamonds, and artwork/antiques.

These collectibles have been chosen for two reasons. First, the majority of dollars invested in real assets, excluding real estate, are invested in one of these collectible groups. Second, and perhaps most importantly, there is an established price/index series for each of these collectibles, thus making a statistical analysis of return performance possible.

Over long periods, each of these collectibles has been known to have performed well when compared against stocks or inflation. This history, however, has been uneven over various subperiods. Our purpose is to analyze recent experience. This should be of interest not only because it is current, but also because it contains some years of remarkably high inflation.

Source: *AAII Journal,* November 1986. Used with permission.

While general conclusions about the investment worth of these collectibles should not be authoritatively drawn from any subperiod, this update should add to our knowledge of their investment worth.

INFLATION HEDGE STUDIES

There has been considerable research investigating the inflation-hedging ability of a variety of investment-grade assets. One study found that between 1953 and 1971, U.S. government bonds and bills, and private residential real estate were a hedge against inflation.

Recent real estate prices, however, may not confirm these results. Another study found that, over nearly the same time period, commodities futures contracts were reasonable inflation hedges. In contrast, a number of studies have found that the nominal returns from common stocks do not match inflation. This is surprising, given that common stocks are claims against real assets.

Gold, diamonds, and artwork/antiques, however, are real assets that may have the potential of providing inflation hedging. Only recently, however, have data series such as the Rapaport Diamond Index (1978) and the Sotheby Art Index (1981) been available to examine these assets.

In the next section, we describe our procedure for estimating an asset's inflation-hedging ability and its relative market performance. In the subsequent three sections we examine the actual returns for gold, diamonds, and artwork/antiques. In the final section, we summarize our findings.

HOW WE CONDUCTED THE STUDY

When data was available for the different assets, we divided our study period into two subperiods. The first subperiod contains the years 1977 to 1980, when inflation was rising and averaged 9.84 percent. The second subperiod is 1981 to 1983, characterized by declining inflation rates that averaged 5.36 percent. These two subperiods were analyzed for both gold and diamonds, although data for the two were not available for the same beginning periods; artwork and antiques were analyzed over one period only, since data only recently became available.

We investigated both the inflation-hedging ability and the returns relative to the market of each asset. An asset is considered an inflation hedge if its return moves closely with the rate of inflation, thus protecting an investor from a declining real rate of return (the asset's return minus inflation).

It should be noted that these collectibles, although real assets, are quite different from other investments. The psychological returns provided by these assets to investors include such diverse factors as prestige, sophistication, and stylishness. In assessing only their monetary returns, we understate their "true" worth to the collector. Our monetary assessment also involves a measurement bias because commission costs, appraisal fees, and storage charges can be substantial for these investments, and we calculate rates of returns only from appreciation in quoted prices.

Our method for estimating the inflation-hedging ability of an asset correlated the monthly rate of return earned by each asset to the inflation rate for that period. What we came up with was a beta statistic much like the one used to compare a security's return with the overall market. Thus, a figure of 1 for "inflation-hedge ability" indicates that the asset is a complete inflation hedge: If inflation increases 1 percent, the asset will, on average, increase by 1 percent; if inflation decreases by 1 percent, the asset will, on average, decrease by 1 percent. A figure below 1 indicates that the asset will be impacted by inflation to a lesser degree, while a figure above 1 indicates that the asset will be more strongly affected by inflation—for instance, 1.5 would indicate that, if inflation rose 1 percent, the asset would rise 1.5 percent. A negative figure would indicate that the asset moved opposite to inflation—in other words, a rise in inflation produced a drop in the asset's return.

The inflation measure used in the study was the Consumer Price Index, as calculated by the Bureau of Labor Statistics.

MEASURING RATES OF RETURN

As a collectible, gold may he held in several forms: coins, jewelry, or bullion. To analyze its performance, we calculated the monthly rates of return based on the closing end-of-month bullion prices quoted in Metals Weeks. In the case of gold as well as the other collectibles, price appreciation is the sole source of return.

In order to calculate the monthly rate of return an investor would receive from diamonds, the Rapaport Diamond Index was used. Constructed by the Rapaport Diamond Corporation, this index is an average measure of the price performance of 25 certified one-carat stones and first became available in August 1978. The monthly rates of return on this index were used to proxy the performance of diamonds in general.

Until only recently, it has been difficult to estimate the rate of return on artwork/antiques. Although yearly announcements of the Sotheby Art Indices were made as early as 1970, monthly announcements of the indices' values were begun only in September 1981. Constructed much like other economic and financial indices, the Sotheby indices measure price levels in the 12 most active sectors of the international art market. An aggregate index for the overall art market is also provided by Sotheby. Monthly rates of return on the aggregate as well as the component indices are used here.

The measure of the stock market performance consists of all stocks listed on the New York Stock Exchange.

In judging investment performance, we calculated the average monthly rates of return on collectibles and compared them against the monthly returns on the common stock portfolio. In comparing returns, it is also important to evaluate the riskiness that is assumed for a level of return. Therefore, we looked at a measure of the variability of the returns—the higher the variability of returns, the higher the risk.

Well-diversified portfolios, on the other hand, may want to use a different risk measure. These portfolios have diversified away most risk except stock market risk—the risk that all investments will move together with the market. A more meaningful measure for these portfolios would be the ''stock market hedge'' factor—beta. Like the inflation beta, the stock market beta measures an asset's return versus the market: A beta of 1 indicates that the asset's return moves in tandem with the market and a 10 percent increase in the market will produce a 10 percent increase in the asset on average; a beta below 1 indicates that the asset will be less influenced by market moves. In contrast to the inflation hedge, however, a hedge against the stock market would move contrary to the stock market—the investor in this instance wants an asset that is *not* influenced by the stock market. Thus, a good stock market hedge would have figures approaching 0, or better yet, figures that are negative.

THE PERFORMANCE OF GOLD

Gold has long been popularly viewed as an ideal medium by which to maintain value during a period of rising prices. In Table 1, we compare the average monthly rates of return on gold bullion to both inflation and the

TABLE 1
Gold versus Inflation, the Stock Market

	Entire Period 1/77 to 12/83	1st Subperiod 1/77 to 6/80	2nd Subperiod 7/80 to 12/83
Average monthly returns			
Gold	1.24%	3.76%	−1.28%
Stock market	1.14%	0.81%	1.41%
Inflation (CPI)	0.67%	0.84%	0.48%
Return variability*			
Gold	8.79%	9.52%	7.27%
Stock market	4.35%	4.38%	4.36%
Gold's hedging ability†			
Vs. inflation	3.33	3.93	−1.84
Vs. stock market	0.52	0.42	0.72

*As measured by standard deviation. This figure represents the amount above and below the average by which two-thirds of all returns fell. The higher the figure, the more variable the returns and the greater the risk.

†Gold returns were correlated to inflation and the stock market to produce a beta figure. Figures approaching 1 indicate a strong similarity in movement. For the inflation-hedge ability, investors desire an asset that moves with inflation; thus, figures approaching 1 indicate a good inflation hedge. For the stock market-hedging ability, investors seek an asset that moves independently of the market; thus, figures approaching 0 or figures that are negative indicate a good stock market hedge.

stock market. During the first subperiod, January 1977 to June 1980, gold outperformed the market and exceeded the inflation rate as well. Its performance during this subperiod was so strong that, despite a dismal second subperiod performance, the overall average monthly rate of return on gold exceeded that of the market and inflation. This performance, however, should be interpreted carefully. The variability of return measure for gold was substantially larger than the market. In fact, with only a slightly higher return but a much higher variability of return figure compared to the market, gold was a rather poor investment compared to the market for the overall period.

The table also pesents the hedging ability of gold. Our measure of asset-hedging ability against inflation is 3.33 for the overall period from 1977 to 1983. That meant that an increase in inflation was magnified three-fold in gold returns. It is even larger for the first subperiod. During the second subperiod, July 1980 to December 1983, it is negative, indicating that the direction was contrary—in other words, as inflation went up, gold went down.

However, gold may be a good addition to diversified portfolios, since the stock market hedge figure shows that the stock market has little impact on gold returns.

In sum, gold did not match the returns on stocks for the whole period, but it did remarkably well during 1977 to 1980. The results are partially explained by a few months of large returns, with gold performing poorly during most months.

DIAMOND PERFORMANCE

During the overall sample period of August 1978 through December 1983, Table 2 shows that diamonds performed rather poorly when compared with the stock market. Not only were the average monthly returns dismal (0.24 percent versus 1.3 percent for the market), but the variability of returns on diamonds was also considerably higher.

In the first subperiod, August 1978 to April 1980, which includes the diamond speculation frenzy of the late 1970s, diamond returns did exceed the market average, but the variability of returns figure exploded to 11.32 percent—significantly above the market average. For the second subperiod, the variability of return was approximately that of the average, but diamonds had an average loss of 2.49 percent.

The findings regarding the hedging ability of diamonds are also presented in Table 2. The hedging-ability figures indicate that there is no meaningful ability for diamonds to adjust to inflationary price changes: In one subperiod, the 6.38 figure indicates a significant effect, while the −3.15 figure for the second subperiod indicates that diamonds moved opposite to inflation. Diamonds also appear to be little influenced by the stock market, indicated by the stock market hedge figure.

Like gold, diamonds appeared attractive during the high inflation years when they outperformed stocks and proved excellent hedges against inflation. Again, their superior performance is due to some months of sharp price appreciation, and so the inflation-hedging figures do not show returns matching inflation in an "average" month. For the overall period, diamonds did not fare well.

TABLE 2
Diamonds versus Inflation, the Stock Market

	Entire Period 7/78 to 12/83	1st Subperiod 7/78 to 4/81	2nd Subperiod 5/81 to 12/83
Average monthly returns			
Diamonds	0.24%	2.96%	−2.49%
Stock market	1.30%	1.42%	1.19%
Inflation (CPI)	0.67%	0.94%	0.40%
Return variability*			
Diamonds	8.91%	11.32%	4.21%
Stock market	4.57%	4.86%	4.35%
Diamond's hedging ability†			
Vs. inflation	4.23	6.38	−3.15
Vs. stock market	−0.08	−0.53	0.45

*As measured by standard deviation. This figure represents the amount above and below the average by which two-thirds of all returns fell. The higher the figure, the more variable the returns and the greater the risk.

†Diamond returns were correlated to inflation and the stock market to produce a beta figure. Figures approaching 1 indicate a strong similarity in movement. For the inflation-hedge ability, investors desire an asset that moves with inflation; thus, figures approaching 1 indicate a good inflation hedge. For the stock market-hedging ability, investors seek an asset that moves independently of the market; thus, figures approaching 0 or figures that are negative indicate a good stock market hedge.

ARTWORK AND ANTIQUES

In Table 3 we present the average returns and variability of returns for the aggregate Sotheby Art Index as well as the 12-component index. As an aggregate, artwork/antiques was outperformed in return by the stock market. On the other hand, the returns were not as variable as the returns on the stock market.

None of the components of the artwork/antiques aggregate index provided a return in excess of the market. Purely in terms of average return, the best performing sector was English silver with a return of 1.16 percent, followed by American paintings with a 1 percent per month performance. In terms of risk, American paintings and English silver had about the same variability in returns as the market. All other assets had lower variability.

TABLE 3
Artwork/Antiques versus Inflation, the Stock Market

| | Entire Period: 9/81 to 12/83 | | | |
| | | | Artwork/Antiques' Hedging Ability† | |
	Average Monthly Returns (%)	Return Variability* (%)	Versus Inflation	Versus Stock Market
Aggregate	0.59	1.02	0.05	−0.06
Old masters	0.68	2.28	−1.25	−0.07
19th century European paintings	0.49	1.26	−0.14	−0.06
Impressionist paintings	0.93	2.01	0.22	−1.14
Modern paintings	0.72	2.37	0.95	−0.09
American paintings	1.00	3.05	0.14	−0.09
Continental ceramics	−0.19	2.22	−2.63	0.11
Chinese ceramics	0.00	1.54	2.18	0.01
English silver	1.16	3.53	−1.85	−0.08
Continental silver	0.32	2.90	−0.35	−0.03
American furniture	0.50	2.23	−0.98	0.00
Continental furniture	0.61	1.26	0.42	−0.01
English furniture	0.72	2.82	−2.01	−0.04
Stock market	1.82	4.28	—	—
Inflation	0.31	—	—	—

*As measured by standard deviation. This figure represents the amount above and below the average by which two-thirds of all returns fell. The higher the figure, the more variable the returns and the greater the risk.

†Artwork/antiques returns were correlated to inflation and the stock market to produce a beta figure. Figures approaching 1 indicate a strong similarity in movement. For the inflation-hedge ability, investors desire an asset that moves with inflation; thus, figures approaching 1 indicate a good inflation hedge. For the stock market-hedging ability, investors seek an asset that moves independently, of the market; thus, figures approaching 0 or figures that are negative indicate a good stock market hedge.

As far as hedging ability is concerned, the table shows that over the sample period, only Chinese ceramics proved to be a significant inflation hedge. Given the positive (although insignificant) figures for impressionist, modern, and American paintings, one might infer some weak hedging ability. The table also indicates that the stock market has virtually no impact on artwork/antique returns.

One note about our inflation-hedging ability figures for artwork and antiques is in order, however: The results may not be correct depending on how one interprets the case of zero price appreciation in the data. A zero rate of return can arise either because there was no price appreciation or because there was no trade and the last prices was assumed still valid. In practice, Sotheby does not discriminate between the two cases. Strictly speaking, the above analysis holds only if all zero rates of return are taken to be genuine cases of zero price appreciation. To see how our results would change if zero rates of return are taken to arise from infrequent trading, we re-estimated a collectible's inflation-hedging ability using an alternate procedure. However, the results did not differ significantly from our previous results and thus are not reported.

One 1984 study examined the historical rates of return from selected artwork and identified some items that do outperform the market and hedge against inflation. But as they note, their results are calculated for specified paintings and hence suffer from a selection bias. It is impossible to assess average investment performance from these individual sale prices. Furthermore, these returns were calculated over holding periods as long as 65 years, which only indicates the long-term hedging ability of carefully chosen artwork. The focus of this article, however, has been the performance of average investments in art during the recent periods of inflation.

CONCLUSIONS

Collectibles are often recommended as hedges against inflation. Based on our findings for the entire 1977 to 1983 period, we found that gold and diamonds failed to be inflation hedges and did not match overall market performance. But during the earlier years, 1977 to 1980, both gold and diamonds performed well relative to stocks and inflation. In the later years, gold, diamonds, and art/antiques fared poorly. Such performance would suggest that these assets are worth considering during high inflation but not during moderate inflation. As the current economic expansion runs its course and federal deficits remain undiminished, there may be renewed fears of inflation and consequent investor interest in these assets. One element of an investment strategy based upon the findings presented here would be to shift portfolio funds into these collectibles as inflation escalates.

On the other hand, our findings do indicate that these assets are relatively good stock market hedges: Their returns are not significantly influenced by the stock market. Of course, any investment should be judged by the risk-return tradeoff, and potential investors should take a close look at the variability of returns, which for gold and diamonds is high.

Finally, as noted previously, our measured returns understate the true complete return to the investor in tangible goods. Simple financial return ignores any "consumption" component of return associated with physical possession of a flawless diamond, an old master's painting, or gold jewelry. Stocks may return more in dollars, but the certificates don't look as nice hanging on a wall.

READING 26

INVESTING IN GOLD

Jeffrey A. Nichols

"When we have gold, we are in fear;
When we have none, we are in danger."
—*John Ray, English Proverbs*

WHO SHOULD OWN GOLD—AND WHY?

More than a decade has passed since the unrestricted ownership of gold
was legalized again in the United States. Yet, it remains a mysterious medium for most American investors, and one that a great many misunder-
stand. Only slowly are investors in this country coming to appreciate the
metal's virtues—as a hedge against inflation, as a vehicle for diversification and enhancement of portfolio performance, and as an insurance policy
against the risks associated with paper assets such as stocks, bonds,
money-market instruments, and the like.

While many investors, particularly pension funds and other institutional buyers, scorn gold as unconventional or nontraditional and hence
unfit, there is no other single asset, from a global point of view, to which
the word "traditional" better applies. After all, gold's investment tradition spans millennia. It has long been coveted by emperors, kings, sultans,

Source: From Jeffrey A. Nichols, *The Complete Book of Gold Investing* (Homewwod, Ill.: Dow
Jones-Irwin, 1987). Used with permission.

and sheiks, and since time immemorial it has been a favorite investment of millions of others as well, whose blood was less "blue."

Looked at analytically, gold is a simple metal designated on the periodic table of elements by an atomic number of 79 and an atomic weight of 196.967. In flesh-and-blood terms, however, it clearly represents a great deal more. This is apparent at once from the way that it pervades our everyday language. "As good as gold" . . . "A heart of gold" . . . "He's got a real gold mine"—these and similar terms have long since entered the vernacular, and all of them conjure up specific and generally positive mental images.

Despite its long tradition and its excellent reputation, gold has been slow to develop as a widespread investment medium in this country. In part, this may be due to lingering doubts and suspicions from the period of more than four decades when its ownership effectively was banned. From 1933 until 1974, Americans were prohibited from buying, selling, or owning gold in any form other than jewelry and collectible coins—and during those years, they developed misconceptions and misgivings. More recently, such clouds have been dispersing, and more and more Americans are now adding gold to their portfolios.

Who should own gold? And why? The answer to the first question is easy: Nearly everybody—everybody, at least, with savings and discretionary income, whether that income is $15 million a year or $15,000. One important premise of this book is that there is a place for gold and gold-related assets in virtually every American's savings and investment program. As for why someone should own gold, the answer may vary from one investor to another, but essentially there are two fundamental reasons: safety and income.

Only during relatively brief intervals of harsh government proscription, such as the period from 1933 to 1974 in the United States, has gold's traditional role been curbed or displaced. And even then, the restrictions have tended to be limited in scope. During the time when U.S. gold investors were suffering repression, for example, gold remained a popular and widely used investment tool elsewhere in the world, serving millions as a cautious nest egg in a portfolio and others as a hedge against inflation or similar insurance against disorder. In my view, gold is the traditional investment vehicle par excellence—and after the episode of disuse in the United States, it is coming into its own here, as well.

The resurgence of gold in this country was triggered by a combination of political and economic factors starting in the late 1970s. Geopolitical tensions were running high, fueled by the American hostage crisis in Iran and the Soviet invasion of Afghanistan. This, combined with the extraordinary surge in world inflation and the associated appreciation in the price of gold itself, served as the magnet that first began to attract the American investor to this market in a serious and significant way. At the same time, some institutional money managers, influenced by modern portfolio theorists, were starting to recognize that the performance of a conventional stock and bond portfolio often could be improved by including gold.

Some investors hold gold sacrosanct, viewing it as the one secure asset in an insecure world. Fearful that conventional financial assets—even our very currency—may be in dire jeopardy and that hyperinflation or worse may lie ahead, the "gold bug" puts his trust in gold and gold alone. But you need not be a gold bug, or rely on the gold bug's logic and emotions, to conclude, as I do, that gold has a legitimate place in your investment program. While I believe that gold should be a part of almost everyone's portfolio, I do not maintain that it holds any theological significance or messianic promise. Note that I said it should be a *part* of a portfolio. Just how big a part depends on your individual needs, desires, fears, and expectations. It is yet another premise of this book that gold investment can be supported by a cool and objective analysis of the yellow metal's attributes and also be the lessons of portfolio theory and experience.

High Returns and Low Variance

Portfolio theory counsels the investor not only to pursue maximum returns but also to seek a minimum variance—in other words, the least possible exposure to one-sided risk. A central tenet of modern portfolio theory, the "efficient portfolio" concept, focuses on the idea that risk can be reduced by diversification. An efficient portfolio is one in which the expected rate of return is maximized for any given level of risk and uncertainty. Here, the risk is measured by the dispersion or variability of possible future returns. A portfolio can be made "efficient" by minimizing the risk associated with any given level of return. In down-to-earth language, all of this can be summed quite simply: "Don't put all your eggs in one basket." In other words, a modern portfolio should be diversified and spread between "hard" and "soft" assets. "Soft" assets include common stocks, bonds, commercial paper, bank certificates of deposit, money market accounts, and the like. A soft asset is a representation, receipt, or claim for a physical item, while a hard asset is the item itself. Thus, shares in a factory are "soft," while the factory itself is "hard."

Gold has the attribute of being a highly liquid asset. While your home and the land on which it sits may rightly be considered hard assets, they normally would not be looked upon as part of your investment portfolio, since few of us would be willing to part with such assets in order to raise quick money. And real estate generally is not fully liquid. Often, it may take weeks, months, or even years to find a willing buyer for a piece of property and realize a price that you, as the seller, consider reasonable. So really, to be of immediate use, part of your hard assets should be fully liquid—and gold, which is traded world-wide and almost on a 24-hour basis, is probably the most liquid hard asset available.

In addition to its liquidity, gold also has another attribute that makes it a valuable part of a portfolio: its "contrariness." And this can be of crucial importance. In periods when the gold market has been free to fluctuate, the price of the metal has tended to move in the opposite direction from the price of "conventional" financial assets, or with little apparent correlation with those assets. This sometimes contrary nature of gold allows it to be used as a hedge against changes in the value of a portfolio. To "hedge" a portfolio means to protect its value against fluctuation by including within it different assets whose price movements are inversely correlated: When the price of one goes up, the price of the other tends to go down, and vice versa. While the price of gold does not always move exactly opposite to the prices of other investments, it does so often enough to permit its use as a hedge against changes in the value of these investments.

You do not own any stocks? All you have is money? This means your "portfolio" is in cash, and part of almost every portfolio is. But even if your portfolio is entirely in cash, then gold can certainly serve you. Just as it has historically shown its contrariness to many other investments, gold's real value often moves as well in a fashion contrary to the value of currency—of money itself. That is what happened in 1979 and 1980, when the U.S. inflation rate soared above 12 percent, sparking a modern "gold rush." Investor demand for gold pushed the metal's price to record highs. In that extreme case, gold was a more than adequate hedge against inflation. It not only maintained its intrinsic worth, but it actually increased in real value, while the buying power of paper currencies was being eroded substantially. Gold's strong performance during the 1970s was not a fluke. It has held its real value—its purchasing power—not only over the short term but also over the centuries, while even the strongest paper currencies have fallen prey inevitably to the ravages of inflation and depreciation.

For many people, gold has been more than just a hedge against the economic uncertainty of inflation: It has meant the difference, quite literally, between life and death. This was the case, for instance, with the "Boat People" who fled from Vietnam after the fall of Saigon. Many of these people were able to survive largely because they had gold stowed away. Indeed, many immigrants from many different countries have been able to reach America—escaping repression, persecution, and even death in their homelands—because a few ounces of gold bought their freedom. Even in ordinary, less dramatic circumstances, gold has served its owners well in regions of the world less stable than the United States and Western Europe. In most countries, whether they are prone to revolution or election, governments often are forced to devalue currency—but gold retains its value through both changes in economic policy and the more dramatic political upheavals. Thus, it is sought by people around the world as a hedge against economic and political uncertainties. Such demand increases the value of gold by forcing the price higher—even for investors in the United States and Europe.

The Pyramid of Investment

Traditionalists hold that a person should view his investments as a pyramid, with conservative assets at the base, more speculative holdings in the middle, and the riskiest investments at the top. In keeping with the shape of the pyramid, the greatest amount of money would be spent on the items in the base—a house, a car, and savings accounts, for example—with progressively smaller sums being allocated for items at the middle and top. Under this approach, stocks and bonds would be placed in the middle, with gold at the very top.

While the concept of an investment pyramid makes sense, I would move at least a part of the gold, especially bullion and coins, to the bottom. Far from being blatantly speculative, gold, in my opinion, can serve as an anchor for a person's whole portfolio. As I have pointed out, it is a valuable form of insurance, especially against inflation and currency depreciation. To counterbalance the gold, an investor might consider buying long-term bonds and placing those, as well, in the pyramid's base. They would provide a hedge against deflation.

Those who can afford it might buy additional gold, perhaps in different forms, for the middle and top of the pyramid. For the middle, I would suggest some gold stocks; for the top, perhaps futures or options. How much you should spend and what form of gold you should buy will depend on both your income and your personal investment philosophy. But I feel very strongly that a truly sound portfolio should include gold in one form or another.

The Types of Gold Investors

There are three basic types of gold investors: long-term hoarders, who may hold gold or related assets for years, perhaps with no intention of ever selling them; medium-term investors, who treat gold like any other industry or investment sector, buying to achieve a capital gain and/or earn income over a period ranging from several months to several years; and short-term speculators.

The word "hoarder" carries something of a stigma—the image of an unpatriotic miser who keeps a stash of coffee while his neighbors suffer through wartime rationing. But, viewed dispassionately, with an understanding of the motives of a gold hoarder in a politically or militarily unstable country, the term starts to lose much of that stigma. The Boat people were hoarders of gold—but, as pointed out earlier, their hoards enabled them to buy their passage to freedom at a time when South Vietnam's currency was nearly worthless outside that country.

For an American hoarder, the stash of gold is a form of protection against a devaluing currency, or simply a "nest egg" to pass on as part of an estate—but a nest egg that will not lose its real purchasing power, as might occur with many other conventional investments. All hoarders share one thing in common: They are not likely to sell except in a dire emergency. For them, gold is not a quick fix—not simply something to be held until the market rises, with the object of taking a profit at the first propitious moment.

If you are a medium-term investor, you probably think of gold just as you would almost any other investment asset: as something to buy when you perceive it to be undervalued and likely to appreciate, and then to sell at a profit. If you are a medium-term investor with a bullish view of gold—that is, you expect its price to rise—you might elect either to own the metal itself, in the form of bullion or coins, or opt to purchase gold-mining equities. Recognizing the value of gold as part of a portfolio but not dedicated to keeping it forever, the medium-term investor is willing to sell if a profitable opportunity presents itself. The medium-term investor might hold gold or gold-related assets for as short a time as a few months or as long as several years.

If you are a short-term investor, then you might be likely to trade gold futures contracts or options—investments that may be held for as short as a few minutes or as long as a few months. As a rule, short-term investments in vehicles such as the gold futures markets are highly risky ventures. Generally, though, they offer the greatest potential profit over a relatively short time span. The short-term investor is interested in gold not as a safety net or hedge investment but rather for its pure profit potential as a trading vehicle. For the short-term holder, gold is nothing more than a source of trading income.

As a rule, each level of investment involves a different portion of a buyer's investment income. The hoarder is a person who tends to view gold holdings as part of savings—as a nest egg. This is not what you might consider risk capital. Again, when I say "hoarder," I do not mean to conjure up visions of a miser in the Silas Marner tradition. I am speaking of any individual or family that saves regularly for the proverbial rainy day by setting aside a fund not earmarked for a house, car, or any other specific kind of purchase. For such an individual or family, I recommend a "golden umbrella" as part of the package of protection. I believe an investment in gold should account for a share of the savings—perhaps as little as 5 percent or as much as 25 percent, depending on the buyer's own emotional attitude toward the metal. This will increase the probability of successfully weathering the storm if that rainy day ever arrives.

The medium-term investor, on the other hand, is willing to accept some risk in order to achieve some return in the form of capital gains. But, in the case of a gold investor, he also is looking to protect his assets. If you are accustomed to making investments in the stock market, you can use those as a basis for deciding how much to invest in gold. My advice would be to determine how much you are willing to invest in any one industry group—computer stocks, natural resources, or banks and financial institutions, for example. This is how much you should be willing to invest in gold-related investments, above and beyond any gold you may be holding as a long-term nest egg.

If you are a short-term investor, you are using the most discretionary part of your income—the part you can afford to risk and lose. The short-termer who invests in the gold futures and options markets or in "penny stocks," another highly speculative vehicle, is not using gold to protect assets or as a form of insurance against possible setbacks in other parts of a portfolio. Rather, he is looking to earn as high a profit as possible in as short a time span as possible. If you are thinking of trying the short-term route with gold, by all means have the bulk of your investments in either long-term or medium-term vehicles.

Just what percentage of your portfolio should be in gold? That is a matter of debate among investment experts. Their recommendations range from as little as 5 percent to as much as 40 percent or even higher. But increasingly, experts agree that precious metals belong in every modern portfolio. Moreover, investors in the gold market have some pretty impressive company. Just as large institutional investors such as pension funds and insurance companies will be fellow shareholders in a blue-chip stock, some institutions also are holders of gold. But, in the case of gold, the scale of institutions is much larger than even the largest pension fund. Among your fellow investors will be the U.S. government, the Union of Soviet Socialist Republics, and just about every other national treasury. In 1985, the U.S. Treasury held more than 262 million troy ounces of gold bullion—by far the largest hoard of any country. As of the end of 1986, the Soviet Union held an estimated 70 to 80 million ounces. Unlike the United States, which sells relatively little gold, the USSR has been a consistent seller since 1953. But while the Russians regularly market a portion of their annual gold-mine output, they still have managed to increase their holdings in most years by retaining a portion of domestic mine production for official reserves. The fact that so many nations with widely varying economic ideologies are heavy investors in gold suggests that the citizens of the countries, where allowed to do so, likewise should participate in the market.

The question for you, an individual investor, is not whether you should participate in the gold markets, but to what extent. Before you can answer that question intelligently, you will have to study the various uses of gold and learn how to evaluate the potential of gold as an investment as well as some of the risks that are involved. You also will have to determine your personal investment objective. Are you a hoarder? A medium-term investor? Or, are you seeking an immediate return? Last but surely not least, how do you invest in gold? You are the only person who can answer questions dealing with your personal view of the world.

One important note on terminology: Gold and other precious metals are measured in troy ounces. The troy ounce is a unit of apothecary weight that is equal to 31.103 grams. By contrast, a standard, British, or avoirdupois ounce is equal to 28.349 grams. Thus, a troy ounce weighs 9.7 percent more than the standard ounce—the kind we normally use to weigh almost everything else, including ourselves. All references to "ounces" here are to troy ounces.

The London Fix

Twice each day, the eyes and ears of the international gold markets turn almost religiously toward London. What is the fix? Ah, that is the question! At one time, London was the center of global gold trading, and the Bank of England was the most important institution in the whole realm of gold. The reason was simple: The United Kingdom controlled South Africa, the world's most important source of gold, and also reigned supreme on the high seas.

The pound may no longer be "sound the world 'round," but for gold traders there will always be an England.

Twice-daily fixing of the gold price in London, a price that forms the basis for many contracts dealing in physical gold, bears about as much relationship to the hustle, bustle, and noise of U.S. gold futures exchanges as a Viennese masked ball does to a rodeo hoedown. Twice each business day, a representative from each of five major London bullion dealers—Mocatta and Goldsmid, Ltd.; Samuel Montagu & Company; Sharps Pixley & Company, Ltd.; Johnson Matthey Bankers, Ltd.; and N. M. Rothschild and Sons—gather at the Rothschild offices and sit around a table, a procedure their corporate ancestors followed 150 years ago. The only concession to modern times is a telephone beside each seat connecting the holder to his gold trading desk.

The chairman—traditionally the Rothschild representative—calls out a price at the beginning of the fixing session. In front of each place, next to the telephone, is a small Union Jack. If the person at one of the seats wishes to buy at the announced price, the flag is pointed down; if selling is the intention, the Union Jack is raised. Aside from the chairman's announcement of the price, the only conversation is on the phones, between the representatives and their trading desks. If everyone is a buyer, the chairman raises the price until there are some sellers. Conversely, if everyone indicates an intention to sell, the price is lowered until some buying is attracted. When there are flags both up and down, each participant indicates how much metal he is willing to trade. If there is a mismatch, the chairman will make proposals to bring the quantities in line. Finally, the price is agreed upon and transmitted from the room at N. M. Rothschild to gold trading desks around the world. (It may be only 1:30 in the morning in San Francisco, but there will be people awake and waiting.)

Recent changes in the international gold market—not the least of which has been the growth of futures trading in New York—have tended to lessen the importance of the London fix, with prices also being "fixed" in Paris, Zurich, and Frankfurt, as well as Asian centers, such as Tokyo, Singapore, and Hong Kong, for example. Other markets have developed in Sydney, Australia, and Sao Paolo, Brazil. But the prices determined in these centers do not carry the circulation and importance of the London figure.

The London fixing process is an example, in microcosm, of the way the international gold market itself achieves balance. When the price is too high, it is lowered until someone is willing to buy. When it is too low, it is raised until someone is willing to sell. Like the gold market itself, the London activity must always achieve a balance—that is, a point where there are both buyers and sellers.

Jewelry

In the gold industry, "karat" refers to the purity of metal. A 24-karat piece of gold, the purest available, is 99.99 percent gold. Lesser purities are expressed in lower karat values, based on a scale where 24 karats is the highest numerical grade. Thus, a 22-karat piece would be $^{22}/_{24}$ths, or 91.67 percent, gold. In some parts of the world, particularly in the Mideast and developing nations elsewhere, government standards require gold jewelry to be no less than 18-karat—that is $^{18}/_{24}$ths or 75 percent pure. Some countries, such as Saudi Arabia and Kuwait, even set a minimum of 21 karat, or 87.5 percent pure. In more developed countries, where gold jewelry tends to be viewed more often as ornament rather than an investment, lower karatage metal still qualifies legally as "gold." The word "karat," as applied to gold, is not to be confused with the word "carat," which is used in the field of gemology. In the case of diamonds and other gems, "carat" refers to the weight of the stone, not its purity.

BULLION COINS

"Tho wisdom cannot be gotten for gold,
Still less can be gotten without it."
—*Samuel Butler the Younger,* Note-Books

Fabricated gold takes many forms. Coinage is one of the oldest, dating back to at least the six century B.C. Even today, it remains a convenient way to own gold for those investors who wish to take possession of their asset. For those, however, who prefer to have their gold stored in an institution, a certificate program or storage account are equally attractive alternate investment vehicles, broadly speaking.

Some gold coins are said to be "numismatic," while others are described as "bullion coins." Numismatic coins are those with collector appeal and a premium that reflects their status as collectibles. The U.S. double eagle is perhaps the most familiar example. Bullion coins, by contrast, are normally bought and sold for just a modest markup over their intrinsic gold value.

This book does not attempt to discuss rare coins, medals, or medallions; it concentrates instead on reviewing gold bullion coins—for these, in my opinion, are a pure play and far better suited to meeting the objectives of mainstream gold investors.

The value of a bullion coin, unlike that of a rare coin, medal, or medallion, is based primarily on how much precious metal it contains and how much that metal is worth at a given moment. When you buy a gold bullion coin, the gold itself accounts for the lion's share of the cost: You pay the spot price at the time of the transaction plus a small added premium to cover such services as production and distribution.

Unlike their numismatic cousins, gold bullion coins are traded much the same as gold bullion bars. Typically, the more widely circulated gold bullion coins—the Krugerrand and the Maple Leaf, for example, and the new U.S. gold pieces—generally sell at wholesale for a premium of up to 3 percent or so over the current spot price of gold. The standard point of reference for determining gold's spot price is the second London gold fix for the day. At retail, the premium usually ranges from 2 percent to 8 percent above spot. The prices of some of these coins are listed in the financial pages of many daily newspapers. But many papers carry the wholesale "offer" or "ask" price of each coin, that is, the price at which a dealer will sell the coin to a retail coin shop or broker, which varies roughly between 1 percent and 3 percent above spot gold. As a rule, however, investors' purchase price will be a few percentage points higher—in line with standard retail markups for each coin.

Before buying a bullion coin, the investor should make sure that the retailer, bank, or broker with whom you will be doing business maintains a two-way market and stands ready to repurchase the coin at a later date. A reputable coin merchant will usually do so. When a retailer buys a coin back, the price he quotes is known as the "bid." The difference between his buying and selling—or "bid" and "ask"—prices is called the "spread." This is much like the spread that a broker might quote on other investment vehicles such as stocks, bonds, or options.

Now, the investor, of course, is concerned not only with how much it will cost to buy a gold bullion coin today but also with how much the coin will return in the future, when he chooses to sell it. Therefore, the spread is a basic consideration in deciding where to buy gold bullion coins in the first place. Typically, the spread between bid and ask is smaller for gold bullion coins than it is for other "hard" or "tangible" assets currently available to investors. In recent years, it has been as little as $1 for a one-ounce coin.

A Growing Popularity

Until a few years ago, gold bullion coins were the province of the relatively affluent. At that time, they were available only in the one-ounce size and some dealers routinely rejected smaller orders—those involving fewer than 10 pieces. Since then, many millions of Americans have awakened to gold's potential. And those who produce and distribute gold coins have sought to broaden the market by making them available in smaller, more affordable sizes and quantities. The Krugerrand, Maple Leaf, and Panda, for example, can be purchased now not only in the standard one-ounce version but also in fractional sizes of $1/2$, $1/4$, and $1/10$ (and in the case of the Panda, $1/20$) of an ounce. The U.S. Congress followed this lead in December 1985, when it authorized the striking of the first-ever U.S. gold bullion coins, for under that law, they are being struck in the fractional sizes, too. The small coins' affordability puts them within the financial reach of every working American, even people of modest means. It also makes them very attractive as gifts.

So, if you are a small or average investor, bullion coins may be the investment for you to buy, particularly if you want to take delivery of your gold and store it in your safe deposit box. In general, I would say this holds true if you earn less than $100,000 per year, want to invest directly in physical gold, and have a long-term orientation toward investments. Obviously, though, this is just a guideline; it is not a hard and fast rule.

Liquidity—the advantage that is lacking with numismatic coins—is the greatest single asset of bullion coins. Being well known and accepted, the popular bullion coins are widely available at stock brokerage houses, banks, and coin shops. In fact, they can be bought (or sold) in virtually every city of any size in the United States or in just about every country around the world at their current bullion value.

The Distribution Chain

Gold bullion coins are made and marketed through a well-organized distribution chain. Think of it as a pyramid. At the top are the issuing countries that fabricate the coins—Canada, South Africa, and the United States, for example. At the base are the coin shops and other retail outlets where they are sold.

Even though they are not made to be circulated as money, some bullion coins carry face values—nominal amounts, well below the value of the metal they contain—and are treated as legal tender by the governments that issue them. The Maple Leaf is a case in point: The Canadian government has assigned it a face value of $50 and made it legal tender in that amount. The new U.S. gold coin has a face value as well: $50 for the one-ounce coin, $25 for the half ounce, $10 for the quarter ounce, and $5 for the 1/10-ounce version. Although it has no face value the Krugerrand, too, enjoys legal-tender status as official coin of South Africa. So does Britain's Sovereign, a small gold bullion coin that, like the Krugerrand, has no statement of value.

The Austrian 100-Corona, Hungarian 100-Korona, and Mexican 50-Peso gold pieces are considered government "restrikes"—remakes of earlier coins, bearing the original dates—and these are not legal tender. Perhaps I should explain what "legal tender" means. It does not mean the coins are in general circulation or that people routinely use them to pay their bills. It simply means the coins are backed by the issuing country. For you as an investor, there may be an advantage to buying legal-tender gold bullion coins rather than restrikes. Legal-tender coins are considered currency and are not subject to sales tax in many states. Even at the moderate rate of only 5 percent, the sales tax on a $400 coin would be $20. That is not an insignificant sum, and remember, it will not be refunded when the coin is resold to a dealer.

Moving down from the top of the pyramid, the next level in the bullion-coin distribution chain, after the issuing countries, consists of primary dealers. Most of the countries have chosen a handful of companies to act as principal agents in distributing their coins. In the U.S. market, firms such as Mocatta Metals, Republic National Bank, and J. Aron/Goldman Sachs act in this capacity. In effect, they are wholesalers: They sell the coins to companies on the next lower tier in the pyramid as well as to major institutional investors.

The primary distributors all maintain active trading desks. The issuing countries require them to make a two-way market in their coins—always standing ready not only to sell them but also to buy them back at a fair price, regardless of market activity at any particular time. This is not to say that if you had two Krugerrands or Maple Leafs and wanted $1,000 apiece for them, you would get that kind of price from a primary dealer. Actually, a primary dealer would not do business with you at all. It would, however, buy several coins from those on lower levels in the pyramid, paying the going price based on the market value of gold itself.

Next in line are the secondary distributors—the precious-metal retailers, national brokerage houses, money-center banks (in cities such as New York, Chicago, and San Francisco), large coin dealerships, and regional wholesalers. These firms purchase bullion coins from the primary distributors in commercial quantities. Precious-metal retailers sell primarily to individual investors, although they also sell to retail outlets such as neighborhood coin shops. National brokerage houses and money-center banks sell chiefly to individual clients and smaller institutional buyers.

The retain store stands on the lowest tier of the coin distribution system. This may be a "mom-and-pop" operation or it may be part of a chain with many outlets. Stores such as these often charge higher premiums; by the time they get the coins, they have already passed through several other layers, and premiums have been added at every step of the way. Nonetheless, these stores are a vital part of the system, simply because their presence makes the coin more accessible to buyers and, at the other end, more liquid for sellers.

Remember, bullion coins are an investment, and you should expect service, reliability, and buy-back assurance from the retailer who sells them to you, just as you would from your stockbroker or commodity futures broker. And, like any other investment, if you deal with a reputable broker, bank, or coin shop, you need not be concerned with the authenticity of your purchase. A professional coin merchant can easily spot a counterfeit coin. Indeed, one of the attractions of gold bullion coins as an investment is the difficulty in fabricating acceptable fakes. The degree of fine detail, the measurements—both thickness and diameter—the color, and, of course, the weight, when taken together, make it virtually impossible for a professional to be fooled by a counterfeit coin. So, deal with a professional you trust. In addition, some depositories that store coins and bullion on behalf of investors will authenticate every coin and bullion bar before accepting it for storage. I must say that counterfeit coins have not been a problem in this country.

Tax Considerations

Bullion coins, despite their legal-tender status, are considered real property in a legal sense and thus are subject to federal capital gains or loss treatment when they are sold. State and local sales taxes also must be considered. As I pointed out earlier in this chapter, legal-tender coins are exempt from sales taxes in some states, such as Florida and California. Even if your state imposes sales tax on bullion coin purchases, you can legitimately not pay this tax by having your coins shipped to a state, such as Delaware, and then stored in a bank vault in that state. As long as your gold coins remain there, your home state (or province if you are Canadian) will not tax them. At most banks and *vault facilities set up to hold precious metals,* storage fees are about 0.5 percent of the metal's value per year—and the sum *includes insurance* at the current market value. Most reputable retail bullion dealers are familiar with how to arrange storage.

Portability is one of the major reasons why bullion coins have been popular around the world. But, unless you are planning to flee across a border, you might want to consider keeping your bullion coins in a *safe deposit box.* This is a secure location, and it is easily accessible whenever your bank is open. Contrary to popular belief, however, the contents of a safe deposit box are *not insured.* All the bank is doing is renting you space under lock and key in its vault. A simple, inexpensive rider on a homeowner's or tenant's policy will cover the contents of your safe deposit box.

Summary

For the investor, gold bullion coins are an easy way to include gold in an investment portfolio. The things you should consider when deciding on a coin are the *premium*—the additional cost of the coin over the price of gold bullion itself; the *spread* or difference between the bid and ask prices of the coin; its *liquidity*—how popular and easily recognizable, and therefore easy to buy and sell, the coin may be; *aesthetics,* if attractiveness is one of your priorities; and *country of origin,* if this is of interest to you.

GOLD BULLION

While gold coins have traditionally been the province of the small-scale buyer and large bullion bars the haven of the rich, well-heeled investor, a variety of new and innovative gold products now offer the consumer a wide range of bullion investments, hybrids, and proxies.

Paralleling this product expansion during the past five years has been the establishment of new types of marketing outlets on Wall Street and beyond. The entry of more banks and brokerage firms as intermediaries offering these innovative vehicles (often patterned after instruments initially developed for other financial markets) have placed gold high on the list of worthy assets, right up there with stocks, bonds, and money markets. Besides bars and wafers, the array of gold alternatives includes certificates of deposit, passbook or accumulation accounts, storage programs, collateralized bank finance, and, although in a separate category, leverage accounts.

The new paper instruments can be transacted with greater efficiency and yield larger profit margins to retailers than the sale of physical gold and, in many cases, they are better suited to investor's needs because they facilitate easy purchase and resale and often carry lower transaction costs for buyers.

For those conservative investors interested in buying physical gold, bullion is available in wafers and small ingots as light as 10 grams (less than one third of a troy ounce) all the way up to bars weighing hundreds of ounces.

As a general rule, buying gold bullion is not economical for the typical American investor in sizes below the 10-ounce bar. If you want smaller quantities, you would be better off buying bullion coins, or what I call "paper gold." But if bigger bullion does fit your budget and your philosophy, you will find there are economies of scale in buying larger bars. In contrast to coins, for example, the only premiums you normally have to pay for bullion bars are brand-name charges—fees for a specific refiner's gold, which represent the cost of fabricating smaller bars. If you buy a 100-ounce bar or the standard-size 400-ounce "good delivery" bar, the chances are good that you will not have to pay any premium at all above the price of the bullion itself—although, as with any investment, you may have to pay a commission to the broker or dealer. This should amount to no more than 1 percent. With smaller bars, of course, you will pay both the commission and the premium. On a 10-ounce bar, the premium may be 50 cents per ounce. On a 1-ounce wafer, it may be as much as $5. Thus, while these two items vary greatly in size, the aggregate premium on both is about the same.

As with the purchase of stocks, a commission is something every gold investor faces. Simply stated, it is what you pay the person who arranges your purchase. Commissions on bullion vary widely. Depending on the size of your purchase, your broker-dealer's competitiveness, and your personal relationship with the firm, it can range from as little as one half of 1 percent of the total cost for large transactions to more than 15 percent—a rate that I consider exorbitantly high. As a rule, you should avoid any firm that charges more than 5 percent, since many reputable retail bullion dealers routinely charge a maximum of 3 percent. Do not confuse commissions with premiums or fabrication fees. These are charges assessed for making gold bars in the size the customer wants, and you may have to pay them even though the bars you buy are mass produced rather than being fabricated just for you.

Gold has to assume some form; consequently, no fee is charged for making a bar in the standard 100-ounce or 400-ounce sizes. For smaller bars, however, there usually will be such a charge. The smaller the bar, the higher per ounce the fee is likely to be. Fabrication charges run from as little as $0.50 per ounce to as much as $5.00 per ounce. Unlike commissions, these charges are usually refunded when you sell your bullion. You may not get back exactly the same amount if you use a different broker, but the buyer will refund at least a portion of your fabrication fees.

Brands

Like most products, gold comes in different brands. The product is pretty much the same: To qualify as gold, the metal must meet the chemical definition; thus, there is little or no physical difference between one refiner's gold and another's, as there would be between different brands of toothpaste. However, some refiners are better known than others and their products are recognized the world over. You should buy only gold that is fabricated by a major refiner—one whose large 100-ounce bars have a "good delivery" rating on the Commodity Exchange in New York or other exchanges. And each bar should be stamped with the name of the producer as well as a number certifying that it has been registered.

Spreads

Most retailers of gold investment products will not only sell you bars and coins but also buy them back from you if and when you decide to liquidate your holdings. As you would expect, a retail gold dealer sells bars and coins at a slightly higher price—the "ask" or "offering" price—than he will "bid" if you wish to sell them back. The difference between a dealer's bid and ask prices is called the "spread." In choosing a place to buy gold, whether it be a local coin shop, your broker, or your bank, make sure that the retailer maintains a two-way market—that is, stands ready to repurchase your bars or coins. And make sure his spread is reasonable and competitive.

Many bullion dealers, including some banks and brokerage firms, simply base their buying and selling prices on one of the London gold price fixes of the day or on the current spot price of the metal on a futures exchange. If the London afternoon fixing price were $340 an ounce, for example, your broker might be a willing seller at $341 and might buy back the metal at $339. In the vernacular of the trade, he would be quoting a $2 spread. Keep in mind that on top of this price, there also might be a fabrication charge and a commission. A retail firm that buys and sells gold may maintain its own inventory or purchase metal as required from a wholesaler. Larger firms that make a market in gold frequently earn a large share of their profit through the bid-and-ask differentials, leaving commissions to cover administrative expenses as well as commissions to individual brokers.

Storage Considerations

There are a few simple rules for investors to follow to assure that the gold they buy will be properly stored. If you purchase your gold from the well-known Wall Street firms or the big-name banks—Merrill Lynch, Dean Witter, E. F. Hutton, Citibank, Security Pacific, to name a few—you effectively have an endorsement of quality and assurance that your gold is being handled responsibly, whether it is in a segregated or nonsegregated account. You should inquire whether you have a direct claim on commingled gold prior to other creditors should the broker become bankrupt. If you do not, find another broker. If, however, you choose not to deal with the big players and wish to rely on a local broker or precious metals dealer to arrange storage for you, it is preferable that you have your gold segregated—that is, identified as your metal and not commingled with the company's bullion or the gold belonging to other customers. The less reputable bullion dealers who went bankrupt in recent years had not segregated their clients' gold; consequently, the bullion controlled by these firms became part of their corporate assets and thus was claimed by creditors when the companies failed.

Many investors who purchase gold bullion or coins wish to take delivery of the metal and store it in their own safe deposit box or under the proverbial mattress, as foolish as that may be. They want the security of having their gold close at hand, and they are also concerned about the risks, real and perceived, of storing it somewhere else.

Unfortunately, in many U.S. states (as in many foreign countries), investors who take delivery of their gold are subject to sales taxes as I discussed in the previous chapter. Others arrange for storage, on their own or through a broker, at one of the major Delaware banks that offer bullion storage facilities. This can be advantageous in more ways than one: You can avoid sales tax up front—and, down the road, when you want to resell your metal, you probably will not have to pay any assay charges as long as your gold never left the bank depository. Typically, annual storage and insurance fees for leaving your gold in a major bank depository should total about one quarter to one half of 1 percent of the gold's value. Since July 1983, U.S. bullion dealers and retail coin shops have been required to report to the Internal Revenue Service all sales of bullion and bullion coins *by investors*. This is in line with an IRS attempt to discourage income tax evasion. Please note, however, that sales by dealers and retailers *to investors* need not be reported to the IRS.

There is another advantage to storing bullion with a major bank depository. The major depositories will not accept bullion (or coins, as I mentioned in the prior chapter) without assurance of its authenticity both in terms of content as well as brand name. So, you will not have to worry about bogus bars if you store your metal or take delivery from a depository at some later date. If you are concerned about the authenticity of your purchase, you might consider the storage or "paper" gold alternative to physical delivery.

Paper Gold

Buying gold bullion may seem like a simple, straightforward sort of process. But just as there have been many new "products" in the equities and futures markets, there are also many ways to purchase bullion.

Many mainstream investors shy away from buying physical gold. For them, one of the best alternatives is to buy gold certificates of deposit. These are offered by a number of major banks and stock brokerage firms. A certificate is a convenient way to own gold without the added concerns for delivery, storage, sales tax, resale, assays, and other details that go with the buying of the metal.

Since you are not receiving segregated bullion, you should buy certificates from nationally recognized firms. Commissions can range from as much as 6 percent of the total value of a certificate down to 1.5 percent or lower. Many sellers also will charge you an annual or quarterly storage fee. This can be either a flat amount or a sum based on the current market value of the metal that's involved. In some programs the holder of a certificate can request delivery of the gold at any time. However, you then may have to pay a delivery charge, as well as a fabrication fee. There also may be no assurance that you will receive a particular brand of gold—though most firms that sell certificates purchase only gold which is deliverable against a futures contract. Be sure that the gold represented by your certificate meets these standards. In other programs it may not be possible to take delivery, but the investor can liquidate his position for the current value of the certificate at any time.

Accumulation Accounts

Another popular alternative to buying physical gold—one which is a cross between bullion and gold certificates—is an accumulation account with a bank or broker. This type of account is similar to a payroll savings withholding plan. In an accumulation account you agree with the broker or dealer to pay a set amount periodically at a given time during the month—perhaps on the last business day. The broker invests your money, purchasing as much bullion as he can, and you are apprised of the actual physical amount of your acquisition at the end of the month, or on your particular "buying day."

Accumulation plans serve as a convenient way to "dollar-average" your purchases. This means that when the price of gold is low, you will get a larger quantity—while at high prices, the quantity will be proportionately less. Accumulation plans are a good method through which to acquire gold for the risk-averse mainstream investor and for the consumer who is interested in increasing his gold savings over a period of time. This strategy has enabled many investors to reap the benefits of lower unit costs for their holdings; and because it takes the guesswork and speculation out of buying bullion, it is an easy way to maintain a portion of assets in gold. Generally, an accumulation plan requires an initial deposit. In some plans, this can be as low as $50 to $100; in others, it can be $500 or even $1,000. This is then followed by smaller subsequent outlays.

GOLD-MINING EQUITIES

> "A gold mine is a hole in the ground
> with a liar standing next to it."
> —*Mark Twain*

Buying mining equities is buying gold in the ground. It combines gold ownership with many of the advantages and disadvantages of investing in securities. For this reason, you should define your investment goals before you buy gold equities or shares in a gold-stock mutual fund. Are you investing for long-term protection against inflation? Are you speculating on a short-term gold-market rally? Perhaps you see the gold-mining industry as just another part of the stock market and believe we are entering a phase of the business and stock-market cycle when this sector will outperform others. Examine your investment objectives carefully before deciding which gold-mining equities, if any, are best for you.

Mark Twain's warning is as valid today as it was a hundred years ago, and there are still plenty of promoters hyping "holes in the ground." But there are also many fine investments and reputable miners. Thus, while "caveat emptor" ("buyer beware") is surely sound advice for someone investing in gold, the prudent investor can do extremely well.

Before investing in mining stocks, you must analyze a series of factors, including gold's price outlook at the ledger sheets and prospects of specific mines. You also should consider minimizing some of the risks by diversifying your mining-share portfolio or investing through a gold-oriented mutual fund.

Many gold-mining companies pay their shareholders regular dividends and so can be a steady source of income. Gold-mining companies also provide a leveraged investment. In other words, your equity value usually rises or falls by a higher percentage than the price of gold. But gold-share investors are taking changes, as well. They not only risk a fall in the price of gold but also accept the hazards that go with mining. A foreign mine, for instance, may expose your investment to political problems and currency fluctuations. In addition, there are risks related to a mine's financial situation—its capitalization, cash flow, and the like; its labor relations; its geology; and even the real possibility of floods, fires, and other calamities.

Various factors, objective as well as subjective, govern the price of stock in a company such as General Motors: How well the auto industry in general has been faring, GM sales figures, management efficiency, the price of the stock compared to company earnings, and the price of GM stock compared to that of other auto manufacturers. These and other factors determine GM stock's investment potential. One thing most GM investors *do not* look at, though, is the price of a Chevrolet or a Pontiac, or any other GM car or truck.

Gold-mining equities are different. With them, you must consider all the factors you would with other investments, plus the present and prospective price of the company's product: the price of gold.

The Importance of Operating Costs

One of the first things most professional analysts and traders look at is a mine's production costs. The cost of producing gold can be as low as $100 an ounce or less, as it is for some of the highest-quality South African producers, or as high as $305 an ounce, as it is at the venerable Homestake mine in the United States. It can even be so high as to make a mine unprofitable at current gold prices.

Investing in a low-cost producer is a conservative approach, but a high-cost producer can give you substantial leverage (in terms of both risk and opportunity) if the price of gold should rise or fall. For example, let us compare the Campbell Red Lake and Dome mines. At Campbell Red Lake, operating costs are about $100 an ounce, leaving a net profit of $200 an ounce when gold is at $300. If the price of gold were to rise from $300 to $330 (an increase of 10 percent), the mine's profits also would rise $30, from $200 to $230. That is an increase of 15 percent. But now let us look at Dome, a higher cost producer, and see what happens there in the same scenario. The Dome mine has an operating cost of almost $260 an ounce, so its net profits are $40 an ounce when the price of gold is $300. But if gold were to rise the same 10 percent to $330, Dome's profits would climb from $40 to $70—a 75 percent increase. So, with an identical 10 percent rise in the price of gold, Campbell Red Lake's profits would show a gain of only 15 percent, while Dome's profits would soar by 75 percent. And, to a large extent, the price of each company's shares would reflect the change in each mine's profitability.

The Making of Gold

We generally think of gold as coming straight out of the ground, but the yellow metal is actually a refined product—the end result of several enriching and purifying processes.

Initially, the gold is found in mined ore. But unless that ore comes from a "placer" deposit—one that exists in a stream bed, where the metal is relatively free from impurities—it has to be separated from its host ore.

When Americans think of gold miners, they tend to picture grizzled old prospectors riding mules, wielding picks, and panning mountain streams for gold nuggets. It is true that this method can lead to the discovery and recovery of gold. But it lacks the economies of scale that make a modern mine financially viable.

Rather than plodding through mountain streams, the modern U.S. gold miner is more likely to be found operating huge earth-moving equipment and stripping away ore in which there may only be microscopic amounts of metal. Or, if he works in an underground mine, he probably spends his workday detonating explosives to shatter massive amounts of ore, then hoisting them to the surface. Either way, the next step is equally unromantic. Once the ore is removed from the mine, it is crushed, ground, and mixed in a water slurry, and roasted in large, pressurized oxidation vessels. This cooking yields a pulp that is then treated with lime and a cyanide solution to "leach" out the gold. Finally, the gold is extracted from the leached solution, refined, and cast into "dross" bars. These may have a gold content as low as 60 to 70 percent or as high as 90 percent.

"Good-delivery" bars—bars that may be delivered to satisfy contracts on the futures exchange—must have a purity of 99.5 percent. To reach that level, the gold in the dross bars has to be further refined, either through a fire-refining process or through the more efficient electrolytic refining—the method that is used to produce gold of 99.9 percent fineness.

Ore Reserves and Grade

After the cost of production, the next thing you should look at is a company's ore reserves. Ore is rock that a company can mine at a profit, and ore reserves are simply the amount of ore on its property. Gold often runs in veins beneath the earth's surface, but in many of the newer open-pit mines, the gold is distributed—frequently in microscopic particles—throughout a large volume of rock. Ore grades must be considered, as well. Essentially, "grade" refers to how much gold each ton of rock contains. Ore grades are an important factor in determining the cost of a mining operation. As I have noted, the best South African mines have about one quarter of an ounce of gold per ton of ore. Ore reserves may be "proven" or "probable." Proven reserves are outlined very carefully by closely spaced drilling and sampling, often along a tunnel that is dug for just this purpose. Probable reserves are less rigorously defined, perhaps through relatively shallow (though closely spaced) drilling from the surface of the property.

Proven ore reserves are much more expensive to determine than probable reserves. Many mining companies will prove out only two or three years of reserves, even though the ore body may have enough gold for many more years of profitable mining. In most cases, the probable reserves will give the company—and the investor—a more than adequate picture of the mine's actual long-term potential.

Generally, the newer mines just coming on stream will have a relatively short life span—in some cases, less than 10 years. Some of the older South African mines *appear* to be nearly exhausted. In these cases, though, the ore-reserve data supplied by a company may not be a good indicator of a mine's life expectancy, since new reserves often are proven each year as old reserves are depleted.

Mutual Funds

If you cannot decide on a single company in which to invest or cannot afford to invest in more than one firm (as you definitely should, in order to main a diversified portfolio), then you should be considering gold-mining mutual funds. A mutual fund pools many people's money and invests it in the financial instruments outlined in the fund's prospectus.

Basically, there are two kinds of mutual funds: open-end and closed-end. Open-end funds are ones in which the number of shares outstanding rises or falls as investor participation expands or shrinks. As an investor in an open-ended fund, you can buy or sell shares at any time at a price equal to the per-share value of the fund's portfolio. This kind of fund often is managed by a major brokerage house. But, just as often, the managers are professionals who specialize in this particular industry.

A closed-end fund is one that has an initial offering period during which a set number of shares in the fund are sold. After the end of that period, the managers take the pooled cash and invest it. While it is possible to buy the shares of a closed-end fund after the initial offering, your investment will not go into the fund itself but rather will be paid to whoever sells the shares. Unlike an open-end fund, where the price per share is tied to the value of the portfolio, the price paid for shares in a closed-end fund after the initial offering will depend upon the supply and demand for these shares among investors in the secondary market. Closed-end mutual funds work like equities in a company. When those equities are first sold, during a period known as an "initial offering," the company takes the investors' money and applies it to its own needs. Any time those shares are bought or sold after the initial offering, the money is exchanged among the individual shareholders, not with the company itself.

An open-end mutual fund, on the other hand, has no real counterpart among investment instruments in the equities market. Because closed-end funds are traded constantly, they usually are listed on a stock exchange, although they may be traded on the over-the-counter market. No matter where they are traded, they must be registered with the Securities and Exchange Commission if they are offered in the United States, as are shares in open-end mutual funds sold in this country.

There are two kinds of open-end funds: load and no-load. A load fund is one in which you as an investor pay a commission when you buy shares in the fund. A no-load fund is one in which no commission is charged when you buy, but in some cases one may be charged when you sell your shares in the fund.

In both open-end and closed-end funds, the manager will charge a fee for administering the fund—a fee that normally is paid out of the portfolio's dividend earnings. In considering a fund, you will naturally want to determine whether this fee is reasonable. You should make this determination based upon the record of the fund's management. That record plus the expected earnings of the fund are the two most important considerations in choosing a fund. If it is an open-end fund or an initial offering of a closed-end fund, your broker will be able to provide you with a prospectus which will detail the management's record and experience as well as the anticipated earnings. If it is an open-end fund or you are buying shares of a closed-end fund after the initial offering, your broker should also be able to give you information on the management as well as the record of the fund since its establishment.

Equities Summarized

Before you invest in equities, there are several points to keep in mind.

First, you must determine the operating costs of the mining property. This figure can be obtained by reviewing a company's annual 10-K filing with the Securities and Exchange Commission if it is a U.S. firm, or it can be obtained through your stockbroker's research department if it is a foreign company. There are many publications that regularly review the operating costs of every gold mine.

Next, determine the mine's ore grade and life expectancy. You should look at the company's physical plant. How is the ore processed? Will maintaining the mine and plant infrastructure require any unusual expenses in the near future?

If it is a foreign company, you should look at the political and social environment to determine the stability of the host country. You also should look at the country's currency situation.

In evaluating an individual company, its price-to-earnings ratio can be helpful in determining whether a share is over- or underpriced.

As an overriding concern, you must analyze the price of gold bullion. Can it be expected to rise or fall? No matter how efficient a company is, or how rich its ore body, it will not make money if the price of gold is below its operating costs; on the other hand, every company will make more money when the price of gold rises. Remember the price of equities of a low-grade company will not rise as quickly as those of a high-grade company at the beginning of any rally in bullion prices but will rise proportionally faster the longer a rally continues.

If you are unable to decide on a particular company or cannot afford to diversify by buying shares in more than one company, consider a mutual fund. Remember, there are basically two types of funds: open-end and closed-end. Within the open-end category, there are load and no-load funds. A closed-end fund is one where you purchase shares from another investor (unless you buy during the initial offering period). An open-end fund is one where you buy from the manager of the fund. A no-load open-end fund is one where you pay no commission when you buy but in some cases pay one when you sell. Factors to consider in both types of funds are the expected yields and the experience of the manager.

PART 7

MANAGING INVESTMENTS

READING 27

USE TIME, NOT TIMING
TO REDUCE PORTFOLIO RISK

Maria Crawford Scott

Market timing is a technique whose success at yielding high returns for investors has been hotly debated. Nonetheless, it is a technique that has proven successful to its promoters—numerous newsletters and even some mutual funds tout the idea.

Its premise is very appealing. How can one argue with the idea that an investor can make the most money if he can simply get in near the bottom of a market, ride the market up, and jump out just before it drops again? The trick, of course, is identifying when to jump in and out, and no one has demonstrated a timing system that has been successful over more than one market cycle in predicting when to move. Several articles in the *AAII Journal* have outlined the difficulties in devising such a system (see, for example, "Putting market timing to the test," by Robert H. Jeffrey in the September 1985 issue). Market timers claim it is possible to devise such a system, and many claim theirs *will be* successful over the long term. This debate will probably continue forever.

However, there is another argument some market timers use to justify their technique that is simply incorrect. And since the concept that this argument runs contrary to is basic to a long-term investment strategy, it is worthwhile to point out the flaw in reasoning.

Source: *AAII Journal*, September 1987. Used with permission.

FIGURE 1
Monthly Returns for the S&P 500 (1986)

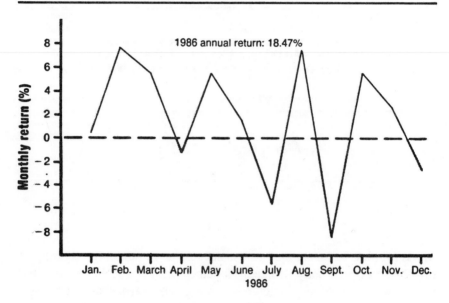

IS RISK REDUCED—OR INCREASED?

Low-risk investing is a basic goal of many investors. Thus, it is logical that some market timers would attempt to classify their technique as low-risk. And that is what some have done.

Their argument runs something like this: The stock market is a risky investment; Treasury bills (including money market funds) are a risk-free investment. Thus, if you park your money in Treasury bills for most of the time and only jump into the stock market occasionally, you limit your exposure to the stock market and thus you limit your exposure to risk.

The flaw in this argument is that limiting your time in the stock market does not decrease your risk. In fact, it does just the opposite—it increases your risk substantially. The shorter the time period that you are invested in the stock market, the more subject you are to violent short-term swings in the stock market. Investing in the stock market over longer time periods tends to smooth out these swings, allowing investors to participate in the overall upward trend in the stock market.

Figure 1 illustrates the point. It graphically depicts the monthly total rates

TABLE 1
How Holding Period Affects Potential Gains and Losses: 1946–1987

Holding Period	Worst Performance		Best Performance		Number of Periods with Losses
	Annual Return (%)	Year(s)	Annual Return (%)	Year(s)	
1 year	−26.5	1974	52.6	1954	10
3 years	−9.3	1972–1975	28.9	1954–1957	2
5 years	−2.4	1970–1975	23.9	1950–1955 & 1951–1956	2
10 years	1.2	1965–1975	20.1	1949–1959	0

Average annual return 1946–1987: 11.4%.

of return for the S&P 500 during 1986. While the overall return for that year was positive—18.47 percent—the monthly returns were volatile. There were four months with negative returns. In fact, the return in *one month* was worse than the worst *annual* return in the last decade: September's monthly return was −8.22 percent, compared to 1977's −7.18 percent.

The concept can be illustrated over a longer time period as well, as Table 1 indicates. Returns were determined for one-year, three-year, five-year, and 10-year periods from 1946 through the beginning of 1987. Rolling time periods were used for the three-, five-, and 10-year holding periods—in other words, for the 10-year periods, returns were determined for 1946 to 1956, 1947 to 1957, 1948 to 1958, etc. The table indicates the biggest decline an investor may have received if he had been unlucky enough to be in the market during the worst time period indicated; it also indicates the biggest gain an investor could have received if he had been in the market during the best time period indicated.

The most striking result, from a risk view, is the change in the biggest declines: The risk of suffering a loss decreases as the investment horizon is lengthened. Investors who remained in the market for only one year would have risked losing 26.5 percent of the value of their investment. They also faced more chances of suffering a loss, since there were 10 time periods that had negative returns. In contrast, investors who remained in the market for 10 years on average faced no risk of an actual loss to their portfolio.

Several studies have reached similar findings. One, in fact, found that extending the holding period reduced risk more than did increasing the number of stocks in a portfolio. The study's conclusion: "The investor who adopts a buy-and-hold strategy, even with a relatively small number of stocks, can reduce the risks of not achieving the long-run market rate of return a great deal more than he could by adding many stocks to his portfolio but only holding the portfolio for a short time." (A summary of these studies appeared in "Diversification: It's about time" in the September 1984 *AAII Journal*.)

OTHER WAYS TO REDUCE RISK

That's not to say that you can't reduce your risk by investing part of your money in Treasury bills. In fact, investing in short-term riskless securities is an excellent way to reduce risk. However, jumping between Treasury bills and the stock market with your portfolio is not the same as a buy-and-hold strategy that invests a portion of your portfolio in Treasury bills and a portion in the stock market. The buy-and-hold strategy subjects only the stock portion of your portfolio to stock market risk, and the risk to that portion can be reduced through various means, such as increasing your holding period and diversifying. The timing method subjects your stock portfolio to the subtantial risks of short-term investing.

Lengthening the time period—time diversification—can also be used to reduce risk when entering and exiting the market. It is the principle behind dollar-cost averaging: Rather than investing or withdrawing a large sum of money at one time, an investor gradually increases or decreases his portion in the stock market. (This technique was discussed in the September 1984 "Investor workshop.")

Time diversification is an extremely important concept, yet it is frequently overlooked because it cannot be measured by any of the standard measures of risk, including beta. But even though it can't be measured, the risks of investing short-term are still there.

Your best bet in stock marketing investing is to keep time on your side: The more of it you are able to use, the less the risk that you will face a substantial loss.

READING 28

THE RELATIVE IMPORTANCE OF ASSET ALLOCATION

Maria Crawford Scott

Stock selection is an activity that takes up a considerable amount of time. As a result, investors tend to concentrate their efforts on stock selection and ignore other less time-consuming aspects of investing.

One aspect that tends to be overlooked is the determination of what portion of an investor's total portfolio should be invested in stocks, bonds, cash, and other investment alternatives. This process is known in financial jargon as "asset allocation," and the proportion invested in the various categories is known as an investor's "asset mix."

Asset allocation is not an area that should be ignored. In fact, it is more important than individual stock selection in determining an investor's total return.

How much more important is asset allocation?

A recent study that appeared in the *Financial Analysts Journal* ("Determinants of Portfolio Performance," by Gary P. Brinson, L. Randolph Hood, and Gilbert L. Beebower, July–August 1986) measured the effects of asset allocation, market timing, and individual stock selection on investment portfolios over a 10-year period and found some rather surprising results.

To conduct the study, the authors first found a universe of 91 pension

Source: *AAII Journal,* October 1987. Used with permission.

funds that had stated investment policies. These policies primarily outline the fund's long-term asset allocation strategy, which is based on the fund's risk and return requirements. The pension funds individually had portfolios ranging from about $100 million to $3 billion; their assets are tax-exempt, and so tax considerations do not enter into any investment decisions.

Based on these stated asset allocations, the researchers determined what returns the funds' portfolios would have returned if no other active investment decisions were made. In other words, "passive" portfolios that merely invested in indexes were set up, where no active security selection or timing decisions were made.

The S&P 500 represented stocks, the Shearson Lehman Government/Corporate Bonds Index represented bonds, and the 30-day Treasury bill rate represented cash. Returns for the individual funds were then determined as if they had invested only in the indexes in the proportions stated in their investment policies. These returns reflect the returns that are due to asset allocation.

Next, the researchers isolated the returns due to timing from the returns due to security selection. First, they looked at the actual asset allocations over the time compared to the stated allocations in the investment policy. The differences represent timing decisions: At a particular point in time, the fund has over- or under-weighted its investments in a particular category—cash, for example—due to short-term timing considerations. The researchers then determined what the individual fund returns would have been if they had invested in the indexes in the proportions indicated by their timing decisions.

The effect of security selection was determined by comparing the actual fund returns for the individual categories with the market index. For instance, a fund's actual common stock return was compared to the S&P 500, with the difference representing the added value (or loss) due to stock selection. The researchers then determined what the individual fund returns would have been if they had made these security selection decisions without making any asset allocation changes but rather had remained invested in the various categories as outlined in their investment policies.

The results? The portfolios based purely on asset allocation decisions returned an average of 10.11 percent, the portfolios based purely on timing decisions returned an average of 9.44 percent, and the portfolios based solely on security selection returned an average of 9.75 percent. In comparison, the actual funds had an average return of 9.01 percent.

The results indicate that the average fund would have been better off if the manager had made the initial asset allocation decision and then left the portfolio alone. The timing decision cost the average fund 0.66 percent per year, and the stock selection decision cost the average fund another 0.36 percent per year (these numbers are rounded). Of course, not all funds shared the same experience. Timing and security selection decisions, in the worst case, cost one fund 4.17 percent per year, while in the best case these decisions produced a gain of 7.86 percent per year over the pure asset allocation decision.

However, the study's conclusions were that, while timing and security selection decisions are important, the bulk of the return of a portfolio is due to the proportions invested in the various investment categories.

MAKING THE ALLOCATION DECISION

The next obvious question is: If asset allocation is so importnat, how does one make the decision? The decision should be based on a numbr of factors, including the investor's own risk tolerance, return requirements, and investment horizon.

One method is to look at the historical performance of the various investment categories. This tends to limit you primarily to stocks, bonds, and Treasury bills (or, for most individuals, money market funds), because of the absence of reliable and practical data for other investment alternatives such as real estate. On the other hand, these three categories form the bulk of most investor's portfolios.

For example, what would be the implications of a portfolio that had invested equally in all three categories?

Over the last 20 years, the average annual return was 10.2 percent for stocks, 7.6 percent for long-term bonds, and 7.4 percent for Treasury bills. A portfolio that was fully invested during this time period, therefore, would have had an average annual return of:

$$10.2\,(33\%) + 7.6\,(33\%) + 7.4\,(34\%) = 8.4\%$$

Another example takes into consideration risk and holding period, and it is based on the data in Table 1. The table provides the best and worst returns over the past 20 years for one-, five-, and 10-year holding periods. It also indicates the best and worst annual returns a portfolio would have

TABLE 1
Historical Performance of Stocks, Long-Term Bonds, and Treasury Bills
(1967 through 1986)

	Annual Return (percent)			
	Stocks	Long-Term Bonds	Treasury Bills	Equally Split Portfolio*
One-year holding period				
Worst	−26.5	−8.1	3.8	−9.65
Best	37.2	43.8	14.7	31.73
Five-year holding period				
Worst	−2.4	−2.2	3.9	−0.19
Best	19.9	22.4	11.0	17.70
10-year holding period				
Worst	1.2	1.7	3.2	2.05
Best	14.8	10.0	9.1	11.27

*33% invested in stocks, 33% in long-term bonds, and 34% in Treasury bills.

received if it had been equally split among the three categories and invested for the indicated holding period.

The table also illustrates the advantages of longer holding periods (see "Editor's choice" in the September *Journal* for a longer discussion) and diversification among the various investment categories.

Two other ways of viewing the asset allocation decision were presented in earlier "Investor workshop" articles. One method uses stock market risk as a guide to building a portfolio (see the August 1985 "Investor workshop"), and another looks at the downside risk of mutual funds (see the May 1987 "Investor workshop").

Most of these methods use historical performance to some degree. Investors, however, should be cautious in forming expectations based on past data. Although history tends to repeat itself, it may not do so in your lifetime.

READING 29

THE BENEFITS OF DIVERSIFYING AMONG MUTUAL FUND CATEGORIES

Jeff Madura
John M. Cheney

The popularity of mutual funds is largely attributed to their diversification benefits. However, because mutual funds often specialize in a particular type of asset category such as common stocks or bonds, a given fund's diversification capabilities are limited to the asset category in which it is concentrated. It would appear, therefore, that investors could benefit from diversifying among the different types of mutual funds.

Diversification among different asset classes—popularly known as *asset allocation*—has become a hot topic in the financial media.

This article illustrates the benefits of this approach as it applies to mutual funds.

THE DIVERSIFICATION STUDY

Most research has focused on the performance of mutual funds and how they compare to a strategy of buying and holding individual stocks. Our research

---

Source: *AAII Journal*, January 1989. Used with permission.

focuses on the potential performance of mutual fund categories rather than individual mutual funds. To assess the possible diversification benefits from mutual funds, six categories of funds were examined in the study:

- International stock funds.
- Small-company stock funds.
- Growth stock funds.
- Corporate bond funds.
- Treasury bond funds.
- Money market funds.

Only those mutual funds that were in existence from January 1978 to December 1987 and appropriately represented one of the six categories were used in the study. The average annual returns, including dividend, interest, and capital gains distributions, were determined for each category of mutual fund. The average annual returns of the international stock funds, small-company stock funds, growth stock funds, and corporate bond funds were compiled by Lipper Analytical Services. The average annual returns of the money market funds were compiled by the Donoghue Organization, and the average annual returns of the Treasury bond mutual funds were compiled by Shearson Lehman Hutton.

RISK AND RETURN

The average annual returns for the various categories are provided in Table 1. International mutual funds generated the highest average annual return, followed by small-company stock funds and growth stock funds. The average annual return of the international mutual funds was more than double that of the corporate bond and money market mutual funds over the period 1978 through 1987.

The risk levels for the various categories were also measured. Risk in this study was defined as volatility of returns. The figure represents the amount by which most actual returns varied around the average return; a higher figure indicates returns were more volatile, while a lower figure indicates returns were less volatile. The risk for the various categories is also presented in Table 1. You can see that the higher average annual returns of the international, small-company stock, and growth stock funds were accompanied by significantly higher risks, as well.

Diversification provides the benefit of greatly reducing risk without

TABLE 1
Average Annual Returns and Risk of Mutual Fund Categories (1978–1987)*

Category	Average Annual Return (%)	Volatility* (%)
International stock funds	20.3%	19.2%
Small-company stock funds	17.0	18.2
Growth stock funds	16.2	14.1
Corporate bond funds	9.7	10.5
Treasury bond funds	10.7	16.4
Money market funds	9.9	3.4

*As measured by standard deviation. The figure represents the amount by which returns varied around the average; the greater the figure, the greater the volatility and therefore the greater the risk.

substantially reducing potential returns. Can diversification among mutual fund categories reduce the high risks associated with the better-performing categories without substantially reducing a portfolio's returns?

That depends in part on how the funds react in relation to one another. These relationships are measured in Table 2, which indicates how the returns of the funds in one category correlated to the returns of the funds in another category. A 1.00 indicates parallel movement—the returns of the funds in the two categories move up and down at the same time and to the same degree; figures approaching zero indicated there is little similarity in movement among the returns of the funds in the two categories, and negative figures indicate that the returns tend to move in opposite directions—when the returns in one category rise, the returns in the other fall.

According to the table, the corporate bond and Treasury bond fund categories are highly correlated; the growth stock and small-company stock fund categories are also very similar. All other pairs of mutual fund categories had low or negative correlations. It is among these latter fund categories that the potential benefits of diversification are large, since poor returns in one category can potentially be offset by better returns in the other category.

THE RESULTS AND THEIR IMPLICATIONS

How would individuals have fared if they had diversified among these categories?

TABLE 2
Correlations among Mutual Fund Categories (1978–1987)*

Category	International Stock Funds	Small-Company Stock Funds	Growth Stock Funds	Corporate Bond Funds	Treasury Bond Funds	Money Market Funds
International stock funds	1.00	—	—	—	—	—
Small-company stock funds	0.30	1.00	—	—	—	—
Growth stock funds	0.38	0.96	1.00	—	—	—
Corporate bond funds	−0.07	0.14	0.14	1.00	—	—
Treasury bond funds	0.07	0.11	0.15	0.97	1.00	—
Money market funds	−0.56	0.12	0.02	0.02	−0.10	1.00

*Indicates how one category behaves versus another. A 1.00 indicates perfect correlation: The returns in one category rise and fall at the same time and to the same degree as the returns in the other.

The combination of categories that could be used is unlimited, each producing a different return at different levels of risk. An "efficient" combination would be one that produced the highest return at a given level of risk. A sample of 10 efficient portfolios with various levels of risk are provided in Table 3; they are listed in order from the maximum-return, maximum-risk portfolio down to the lowest-return, lowest-risk portfolio. The maximum-return portfolio is represented by international mutual funds, and the other portfolios that emphasize return concentrate on international, small-company, and growth stock funds. Conversely, the proportion invested in money market funds is higher for low-risk portfolios, because of the lower risk in the returns of money market funds.

While small-company funds achieved high returns, they were included in only one of the 10 portfolios because of their high risk. Their returns were more highly correlated with money market funds when compared to the international mutual funds, which were negatively correlated with money market funds. Therefore, even though international mutual funds were more risky than small-company stock funds, they could be more effectively combined with money market funds to achieve lower portfolio risk. It is also interesting to note that only three or four of the six categories of funds are necessary to form any single particular, efficient portfolio.

When comparing Table 3 to Table 1, the following conclusions can be drawn:

- A combination of four categories of mutual funds can achieve a portfolio that has fully 78 percent less risk than the risk (13.6 percent) of the average mutual fund category taken alone.
- A combination of international stock, small-company stock and growth stock mutual funds achieved a portfolio return that is only 1 percent less than that of the international funds alone, but with 18 percent less risk.
- That same combination of international stock, small-company stock and growth stock mutual funds achieved a portfolio return two percentage points greater than that of small-company stock funds alone, yet with 13 percent less risk.
- A combination of international stock, growth stock, and money market mutual funds achieved a return similar to that of small stock funds alone, yet with 35 percent less risk.
- A different combination of international stock, growth stock and

TABLE 3
Examples of Diversified Mutual Fund Portfolios

Portfolio	Return (%)	Volatility* (%)	Percentage Allocated to Mutual Fund Category					
			International	Small-Company	Growth Stock	Corporate Bond	Treasury Bond	Money Market
Max. return, max. risk								
1	20.3%	19.2%	100.00%	0.00%	0.00%	0.00%	0.00%	0.00%
2	19.3	15.8	68.4	29.2	2.4	0.0	0.0	0.0
3	18.2	13.7	53.9	0.0	42.3	0.0	0.0	3.8
4	17.1	11.8	47.8	0.0	35.7	0.0	0.0	16.5
5	16.1	9.9	41.7	0.0	29.1	0.0	0.0	29.2
6	15.0	8.1	35.6	0.0	22.4	0.0	0.0	42.0
7	14.0	6.2	29.5	0.0	15.8	0.0	0.0	54.7
8	12.9	4.5	23.4	0.0	9.2	0.0	0.2	67.2
9	11.8	3.0	17.4	0.0	2.5	3.3	0.0	76.8
Min. return, min. risk								
10	10.9	2.4	10.1	0.0	0.0	6.4	0.0	83.5

* As measured by standard deviation. The figure represents the amount by which returns varied around the average; the greater the figure, the greater the volatility and therefore the greater the risk.

money market mutual funds achieved a return similar to that of growth stock funds alone, but with 29 percent less risk.

- The lowest-risk portfolio achieved a return similar to that of the Treasury bond funds, but with 85 percent less risk.
- The lowest-risk portfolio of mutual funds also achieved a portfolio return above that of the corporate bond funds, and with 77 percent less risk.
- Surprisingly, the lowest-risk portfolio of mutual funds achieved a return of 1 percent above money market mutual funds, with 29 percent less risk.

It should be added that these portfolios are merely illustrations, and are not suggested combinations. The actual performance figures indicated here are historical, and may not be indicative of future returns. The results demonstrate, however, the substantial benefits that can be gained from diversifying among mutual fund categories.

In reviewing this data, investors should keep several other points in mind.

First, the use of a group of mutual funds for each mutual fund category was intended to avoid a possible bias that could result from selecting a single representative mutual fund from each category. Because the data base was composed of numerous mutual funds within each category, an individual investor may obtain different results if a particular fund is used for each of the six categories. However, in this instance the results may present an even more pronounced benefit from diversification among mutual fund types, since an individual mutual fund's variation in returns may exceed the variation of a group of funds within that category. Thus, our study may understate the gains an individual investor may find from diversifying among fund categories.

Second, to the extent that relationships among the funds change, the benefits of diversification may change. However, unless there is a fundamental change in the relationships over time, substantial benefits are likely to remain.

Even a simple approach that put equal amounts into the various mutual fund categories would likely offer some risk-reduction benefits without substantially affecting return.

READING 30

MULTIFUND INVESTING

Michael D. Hirsch

THE SOLUTION TO THE PROBLEMS OF VOLATILITY AND COMPLEXITY

The investment markets today are marked by sharp turns in direction and by market movements—or by segments of a cycle—of short duration. This places the traditional portfolio, broadly diversified across a wide cross section of stocks and/or bonds, at a distinct disadvantage. Such portfolios simply cannot be restructured quickly enough to reflect the rapid changes in market sentiment. As a pundit once quipped, "It would be like trying to turn a supertanker around in the middle of the ocean."

How to Create a Compact, Manageable Portfolio

It would be imprudent to sacrifice the safety provided by diversification in an attempt to cope with a volatile state of affairs. Just the opposite is true— the more volatile the market, the greater is the need for risk-aversion. The question, then, is quite basic: Is it possible to create a compact, manageable portfolio without sacrificing diversification? The answer is an unqualified yes! You can do so through mutual funds.

If you own a single share of a mutual fund, you automatically own a

---

Source: From Michael D. Hirsch, *Multifund Investing* (Homewood, Ill. Dow Jones-Irwin, 1987). Used with permission.

representative portion of a broadly diversified portfolio (the underlying stock/bond portfolio of that fund). And yet, since your means of ownership is that single share, you have the compactness necessary to cope with volatility. But even that compactness is not in itself the answer. For in addition to compactness, investors also need liquidity.

By liquidity we mean those financial assets that can be readily converted into cash or other forms of financial assets. By comparison, a unit in a real estate limited partnership is compact since a unit holder has a pro-rata share in a property or group of properties. But such an asset is not liquid. There is no available means of quickly converting that ownership position into cash. Compactness, therefore, is only half the answer to volatility; the key is liquidity.

In terms of stock and bond investing, *there is no more liquid means of participation than mutual funds*. They are the every epitome of liquidity. For years it was believed that stocks listed on national exchanges provided all the liquidity one would normally require. A specialist managing the order book on the floor of the exchange was assigned to each issue and empowered to maintain "orderly" markets. Theoretically, if a buyer were willing to pay the offering price, or a seller were willing to accept the bid price, the specialist would supply the necessary liquidity by selling short the shares to the buyer if insufficient shares for sale were available. Or that same specialist would buy the shares from the seller for his own account if enough buyers were not available.

But as market specialist Stephen C. Leuthold correctly points out, in this day of institution-dominated markets when buyers and sellers are dealing in tens and hundreds of thousands of shares, no specialists in their right minds would commit their own capital to provide liquidity and maintain an orderly market. Instead, what we have of late are stampedes, with all the concomitant panic. If you are the holder of 50,000 to 100,000 shares of a suddenly out-of-favor stock, and if you know that there are dozens of your peers in a similar position, prudence has of late come to mean, "Get me out at any price." This leads to an order imbalance, which remains until the specialist is able to determine how low price levels must drop for buyers to be found in order to satisfy the rampaging herd's desire to get out at any price. Only in a manner of speaking, then, are stocks still liquid if you are satisfied with receiving up to one third less for your shares than they were worth but one day earlier.

Mutual funds, on the other hand, provide true liquidity. And here again, we can look to the Investment Company Act of 1940 for the reason.

According to a provision of that act, all open-ended mutual funds must honor all buy-and-sell order on the day they are received. The fund itself becomes the other side of the trade. If you wish to buy shares, the fund simply issues new shares. If you are a seller, the fund merely redeems those shares. More important, all this occurs with absolutely no impact on price! Remember, the mutual fund is a large elastic pool of capital, representing the combined assets of many investors. If at the close of business on a given day, the fund has net assets of $100,000, and there are 1,000 shares outstanding at that point, the net asset value per share is $100. If a new investor comes along and wishes to invest $1,000 in the pool, the fund issues 10 new shares at $100 per share. The fund now has net assets of $101,000 and 1,010 shares outstanding. (The reverse occurs when you wish to sell out of a fund position.)

Thus there is no fear of getting caught in a sudden stampede, or of attempting to sell shares on the floor of the exchange and receiving the report "stock ahead." In addition, you will not witness rapid shifts in price strictly because of buying or selling pressures, not because of fundamental reasons. Theoretically, if the vast majority of a fund's shareholders sought to liquidate on a single day, the management company would find itself in a bind because it would be forced to sell off an appreciable portion of its underlying portfolio quickly in order to raise sufficient cash. Yet since 1940 this problem has never occurred—probably because a typical fund's list of shareholders is such a diverse group of individuals and institutions. But if that problem were to occur, the fund shareholder would receive at the worst a pro-rata portion of the fund's underlying securities in lieu of cash. Short of this exceptional case, the serious investor knows, therefore, that through mutual funds he or she can move as rapidly as the market itself.

Telephone Exchange Privileges

Since a sufficient number of mutual funds are currently available that provide telephone exchange privileges (whereby investors can switch from one fund to another fund within the same mutual fund complex by placing a phone call), there is nothing hindering investors from altering the complexion of their portfolios with no more than one or two telephone calls. For instance, let us say that an investor has grown wary of the stock market's prospects. Through the traditional approach, changing his or her portfolio composition would require the sale of perhaps 10 or 20 security positions. When proceeds from those sales became available, the investor would have to purchase an equal dollar amount of bonds or short-term money market investments. With mutual funds, however, the investor can use exchange privileges to accomplish the same result by placing a telephone call to the fund's shareholder service number and by instructing them to transfer a certain dollar amount or an entire position in a growth or aggressive growth fund into that group's bond fund or money market fund.

In most cases the cost of this transaction will be no more than a nominal service charge (about $5). Besides the convenience afforded, the cost savings for an active investor are significant. There is no chain of commissions on 10 to 20 sell orders nor a series of commissions to buy the replacement positions.

Letters of Instruction

If the individual is considering an investment in a fund that is not part of a family of funds, or in a group that does not provide telephone exchange privileges, all that would be required to achieve the same effect would be a properly prepared letter of instruction to the fund's transfer agent. "Market timers," people who invest in three or four funds at a time, have letters of instruction to liquidate readied and properly certified on the day following purchases. When the signals tell them that it is time to get out of the market, they dash off to the post office or one of the express letter services to execute their changes. According to this scenario, total portfolio modification can be accomplished by Decision Day plus one. In either case, by using the telephone or express mail, investment decisions implemented through mutual funds can be quickly modified or totally altered.

The Liquidity Factor

Liquidity is the antidote to volatility, and liquidity is exactly what mutual funds provide. At the same time, there is no sacrifice in diversification associated with the compactness of funds. On the contrary, the typical mutual fund portfolio is much more diversified than the typical individual or professional investor's portfolio. So the safeguards of diversification are retained, while the benefits of compactness and liquidity are gained. There is, thereby, a certain efficiency to mutual funds that lends itself perfectly to the current volatility in the investment world. Multifund investing carries this notion a step further.

Let me give you here an example drawn from my own experience. I am currently managing approximately 200 client portfolios with a wide range of investment objectives. A typical portfolio is invested in 10 to 20 mutual funds. When our firm's Investment Policy Committee decides to alter our investment philosophy, those changes will be reflected in all our clients' portfolios within 24 hours.

Since mutual funds provide both diversification and compactness, we can take advantage of this efficiency and create "superdiversification" by constructing a portfolio of funds rather than by investing in only one or two funds.

In-Depth Coverage of the Entire Spectrum of Investments

Mutual funds are equally noteworthy in their ability to overcome the difficulties created by complexity. The scope of investment alternatives has exploded in a little over 10 years' time. Formerly we had to deal only with a handful of stocks and bonds, which were rather simple, straightforward investments. By contrast, we are overwhelmed today by numerous disciplines, each of which has developed an intricacy of its own. The result is a stock and bond market that, in reality, is now a series of submarkets. Institutions and individuals are attempting to cope with this expansion in different ways. Neither the full spectrum school nor the investment boutique has proved completely successful.

But mutual funds allow us to cope with the present-day marketplace because from among the over 1,300 nonmoney market funds currently available, we can find in-depth coverage of the entire spectrum of investments. In addition, the coverage is provided on a most timely basis. Let a new "discipline" surface, and within a short time there will emerge at least one fund through which the investor can have access via professional management to that particular area. For instance, shortly after the development of sophisticated, covered option-writing programs, the market was presented with the first of many option income funds. The first medical technology fund came out of registration in 1979. At that time many investors were not yet conversant with this emerging area, but there are now over half a dozen such funds.

An institution—whatever its size and whatever its budget for staff—need no longer wonder how to provide broad-based coverage. All the coverage it needs can come through the new, expanded world of mutual funds. An institution's research staff now resides off premises; it is a 1,300-member "farm team," standing by at the ready to allow the fiduciary to access whichever segments of the market spectrum are deemed prudent for a specific client or group of clients. In addition, this access is available through a most efficient conduit: the open-ended fund. If the concept is adopted to the extent I propose in Part Three of my book—*Multifund Investing*—there will be no need at all for a research team. For example, the investment department of my own institution does not have a single analyst on its staff.

Obviously, the same premise holds true for individual investors as well. Yes, there are individuals who continue to feel capable of selecting individual securities, some via brokerage house research reports, other via intensive reading of financial journals, yet others by tips and recommendations from friends and associates. But for those who are not comfortable with such methods, the necessary answer is mutual funds. Whatever your objectives, whatever your ability to absorb risk, there is a mutual fund to fit the bill. And because of the efficiency of the funds, however hectic your lifestyle may be, a full range of investment alternatives can be built into an investment portfolio at a minimum of effort. No need to spend hour after hour of your time poring over publications and research reports and then relying on someone else's judgment. (It is only fair to point out that the authors of such articles and reports have much less at stake than the managers of mutual funds.) Instead, your total investment needs can now be accomplished through a compact portfolio of funds.

There are a number of additional considerations worthy of attention. One is the quality of the advice being offered. Let us assume that an institution has focused on deep discount bonds as an investment area it believes it must make available to its clients. A search would be conducted to find a qualified analyst or portfolio manager with an established reputation in this discipline. Obviously, this person's recognized talents and expertise will dictate his or her salary level. Conversely, whatever that firm's salary limitations for a single analyst or portfolio manager will dictate the level of the "quality" advice it can provide to its clients.

On the other hand, compare this state of affairs to that faced by an institution or individual that has decided to use mutual funds in lieu of analysts or portfolio managers. Here, as well, a search must be conducted. Assuming the search identifies a suitable "candidate"—in this case, a fund—the hiring process entails no more than a purchase order. What can you do if the candidate should later prove unsuitable? A phone call or sell order will end the relationship. From a dollars-and-cents point of view investment talent can now be added to your staff without expanding the salary budget, without incurring such items as a benefits package, travel and entertainment costs, office and telephone expenses, or the need for a support staff. By contrast, funds are a ready-made staff, and they do not involve fixed overhead expenses.

Institutional and individual investors, therefore, have at their beck and call a fully staffed team of specialists who are prepared to provide in-depth coverage of the complete spectrum of investments. This team is put together by simply placing phone calls or purchase orders. It involves no fixed expense except for the period of time it is being used; each fund has its own built-in expense ratio. The team can be upgraded, expanded, or shrunk again and again merely as the result of a telephone call or sale order.

The fact that mutual fund investors have no fixed expenses except during the period they invest is something that merits further consideration. For this aspect clearly differentiates the traditional approach from the mutual fund approach. Let us assume that an institution has hired an analyst to cover high-tech stocks, and that later on the investment policy committee feels it is imprudent to have any high-tech exposure in client portfolios. That institution is now faced with the following questions: (1) What is the cost of liquidating all current high-tech positions in the portfolios? and (2) What can the firm do with its high-tech specialist during the time the committee decides to stay out of high-tech stocks? Such analysts are not blue-collar workers who can be temporarily laid off during a work slowdown! One does not let highly paid professionals sit around with their hands folded in their lap. Instead, what is much more likely to happen is that stocks from each niche covered by the firm's analysts will find their way into that firm's clients' portfolios. This is because exposures to niches are often cut back, but rarely lqiuidated completely. It is fairly easy to explain to a client why a certain position has been reduced instead of liquidated; it is far more difficult to rationalize the existence of an idle staff. The ultimate detriment is to the client.

This problem does not arise with mutual funds. Ridding one's portfolio of a suddenly undesirable investment discipline involves no personality conflicts, no idle staff considerations; it involves no more than the sale of a single fund holding or a few funds. There is no pressure because of a fixed overhead because there is no overhead at all! The cost of acquiring mutual fund talent is fixed only for the time during which an investment is made. Most funds maintain expense ratios hovering around 1 percent; by law they are capped at 1.5 percent. In other words one can have a $1 million portfolio managed for no more than $10,000 per year. This is obviously much less than the costs associated with placing a qualified analyst or portfolio manager on staff on a permanent basis.

At this point let us sum up briefly why mutual funds are such unique instruments for an investment world in a state of constant and rapid flux:

1. They offer complete, in-depth coverage of the full spectrum of investment possibilities.
2. Funds are a compact, liquid, and efficient investment vehicle.
3. There is no fixed overhead cost to investors, except for the period of time during which the investment is in place.
4. The mutual fund universe provides an adequate, easily accessible list of substitute candidates.
5. As various disciplines and market segments gain or lose favor, mutual funds offer a total ease of entry and exit for investors.

THE INVESTMENT PYRAMID

Newfangled Portfolio Theorems

As we have seen, the investment world has become a difficult place, and most investors have become skeptical of the old-fashioned, seat-of-the-pants approach to investments. Therefore, it is not surprising that a new school of thought has developed. Its followers would have us believe that the individual investment manager cannot bring value-added to the process. Instead, a rigidly dogmatic approach is suggested. Under the banner of "modern portfolio theory," some of these theorists categorize stocks and bonds under such terms as *alphas* and *betas*. Investors are asked to decide on their risk-tolerance level, examine the historical risk characteristics of each issue, mix them in the proper proportion, and then *presto*—an instant portfolio is born!

Discourses on such portfolio theorems run into the hundreds of pages. Even certain sections of academe are getting into the act. Weighty journals now abound to provide scholarly dissertations on various aspects of the "science" of investment management. We live in the age of computers, so why shouldn't we believe that investment portfolios can be custom-made by computer like virtually everything else today? What is improbable about creating the CAD-CAM of Wall Street?

I for one do not accept this "new religion." The method we will describe in the following pages is based on a simple, straightforward approach that has been tried and successfully tested for over 10 years. You do not need an advanced degree in computer technology to understand it, nor do you need to read hundreds of pages of explanation because it consists of only four basic steps. As many an observer has commented, this approach appears to follow the KISS method (Keep It Simple, Stupid).

We are often asked, "If your method is so simple, why do many so-called experts seek to confuse the issue with complicated, hard-to-understand methods?" I have no solid answer other than the observation that if such methods do not deliver the projected results, their proponents can always "hide behind the computer" to explain their errors. Perhaps these people fear that simplicity would not allow them to rationalize their annual six-figure retainers. If the clients clearly understand what's going on—or feel that they can handle their investments by themselves—the rationale for high consulting and management fees might be in jeopardy. As a result, the so-called experts create layer upon layer of investment "technology," regression analysis, and standard deviations. They especially keep in mind the fact that "an ignorant client is the best client."

The Right Solution: The Investment Pyramid

Let me now call to your attention the investment pyramid depicted in Figure 1. The entire process of portfolio construction consists of just four steps. We will examine each of these steps in greater detail. At this point we want to give a quick overview of the pyramid. Even a cursory glance at Figure 1 shows that we are dealing here with a method of building portfolios that proceeds from the top downward. Step 1, at the top of the pyramid, involves objective setting; Step 2, asset allocation; Step 3, sector allocation; and Step 4, mutual fund selection. Each step leads naturally to the next one.

The process goes from the general to the specific. We begin with a very basic concept of what we want from our investments; we add the necessary details; and we end up with a fully structured portfolio. As we shall see later, the linkage between these steps is truly from the top downward. Changes at a step higher up on the pyramid automatically force changes in the step or steps below, but not vice versa.

From another perspective this process is like a building project. Admittedly, this building is unusual in that it is being constructed from the top downward. But as if we were constructing a building, we would start with an "artist's rendition," that is, by setting our investment objectives.

FIGURE 1
The Investment Pyramid

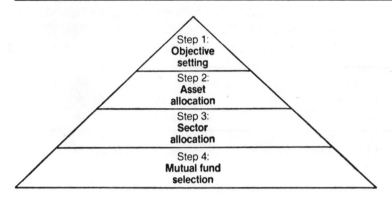

Next we would develop more detailed "line drawings," that is, we allocate our assets. Then we would draw up "engineering plans" or allocate the sectors of our portfolio. Finally, we would "put up the structure," that is, we select our mutual funds. Steps One to Three are like a building structure to which we have to add "bricks and mortar," namely, the mutual funds selected for the portfolio. Keep in mind that any building of unsound structure to which we add quality materials would be doomed in advance to failure. The same would be true if we were to apply subpar bricks and mortar to a building with a sturdy framework. We need to pay careful attention to details at every step of the investment process.

Additional features of this four-step process bear further study. The first is obvious: As our building blocks we have replaced stocks and bonds with a carefully selected group of mutual funds. The reason for this decision is by now quite clear. In today's investment environment stocks and bonds can be likened to subpar materials.

The Proper Emphasis

Next comes the question of emphasis. In the traditional approach stock and bond selection is such a time-consuming process that little time is left over to set our objectives, allocate our assets, and allocate sectors of our portfolio. Mutual fund selection—the substitute for stock and bond selection—is perhaps the least time-consuming step of all if it is done properly. This allows us to focus our attention on the critical Steps One through Three.

These steps are critical because a number of studies have clearly shown that the most effective use of a portfolio manager's time is spent on asset and sector allocation, not on stock and bond selection! One study, in fact, concluded that over 60 percent of the incremental returns provided by a group of investment managers was the result of proper asset and sector allocation. Less than 10 percent could be attributed to correct stock and bond selection. (The balance is accounted for by miscellaneous factors.) Success with one's portfolio has little to do with selecting individual issues. Every rule has its exception, and this one is no different. Yes, there are disciples of Graham & Dodd—those well-known advocates of investing in basic value stocks—who spend 100 percent of their time on stock selection, and do so very successfully. But they are the exception.

Although it may be hard for us at first to accept the fact that the selection of stocks and bonds plays only a minor role in successful investing, let us consider the following situation: When the market declines, as it did between 1973 and 1974 and between 1981 and August 1982, how might portfolio managers have better spent their time? Should they have decided whether to own stock in General Motors Corporation or Ford Motor Company? U.S. Steel or Bethlehem Steel? Philip Morris, Incorporated, or R. J. Reynolds Tobacco Company? Alternatively, shouldn't they have decided whether to be in equities at all or in cash equivalents? From the late 1970s to the early 1980s, while interest rates were rising precipitously, how did the bond managers better spend their time—researching various credits of the same rating and similar maturities, or by determining whether to be at the long end of the interest rate curve or at the short end? The evidence and logic are clearly in favor of asset and sector allocation, not stock and bond selection.

In a rising market most securities appreciate in value; in a declining market the reverse is true. Finding minuscule differences between different issues in either environment is futile. Portfolio managers who correctly spent their time on asset allocation between January 1973 and September 1974, and who determined to stay out of the stock market completely, would have outperformed the most astute stock picker who determined to stay fully invested during this period. By shifting the emphasis away from stock and bond selection and toward portfolio construction, the investment pyramid forces a focus on the critical steps.

Two Teams of Specialists: Portfolio Managers and
Mutual Fund Managers

Finally, perhaps the most noteworthy characteristic of this four-step process is the development of a new notion. What we see here is a breaking out of separate and distinct investment functions. On the first level there is portfolio management, the proper structuring of the overall portfolio. On the second level we have stock and bond selection. However, each is a full-time undertaking. Those attempting to fulfill both roles simultaneously, particularly in a volatile, complex marketplace, are doomed to failure. Each role requires the total devotion of the practitioner. Instead, what we propose here is something quite different. Portfolio managers, or individual investors, who until now have attempted to wear both hats, will give up one hat. They will perform the function we now call portfolio management, or portfolio design, and when it is time to perform the second function—stock and bond selection—they will call upon a second group of professionals, the mutual fund managers, to whom we will delegate this responsibility. The portfolio manager, rid of the responsibility of selecting stocks and bonds, can tap the expertise of a 1,300-member farm team of stock and bond fund managers to perform this role for him.

As I wrote in a 1984 article in the *American Banker*:
This farming out should not take on a negative connotation, but rather a very positive one. Typically, the individual portfolio manager can at best devote only a few minutes per day to any of the myriad number of investment sectors that have developed into full-time enterprises in recent years, such as options, convertible bonds, medical technology, etc. By delegating the stock and bond selection process, we now have a portfolio manager who can call upon the services of a group of carefully selected specialty mutual fund managers who devote 100 percent of their time focused solely on their areas of specialization.[1]

That is the crucial link—two teams of specialists consisting of portfolio managers and mutual fund managers who work in tandem to the ultimate benefit of the investor. Each team devotes itself full-time to its area of expertise, with no duplication of effort! Portfolio managers spend none of their time on stock and bond selection; mutual fund managers spend none

---

[1]Michael D. Hirsch, "Mutual Funds: Key to Investment Management," *American Banker*, April 16, 1984.

of theirs on objective setting or asset and sector allocation. Again, a rule with exceptions. There are a number of mutual funds that perform active asset allocation, but they are an extremely small minority.

CREATING A MULTIFUND PORTFOLIO

So far our discussion has focused on the theory of multifund investing. Let us now take all this information and build a real portfolio by applying the principles. We will select a prototypical case, keeping in mind that the same process applies regardless of our objectives. We will follow the four-step process described in the investment pyramid (see Figure 1).

The investors are a middle-aged couple who have enough money in savings to take care of emergencies. A separate savings account has been set up to pay for the projected college expenses of their two teenaged children. The couple own their own home, and their current mortgage payments represent a reasonable 25 percent of the annual family income. A benefits package provided by the husband's employer will take care of all contingency situations, such as major medical, disability, and dental expenses, as well as life insurance payments.

Objective Setting

The couple's assets available for investment, therefore, are primarily targeted for retirement planning. Both husband and wife are currently working, but would like to retire in approximately 10 to 15 years. By that time the children will have finished their schooling and be self-supporting. Additional savings accumulated over that period will supplement the current pool of capital for retirement purposes. In analyzing their situation by themselves or with the help of a financial counselor, the couple realize that their investment temperament is somewhat conservative. They are willing to devote some portion of their investable assets to growth-oriented investments, but in moderation. They would not be comfortable with any undue risk. In other words, they want to see their retirement nest egg grow as much as possible, but within reasonable bounds. The capital additions to the investment pool while both husband and wife are still working negate the necessity of sacrificing safety for the sake of accelerated growth (see Figure 2).

Such investors should adopt a balanced growth-and-income objective.

FIGURE 2
Step One: Objective Setting

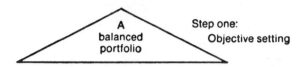

This is a middle-of-the-road approach, not too conservative and not too aggressive. Equal emphasis should be placed on growth and income. The income is obviously not for current purposes. (In fact, we will invest all income as it is earned.) Indeed, the income will act as an anchor on the portfolio, muting risk and providing a measure of safety. This is because income-generating instruments, in general, are more risk-averse than growth vehicles. Such an objective seems to fit the investors' temperament.

Asset Allocation

Now that the objective has been determined—a balance between growth and income—we can turn our attention to Step Two: asset allocation. Looking at the factors that help us develop this allocation, we find that the economy is in a healthy state; it came out of a recession 12 months earlier. Prospects for sustained economic growth are favorable, and the Federal Reserve Board is maintaining a fairly reasonable stance on the growth of the money supply. Nor are there any indications of a forthcoming tightening of interest rates. These rates have been stable to slightly lower for some time, although according to the theory of the historic economic cycle, there should be some fear of higher rates in the next 9 to 15 months. At that point the recovery should be gaining additional momentum, thus placing a demand pressure on rates.

Nothing of particular significance is occurring on either the international or domestic political fronts. No tax or spending bills of any consequence are before Congress. The White House is not talking about new economic initiatives. Overall, we are left with a mildly optimistic scenario. Since this is a hypothetical example, we have simplified the fundamental analysis that has to be performed before creating an intelligent asset

FIGURE 3
Step Two: Asset Allocation

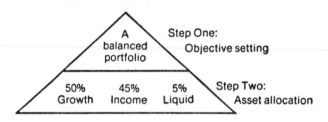

allocation. Our analysis is based on the assumptions that the investor follows the fundamentalist school and is not a technician.

Now let us take a look at the investment markets themselves. The stock market is in the midst of a prolonged advance that reflects the healthy state of the economy. This rally, with intermittent corrections, has a fairly broad basis, and most market sectors have participated in it. On the fixed-income side, the bond market is also experiencing a significant rally, moving in line with the lower trend in interest rates. Recently, however, the bond rally has been faltering, as fears of a rebound in rates have surfaced.

This is the atmosphere in which we will create a balanced asset allocation. Since conditions for equity investment appear favorable, we will allocate 50 percent of the assets to growth investments. Until the upturn in rates is confirmed, we need not react prematurely. (We will keep in mind the liquidity of mutual funds and our ability to shift gears quickly if the need should arise.) Therefore, we will devote 45 percent of the assets to income investments. The remaining 5 percent will be kept liquid. This is a balanced asset allocation that places equal emphasis on growth and income (see Figure 3).

Sector Allocation

Let us now proceed to the sector allocation. The short-term view of the environment presents an equally compelling argument in favor of both equity and debt investments. Accordingly, in our sector allocation for the 50 percent intended for growth, we will put 25 percent into agressive-growth funds and 25 percent into conservative-growth funds. Although these investors are risk-averse, it is not unreasonable to have 25 percent of their portfolio in aggressive funds. If we were dealing here with investors with a growth or maximum growth objective, both the asset allocation and the sector allocation would be appreciably different. Assuming a similar economic and market environment, we would recommend putting perhaps 45 percent of the investment assets in aggressive-growth funds and 15 percent in conservative-growth funds for growth investors. But if they were maximum growth investors, we would recommend putting 60 percent into aggressive-growth funds and 20 percent into conservative-growth funds.

What about the 45 percent allocated for income-oriented investments? Inasmuch as we are attempting to maintain a balanced approach, the bulk of this allocation will go into fixed-income funds. However, since prospects for the equity market remain favorable, some allocation will be made to equity income, namely, 10 percent to equity-income funds and 35 percent to fixed-income funds. In turn, since our projections for the interest-rate environment remain positive, of the 35 percent targeted for fixed income, 25 percent will go into long-term funds (a mix of high-grade and lower-grade funds) and 10 percent into intermediate-term funds. That presumes a flat yield curve from the intermediate-term to the long-term. If there is an appreciable yield differential between the two, perhaps only 5 percent will be placed in intermediate-term bond funds.

As for the 5 percent targeted for liquid funds, let us assume that we are dealing with an environment without any scares in the financial system. In that case this 5 percent will go into a general money market fund. If our investors are "nervous," a prime or government-only fund can be used.

Finally, if our investors are in a high tax bracket, the 5 percent allocation to liquid might be placed in tax-free money market funds. This proposal also applies to the sector allocation for fixed income. Suitable tax-free bond funds can be substituted for taxable corporate bond funds. There is a broad array of choices available to us today in the universe of mutual funds: we can choose among a variety of long-term, short-term, high-grade, and low-grade tax-free funds.

A cursory overview of the suggested sector allocation might lead us to conclude that this portfolio is not balanced but rather tilted in favor of equities. As we can see in Figure 4, we plan to put 25 percent of the assets into aggressive-growth funds, 25 percent into conservative-growth funds, and 10 percent into equity-income funds; this means a total of 60

FIGURE 4
Step Three: Sector Allocation

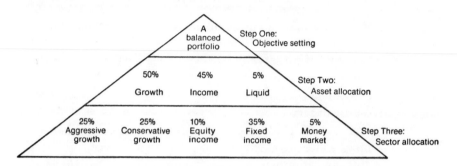

percent of the portfolio would be in equity-oriented funds. But this is not the case. If we were to examine the underlying portfolios of each of the aggressive-growth funds, conservative-growth funds, and equity-income funds, we would find that some portion of each fund's assets are invested in fixed-income or money market instruments. Therefore, the portfolio is truly balanced fairly evenly between growth vehicles and income vehicles.

Mutual Fund Selection

We have now reached the final stage of multifund investing, when we select from our core group of mutual funds to create the multifund portfolio. Keep in mind that we do not want any single fund to have an undue influence on the total portfolio. In addition, each sector has to be invested in funds with a variety of investment styles so as to provide further diversification of the portfolio.

There will be four funds in the aggressive-growth sector. Fund A's style is to invest in emerging growth stocks. Fund B invests in small capitalization stocks, Fund C in deep cyclical issues, and Fund D in potential turnaround situations. We will invest 6.25 percent of the assets in each fund, for a total of 25 percent.

There will be three funds in the conservative-growth sector. Fund E invests in companies with established manufacturing (or service) lines, that is to say, in companies that are either industry leaders or among the top three in a particular industry. Fund F invests in basic value issues (issues with a lower price/earnings ratio and a higher dividend rate than the Standard & Poor's 500 Stock Average). Fund G is a "stock picker," which means that it does not have a preconceived bias toward any particular industry, nor does it use financial screens. At the same time Fund G does not invest in more speculative issues. We will invest 8 percent of the assets in two of these funds, and 9 percent in the third fund. Since aggressive-growth funds bring more risk to the portfolio than conservative-growth funds, we have decided to use one more aggressive-growth fund than conservative-growth funds (even though on a percentage basis both groups have an equal weight in the portfolio).

We will use two funds in equity income. Fund H always keeps a preponderance of its portfolio in equities. Fund I will mix and match its portfolio between equity issues and debt issues, although there will be a slight bias toward equities. We will invest 5 percent of assets in each of these funds.

There will be four funds in the fixed-income sector. Fund J will be a long-term, high-grade bond fund. Fund K is a long-term, lower-grade bond fund. Fund L is a mixed-grade, mixed-maturity bond fund, while Fund M is an intermediate-term bond fund. In addition, all these funds are available in tax-free form for investors who can benefit from such an exclusion. We will invest 9 percent in Fund J, 8 percent in both Fund K and Fund L, and 10 percent in Fund M.

Finally, Fund N will be either a general market fund or a prime market fund. Alternatively, it may consist of a government-only money market fund. Figure 5 describes the mutual fund selection of this balanced portfolio. It also shows the completion of the investment pyramid.

The portfolio shown in Figure 5 is both a finished product and the quintessence of multifund investing. It is compact, streamlined, efficient, and totally flexible. It is also easy to look after, as there are only 14 positions to monitor, not 30 to 40 stocks, 10 to 20 bonds, and 3 to 6 cash instruments. This portfolio has all the characteristics required to cope with a volatile, complex investment environment. And, of course, it is simple and straightforward to assemble either by part-time individual investors or full-time professionals.

Have we had to sacrifice anything in creating this new portfolio in terms of safety, prudence, or diversification? As we shall see in the next chapter, a multifund portfolio is the ultimate in risk-aversion and safety. Critics might believe—mistakenly—that there is safety in numbers, and

FIGURE 5
Step Four: Mutual Fund Selection—The Completion of the Investment Fund

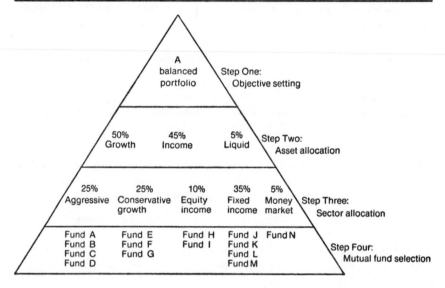

that something has to be lacking in a portfolio with only 14 mutual funds. But if we total up the underlying stock, bond, and money market equivalents in these 14 funds, and if we keep in mind the care taken to prevent any duplication of investments, we will discover that this portfolio provides indirect ownership of *hundreds* of stocks, bonds, and money market instruments. A multifund portfolio offers both compactness and greater diversification.

What about the problem of complexity and the need of investors to shift certain stocks and bonds? We have here a portfolio of 14 themes, not one or two as in the traditional portfolio. Which type of portfolio is better equipped for today's complex marketplace? If any of these 14 choices have to be changed, if the asset and/or sector allocations have to be adjusted, or if we modify objectives, we can do so with one or two phone calls. What is the reason for this flexibility? We are investing through mutual funds, the most liquid method of participating in the equity and debt markets.

THE TRIPLE SAFETY NET

Multifund investing has worked for an extended period of time in many different market environments and for investors with a wide array of goals and objectives. It has delivered consistent, above average returns while many other approaches to investment have floundered. What is the reason for this extraordinary record? What explains its consistency, its steadiness in the most turbulent conditions? Some previously enumerated features, such as compactness, efficiency, and flexibility, provide only part of the answer. A feature unique to multifund investing is the true explanation: *A multifund portfolio is diversified on three separate levels.*

It is an axiom of investing that the greater the diversification, the lower the risk. To repeat, if we invest all our assets in a single stock, we are at far greater risk than if we invest them in 10 stocks. If our assets are invested solely in equities, they are at far greater risk than if they were spread across a variety of stocks, bonds, and money market instruments. If all our assets are invested only in a limited number of financial instruments, they are at greater risk than if they included both financial assets and hard assets such as real estate, oil and gas, or collectibles. In terms of diversification, there truly is safety in numbers.

The traditional stock/bond portfolio's diversification is limited to the number of different stock and bond issues purchased for the portfolio. It can be said to be diversified on only one level or plane. The multifund portfolio, by comparison, achieves diversification on three separate and distinct levels. And if we accept the principle that the greater the diversification, the lower the risk and the higher the safety, then a triply diversified portfolio would obviously be the answer to success in a market environment that has become ever more treacherous. Let us call those three levels of diversification the *triple safety net*.

Level One: Each Investment within the Portfolio Is in Itself Diversified

Very simply put, if an investor were lazy and purchased only one mutual fund (instead of going to the time and trouble of creating a multifund portfolio), this fact alone would provide the same degree of diversification as the traditional stock/bond portfolio. Each investment in our portfolio is a mutual fund; each mutual fund is a diversified portfolio of stocks and/or bonds. A one-fund portfolio provides similar diversification to (or better diversification than) the traditional portfolio. A portfolio of funds will provide far greater diversification.

Level Two: Diversification across a Broader Array of Asset Types and Market Sectors

As stated earlier, a portfolio invested in a single-industry group contains far more risk than one more broadly invested across a wide cross section of the market. Since mutual funds are concentrated portfolios of whichever market sectors or asset types we choose to include in our multifund portfolio, they allow us to capture a far broader assortment of alternatives from the expanded spectrum of investments available today.

If we restudy the fixed-income sector of the model portfolio in the previous section (see Figure 4), we can focus more sharply on this issue. Instead of looking upon fixed-income funds as a sector of a larger portfolio, we should consider them as a portfolio within themselves. In addition, let us compare this sector to a fixed-income portfolio invested directly in bonds. While the traditional portfolio may contain perhaps as many as 30 to 40 bond issues, it is limited in diversification. Why? Because the investor or portfolio manager assembling a list of investments may apply a certain point of view over the entire portfolio. If that individual is optimistic about the future course of interest rates, he or she will probably invest the vast majority of holdings in the portfolio in long-maturity bonds—many of which may be of lower quality. If the investor is pessimistic about the rate situation, the portfolio may be dominated by shorter-term, higher-grade issues. In other words, while the portfolio might contain 30 to 40 investments, in reality most of its issues may be similar to each other.

By comparison, let us look at a fixed-income portfolio of mutual funds. Keep in mind that we are using the fixed-income sector of a balanced portfolio. If we were reviewing the fixed-income sector of a maximum-yield portfolio, we might be considering seven or eight funds, instead of four. But the point still comes across. We no longer have a single investor or portfolio manager dictating the composition of our bond portfolio. Instead, we have four portfolio managers making those decisions, each insulated from the others. So no one prejudice will affect the overall composition of our fixed-income portfolio. The result is a multifaceted bond portfolio that effectively captures as many different niches within the broad category called *bonds* as we choose.

Using four carefully selected fixed-income funds, we can gain exposure to long-term, high-grade bonds; to long-term, lower-grade bonds; to mixed-grade, mixed-term bonds; and to intermediate-term bonds. As investors with a maximum-yield objective, we could have added funds invested in convertible bonds, deep discount issues, zeros, Ginnie Maes, or any number of alternatives. The flexibility provided by a multifund portfolio facilitates the efficient representation within a single portfolio of as many different asset types and market sectors as we choose. This is an additional form of diversification.

Level Three: Diversification within Sectors by Investment Style

We have stressed the need to identify clearly each fund candidate's investment style. This allows us to build in the final level of diversification. We are not going to select at random three or four funds that will represent the aggressive-growth section in our overall portfolio. We will not select a variety of equity-income funds for our multifund portfolio strictly on the basis of their past performance. Instead, we will take the time and effort to define clearly what makes each fund tick and what differentiates it from every other fund in the portfolio, particularly those in the same sector.

As we have said a number of times, investment styles and themes come and go. This level of diversification ensures that a total sector of our portfolio will not underperform because a single investment style has fallen out of favor. Let us assume that our sector allocation to aggressive-growth funds was proved accurate by subsequent market behavior, but that instead of investing in four aggressive-growth funds, we chose only one. If that fund represented a style that was currently out of sync with the investing public's preferences, our entire sector might underperform. This is hardly theoretical. Let us assume that at the beginning of 1984 the balanced investors described previously had chosen a high-tech fund for the 25 percent of assets to be invested for aggressive growth. In retrospect, their sector allocation would have proved to be totally accurate, but its performance would have ended up as subpar.

The success or failure of a multifund portfolio is not determined by the investment acumen of one investor or one portfolio manager. Instead, it results from the combined expertise of 10 to 20 different professionals, each of whom has a totally different perspective on investing. Each professional views this amorphous process called stock-and-bond investing from a totally different vantage point. That is the ultimate beauty of the multifund approach. Let us assume that one, two, or three of these managers "bomb out." This should be no surprise since we know that there can never be a situation in which every investment style represented in our portfolio will be in the ascendancy at the same time. Even so, our portfolio as a whole will still succeed. This is because we have 9, 10, 11, or 12 other styles in the portfolio, each of which is managed by professionals with an above average track record. And they can take up the slack. Just think, if our portfolio has just one more winning style than it has styles on the losing side, the whole portfolio will end up as a plus! If there are 14 well-chosen funds in the portfolio—funds with long-term above average performance histories—and if all of them perform proportionately and only eight of them achieve a gain, the portfolio will succeed. We will enjoy safe, consistent returns, regardless of the market's direction or our own objective. Why? Because of the triple safety net of multifund investing.

As the investment world becomes more and more volatile and more and more complex, the paramount consideration in any portfolio will be to reduce risk and maximize safety. By providing three separate and distinct levels of diversification, the multifund portfolio has built in the essential characteristics for success in such an environment.

Is multifund investing revolutionary? Perhaps it was revolutionary when first launched in the mid-1970s. But today most people in the pension fund world are investing their assets according to the same principles. Estimates within the investment community are that upward of 70 percent of Fortune 500 companies are using the services of independent pension consultants to assist them with their pension plans.

What, then, is the role of the independent pension consultants? Their duties include the following: (a) helping clients to set their investment objectives; (b) preparing asset allocation models; and (c) performing a search for appropriate managers for the clients' assets. In performing the search for appropriate managers, the independent pension consultants have a number of tasks to carry out:

1. They must do research on the hundreds of independent investment counselors, bank trust departments, common accounts of insurance companies, and others who provide investment management services to pension plans.
2. They must identify the superior performers and their areas of expertise.

3. They must suggest to the plan sponsors a team of managers that can implement the total range of asset allocation developed for a particular plan.

The buzzword for this approach is *multimanager, multistyle investing*.

In effect, multifund investing provides the same objective setting, the same asset allocation and sector allocation, and the same multimanager, multistyle portfolio structuring. The only difference is the use of mutual funds in lieu of private account managers. The multifund portfolio enables investors of any size or any level of sophistication to enjoy the benefits of this investment approach. In fact, even those in a position to utilize account managers are probably better off using multifund investing.

Most major investment management firms serving the world of tax-exempt plans also have publicly available mutual funds that offer exactly the same investment expertise. Included are such firms as Delaware Investment Advisors–Delaware Funds, Capital Guardian Trust–American Funds, and Fidelity Trust–Fidelity Funds.

Let us summarize here. For individual investors and sponsors of smaller plans, multifund investing provides access to the same state-of-the-art investment thinking as heretofore was only available to sponsors of large plans. It allows bank trust departments and investment counseling firms to offer clients a comprehensive approach by providing through one source what would otherwise only be available through a team of managers. It provides sponsors of large plans with access to the same investment expertise they are probably receiving through their present manager lineup, but in a far more efficient fashion.

What about the Danger of Overdiversification?

At this point, we need to answer a question that has been raised about overdiversification. A number of studies have concluded that diversification to reduce risk works only up to a certain point. It is generally believed that—so far as stock portfolios are concerned—the maximum benefit accrues in a portfolio of 30 to 40 stocks. Beyond that number, according to these studies, there seems to be no perceptible advantage to diversification in most cases. (Perhaps this occurs because of the unwieldiness of broadly based portfolios.) So the question arises whether a multifund portfolio that indirectly invests in hundreds of stocks and bonds might not be overdiversified.

Our answer is no. The studies on the maximum level of efficient diversification are probably correct, but they apply only when direct investments are made in stocks and bonds. This is because too many issues in a portfolio place too much of a strain on the portfolio manager. A portfolio with 60 to 75 stocks demands too much time and attention. But a multifund portfolio contains only 10 to 20 funds that have to be followed. There is no strain, and there is no "washing out" (because an overdiversified portfolio may have as many losers as winners). Because of the efficiency of multifund investing, we can enjoy the benefits of broad diversification without suffering any negative effects. As Solveig Jansson wrote in 1978, this investment approach is not overdiversification but "super-diversification."[2]

What about Indexing?

A second question concerns indexing. As we said earlier, many investors who feel despair over their inability to "beat the market" have turned to indexing. This means buying a group of stocks or bonds in direct proportion to their representation in a broad market index, such as the Standard & Poor's Stock Average, the Dow Jones Industrial Average, or the Shearson/Lehman Bond Index. As a result, these investors hope that their investments will always approximate those of "the market" as represented by one of those indexes. Since a multifund portfolio captures so many different market sectors, is it really no more than a superindex fund?

To reply to this question, we need to point out that indexing implies a goal of matching market returns by creating a market portfolio. Multifund investing does not seek market returns. By investing in mutual funds with consistent, above average performance, the goal is to achieve market returns plus. The total number of market niches represented in the portfolio is immaterial. If we were to purchase within each sector an index fund, the claim would be true that a multifund portfolio is no more than a superindex fund. But this is not the case. In each sector we invest in funds with above average records. The cumulative effect, then, is that as

---

[2]Solveig Jansson, "Portfolio Strategy," *Institutional Investor Magazine*, December 1978.

long as more than half of the funds selected perform up to expectations or historical norms, we have at a minimum created a superindex fund plus. This is exactly what every investor wants!

A SUMMARY

Since the early 1970s the investment markets have experienced a number of significant changes. Volatility and complexity have so altered the nature of the markets that the traditional methods of investing through broadly diversified portfolios of stocks or bonds have been unable to achieve the investors' objectives. Because of volatility portfolios must now be adjusted over a far shorter period of time. Because of complexity portfolio managers have to absorb critical information over a much wider spectrum. Since these change have occurred almost simultaneously, the problem has been exacerbated even further.

We have explored the inherent strengths of the open-ended mutual fund as a potential solution to these problems. Since mutual funds provide what in effect is instant liquidity along with an extremely compact and flexible investment vehicle, investors can cope with volatility. In view of the new dimensions of the fund industry, which offers over 1,300 nonmoney market, stock, and bond funds, investors are now provided with a range and depth of expertise unmatched by other potential avenues. The entire range of investment alternatives from the most mundane conservative-growth stocks to the most exotic option strategies and medical technology can be captured through one or more funds. Combined, these two major characteristics of mutual funds—their liquidity and the depth of coverage they provide—make them perfect investment vehicles for a volatile, complex market.

Next we took the concept a step further into multifund investing. Instead of considering the purchase of a single fund or a randomly selected group of funds to achieve our objective, we described the following simple four-step process by which we could create a cohesive multifund portfolio of 10 to 20 funds:

1. **Objective setting.**   This means obtaining a clear understanding of an investor's goals as well as of his or her ability to absorb risk.
2. **Asset allocation.**   On the basis of our investor's objective, we consider how various factors, such as developments in the econ-

omy, the political situation, the monetary situation, and the market, might affect investments over the next 9 to 15 months. We then develop a plan for deploying the investor's assets among growth, income, and liquid investments.

3. **Sector allocation.**   This involves adding detail to the portfolio matrix by further defining how we are to deploy the assets. We further determine whether growth-oriented assets should be invested in aggressive-growth or conservative-growth funds; whether the income assets should be invested in equity-income funds or fixed-income funds; and finally what type of money market funds should be utilized for liquid investments.

4. **Mutual fund selection.**   We learn that there is a wrong way and a right way to carry out mutual fund selection. The wrong way is to pursue high-flyers and passing fads while the right way is to identify consistent funds that have been above average in performance. We need to go beyond the historical performance numbers in order to understand the unique characteristics of those funds, such as the investment type and philosophy of their managers. We should then assemble a group of complementary styles and philosophies in a single portfolio so as to provide our investor with the maximum in safety and consistency.

Last, we have delved further into the reasons why multifund investing has been able to deliver consistent returns over such an extended time period, regardless of the investor's objective and the market environment. We conclude that a multifund portfolio provides three distinct layers of diversification, the following triple safety net:

1. Each investment within the portfolio is itself diversified.
2. A far greater diversification than the traditional stock and bond portfolio is achieved in the portfolio by capturing many more asset types and market sectors.
3. Within each sector we can achieve a third layer of diversification by investing in a cross section of funds with distinct, complementary investment styles. As a result, no one investment bias or school of thought determines the success or failure of the portfolio. Instead, we can draw on the combined, but totally independent investment expertise of 10 to 20 full-time professionals.

As the investment markets become increasingly volatile and complex, the treacherous aspects of stock and bond investing will increase, while the overriding advantages and safety features of multifund investing should become more important to the investing public. At first thought multifund investing may appear too radical a change in direction for traditionalists to accept. But the record of success of multifund investing speaks for itself. Its ability to deliver what other approaches cannot requires a serious consideration by all investors, regardless of their level of sophistication.